Battle for the Bundu

BATTLE FOR

THE FIRST WORLD WAR IN EAST AFRICA

THE BUNDU

by CHARLES MILLER

MACMILLAN PUBLISHING CO., INC.

NEW YORK

Library of Congress Cataloging in Publication Data

Miller, Charles, 1918-
    Battle for the Bundu; the First World War in
East Africa.

    Bibliography: p.
    1. European War, 1914-1918—Campaigns—Af-
rica—Tanganyika. I. Title.
D567.G3M45   940.4'16   73-14013
ISBN 0-02-584930-1

Macmillan Publishing Co., Inc.
866 Third Avenue, New York, N.Y. 10022
Collier-Macmillan Canada Ltd.

First Printing 1974

Printed in the United States of America

For Isabel

Contents

Acknowledgments

I wish to thank the following individuals and organizations for their kindness in permitting me to reproduce textual material or illustrations, or for assistance in obtaining background information: Arbeitskreis für Wehrforschung; Bilderdienst Süddeutscher Verlag; Mrs. Gunn Brinson; Bundesarchiv; Cambridge University Press; Chatto & Windus; Dr. Theresa Clay; Lt. Col. Josef M. Engelhardt, Defense Attache's Office, German Embassy, Washington; Faber & Faber; Robert Hale & Co.; David Higham Associates; Hutchinson Publishing Group; Imperial War Museum; Koehlers Verlagsgesellschaft; Library & Records Dept., Foreign & Commonwealth Office; Longman Group; Macmillan—London; John Murray, Ltd.; Naval Home Division, Ministry of Defence; Pictorial Press; Radio Times Hulton Picture Library; Ullstein Verlag.

On a more personal level, I am specially grateful to Herr Ludwig Boell (formerly Oberleutnant Boell of the Schutztruppe) for his patience and cooperation in dealing with a small tidal wave of queries; and to Dr. Wolfgang Budich for invaluable translations. I am at the very least equally indebted to my editors, Stephanie Erickson, and Jody Ward, for the kind of backstopping that only editors can provide, and—as always and above all—to Gunther Stuhlmann, my agent, for consistently useful advice and priceless moral support.

None of the abovementioned, of course, are in any way responsible for my mistakes—and I presume I have made more than one. My aim in writing this book was to describe, in a general way, the East African campaign of the First World War—and how a modestly immense Allied army tried to cope with a midget German force led by an obscure Prussian officer who could have conducted post-graduate courses in irregular warfare tactics for Che Guevara, General Giap and other more celebrated but far less skilled guerrilla fighters. The very last thing I wanted to do (or, for that matter, could have done) was turn out a work of scholarly or military expertise. While a good deal of my time and effort went into conventional research, I also drew heavily on literary license and educated guesswork. One reason for this was that the sources which I consulted—whether written by men on the spot or by specialists trained in distilling fact from battlefield confusion—seldom agreed on anything. This state of documentary disorder is best described by a British officer who fought in East Africa and later tried to compile the campaign's records for the War Office, remarking that he "found accounts of battles which differed not only as to the hour, day and even week when they occurred, but also in every other possible detail." To put it mildly, so did I.

Perhaps I should have approached my task by adhering rigidly to the facts in Lt. Col. Charles Hordern's *Official History of the Great War; Military Operations; East Africa* and Ludwig Boell's *Die Operationen in Ostafrika,* which probably come closer than anything else to being the definitive British and German studies of the campaign. However, Hordern died before he could finish his voluminous account, which goes no further than 1916, while Boell's monumental work, although published in 1951, did not become available to me until I had practically finished my own manuscript. But even if things had been otherwise, I suspect that I would have chafed under the restraint of writing only about what "really" happened. Errors? So be it. I leave the crossing of "t's" and the dotting of "i's" to those conscientious military scholars who revel in such pursuits.

Certainly it was more fun to concentrate on the less formal but infinitely more human works. No official report can bring across the weight of what the Germans were up against as does von Lettow, the Schutztruppe commander, in his personal memoirs of the campaign. Meinertzhagen's diaries are more than just the product of a brilliant professional British (not German) soldier who fought in East Africa; they also happen to make perfectly delicious reading. Certain so-called popular histories also proved invaluable—notably Peter Shankland's *The Phantom Flotilla*, which sets forth the facts of the Lake Tanganyika naval expedition no less accurately and far more engagingly than any Admiralty document; my own account of that goofy but intrepid undertaking leans heavily on Shankland's book. Even fiction played a useful role: exceptionally well-informed novels by David Bee, Elspeth Huxley and Francis Brett Young went a long way toward bringing home to me the squalor, misery and high adventure of a forgotten war.

In short, the idea behind this book was to create a faithful overall impression of the spirit rather than the letter of the East African conflict. For spirit, it seems to me, is the quality to be played up in writing about what may have been the most bizarre campaign ever fought in the history of tropical warfare.

Battle for the Bundu

Prologue

Beachhead

WITH ENGINES AT SLOW AHEAD, the fourteen ancient transports of the British troop convoy reeled drunkenly in the oily Indian Ocean groundswell, the horizon just barely masking the knotted mangrove swamps that fronted their military objective on the coast of German East Africa. Below decks, in the cramped, badly ventilated holds which comprised the troops' quarters, some seventy-five hundred Indian army sepoys and a few hundred British soldiers staggered, slipped, crawled and lay prone in shifting pools of their own vomit. It was early evening on Sunday, November 1, 1914. Since October 16, when the convoy had weighed anchor in Bombay, it had been unable to proceed at more than seven knots—the speed of its slowest vessel, a pipestem-funneled antique of nineteen hundred tons. This creeping pace across two thousand miles of lurching watery mountain range had been tolerable only to the strongest stomachs. After a fortnight of retching, Indian Expeditionary Force "B" was hardly in a state of combat readiness. But in the main saloon of the S.S. *Karmala*, a converted P. & O. liner serving as headquarters transport where the force's staff and line officers were now assembled for an eleventh-hour briefing, the atmosphere was electric with anticipation. The Great War was three months old. Kluck's First Army had overrun Belgium, the Germans had been rolled back at the Marne, the Russian army was reeling from the blows which Hindenburg had dealt it at Tannenberg and the Masurian Lakes. But in East Africa, where only a few brief skirmishes had taken place, there had been no decisive actions, and Force "B's" impending assault on the German port of Tanga was expected to change all that.

Not that the landing itself could be anything more than a drill. The force commander, Major General Arthur Edward Aitken, quickly recapitulated the plans of the operation. On the following morning, the convoy would approach the harbor under the guns of the Royal Navy cruiser *Fox*. No more than token resistance was to be expected. Tanga was held, under what amounted to open city terms, by a few dozen German army officers and fewer than four hundred *askaris*—African soldiers. They would have no real option but surrender. Even if the commander of the toy garrison did choose to fight back, his defenses would be quickly smashed to pieces by the artillery, machine guns, rifles and cold steel of two Indian brigades.

Aitken was a thickset man, exuding gruff assurance. He tugged at his Kitchener mustache and smiled as he completed his summary. Any questions, gentlemen? No: regimental and battalion commanders knew their allotted dispositions. The broader outlines of the operation were also quite clear, having been discussed and examined at length in a staff meeting a day earlier at the British port of Mombasa. Here a coordinated pincer movement had been worked out. From Tanga, Force "B" was to advance northwest for about two hundred miles, along the route of the Germans' Northern Railway, which followed a winding path beneath the densely forested Usambara Mountains, to the town of Moshi in the foothills of Mount Kilimanjaro. At Moshi, a linkup would be made with the five thousand troops of another Indian force—which by then would have completed a synchronized enveloping thrust across the border from British East Africa—to deal with the main German command, estimated at well under three thousand rifles. No detail had been overlooked. All that remained was debarkation, advance and the swift capitulation of the vastly outnumbered German army. The entire operation was expected to end before Christmas.

No questions, then? Very well, dismiss—and good hunting. The saloon, already heavy with cigar smoke, now became filled with low-keyed laughter and the clink of brandy and whisky glasses as officers toasted confusion to the Hun. With little fighting and minimal casualties, the Union Jack would soon be flying over the colony of German East Africa. Tanga was to be the beginning of the end.

PART I
THE OVERLORDS

I

Mikono wa Damu

OTTO VON BISMARCK, the architect of modern Germany, is also rightly credited as the man who gave the Kaiser his vast overseas empire. But it was an empire that the Chancellor himself never wanted. To think of Bismarck as a ravenous imperialist is to do a disservice to the grandmaster of nineteenth-century *realpolitik*. More clearly than any other contemporary European statesman, Bismarck recognized that colonial holdings were a prohibitive luxury. Shortly after the establishment of the German Empire in 1871, he made it plain that the word "empire" implied no overseas ambitions. "For Germany to acquire colonies," he said, "would be like a poverty-stricken Polish nobleman providing himself with silks and sables when he needed shirts." A decade later he put it even more plainly: "As long as I am Chancellor, we will carry on no colonial policies." Even as late as 1889, when the Reich embraced more than three-quarters of a million square miles of Africa, not to mention substantial estates in China and the southwest Pacific, Bismarck could still declare: "*Von Haus auf bin ich kein Kolonialmensch*"—from my whole background I am not a colonial animal.

If this seems paradoxical, the fact remains that the influential ideologues of Germany's colonial movement—which began making itself felt as early as the 1860s—never found a passionate advocate in Bismarck. The Chancellor was decidedly cool to the almost universally accepted proposition that overseas holdings would gain raw materials for German industry and new markets for German manufacturers. Nor did he respond to what many regarded as an even more urgent reality: that colonies would provide a national outlet for German emigration, thus stemming the tide of an exodus which saw several million subjects of the Emperor become American citizens in barely half a century. Bismarck appeared to think that Germany was well rid of such leave-takers. "I am not anxious to know," he once said, "how people who have shaken the dust of the Fatherland off their feet are getting on." Perhaps curiously, he did not even salivate to the emotional appeal of "a place in the sun," as the imperialist Bülow put it, for German national vainglory. Given the near-absolute power which Bismarck wielded as Chancellor, he could in all likelihood have resisted expansionist importunities as long as he held office.

But if he so clearly perceived the sham and deceptive allure of the philosophies which animated nineteenth-century imperial expansion, why, then, in 1884, did Bismarck yield, or seem to yield, to imperial persuasions? For it was in that year that Germany, at the Chancellor's personal instigation, laid the foundation of its empire in Africa. Almost overnight, in a period of less than three months, German spheres of influence surfaced in South West Africa, Togoland and the Cameroons. Bismarck's policy *volte-face* jolted the foreign ministries of all Europe.

Most noticeably in England. For England in fact was the whole idea. If one asks why Bismarck suddenly staked out claims for Germany in Africa, the oversimplified but still correct answer is that he wished only to cause Great Britain a temporary setback at the European political card table.

And it may be that no one was more startled than Bismarck himself when, after the Imperial Eagle had been raised in western and southern Africa, he discovered that the Reich had simultaneously gathered in a more than generous chunk of East Africa.

This annexation had been brought off, without his sanction or knowledge, by one Dr. Carl Peters, a frail scholar and sulphurous-tempered bully-boy who was possessed of an imperial gluttony matched by no other empire builder of the era, Cecil Rhodes not excepted. Although he held a Ph.D. and wrote papers on metaphysics, Peters was basically a man of action—the driving force, in fact, behind his country's expansion in eastern Africa. In 1884, as the head of a private organization called the Society for German Colonization, he set his sights on an immense no-man's-land in East Africa which was ostensibly ruled by an Arab sultanate on the island of Zanzibar. Leading a small expedition through the dense thorn of this region, Peters busily and unabashedly waved imposing "treaties" of "protection" under the eyes of several dozen unlettered African chiefs. It was like taking candy from a baby. After less than three months of alternate cajoling and fist-shaking, Peters emerged from the bush with X-marks on documents making the Society landlord of some sixty thousand square miles of the Zanzibar Sultanate's mainland property. All that remained was to obtain Bismarck's blessing.

Bismarck never liked or trusted Peters. (Once, when Peters urged him to claim part of Madagascar, he snapped back: "Do you manage German politics or do I?") In 1884, however, he recognized Peters' acquisition as an opportunity to give the British lion's tail an extra twist, and therefore, with a deaf ear to the protests of the Sultan of Zanzibar, he prevailed on

Kaiser Wilhelm I to grant a charter to the Society, which then became the German East Africa Company. Since colonial government by chartered business concerns was a common instrument of nineteenth-century imperialism, German claims in the region gained a facade of legality.

Between 1884 and the outbreak of the First World War, German rule in East Africa passed through three separate and distinct stages. The Company's stewardship, lasting until 1891, was the first. Outwardly, the enterprise appeared to flourish as cotton and rubber plantations sprang up along the coast, while jubilant communiques from Peters sang the praises of Germany's equatorial land of Goshen. During this period, Peters also mounted no fewer than sixteen expeditions to gobble up more East African real estate. He did his work well. By 1890, the Imperial Eagle flew over a region nearly three times the size of Germany itself—a land later to become the nations of Tanzania, Rwanda and Burundi.

It ran the gamut of climate, terrain, flora, fauna and demography. The coast was a six-hundred-mile embroidered tropical hemline of gold-emerald coco palms, ivory beaches and green-black mangrove swamps, punctuated at frequent intervals by the convoluted deltas of great rivers. The north of the colony was alternately dead and lush: waterless deserts flanked a rich volcanic highland region dominated by the layer of icing on the flat nineteen-thousand-foot summit of Kilimanjaro, Africa's tallest mountain. Twirling south from Kilimanjaro, like the tail of a comet more than four hundred miles long, were the fertile, heavily timbered Pare, Usambara, Nguru and Uluguru ranges, which in many places resembled the Alps in summertime. In the center of the country, cool airs caressed an immense tableland on which temperate-zone cultivation flourished. Deep in the interior, along the southwest border, a wild upheaval of titanic crags vaulted nearly two miles into the sky between the miniature oceans known as Lakes Nyasa and Tanganyika.

Also scattered across the entire country were horizonless tediums of clawlike thorn, known variously as the *nyika*, the *pori* or the *bundu*. Alternating with these wastes were throw-rug patches of savanna, dotted with flat-topped acacia and grotesquely fat baobab trees. Such regions were really great zoos, where elephants, lions, giraffes and uncountable other species of wild game coexisted in uneasy majesty. There was also a modest human population of some seven million Africans, subdivided into one hundred-odd tribes, from the lion-killing Masai of the north to the warrior Wahehe of the central plateau to the agrarian Makonde near the mouth of the Rovuma river on the southeast border. The variety of Germany's East African estate seemed limitless.

But for all its size and promise, the German sphere under Company rule was little more than a status symbol and the Company's own prosperity a myth. Eastern Africa in the late nineteenth century did not yield large or

swift returns on investment. Although the Hamburg mercantile houses
which managed the Company had spearheaded earlier German commercial
enterprises along the East African coast, they could not attract the kind of
massive loan capital needed to exploit the resources of the interior. Simple
trade was one thing; economic development—with its costly attendant
infrastructure—another matter entirely. Apart from a handful of plantations, some warehouses in a few ports and a small sprinkling of widely
separated trading posts that could be reached only after weeks of arduous
foot safari, one would hardly have known that a German presence existed
in East Africa.

One of the main reasons for the Company's failure to get off the ground
was the coast, which, by earlier agreements with Zanzibar, remained under
the Sultan's nominal rule. This meant that all ports were subject to customs
duties and import taxes accruing to the Sultan—which in turn had the effect
of reducing profits and further discouraging investment in the hinterland.
It did not take long for the Company's directors to realize that unless they
could get a slice of the coastal pie, their enterprise would probably dry up.
Accordingly, they set about changing the rules, and in 1888, the Sultan of
Zanzibar—no doubt influenced by the German gunboat anchored off his
palace—consented to a new treaty. Under its terms, collection of customs
duties was leased to the Company for fifty years. In effect, this gave the
Germans sovereign status on the coast.

But the transfer of power backfired almost at once. Arab slave and ivory
trading families, who had long held lucrative sway over the coast, did not
take kindly to their new masters, especially when the Company initiated
anti-slavery measures which threatened not merely a traditional source of
wealth but an entire way of life. Tensions were exacerbated by the Company's often undiplomatic and sometimes needlessly harsh behavior toward
the coast population as a whole. Indeed, the ink had hardly dried on the
customs duty agreement when resentment of the infidel overlord reached
boiling point in a sort of reverse crusade. Led by a fire-eater named Bushiri
bin Salim, a ragged but large and well-armed horde of Arabs and Swahilis
swore a collective oath on the Koran that they would not rest until the last
German had been driven into the Indian Ocean. A holocaust swept the
coast. Company warehouses and plantations were put to the torch. Bushiri's
mobs gunned down Germans and other Europeans on the streets of the
main ports. Without troops or the funds to raise them, the Company directors were left with no choice but to appeal to their government for help.

Here was Bismarck's chance to divest himself of at least one imperial
burden. He did not seize the opportunity. Despite his distaste for colonial
adventures, the Chancellor could ill afford a capitulation to the forces of
slavery—and the effect of such a surrender on Germany's prestige in
Europe. Instead, Bismarck summoned a distinguished German soldier-ex-

plorer, Captain Hermann von Wissmann, and gave him the explicit instruction: *"Siegen sie"*—Go out and win.

Wissmann acted swiftly, recruiting six hundred askaris from the British-controlled Sudan and hastening them by troopship to East Africa. Bismarck, too, went to his English colonial rivals for cooperation. Always ready to lend a helping hand where the suppression of slavery was concerned—although slavery in this case was really a side issue—the British government consented to a joint Anglo-German naval blockade of the coast. In less than a year, Bushiri was hanged, the rebels were dispersed and the Company had become a basket case. In 1891, without visible enthusiasm, the Kaiser's government assumed formal responsibility for the administration of German East Africa, with Wissmann as the first governor. Thus began the second period of German rule in that country.

As a department of the Foreign Office, the colony began to show some signs of progress. A trickle of settlers started planting coffee, sisal and other crops in the temperate foothills of Kilimanjaro and the Usambaras. To move their produce, work began on a meter-gauge railway running north from the port of Tanga, and a pier was built in the harbor itself. The government encouraged research in tropical agriculture and medicine. Officialdom took on at least a semblance of order with the appointment of a district commissioner in each of the territory's two dozen administrative areas.

The Foreign Office even allowed a degree of African autonomy at the local level. Headmen were made precinct representatives of the Kaiser; along with the title of *jumbe*, each received a *jumbenschein,* or certificate of authority (embossed with the Imperial Eagle), a white gold-faced robe and a gold-headed staff of office. Minor legal disputes were adjudicated by the African village magistrate known as a *wali*. A uniform system of hut taxes was imposed, and levied in every accessible settlement by an Arab or Swahili collector called an *akida*. In due course, some of the fruits of this revenue were seen in the opening of schools and clinics for Africans.

In reality, however, the colony was standing still, for the government had no intention of burdening the German taxpayer with the cost of developing a raw wilderness. In 1901, a decade after the Company's dissolution, German East Africa's total annual overseas trade amounted to a trickle of exports buried in an import avalanche. The moderately efficient hut tax and customs apparatus yielded about a million dollars in yearly revenues, but administrative expenditures came to twice that figure. The port of Dar es Salaam, chosen as the territory's capital because of its splendid natural anchorage, was always filled with Arab sailing dhows but seldom berthed an ocean liner, since the government showed little disposition to underwrite badly needed wharves, cranes and other modern harbor facilities. The railway from Tanga had advanced barely thirty miles inland; the Tanga pier had become a heap of rubble. Nor had many settlers been attracted. In 1901, the European population of German East Africa stood at less than two thousand, and a large percentage of the residents were not colonists but government officials. The country was hardly living up to its highly vaunted promise as an outlet for German emigration.

Not the least of the deterrents to the setting down of roots was the colony's state of unrest. Dar es Salaam, Tanga and other coast ports may have spilled over with minor Foreign Office bureaucrats, but the actual keeping of the peace in the interior was entrusted to seventy administrators —or about one official for every one hundred thousand inhabitants. And the difficulty of their task was compounded by their methods of enforcing Pax Germanica. To put it charitably, these methods were severe; it can almost be said that for a decade and a half, they kept German East Africa on the lip of a volcano.

Not that the Germans held a monopoly on the mistreatment of Africans. During the war, the Allies were to make much of the Hun's bestiality toward blacks, but this was only to be expected from propagandists who concocted yarns about nun- and baby-raping. Early German administrators and settlers in Africa did no more than implement honestly held—if horrendously wrong-headed—beliefs about "natives" which were shared by most whites of the era. In all likelihood, the Germans behaved only a little more harshly toward their lesser breeds than did the British and French, and they were probably models of forbearance alongside the Belgians and Portuguese. Most of the Germans' uniquely bad odor arose from the misdeeds of one man. Carl Peters was celebrated not only as an empire builder but as a sadist. His penchant for flogging and hanging Africans on the smallest provocation—sometimes, it seemed, on none—eventually proved too much even for a nation that was supposed to thrive on blood and iron. "What have you achieved," thundered Baron von Eltz in the Reichstag, "by perpetual fights, by acts of violence and repression? You have achieved, Herr Doktor—I have it from your own mouth in the presence of witnesses—that you and the gentlemen of your retinue cannot go five minutes' distance from the fort without military escort. . . . You have cut the knot with the sword and have transformed this most beautiful country into a battlefield." In 1897, for his acts of cruelty, Peters was dismissed from the colonial service. But the damage had been done: Africans would not soon forget *Mikono wa Damu*—the man with blood on his hands—and as a result, Germany's image as a "civilizing" force among "savages" became badly tarred with Peter's brush.

Even so, early German overlordship in Africa could not have been called benign. The Foreign Office at this time did not atract the most high-minded colonial civil servants. German district commissioners tended to give muscle priority over patience and diplomacy in the management of subject peoples.

Nor was their outlook frowned on by higher authorities. To encourage settlement, the government made large-scale concessions of African land—particularly in the fertile northern regions—to farmers and private firms, riding roughshod over traditional laws of tribal ownership. As often as not, administrators and colonists alike looked on the African as a raw material to be exploited. The Tanga railway and pier, as well as the few other public works which the government undertook, were built by forced, often unpaid labor. Field hands and domestic servants on European farms were also shanghaied.

Working conditions, to understate the case, were unattractive. Africans in German employ toiled twelve hours a day, seven days a week, received a few handfuls of rice or stale maize meal for their daily fare. At the slightest hint of malingering, a laborer could be chained up for several days without food or water, or be given the notorious *"hamsa ishirini"*—twenty-five lashes with a hippopotamus-hide whip called a *kiboko,* which could expose a man's backbone in a single stroke. In 1907, when the German colonial administration underwent drastic reforms, the newly appointed colonial secretary, after visiting German East Africa, remarked that "it makes a very unfavorable impression on one to see so many white men with negro whips."

Even African local rule was a charade. For all his printed credentials and robes of office, the jumbe was little more than a hostage. He held no real powers but was expected to recruit the men—and sometimes the women—of his village for forced labor tasks, and also to see to it that every householder paid the hut tax promptly to the akida. If the jumbe's quota fell short by so much as a single worker or a single rupee, he was instantly triced up and given his dose of *"hamsa ishirini"*—usually by the akida himself. For it was in the office of akida that Germany's real authority among the tribes rested. No government official was more loathed and feared, even though the akida, while seldom a black African, was not a white man either.

But the subjugated tribesmen knew that the akida was only the instrument of a higher jurisdiction which they found intolerable—and which they were prepared to resist with all the force at their command. For a while, it almost appeared as if that force might prove too much for the Germans.

The first clash was also the longest and most fiercely fought. Oddly enough, it involved the tribe most distantly removed from forced labor, the hut tax and the kiboko. In the remote central highlands, the masters of all they surveyed were the Wahehe, an intensely xenophobic nation of six-foot warriors—no less intelligent, brave, proud or arrogant than any Junker. Led by an aristocratic Sandino named Mkwawa, the Wahehe held the neighboring tribes of the region in perpetual semi-slavery, and for many generations no one had dared to challenge their authority. But to the German administration it was clear from the outset that if Foreign Office rule were to become the law of the land in the new colony, the Wahehe must be domesticated. Accordingly, in the summer of 1891 a punitive expedition was mounted against them.

The force consisted of 360 askaris, a field piece and a machine gun, more than enough firepower to make short work of any primitive army no matter how large. So confident, in fact, was the column's commander, the veteran Captain Emil von Zelewsky, that he did not even trouble to open his ammunition cases and assemble the machine gun as his troops approached the Wahehe capital of Iringa.

It was an appalling act of recklessness. A very smart guerrilla tactician, Mkwawa had sent out spies and scouts to observe every step of the enemy advance, while his own army converged swiftly and silently in the concealment of the thick undergrowth. Zelewsky never had a chance. Shortly before dawn one morning, Mkwawa and four thousand Hehe warriors burst from the dense thorn on both sides of the column's dirt footpath and within minutes had cut the German force to pieces with their muzzle-loading rifles and spears. A few of the askaris were able to jam cartridges into their own rifles, rally round Zelewsky and stem the onslaught for a few brief moments. But it had to be a reenactment of Custer's last stand; Zelewsky emptied the chamber of his revolver into Mkwawa's whooping phalanx and then thumped to the ground with a spear blade in his throat. Only a handful of men from the column's rear guard managed to escape annihilation.

Of course the massacre could not go unpunished, and another German officer was assigned to the taming of the Wahehe. The pugnacious Captain Tom Prince had been born a British subject; his boyhood idols were Nelson, Wellington and Gordon. But he also had a German mother, and after failing to secure a commission with a British regiment, entered the Military School at Kassel. In German East Africa, his volatile temperament quickly won him the sobriquet *"Bwana Sakarani"*—the wild one—among his askaris. It is said that when he arrived on the scene of the earlier Wahehe ambush, he stood over Zelewsky's skeleton, held the skull before him and swore an enraged oath to wreak a terrible vengeance on Mkwawa and his entire nation.

Seven years of attrition followed. Prince's troops, although vastly outnumbered by the Wahehe, were better armed. In uncountable skirmishes and pitched battles, they slowly blunted the tribe's fighting edge and converged in gradual stages on Iringa, eventually capturing the fortified capital in 1894. But Mkwawa, the symbol and sparkplug of resistance to the white intruder, remained at large. So long as this stubborn and brilliant soldier could rally even a handful of tribal warriors to his cause, an immense region of German East Africa would be German in name only.

At one time during the seven-year standoff, Prince took a brief leave in Germany and returned to East Africa with a wife. She may have exercised a temporizing influence over him, for he presently began applying political intrigue to divide the Wahehe against each other. In the process, the couple came to know and like many members of the tribe's royal family. When one puppet king proved loyal to Mkwawa and was hanged for treason, Magdalene Prince wrote: "I wept bitterly, and even now I am mourning for the black gentleman, though my reason struggles against it. He could not betray his Mkwawa blood; Tom is quite upset too."

Over the long haul, Prince's kid gloves seemed to pay more dividends than his iron fist, as growing numbers of Wahehe showed less inclination to defiance. Many even came to look on Prince, rather than Mkwawa, as the tribe's ruler. And hostilities ceased altogether in 1898, when Mkwawa himself was trapped in the bush by a German sergeant—although the proud king blew his own brains out rather than be taken prisoner. His skull was sent to Germany and put on display in a museum. Prince was eventually awarded the hereditary title "von."

But the uneasy peace that settled over Iringa did not seem to infect the rest of the country. German askaris were continually on the march against other refractory tribes. In the central region, the Wagogo proved not much less martial than their Wahehe neighbors. Many bullets and lives were expended in hard-fought battles with the Wachagga on the slopes of Kilimanjaro. Isike, King of Unyanyembe, emulated Mkwawa by committing suicide before the Germans could capture him when they stormed Tabora, Unyanyembe's fortress-capital, after a long and bloody siege. Machemba, ruler of the Yao nation in the southwest, defied the Germans to do their worst. "I do not fall at your feet," he replied to a surrender ultimatum, "for you are God's creatures just as I am. . . . If you are strong enough, then come and fetch me." Between 1889 and 1904, upwards of seventy-five punitive expeditions were mounted in various parts of German East Africa—which meant that some new tribal disturbance broke out approximately every ten weeks.

And the worst was yet to come. In 1905, the entire southern half of the colony erupted in a rebellion that threatened for a time to drive every white oppressor into the sea.

It began harmlessly enough, when a few witch doctors near the southern post of Liwale began peddling a magic water which they claimed would guarantee personal health and bountiful harvests. Soon, however, the pharmacists let it be known that their product had other attributes, including the power to protect the consumer from gunfire by turning bullets into water.* Given so infallible a shield against enemies, and given enemies like the Germans and their Arab-Swahili akidas, it was not surprising that some sort of plot should have been hatched.

---

* This particular theory of ballistics has prevailed for some time; it was most recently tested by Congolese rebels in the 1960s.

What was unusual, however, was the swiftness with which it spread, the secrecy in which it was cloaked and the suddenness of the outbreak itself. Moreover, since the tribes of the Liwale region were generally thought of as the most docile in the colony, the Germans were caught completely unprepared. The first sales of the water were made in mid-July of 1905. Early in August a party of Benedictine missionaries was attacked and murdered near Liwale. A few days later, Liwale itself fell in a massed moonlight assault, and German garrisons in other isolated posts soon found themselves under siege. By September, tribal armies were mobilizing across the south, and nearly every white man and Arab in the region had become a headless or otherwise mutilated corpse. For a short while, even Dar es Salaam and the other large settlements in the north went on the alert. Mau Mau may have been a peaceful protest demonstration alongside the 1905 uprising that came to be known as the Maji-Maji rebellion.†

The fury of the insurrection was exceeded only by the barbaric thoroughness with which the Germans stamped it out. Under the orders of the governor, Graf von Götzen, the small colonial army and police force cut the heart out of the movement—and out of the entire region—in a systematic scorched-earth campaign which witnessed the burning of every cultivated acre and nearly every village across a territory the size of Germany itself. By early 1907, when the Maji-Maji leaders had been rounded up and hanged, the southern half of the colony was a vast smoking ash heap. In the famine and disease that pounced down on the gutted land, more than 100,000 men, women and children died. Nearly two decades would have to pass before much of the south ceased to be a disaster area.

Even after the suppression of Maji-Maji, however, German East Africa remained a powder keg. Would the next uprising witness another ghastly pyrrhic victory, another disemboweling of the land? Could any tribe be trusted? An official directory of the colony's districts about this time listed the African communities that had not joined in the southern revolt. There were practically none. For the protection of German administrators and troops in isolated stations, the government posts known as *bomas* were surrounded by high stone walls with battlements, very much like Beau Geste forts. As long as this state of affairs prevailed, German East Africa could not be expected to attract investments or settlers. It would not be very different from an armed camp.

As it happened, Maji-Maji proved to be the last of the major uprisings in the colony. After 1907, German East Africa entered into an era of relative tranquility. One reason for this was the maturing of the *Schutztruppe*, the colony's defense force.

Colonial rulers of the late nineteenth century had a favorite expression for the pacification of hostile peoples. They called it "teaching the natives

† *Maji* is the Swahili word for water.

a lesson." In German East Africa, this may have worked the other way around. It so happened that many of the tribes in that colony not only resented foreign domination but were better fitted to do something about it than most inhabitants of neighboring white-ruled lands. To the north and northwest, in British East Africa and Uganda, there was comparatively little tribal unrest. Under the animal brutality of the Portuguese to the south, one might have expected the subject peoples to rise in revolt against a white domination backed up by a few guns and less competence, but the tribes were supine. Only the Germans, despite the vaunted Prussian military know-how, seemed almost powerless to maintain order among the small but violently dissident chiefdoms in their uneasily held East African possession.

Some idea of what the Germans were up against can be found in passages from a field service manual prepared for the Schutztruppe, voicing a respect for the primitive adversary that bordered on admiration:

His mobility and incredible marching powers, coupled with accurate knowledge of the country, make him able to carry out apparently impossible detours. He has no fixed line of retreat, for after a defeat his forces break up into small parties, which retire in all directions, and concentrate again at points previously agreed upon, often in the rear of the victorious troops. . . . After discharging their fire-arms, the natives retire hastily . . . to get ahead of the column so that they may repeat their attack. . . . By constantly harassing their enemy in this way, they hope, while avoiding serious losses on their own side, to tire him out, compel him to expend his ammunition and gradually reduce his power of resistance till he can be finally overwhelmed by an energetic spear-attack. . . . The natives think themselves beaten in a fight only when they have suffered great losses: flight and escape with small losses they regard as a success. . . . Only in exceptional cases has it been possible to take them by surprise. . . .

In short, the Germans were facing a brilliant guerrilla foe, a master of the hit-and-run tactic, and this left the military commanders in the colony with little option but to borrow a page from the enemy's book. During the struggles against the tribes, adversity became the mother of invention, giving slow but visible birth to a remarkable colonial army. The Schutztruppe was remarkable because of the thoroughness with which the men who led it learned their trade from the tribal warriors whom they sought to tame.

One of the most conspicuous ways in which the Germans emulated the enemy was in the recruitment of a black rank and file. This practice was not unique among the colonial powers, for the climate alone argued eloquently against European troops. ("A white force," as one German officer put it, "would be nothing more than a walking hospital.") But the Germans, under harassment of unmatched intensity, had more reason than anyone to recognize that the best men to rely on in bush fighting were those who had invented it. In the early days, the bulk of the enrollment had come from the Sudan, long known as a mother-lode of Africa's finest soldiery. But these troops, being foreigners, were mercenaries in the purest sense of the word. German field commanders soon began looking closer to home: the courage and skill—not to mention knowledge of terrain—shown by the enemy within the borders of the colony amply demonstrated that here was the real backbone of the Schutztruppe. Provided, of course, that with the right incentives of pay, privilege and prestige enough tribal soldiers could be induced to change sides.

Slowly but steadily, this was what happened. After Mkwawa's power had been smashed, large numbers of Wahehe began joining up. New askaris also came from the Angoni tribe, an offshoot of the once-dreaded South African Zulu nation. There was lively recruiting among the Wanyamwezi, Wagogo, Wasukuma and other peoples with long and proud martial traditions. Such fighting men hardly needed instruction in tactics which, to them, were conditioned reflex.

But they had a great deal to learn. Even to a spear-thrower, the art of wielding a bayonet, with its grotesque, unfamiliar thrusts and parries, did not come readily. A breech-loading rifle could mystify even the sharpest-eyed owner of an old Arab muzzle-loader. Machine guns and field artillery pieces were simply witchcraft. Hours and days and weeks and months had to be spent impaling straw dummies with bayonets, shredding wooden targets with lead. Only gradually did inexperience give way to savvy, but in due course, the Schutztruppe askari came to call his rifle his "*bibi*"—his wife.

Nor did training stop with weapons. Newly enlisted askaris were a heterogeneous, undisciplined lot, often carrying out tribal vendettas within their own companies. To become a single force with a single purpose, raw black recruits had to learn not only European military formations but all the ways of a white man's army. No German private at home was more thoroughly and rigidly indoctrinated. Basic training was structured on the standard German infantry drill regulations and modified only when absolutely necessary. (Direct commands, for example, were barked out in German, lengthier orders or explanations delivered in Swahili.) Bugles had the men on their toes around the clock, hastening them—always at double time—to company assemblies, to lectures on rifle and machine gun maintenance, to issues of equipment, to the rifle range, to seemingly perpetual spit-and-polish inspections of weapons, barracks, uniforms and kit. For endless hours, the askaris goose-stepped up and down parade grounds as screams of "*Links! Links!*" echoed in their ears. Instant flogging corrected the slightest infractions of Prussian discipline.

But the last thing the Germans wished to do was break the men's spirit. Nor did they. German officers scrupulously refrained from interference in the black enlisted man's private life, offered personal advice only when it was sought, respected tribal religions and customs. Pay scales were generous: up to thirty rupees (about $9.90) per month for privates, 150 rupees ($50) for African noncoms—at least twice what askaris in the neighboring

British colonies received. The ordinary soldier was seldom required to do fatigue duty or other menial work, but usually supervised forced labor gangs. (He also had his own personal servant, called an "askari boy.") There was even a house organ for the troops: a Swahili language newspaper called *Kiongozi* (The Leader). The few men who could read were always mobbed by huge listening audiences on publication days.

All this was intended to create a high level of esprit, to inculcate in the troops the awareness of belonging to an élite corps, to wean them away from tribal bonds and win their first loyalty to the Kaiser. It worked. In his smart khaki jacket, trousers and puttees, shining black leather belt and ammunition pouches, Foreign Legion-type kepi with the bright gold Imperial Eagle on the front, the Schutztruppe askari came to see himself as part of a black master race.

He reveled in this distinction and abused it freely. A Schutztruppe private wishing to spend a night in a strange village would have his "askari boy" deliver a cartridge to the local jumbe. This was the universally recognized— and dreaded—peremptory order to the jumbe to make four beds: one for the askari, one for his rifle, one for his ammunition pouch and one for his uniform. It also meant that the jumbe was to furnish the soldier's bed with a "blanket"—meaning a woman or women. Unless he wished to feel the bite of the kiboko, personally wielded by the askari himself, the jumbe would hasten to comply. Even the German officials and their puppet akidas came to be less feared and loathed than the Schutztruppe askari.

And the government smiled. Once again, the time-tested colonial practice of divide and rule was paying dividends.

Regardless, however, of inherited African fighting skills and acquired Western discipline, the Schutztruppe askaris could be no better than the officers who led them. Unlike the German colonial civil service, the Schutztruppe officer barrel contained few bad apples. A two-and-one-half-year term of military service in Africa counted double toward pensions, and misfits were carefully weeded out. A minimum of three years' active duty plus an unblemished record were required before any candidate could approach the Schutztruppe selection board. The medical examination was probably the most rigorous in the German army. Character, intelligence, initiative and, above all, leadership were also sought out and tested exhaustively, and the end product was a colonial officer aristocracy unsurpassed by any other imperial power.

But like the black troops who were taught to strip machine guns and operate field telephones, newly arrived Schutztruppe officers also had much to learn. As cadets at Kassel, they had studied Clausewitz and Schlieffen; in East Africa they took a postgraduate course in the much more ancient strategies of unknown, aboriginal field marshals. Their education came the hard way, and it was thorough. Leading companies and patrols through the bush, officers soon learned that the tribal enemy's most effective offensive tactics were daylight ambushes from dense thorn or man-high grass, night or dawn rushes across open ground. These attacks, as often as not, were launched on a column from all quarters—with the officers always the principal targets.

After a few such actions, the fledgling commander came to know—and respect—the range and accuracy of enemy poisoned arrows, spears (both the throwing and stabbing types) and muzzle-loading rifles. He was made to realize that his column was particularly vulnerable while pitching or breaking camp. He learned what weapons to hit back with: at night, cold steel was preferable to rifle or machine gun fire; in daylight actions, especially when the Germans attacked, massed volleys had a more devastating effect than independent fire. Experience taught officers to curb their over-confidence during pursuit: as often as not, the "fleeing" enemy was simply leading the German force into another ambush.

The Schutztruppe officer was never allowed to forget his foe's intimacy with the terrain, his artistry with natural cover. A great deal was learned about such "primitive" obstacles and booby traps as log barricades on forest paths, tangled thorn *zaribas* that stopped an assault more effectively than barbed wire, camouflaged pitfalls lined with needle-sharp bamboo stakes. Unceasing vigilance on the march became intuitive to German company and platoon commanders. They never allowed machine guns or field pieces to be carried in sections—not after what had happened to Zelewsky. Columns never halted in thick bush or tall grass; when they did stop to rest, the askaris never stacked their rifles but held them ready to fire. Orders were often given to shoot any porter who laid down his pack while marching. Locally recruited guides could seldom be trusted; when passing through enemy country it was not uncommon to have guides roped together so that they could not escape and reveal the German route of march. Field exercises, in short, were the real thing with a vengeance. And the officers proved apt pupils. They had to. The slow learner could become a corpse very quickly.

In seeking to cope with tribal mobility, the Schutztruppe had to become even more mobile, or at least try to. The result of that effort may have been the enemy's most valuable contribution to the German force: a basic combat unit unique among all colonial armies. This was not a division, regiment or even a battalion, but the small independent command known as the field company. It consisted of seven or eight German officers and NCOs and 150 to 200 askaris—including two machine gun teams—and was often beefed up by large numbers of tribal irregulars called *ruga-ruga*. With several hundred porters toting ammunition and food, with two collapsible boats for quick passage of river barriers, with its own surgeon, even with its own cobblers, the field company was almost totally uninhibited by supply lines. While it sometimes formed part of a larger (though still flexible) group called an *abteilung*, it was logistically autonomous, and able to make long forced marches much more swiftly than the conventional rifle company with its complex administrative and supply links to battalions and regiments. It also had an essentially loose-jointed internal organization which permitted it, if necessary, to emulate the tribal foe and scatter when outmaneuvered, then reform quickly and counterattack. In effect, the Schutztruppe field company was a self-contained micro-army.

The force never forgot its debt to the "natives" who taught the Germans their lesson. Perhaps the highest compliment paid to the enemy was this observation in the Schutztruppe field manual: "Apart from wars against native rebels, our Protectorate Force must always reckon with the possibility that it may find employment against the troops of foreign Colonial powers. In that case the tactics of European warfare will in the main be applied, but at the same time it will be in many ways expedient to take lessons for such wars from the native methods, which have grown up out of the nature of the country, and to avail ourselves of such lessons as occasion may serve."

The writer may not have realized his gifts of prophecy.

As the Schutztruppe evolved into a well-oiled engine of bush warfare, its gradual subjugation of the hostiles did not witness a corresponding letup in German mistreatment of the colony's black population. If anything, excesses grew worse, and in due course the whole question of German rule in all of its African possessions became a political hot potato in Berlin. In 1906, a wave of anti-colonial feeling began to gather momentum in Germany with increasing press and eyewitness reports of repression in the African territories. Ordinary citizens were shocked to learn not only of the methods used to stamp out the Maji-Maji uprising but the near-genocide attendant on General von Trotha's campaign against rebellious Herero tribesmen in South West Africa, where, according to one German historian, "we solved the native problem by smashing tribal life and by creating a scarcity of labor." The result was the only general election in German history that turned on a colonial issue, as opposition Catholics and Social Democrats sought to bring down Prince von Bülow's conservative government with salvoes of documented atrocity stories and charges of general maladministration in Africa. Although Bülow managed to survive, his liberal opponents gained so much clout in the Reichstag that the entire colonial apparatus underwent a complete overhauling. Thus the stage was set for the third and most promising period of German rule in East Africa.

While the streamlined Schutztruppe may have inhibited rebellion, German East Africa's progressive regime did something even more important: it encouraged willing and even cheerful compliance with the law of the land. Wielding the new broom was Dr. Bernhard Dernburg, newly appointed head of a newly created Colonial Office which took over the reins from the Foreign Office. A hard-nosed idealist, Dernburg accomplished in less than five years what previous German administrations had failed to do in two decades. During his incumbency, incompetents and sadists were screened out and summarily removed from office. Not a few had to stand trial for acts of cruelty or malfeasance. Replacing the misfits was a new breed of efficient, humane colonial civil servant, usually the product of Dernburg's own creation, the British-modeled Colonial Institute in Hamburg. Among the most capable of the reformers was Albrecht von Rechenburg, East Africa's new governor. Dernburg had declared that the indigenous African was "the most important factor in our colonies," and Rechenburg put teeth in that statement by enforcing stern measures to curb racial oppression and promote African welfare.

By present-day standards, these reforms might suggest the work of a feudal baron in a magnanimous frame of mind toward his vassals, but in 1907 they were revolutionary. The use of forced, unpaid labor went on the books as a criminal offense. All settler work contracts with Africans had to be drawn up under government supervision. Flogging, although not outlawed, was permitted as punishment only for a few serious crimes, and even then could not be administered unless in a doctor's presence. New land laws sharply curtailed wanton expropriation of tribal acreage by white farmers and plantation owners. African cultivators themselves were encouraged to grow cash crops, with technical aid from trained agronomists, guaranteed prices and government assistance in marketing the produce. Rechenburg's administration launched a new era of black goodwill toward the German overlord.

There was a practical as well as a humanitarian side to the reform movement. Dernburg, a former director of the Darmstadt Bank, set himself the task of making the German colonies into paying propositions—with the help of public funds if necessary. Although he did not quite bring this off, he went far toward priming the pump. In 1908, the Northern Railway, which had been dragging its tracks from Tanga for nearly twenty years, received a vote of twelve million marks to hasten its progress; in 1911, it was completed. Work also gathered momentum on the colony's main trunk line, the seven-hundred-mile Central Railway linking the coast with Lake Tanganyika. The first tracks had been laid down in 1905. By 1912, railhead had arrived at Tabora, four hundred miles inland, two years ahead of contract schedule, and reached the lake in 1914. This made Germany a competitor for interior markets which had previously been all but monopolized by Belgian traders in the Congo.

In anticipation of the hinterland commerce which the Central line would tap, Dar es Salaam, the coastal rail terminus, blossomed into the country's main port. Bristling at last with its overdue wharves, electric cranes, railway freight sidings and warehouses, Dar was capable of handling even the eight-thousand-ton passenger steamers of the Deutsch-Ostafrika and Oster-reich-Lloyd lines—the latter running a direct service between German East

Africa and Japan. Harbor facilities also expanded in Tanga, Bagamoyo, Kilwa, Lindi and other ports. The developing infrastructure swiftly made its worth felt in the beginnings of a modest overseas trade. When Dernburg took office in 1907, the value of German East Africa's exports stood at barely twelve million marks; five years later the figure had almost tripled.

Dernburg also made enemies, particularly in the settler community. While the colonist farmers could applaud the stimulus given to railways and harbors, the consequent easier access to markets and the higher prices for their crops, the reforms—cutting off a source of cheap land and cheaper labor—stuck in their craw. By energetic lobbying, they eventually succeeded in having Dernburg and Rechenburg removed—for whatever good that may have done them. Dr. Solf, Dernburg's successor in the Colonial Office, simply picked up where Dernburg had left off, founding his policies on the proposition—far in advance of its times—that "the natives have a right to demand that they be regarded by the more highly developed races as an end and not a means." As for the new governor of German East Africa, Dr. Heinrich Schnee proved to be the most liberal of all German colonial administrators. "The dominant feature of my administration," he made it clear, was to be "the welfare of the natives entrusted to my care."

Indeed, Schnee's stewardship saw the flowering of what was probably Germany's most noteworthy contribution to African betterment: a small but successful educational program. One thousand government-assisted elementary, secondary and vocational schools, with a total enrollment of about sixty thousand, may not have been much for seven million functional illiterates, but they were approximately one thousand more schools than the enlightened British colonialists next door could claim. Instructor qualifications, curricula, textbooks, teaching materials, all met standards unmatched anywhere else in tropical Africa. As late as 1924—long after the colony had become British—the visiting American Phelps-Stokes Commission reported: "In regards to schools, the Germans have accomplished marvels. Some time must elapse before education attains the standard it had reached under the Germans."

Foreign praise was not confined to social advances. The Biological Agricultural Institute at Amani in the southern Usambaras was described in a postwar British study as "a tropical scientific institute superior to anything in the British colonies or protectorates." At Amani, a staff of specialists conducted soil analyses, developed plant hybrids, experimented with fertilizers, studied vegetable pests, ran courses in agronomy for settlers and Africans and performed a host of other tasks aimed, as one official put it, at "encouraging . . . the production of those raw materials which Germany must still draw from foreign lands for the sustenance of its people and industries." The findings at Amani and other research stations in the colony were not kept secret but shared with agriculturists of all nations. So, too, were medical discoveries: doctors the world over benefited from pioneering work in tropical diseases carried out in German East Africa by such bacteriologists as Ehrlich and Koch. Ehrlich's .606 became a standard therapy for sleeping sickness and relapsing fever. On the basis of its achievements in medicine and agriculture alone, the German presence in East Africa seemed more than justified.

Nor did economic progress lag. Although Dernburg and Solf were never quite able to bring German East Africa out of the red, the colony was far from being indigent. Thanks in great part to Amani and the new railways, the seven years preceding the war witnessed something like an agricultural bonanza. From the broad verandas of their farmhouses in the Usambara mountains, settlers looked down on a sea of cultivation. One hundred thousand acres lay under sisal alone—the country's biggest money-maker. The volcanic soil of nearby Kilimanjaro nourished two million coffee trees which yielded over a thousand tons of high-grade beans every year. Despite a fall in prices, rubber paid well; nineteen million trees grew on two hundred thousand acres. There were also thirty-five thousand acres of cotton, not to mention huge fields growing tobacco, cereals, sugar and a multiplicity of other farm products. The land basked in a climate of plenty.

Whatever the Germans made in their colony was made to last. It was also very German. The settler farmhouses were solid, roomy structures of stone and timber, exuding comfort, suggesting many generations of large, robust apple-cheeked families to come. Wilhelmstal, the summer capital, nestling in the dark green, tumbling slopes and shadowed valleys of the Usambaras, might have been a cozy Bavarian hamlet. The big coastal ports, in their own torrid way, could be likened to miniature Hamburgs and Bremens. Dar es Salaam was the showcase city of all tropical Africa. Any other colonial capital, even Britain's modern, fast-growing Nairobi to the north, was a shantytown by comparison.

July of 1914 was Dar es Salaam's moment of glory. The Central Railway had at last reached Kigoma on the eastern shore of Lake Tanganyika, and the Germans celebrated the event with a mammoth exhibition in the capital. Trade fair, agricultural show and carnival rolled into one, it was attended by thousands of visitors, not only from the neighboring colonies but many European countries as well. As their steamers entered the narrow neck of the harbor, the tourists saw a frieze of modern office buildings and church steeples along the broad palm-lined waterfront. Ashore, they gaped at the Governor's Palace with its imposing arrangement of tall white colonnades and graceful oriental-style archways. Going to the farm products exhibit at the Botanical Gardens, they welcomed the shade of the carefully tended acacia and mango trees bordering the wide avenues on which they rode in electric broughams or rubber-tired rickshaws. They played billiards and drank schnapps at the Dar es Salaam Club, enjoyed sauerbraten, kassler rippchen and knockwurst at the Kaiserhof Hotel and the Roumanian Cafe at the Burger Hotel, sampled the products of the Schulz-Brauerei in any

number of beer gardens. There was even a touch of the Fatherland in
African garb: cotton robes, *kangas* and *kikois* were adorned with gaudy
color prints of the Graf von Zeppelin's newest dirigible airship. For visiting
Germans, Dar es Salaam must have induced a strong sense of *déjà vu*.

For better or worse, Germany was in eastern Africa to stay. "Take it
all in all," as Peters once remarked, "German East Africa is perhaps not a
colony of the first class. It is not a British India, nor may it be compared
with the rich islands of the Malay Archipelago, or the West Indies. But it
offers splendid openings in several directions, and if properly managed it
may be developed into a wide and very important field for German enterprise, and take its great share in the commerce and prosperity of the world."

The future looked sunny.

2

The Stepchild

LONG BEFORE CARL PETERS presented Bismarck with the surprise gift of German East Africa, there had been a powerful British presence in that part of the continent. England's earliest involvement in eastern Africa came about indirectly, at the end of the eighteenth century, as the result of a successful ploy aimed at thwarting Napoleon's designs on India. This was brought off in a treaty with the tiny but strategically situated Persian Gulf state of Oman, whose domains also happened to include Zanzibar. And, since Zanzibar was the African focal point of the most massive slave-trading apparatus on the Indian Ocean, the rulers of the little island soon came under pressure from their British allies to abolish the traffic. Although there was not much choice but to comply, Byzantine evasions and outright violations of various anti-slave trade treaties delayed the process for the better part of a century. To counter this dodging, the British Foreign Office made a practice of appointing conspicuously forceful diplomats to Her Majesty's Consulate in Zanzibar, with the result that the consul in time became the de facto ruler not only of the island but of a vast mainland region claimed by the Sultanate.

Concurrently, British explorers were drawing back the curtain of the East African interior and a swarm of British missionaries was teaching the savages to read and understand that nakedness would send them straight to hell, while British Indian subjects busily consolidated long-standing commercial interests on the coast. To all practical purposes, eastern Africa for the first four-fifths of the nineteenth century was British territory.

Except that Britain wanted no part of it. Zanzibar and the coast ports, to be sure, had strategic usefulness as outposts on the southern route to India, and there was also the unshakable British commitment to suppressing the slave trade. But no one saw these things as incentives to possession. East Africa seemed to have few natural resources worth exploiting. Whatever trade the country offered could be enjoyed without the burden of formal annexation. The climate and diseases were an electrified steel fence against colonization. No British statesman in his senses wished to incorporate this vast millstone into the Empire.

It was an attitude that changed almost overnight, after Peters' intrusion and Bismarck's claim to an East African sphere of influence. Although the complexities of Europe's political cold war dictated a passive British stance on the actual German annexations, this was soon counterbalanced by the reasoning—if that is the word—which animated so much of the so-called scramble for Africa. It would violate every canon of imperial nonlogic to sit by and allow the Germans to become undisputed king of the same hill which Britain had been spurning for eight decades. To protect interests which were not really threatened, the British Foreign Office concluded that the lion, too, must have its share of East Africa. Bismarck offered no objection, and in 1886 a Delimitation Commission, representing Britain, Germany and France, consented to a British sphere of influence just north of the Kaiser's bailiwick—in the region which was later to become Kenya.

With that done, Whitehall washed its hands of the Empire's unwanted stepchild. Its only real concern with the sphere was that a British presence be visible there, thus inhibiting the imperial designs of other European powers. Whether the country was developed or not was of small moment, since it could be administered—at no cost to the British taxpayer—by private interests. Accordingly, a Royal Charter was granted to Sir William Mackinnon, a monkey-faced Scots businessman and philanthropist whose Imperial British East Africa Company took over the management of the sphere.

Foreign Office indifference to the fortunes of British East Africa was equaled only by Mackinnon's zeal for his charge. He lost no time in launching schemes designed not only to tap the country's resources but also to deal the slave trade its death blow. The only shortcoming of these programs was that they failed to work, and it was not long before Mackinnon and his directors found themselves on a collision course with bankruptcy—with no prospect of being bailed out by the government which they served as surrogate landlords in East Africa. Indeed, the Company was to founder, but only after Britain did another official about-face with the surfacing of a second threat from Germany—or, more correctly, from Peters.

To the west of the British sphere, on the lush northern shore of Lake Victoria, lay the ancient African kingdom of Uganda. In 1888, Peters led an expedition across the upper edge of Mackinnon's territory to annex Uganda for the Fatherland. This was no ordinary filibuster because Uganda was no ordinary slab of imperial real estate. The country straddled the headwaters of the Nile, and this invested it with a certain uniqueness. A belief was then gaining currency among European colonial statesmen that whatever power dominated the Nile source could somehow stem the river's flow, transform its delta into a desert and thus become master of Egypt. This in effect meant control of the Suez Canal and the route to India. Small matter that the hypothesis was one of the more spectacular absurdities in the history of geopolitical thinking; anything with the remotest bearing on the security of India was a panic button for even the most level-headed Victorian politician. When Peters' plans became known, Britain felt compelled to act swiftly.

She was fortunate. At that particular moment, Germany considered that her own European political interests would be best served by an amicable England. Accordingly, Count Caprivi, Bismarck's successor, seized the opportunity to repudiate Peters' claim and accommodate Lord Salisbury, the British Prime Minister. By the Anglo-German Treaty of 1890, the black ruler of Uganda—who, of course, had not been consulted—found himself a ward of Queen Victoria. This gave new importance to the older and previously neglected British sphere in the east simply because it could serve as the corridor for a railway that would hasten British troops to Uganda if some hostile power ever tried to sabotage the Suez Canal via the back door.

Much confusion and acrimony marked the early stages of the railway's planning, which encountered strong resistance in Parliament from a small but vocal anti-imperialist Opposition. Actually, however, the line was only a side issue to a larger and more fateful question, turning on the difference between a sphere of influence and a protectorate. The first was a quasi-official holding which entailed little government responsibility or expense; the second was formal ownership and cost the taxpayer a great deal. Should the British sphere in East Africa be transformed into a protectorate? For nearly two years, this was England's most hotly contested political dispute; only Irish Home Rule inspired more eloquent invective on the floor of the House of Commons than did the raging marathon debate over possession of an uninviting equatorial wilderness.

But the "Little Englanders" could only fight a delaying action; Britain's jingo tide was at full flood, and in 1894, Parliament voted to annex the East African sphere. For administrative purposes, the country was divided into two protectorates—British East Africa (including Zanzibar) and Uganda—but in any case, the entire region was now officially in the Empire, and all obstacles to the building of the railway were removed.

Or almost all. For more than half a decade, nature waged unrelenting war against the army of British engineers and Indian laborers who dragged the tracks across 680 miles of desert, thorn, mountain and swamp. The builders also had to cope with an unending deluge of criticism and obstructionism at home, where the Little Englanders continued their efforts to derail the line by blocking its funds. But somehow the tracks crawled ahead. On December 20, 1901, the wife of the railhead engineer drove in the last spike of the Uganda Railway at the very edge of Lake Victoria's eastern shore.

British statesmen could now rest easily with the knowledge that they had fiinally secured their hold on the headwaters of the Nile.

With or without the line, there was actually little likelihood that Uganda would ever be invaded once it had become a British protectorate, and from that standpoint it could be said that Parliament had thrown five million pounds—the cost of construction—on a tropical trash heap. But the railway did something that no one had anticipated. In traversing the Great Rift Valley, which bisects present-day Kenya, the tracks passed across a previously inaccessible highland region that was just as temperate and fertile as the plateau and mountain zones of German East Africa. Not only could every imaginable tropical and temperate plant be grown on the Rift in abundance, but the soil and its grasses were tailor-made for large-scale livestock farms. Within two years of the railway's completion, the country once dismissed as no more than a passageway to Uganda had a white settler population of nearly five hundred. Less than a decade later, some three thousand British, Canadian, Australian, New Zealand and South African farmers had put down roots in the highlands of British East Africa.

It was a unique community, probably the most aristocratic in the annals of colonization. The names on the title deeds of many settler farms could have filled several pages of Burke's Peerage. The vast wheat fields, sheep pastures and coffee plantations on the highlands were studded with cricket pitches, tennis courts and polo fields. Additional tone was furnished by a steady stream of upper-crust transients whose opulently outfitted big-game hunting treks helped make British East Africa into a resort not much less fashionable than the Riviera.

But the atmosphere of sport and high living was deceptive, at least in the protectorate's infancy. If the visitors were rich, the settlers, their blue blood notwithstanding, were not. They played hard but they worked much harder. The early years of colonization in the highlands witnessed a never-ending struggle—often a losing one—against drought, floods, plant pests, livestock diseases and a near-total absence of markets for the scant produce which the settler farms managed to yield up. Unlike their German neighbors, the colonists in British East Africa had no Amani to help them over the rough spots. Not a few settlers went bankrupt and had to sell out. But they did have the soil, and the soil, in the long run, could not fail them. By 1914, there was no longer the slightest doubt that a highland farm or ranch was the soundest of investments. Like the Germans across the border, the British settlers in East Africa had found a new home.

One thing British East Africa always had going for it was a relatively friendly tribal population. Despite some inevitable acts of brutality, the white settlers on the highlands for the most part expressed their Anglo-Saxon superiority over the "natives" in a kind of arrogant paternalism which probably generated less resentment than did the harsher Prussian attitudes on the other side of Kilimanjaro. But not all the tribes accepted their new masters without a fight, sometimes a very hard fight, and although the protectorate government had to cope with few serious uprisings—certainly none on the scale of Maji-Maji—a certain amount of military muscle was needed. The King's African Rifles provided it.

Like the Schutztruppe, the KAR had originally been an all-Sudanese force and had gradually absorbed local tribesmen until the bulk of its rank and file was recruited from within the two protectorates. But three factors may have put the KAR at a disadvantage alongside the German troops. One was the Schutztruppe's organization into field companies, far more mobile than the KAR battalions. The Germans also held a conspicuous edge in firepower, with two machine guns per field company and only one to each KAR company. Finally, the Schutztruppe could claim far more actual combat experience, arising from the near-perpetual rebellions that took place in German East Africa before 1906. For all this, however, the KAR had no reason to feel inferior. If its fighting record was not extensive it was still of the highest order. If its training did not quite meet the Schutztruppe's rigidly enforced standards, neither did it fall very far short. The British officers, usually products of Sandhurst, were first-class leaders and seasoned hands at bush warfare—having gained their experience not only in East Africa but also in other British possessions on the continent. On the strength of their personalities alone they always brought out the best in their men. Indeed, general esprit in the KAR was probably far above that of the Schutztruppe.

In 1906, a KAR company commander—who will be heard from again—paid a visit to German East Africa and took the opportunity to compare the two forces. "I do not doubt," he wrote, "that the Germans have created as fine a military machine out here as they have done at home. . . . They are every bit as good as our K.A.R. but lack the ties which exist between officer and man. In the K.A.R. it is a bond of genuine friendship. Among the Germans it is the tie of iron discipline. War alone can prove which is the most effective."

PART II
THE ANTAGONISTS

3

Manowari na Bomba Tatu

O<small>N</small> J<small>UNE</small> 6, 1914, the star attraction of the Dar es Salaam exhibition arrived in the port. The thirty-four-hundred-ton S.M.S. *Königsberg* could not fail to command admiration wherever she sailed. One of the Imperial Navy's most modern light cruisers, she had been chosen, shortly after her commissioning in 1906, to escort the Royal Yacht *Hohenzollern* on Kaiser Wilhelm II's state visit to England. *Königsberg* herself did not look unlike a yacht. The slim, almost svelte lines of her 375-foot hull hardly bespoke the punch carried in her main armament of ten 4.1-inch guns and her twin torpedo tubes. This firepower, along with a speed of twenty-four knots, made *Königsberg* the most formidable seagoing engine of destruction in the western Indian Ocean.

Before her arrival, Germany's naval might in East African waters had not been very menacing, consisting as it did of an aging gunboat and an even more venerable survey vessel. Together, these two warships represented less than the threat of a water pistol to even just one of the three arthritic cruisers comprising the Royal Navy's Cape of Good Hope Squadron, whose area of operations also embraced the East African coast. But *Königsberg* made it a new ball game.

Not that her mission was to intimidate the British; little international tension existed in those brief spring weeks before Sarajevo. But there was nothing to be lost and much to be gained from showing the flag—and flexing the muscles—for the Kaiser's black subjects in German East Africa. At Dar es Salaam, Tanga, Bagamoyo, Kilwa and other ports, Africans packed the waterfronts to watch the sleek white titan glide silently into the harbor and then make coconuts fall from the palms with the thunder of her salutes. Once at anchor, *Königsberg* became open house to thousands of tribal visitors. They marveled at her long guns, her bright decks, her gleaming engines and—above all—her three towering funnels. "For [Africans] to establish a warship's size and power," wrote *Königsberg's* captain, Commander Max Looff, "the number of stacks is all-important." The German cruiser soon became known up and down the coast as *manowari na bomba tatu*—the man-of-war with the three pipes.

The first part of *Königsberg's* East African cruise was not much different from a holiday. The picked crew of 322 officers and men received VIP treatment at every port. They were entertained at government residences and private homes. On sightseeing jaunts, they sampled coconut milk, bought African carvings and other curios like any tourists. Looff and others found time to try their hand at big-game hunting in the interior. And although gun drills and other exercises were still carried out scrupulously, they seemed less like a rehearsal for war than a feature of the Dar es Salaam exhibition. But by mid-July, even as cables from the German Foreign and Colonial Offices soothed Governor Schnee with reassurances minimizing the threat of hostilities, Looff was receiving entirely different instructions from the Admiralty in Nauen. In brief, *Königsberg* was expected, in the event of war, to launch immediate attacks on enemy shipping in the Indian Ocean.

Such a mission would hardly surprise the British, very much alive to *Königsberg's* potential as a commerce raider. To be sure, the likelihood of a major naval campaign in East African waters seemed remote. Nowhere on the seas, in fact, was Germany in a position to challenge the might of the Royal Navy. (U-boat warfare was yet to come.) But neither was the Imperial fleet impotent. The battle cruiser *Goeben* and the light cruiser *Breslau* were already prowling the eastern Mediterranean; their presence in that theatre would shortly help win Turkey over to the Central Powers. Admiral Maximilian von Spee's East Asia Squadron steamed at large in the western Pacific, ideally situated to disrupt Royal Navy dispositions anywhere between the Indian Ocean and South America. And looming very large on the German Admiralty's planning boad was the strategy known as *kreuzer-krieg*.

What this called for, simply, was hit-and-run forays against Allied merchant shipping by fast, heavily armed cruisers which operated independently of any fixed naval base or coaling station, replenishing fuel and other supplies from the bunkers and holds of the prizes they sank. It was believed that the Indian Ocean would be particularly vulnerable to such raids, since the Royal Navy was expected to concentrate its power in home waters. Already, the cruiser *Emden* was poised to cut her immortal swath of destruction along the sea lanes from the upper Bay of Bengal to the Dutch East Indies. And on the East African coast, the Germans had *Königsberg*.

But what would *Königsberg's* destination be if—or rather when—war broke out? Would she steam north, toward the convoys bound from India to Aden en route to the Red Sea, or south toward the busy shipping lanes around Madagascar and in the Mozambique Channel? Just what were Looff's orders?

The British worked hard to find out, mainly through their consul in Dar es Salaam, Norman King. The most popular member of German East Africa's diplomatic community, King played a sparkling game of bridge, and in idle conversation between rubbers at the Dar es Salaam Club he had been able to collect a great deal of useful information on German troop and ship movements. In *Königsberg's* captain, however, he ran into a stone wall. Looff found himself baffled and shocked when King approached him casually one day and showed "the unbelievable impudence to wish to question me . . . about my intentions in case of war—with Russia!" After that encounter, Looff ordered his officers to keep a wide berth of "the spy consul." But as July drew to a close, so, too, did the time for prying and speculation. Whatever Looff's secret orders might be, he must be prevented at all costs from carrying them out.

On July 27, the Royal Navy's Cape Squadron was anchored in the harbor of Port Louis, Mauritius, on a routine cruise, when the squadron commander, Rear Admiral Herbert King-Hall, received a wireless message advising that *Königsberg was* expected to leave Dar es Salaam at any moment. War or no war, the German cruiser was to be kept under tight surveillance. King-Hall immediately ordered his ships to weigh anchor and steam north for Zanzibar. From there, they would move to maintain a permanent watch off Dar es Salaam, thus blockading *Königsberg* in the event of hostilities— or sinking her if she chose to come out and fight.

The fifteen-hundred-mile voyage was a busy one, as crews scraped and painted energetically to change the squadron's complexion from white to wartime gray. But the cruisers themselves steamed at a sluggish pace. King-Hall's flagship *Hyacinth,* fastest of the squadron, could log no more than twenty-one knots at her best, while the other two ships, *Astraea* and *Pegasus,* did well at twenty. These speeds were further reduced by a curious regulation which forbade the use of Welsh coal on the Cape station; only patent blocks of inferior Natal coal were permitted in the ship's bunkers. And even more time was lost when the squadron put in at the port of Diego Suarez, on the northern tip of Madagascar, in a vain search for coal that would not foul the boilers. Thus it was not until early in the evening of July 31 that the three cruisers took station off Dar es Salaam.

Looff, meanwhile, had not been idle. That same afternoon, the DOA liner *Tabora* had arrived in Dar es Salaam from Zanzibar, with news that the British squadron would probably arrive the following day. Looff had already made *Königsberg* ready for sea. He had also arranged a fueling rendezvous with the twenty-five-hundred-ton steamer *Somali,* which had been converted into a collier. There was nothing to keep him in Dar es Salaam. At 4:30 P.M. on July 31, with her crew at action stations, *Kö-*

nigsberg steamed out of the harbor and into the Indian Ocean. The Royal Navy's coal crotchet had saved the German cruiser from being bottled up.

By just ninety minutes. The sun had barely dropped beneath the fast-vanishing land astern when the officer standing lookout on *Königsberg's* foremast signaled the head-on approach of King-Hall's squadron. As Looff maintained his cruising speed of twelve knots, the British warships swiftly deployed around him: *Astraea* on the port beam, *Pegasus* ahead, *Hyacinth* astern, each at a distance of three thousand yards, each also holding at twelve knots. If war should suddenly be declared, Looff could never take *Königsberg* out of range in time. Singly, none of the three old British cruisers could stay afloat long under the German's 4.1-inch broadsides; but together they could pound *Königsberg* into junk.

For three quarters of an hour the procession continued out to sea. It was almost as if the four cruisers were steaming together in a peacetime exercise. But Looff had an ace up his sleeve. He had ordered his chief engineer to get up steam for twenty-two knots, but not to make smoke—which would arouse suspicion. Then he waited for his chance.

It came when a sudden squall pounced down from the southwest, cutting visibility to only a few feet. Looff snapped out a string of orders. Instantly, *Königsberg's* bow wave became a hurting white comber as the cruiser swept sharply around, 180 degrees to starboard, and her engines put the full bite of 13,500 horsepower into her propellers. Before King-Hall could realize what had happened, the British screening formation was broken. Invisible to each other in the storm, *Königsberg* and *Hyacinth* passed in opposite directions at a combined speed of nearly sixty miles an hour. After about ten minutes, when the squall lifted, the British cruisers were well out of range and night had fallen.

At this point, Looff ordered the helm over again, ninety degrees to port, or due south, and *Königsberg* continued to pile along, at just under twenty-three knots, for an hour. Then it was safe to order the ship seaward again, and to cut her speed back to twelve knots. On August 1, as the sun rose over an otherwise empty ocean, Looff ordered a fourth change of course: due north toward Aden. He had now put at least one hundred miles of blue water between himself and King-Hall's plodding cruisers. It might just as well have been one thousand.

Whether or not *Königsberg* would go commerce raiding, however, remained a moot point. On August 1, Germany was still at peace with the world. August 2 and August 3 went by with no news from Dar es Salaam. The cruiser's wireless room was strangely silent. Looff did not know that the British had been delaying cable messages that passed through their African colonies en route from Berlin to German East Africa, and that they had been trying—usually with success—to jam wireless transmission between German stations. For all that Looff could tell, *Königsberg* was ploughing north on a fool's errand, her coal supply dwindling, a heavy sea making up.

On Tuesday, August 4, *Königsberg* had lifelines rigged along her decks as she plunged and reared through the towering white-maned waves, continually shipping solid water over the bow while the wind bucketed the canvas dodgers on her bridge. From every part of the cruiser came an irregular cacophony of bumps and crashes below decks, the shrill nagging of wind against stays and spreaders, the almost human groan of steel frames under stress. But the radio shack remained mute. Only an infrequent and incoherent cackle suggested that *Königsberg* carried wireless.

On August 5, the skies cleared but the seas grew even heavier. *Königsberg* was now just southeast of Cape Guardafui, the eastern tip of Africa's "horn," and only a few hours' steaming from the main shipping lanes between India and the Red Sea. Crews stood at action stations, lookouts fanned the horizon with their binoculars, Wireless Officer Niemyer continually fiddled with his dials. Not even a smudge of smoke appeared on the lenses, not so much as a dit came out of the radio shack.

Then the sun went down and the wireless began to chatter. It kept repeating a single word: EGIMA. That was the prearranged secret code—one day late. Germany was at war with Britain, France and Russia.

To at least one member of *Königsberg's* crew, this seemed an insufficiently Wagnerian way of heralding Armageddon. "Strange," wrote Lieutenant Richard Wenig, a youthful gunnery officer. "The moon shines as before, the sea roars, the rigging wails—nothing has changed! How is that possible? Does not the moon have to hide in the clouds, does not the sea have to darken? Nothing! They smile at human affairs; what does the quarrel of atoms mean to the universe!"

But Looff had no time to ponder the indifference of the cosmos. At any moment, Allied merchant ships or troop convoys might appear on the horizon, easy prey for *Königsberg's* guns. The leopard had begun to stalk the antelope herd.

4

The Junker and the Egghead

O NE POTENTIAL victim which may have crossed *Königsberg's* path just before hostilities was the British passenger liner *Pentakota,* which entered Mombasa's Kilindini Harbor on August 4, after a routine voyage from Bombay. *Pentakota* carried no wireless and everyone aboard had been out of touch with world events for over a week. As the ship came to anchor, Second Officer Clement J. Charlewood noticed a curious sight. Also moored in the harbor were large numbers of Arab dhows flying the American flag. They, too, had just arrived, bringing in British, French and Belgian nationals from German territory, only hours before the declaration of war that would have seen them interned.

With hostilities, Charlewood's Royal Naval Reserve commission automatically became activated, and he combed the bazaars of Mombasa's Old Town in search of an Indian tailor who might have just enough gold braid for the single sub-lieutenant's stripe required on each of his shoulder boards. He was more fortunate in finding the material than was Mombasa in defending herself against possible German attack. Mounted near the port's lighthouse was a pair of antiquated naval guns with a range of about one thousand yards; they would be as useful as air rifles should *Königsberg* open up from eight miles offshore. There were also one or two dozen KAR askaris to throw back any massed land assault, and Charlewood was ordered to patrol the harbor entrance in command of a tugboat whose crew consisted of volunteer bank clerks. Mombasa was probably safe from any bombardment by the Ruritanian navy.

A state of even less readiness existed in British East Africa's interior. Nairobi went into a panic after someone reported seeing a German plane over the city. In fact, the East African Luftwaffe consisted of a single biplane which had been sent out for the Dar es Salaam exhibition, and which had crashed on its first flight. But for several days, Nairobi responded to impromptu air raid alerts as citizens spotted birds, locusts and even the planet

Venus, which was unusually bright that summer. Eventually, calm was restored and the townspeople could even laugh sheepishly at the verse that the scare had created:

> I thought I saw an aeroplane
> Upon the Athi plain.
> I looked again and saw it was
> A Kavirondo crane.

But this only reflected the colony's almost total unpreparedness, particularly on the most vulnerable target of any enemy thrust: a 150-mile section of the Uganda Railway which ran parallel to—and less than 50 miles from —the German border. In August of 1914, there were two KAR battalions in British East Africa and Uganda, with a total strength of twenty-four hundred officers and askaris. Nearly all of this force, however, was on patrol or garrison duty in remote northern regions near the Sudanese and Abyssinian borders. Only two half-companies—fewer than 150 men—in Nairobi were available to move down and protect the exposed section of the railway. It would take at least two weeks of forced marches to bring the main body of the KAR into position. In short, the war had caught British East Africa with its pants down. It was only by a curious stroke of good fortune that the German forces—numerically about equal to the KAR—were unable to pounce on the railway immediately.

The Schutztruppe failed to launch its blitzkrieg mainly because the Governor of German East Africa did not want to go to war.

One day in January of 1914, a young Schutztruppe platoon commander went AWOL from his field company near the British border to spend an afternoon drinking beer in the large German settlement of Moshi. While walking toward the town, he fell in with another European, a tall, well-built civilian who was chewing on a stick of sugar cane. The two chatted idly, and in the course of the conversation the officer mentioned his French leave, adding that he hoped the newly appointed commander of the Schutztruppe, who had just arrived in the colony, would not hear of it. I'm told, he said, that this fellow von Lettow can be a perfect bastard about such things. The other man seemed amused. As they approached the outskirts of Moshi, which was also a military post, the youthful lieutenant was surprised when several senior officers saluted him, astonished when his companion returned the salute. Then he blanched, stopped dead in his tracks and came rigidly to attention. At ease, at ease, said the other, smiling. What you told me was told to a comrade. He certainly won't inform the commander.

The son of a Prussian general, Lieutenant-Colonel Paul Emil von Lettow-Vorbeck looked every inch the Junker. A snapshot taken at Moshi in 1914 shows him relaxing in a wicker armchair on a settler's veranda. In another photograph, made four years later, he is taking his ease in a British officer's camp chair as a prisoner of war. Although both pictures find him seated, he somehow seems to be standing at attention. The hair on his balding skull is as short as any military barber can crop it. His brows angle inwardly toward a large beaklike nose and the eyes of a bird of prey. Beneath a severely trimmed mustache, sharp lines draw his thin lips into an expression suggesting that the smile with which he favored the truant lieutenant was a very rare indulgence. In von Lettow, one saw the Imperial Eagle come to life.

Von Lettow did not only look the part. In 1914, he was forty-four years old and had served in the German army for a quarter of a century, holding posts which qualified him almost uniquely to lead the Kaiser's forces in East Africa. During his tenure as a General Staff officer, he had made a point of studying the military aspects of German colonial policies. The naval strategy of any East African campaign would not be unfamiliar to the man who had done detached duty as commander of the Marine Battalion at Wilhelmshaven, taking an active part in maneuvers and exercises of the German fleet. He had been given a first-hand look at his future enemies while fighting alongside the British in the Boxer Rebellion; the main impression he took from this episode was what he described in his memoirs as "the clumsiness with which English troops were moved and led in battle." Von Lettow had also studied another future adversary while on detached service with pre–Boer War South African forces under the great commando leader Louis Botha. The Afrikaners gained a different verdict; von Lettow found that "the excellent qualities of this low German race, that had for generations made its home on the African veld, commanded my respect."

Von Lettow's introduction to bush fighting tactics came the hard way during the Herero uprising in South West Africa, where he was severely wounded in one eye. After being assigned to German East Africa, he rapidly won the unqualified respect of his officers and men—although their personal affection for him, which was enormous, may have been diluted at times by his apparently well deserved reputation as a martinet. "Understanding of human nature did not seem to be von Lettow's strong suit," wrote a member of the Schutztruppe medical staff, while another subordinate remarked that "life in his immediate neighborhood was a trifle oppressive." Even so, von Lettow may have been almost unique among Prussian officers in that he was often capable of unbending, and in his nice gift for looking the other way at the right time—as illustrated by the encounter with the AWOL lieutenant at Moshi. And complaints against his occasionally harsh discipline were never leveled by the black troops, who all but worshipped him, and whose esteem was fully reciprocated. It is probable that no white commander of the era had so keen an appreciation of the African's worth not only as a fighting man but as a man.

Arriving in Dar es Salaam shortly after New Year's Day of 1914, von Lettow immediately set about bringing his new command to a war footing.

He could not afford the luxury of wishful belief that the mounting European tensions of the preceding decade would be resolved peacefully. He had to assume that war would come, and he had to make the Schutztruppe ready for it. But this was no simple matter. It meant a careful study of the vast terrain where the force might have to march and fight; it meant personal inspection visits to fourteen field companies scattered from Kilimanjaro to Lake Nyasa, from the Indian Ocean to the volcanoes below the Mountains of the Moon. Only a microscopic fraction of this vast territory could be reached by railway, practically none of it by road. For a thorough reconnaissance, von Lettow had to make three separate journeys—by trains, aboard warships and lake steamers, and, mainly, on foot, tramping across more than one thousand miles of bush. The entire survey occupied the better part of half a year.

Von Lettow's findings gave him a certain amount of optimism. Schutztruppe morale was conspicuously encouraging. So, too, was the attitude of the white colonists toward the impending war. Most of the German farmers had already formed rifle clubs which trained regularly as para-military units; they were soon to be incorporated into the force as *"Schützenkompagnien"*—sharpshooter companies. Many settlers, moreover, were retired army officers; some of them, including Tom von Prince—the legendary *"Bwana Sakarani"*—had been classmates of von Lettow at Kassel. Here was an unmatched reservoir of future leadership.

But other things left much to be desired. Many of the Schutztruppe's best African NCOs had been lured into the police force, which von Lettow called "a travesty of a military organization." He was also greatly disturbed by the "pretty low level" of his own troops' marksmanship with both rifle and machine gun. The former weapon created the most vexing problem, not so much because of the askaris' tendency to fire high—a failing common to nearly all colonial African soldiers—as because the rifles with which the force was armed were woefully inadequate. Manufactured three decades earlier, these single-shot .450-caliber Mauser museum pieces, with their thundering reports and black-powder cartridges that gave off huge clouds of smoke, had been considered satisfactory against tribesmen carrying spears or muzzle-loaders. But von Lettow realized that in modern warfare the Model 71 rifle would be practically an enemy secret weapon, since the smoke alone must instantly reveal the German soldiers' positions, not only to a seasoned African fighter "but even to the European accustomed to office work." In 1914, only three Schutztruppe field companies carried modern rifles; von Lettow was able to rearm three others before the war broke out. But the remaining eight companies would have to rely on weapons which seriously weakened the force's firepower.

Von Lettow's overriding concern, however, was with strategy. The inspection tours gave him a clear picture of the kind of country in which he must wage war, and he saw that in this topography lay both his weakness and his strength. While he knew that a major conflict of the powers would be settled on the battlefields of Europe, that any East African campaign would go all but unnoticed, he asked himself "whether it was possible in our subsidiary theatre of war to exercise any influence on the great decision at home."

At first glance this seemed quite unlikely. Von Lettow did not delude himself with the fancy that the Schutztruppe stood the remotest chance of victory in East Africa. With a declaration of war, the Royal Navy would block off any troop reinforcements from Germany, while the British and presumably the Belgians would be free to pour in men and guns until they held the required numerical edge.

Recognizing, therefore, that he was powerless to reduce the odds against him, von Lettow began to evolve a strategic plan aimed at increasing them. If the Schutztruppe was inevitably to be outnumbered by, say, two to one, why not make it five or even ten to one? Might it not be possible to adopt tactics that would compel the enemy to bring in the largest possible force, thereby diverting troops and resources from the arena where they would be most desperately needed?

Clearly, the trick could not be brought off by taking a passive stance: "hostile troops would allow themselves to be held only if we attacked, or at least threatened"; it was imperative that the Schutztruppe "grip the enemy by the throat and force him to employ his forces for self-defence." This in turn raised the question of just where the jugular was situated. The answer came readily: "One thought at once of the frontier between German and British East Africa"—or more specifically, that hundred-mile stretch of the border within raiding distance of the Uganda Railway, "the main artery of the British territory." Concerted German attacks on that most sensitive strategic nerve should bring in swarms of British troops.

This border area, moreover, was strategically crucial not only as a jumping-off place for Schutztruppe assaults on the Uganda line. Von Lettow also recognized it as the vital sector of defense against any large-scale British drive into German East Africa. It had to be: the Germans' own Northern Railway from Tanga had its inland terminus at Moshi in the foothills of Kilimanjaro. And Kilimanjaro straddled the border.

A superficial glance at a map might have given the impression that the Northern Railway was all but immune from attack. Unlike the Uganda line, it ran away from the border and not alongside it. A direct British thrust at the Moshi railhead would be blocked by the mass of Kilimanjaro, flanking moves across the frontier northwest of the mountain would run into an immense, waterless volcanic region, while any drive below the border from the east would come up against the Pare and Usambara ranges, a natural fortress behind which the German railway ran south for nearly two hundred miles. But it was this seemingly impenetrable region which in fact offered the British their easiest avenue of land access to the enemy colony.

Dividing the northern end of the Pare range and the southern slopes of Kilimanjaro was a sort of pass about twenty miles wide. In its center lay the British border post of Taveta, from which a rough wagon road ran east, across sixty miles of thorn, to the Uganda Railway station at Voi. An invading force, detraining at Voi, could not only cross the border through the "Taveta Gap," as it was called, but in all probability could throw out a tight enveloping column to hug the northern flank of Kilimanjaro and descend on Moshi from the west. In short, two corridors of enemy penetration lay on either side of the mountain, barely fifty miles apart. This meant that the Kilimanjaro region, with Moshi as the principal base of operations, had to be the nerve center of German strategy in any East African campaign. It also stood to reason, therefore, that here was where the Schutztruppe must be concentrated.

And it was over the question of Kilimanjaro that von Lettow ran head-on into Governor Schnee.

It would have been quite unnatural if Schnee had not regarded war as the worst possible calamity that could overtake German East Africa. Even after Sarajevo, he was resolutely set against the colony's embroilment in a conflict that promised to undo everything which his social and economic reforms had accomplished. The outbreak of the war itself did not shake his resolve to refrain from any remotely provacative act on the part of the German East African government. This policy was neither totally isolated nor totally unrealistic. In British East Africa a somewhat similar anti-war feeling existed among the settlers, who had no wish to see the budding fruits of their arduous farming labors go down the drain of a remote European quarrel. British East Africa's governor also shared these sentiments outspokenly. But Schnee hoped to do more than just ignore the war by inaction. He intended to stay out officially, invoking a legal precedent that had been established three decades earlier. In the Neutrality Clauses of the 1885 Congo Act, to which all colonial powers were signatories, it was specified that in the event of a European war, the African possessions of the belligerents might remain neutral. It was on this agreement that Schnee pinned his hopes. Actually, however, the clauses contained a catch requirement: the consent of all parties concerned. Since it was generally believed that Germany rather than the Allies would benefit from African nonbelligerence, Schnee never really stood a chance of keeping his colony aloof.

But he tried manfully in other ways, and one of the most visible results of his effort was seen at the outbreak of the war, when the Schutztruppe found itself deployed far from the positions it should have taken up— months earlier—in the Kilimanjaro area. Had the force been concentrated here, the unready British in all likelihood would have sustained a stinging initial setback.

Von Lettow had not accepted Schnee's policy supinely. As the crisis in

Europe approached its boiling point, the Governor's Palace in Dar es Salaam became the scene of a raging marathon dispute between soldier and egghead over the disposition of the Schutztruppe. In his frustrated anger, von Lettow found it hard to observe the formal courtesies expected even of the Schutztruppe's commander toward the Emperor's own viceroy in East Africa. He stopped short only of open insubordination. His requests sounded almost like direct commands as he told Schnee that not a day must be wasted in hastening the bulk of the force from its scattered garrisons to the one sector where its presence was vital. Schnee refused out of hand. Massing the Schutztruppe on the border was precisely the kind of belligerent gesture which he had no intention of making. Von Lettow in turn would not accept this. So persistently and furiously did he press Schnee on the deployment issue that other officers nicknamed him the "Mad Mullah," after a Somali guerrilla leader who had been driving British forces to distraction for a decade.

The intensity of the clash was never more forcibly dramatized than in an event that took place shortly after the war began. Oddly enough, the scene was not Kilimanjaro but the coast. On August 8, two of King-Hall's cruisers, *Astraea* and *Pegasus,* shelled Dar es Salaam as a prelude to demanding acceptance of an agreement whereby German East Africa's coastal ports would become open cities. Intending to resist, von Lettow immediately ordered seven field companies to march on Dar es Salaam, and sent a Schutztruppe officer ahead under a flag of truce, to inform the British that "negotiations . . . must be conducted through me alone." But just then he received orders from Schnee to withdraw the force. The governor, it seemed, had already accepted the British terms—without even informing the commander of the Schutztruppe. Von Lettow could only swallow the humiliation, although with the greatest difficulty: "For a soldier it was not inspiring to find that here, under the eyes of a thousand good troops, an agreement had been concluded which forbade us to undertake any hostile act in Dar es Salaam, while the enemy was not so bound, and that we had received no information of a step of such great military importance."

In the end, though, Schnee capitulated; even he could not pretend indefinitely that the colony was at peace. By mid-August, "the holder of the supreme military power," as von Lettow mockingly referred to Schnee, "was successfully persuaded to agree to moving the bulk of our forces to the Northern Railway." Von Lettow believed that Schnee had consented to the move "not so much from the conviction of [its] usefulness than from the desire to get rid of me in Dar es Salaam." The "Mad Mullah" had prevailed. And "relations with the Governor remained sultry." They were to stay that way.

Schnee's change of heart certainly had nothing to do with the first German offensive of the campaign. On August 15, Taveta fell to the three hundred askaris of two Schutztruppe field companies, as the twenty-four-man garrison of the British East Africa Police fired a token volley and retired in good order on Voi. This gave von Lettow the distinction of being the first and only German commander of the war to occupy British soil. It gave him little else. The two companies that took Taveta had already been stationed at Moshi, but in mid-August, the main body of the Schutztruppe had yet to be moved up to the Kilimanjaro front. There were still nowhere nearly enough troops in that sector for further thrusts of any importance.

Concentrating the force in the north was a very laborious business. Several field companies had to march more than three hundred miles before they reached Dar es Salaam or other points on the Central Railway. And the line itself was of little use in hastening troops and supplies up to Moshi, since it had no connection with the Northern Railway. In peacetime, passengers and freight had been carried by sea from Dar to Tanga, whence they moved up-country on the Northern line; but now the ports were sealed off by the Royal Navy, and it therefore became necessary to start work on a military road across 150 miles of broken, mountainous country between the two rail arteries. This meant troops needed two weeks—or ten days if they stepped off—to cover a mileage that a train could swallow up in less than twenty-four hours.

At first, the columns seemed to crawl. It was one thing for field companies to maneuver swiftly and independently in combat, but when they became elements of a massed army on a forced march over a narrow road, serious problems arose. During the move north, wrote von Lettow, "the march and supply of a single company in the conditions there prevailing required about the same consideration as would a division in Germany."

But von Lettow also had a stroke of luck at this time when he enlisted an officer who outranked him by three grades. Just before the outbreak of the war, Major General Kurt Wahle of the Saxony army had arrived in the colony to visit his settler son and see the Dar es Salaam exhibition. With the Royal Navy now blocking off his return to Germany, he was glad to serve under von Lettow as Inspector of Lines of Communication. Later in the campaign, Wahle was to take over a combat command which gave the enemy some bad headaches in the western and southern theatres of operations, but he probably made one of his important contributions to the East African war effort as the architect of the Schutztruppe's logistics apparatus. His organizational skills and resourcefulness were mainly responsible for what almost amounted to a miracle of troop movement. Barely a month after Schnee had agreed to unleash the Schutztruppe, the larger part of the force had taken up its positions on or near the Kilimanjaro front.

But by now, the British, too, were more or less ready. Recovering from their initial surprise, they had rushed the two KAR battalions down from the northern frontiers and deployed them at key posts along the railway. Further precautions against attack had been taken by improvising a pair of armored trains which regularly patrolled the line's most vulnerable section. And the KAR was no longer the only British force in the field. In London, the Committee of Imperial Defence had approved the dispatch of four thousand Indian troops to East Africa; led by Brigadier General James Marshall Stewart, the first contingents debarked at Mombasa on September 1. Before the month was out, upwards of five thousand Indian, African and British soldiers were on hand to launch an offensive. The Schutztruppe was now outnumbered two to one.

To von Lettow, this could only be an encouraging first step toward his larger objective.

5

Killer Guppy

T HE FIRST THING that Commander Max Looff did after *Königsberg* received the EGIMA code message signaling the declaration of war was to order the word passed to all German merchant ships within wireless range. Their captains were instructed to make directly for Dar es Salaam or the nearest neutral port. Then, as if in compensation for the previous five days' inactivity, Looff suddenly found himself busily occupied on the enemy shipping approaches to the Red Sea.

On August 6, the sun rose over perfect raiding weather. The heavy seas had flattened out during the night. The sky was cloudless, visibility limited only by the horizon. It was not long before *Königsberg's* lookout signaled smoke off the starboard bow. The cruiser at once bore down on her prey. It proved to be the North German Lloyd liner *Zieten,* carrying one hundred German marines homeward bound on leave from China. *Zieten* had already received Looff's message and was now headed for Dar es Salaam, where the marines would join von Lettow's force. Now the lookout sighted another column of smoke. Flashing a "stand by" signal to *Zieten, Königsberg* made for the new ship, which hove to promptly. She was the German *Hansa*, also complying with Looff's radioed instructions. The enemy sea lanes appeared uncommonly friendly.

Still another vessel was then spotted, but this one did not heave to. On being requested by wireless to identify herself, she immediately changed course. Looff ordered her to stop. Smoke tumbled from her funnels as she got up steam for headlong flight. This meant that *Königsberg* must also increase speed—to Looff's great ire, since his coal supply was beginning to run short. In a few minutes the enemy ship was in range, and a 4.1-inch shell screamed across her bow. That quickly stopped her engines and brought her colors to the masthead. Looff gaped at the German merchant flag: the Hamburg-bound *Goldenfels* had mistaken *Königsberg* for a British cruiser. There was nothing to do but signal an exasperated "Godspeed."

But the day was not over. Shortly after sunset, the lookout's night glasses made out a fourth wisp of smoke. *Königsberg* drew alongside a large passenger ship and was hailed cheerily by her captain in German—with a Japanese accent. The quarry this time was a neutral Nippon Yusen Kaisha liner, on which Looff himself had once voyaged to the Far East. He managed to return the greeting with a show of courtesy.

By now, the German Admiralty might have forgiven *Königsberg's* captain if he had disregarded the day's final column of smoke, which was sighted shortly after the Japanese vessel had resumed her course. Dutifully, the ship hove to at the cruiser's signal, and once again the skipper greeted Looff as an ally. But this time the joke was on the enemy: the officers of the *City of Winchester*, preparing to welcome a British warship, suddenly found that their sixty-six-hundred-ton freighter had become the first Allied prize of the war to be taken on the high seas by the Imperial Navy.

City of Winchester carried a cargo of tea valued at about two million dollars, and the bottom dropped out of the London tea market when news of the ship's capture reached England. But Looff cared less about the prize's holds than her bunkers. In six days of cruising, *Königsberg's* coal supplies had dropped from 850 to 200 tons; a full three days' supply had been burned up in the single hour she had spent breaking away from King-Hall's squadron at top speed. Now, four hundred tons of coal—nearly half her bunker capacity—could be taken aboard from *City of Winchester*. But when Looff inspected the coal, he found himself experiencing King-Hall's earlier frustrations over inferior fuel, for the British freighter burned only the lowest-grade Bombay coal—"poison for our boilers," as Looff put it. But he also knew he could not be choosy. For the rest of the night and most of the next day, the crews of both ships coughed unceasingly on the cheap black dust as they heaved coal aboard the German cruiser. In due course, *City of Winchester's* crew was transferred to *Zieten*, which then made off for Dar es Salaam, while the British vessel went to the bottom with two shells below her waterline.

But it was vital to Looff that he refuel again as quickly as possible. The new coal supply not only threatened to damage his engines but gave *Königsberg* barely a fortnight's cruising. A rendezvous with the collier *Somali* had been arranged; it was to take place in mid-August. But at least one more enemy prize before that time might yield up a less abrasive coal, even enable *Somali* to hold her own reserves for a later meeting. No more ships, however, were sighted: the Royal Navy seemed to have temporarily halted or diverted British Red Sea merchant and troop traffic. And the Bombay coal burned much too swiftly. The meeting with *Somali* fast became imperative.

On the night of August 12, *Königsberg* approached the rendezvous off the southern coast of Arabia in a half-gale. Waiting to meet her was not

Somali but a cruiser of the Royal Navy's East India Squadron, whose captain had acted on an educated guess. Thanks to the heavy weather, Looff barely managed to duck the enemy salvoes and vanish into the night. *Somali* was now instructed by wireless to join *Königsberg* in the lee of Socotra Island, a barren heap of rock and sand about six hundred miles east of Aden. The new rendezvous was set for August 19, giving Looff another week to seek out the now desperately needed enemy prize. The seas remained empty, making a mockery of *Königsberg's* five-thousand-mile cruising radius. When the warship's anchor rumbled out at the meeting place, the stokers were literally scraping the bottom of the bunkers, and the entire crew had gone on a strict water ration. *Königsberg's* drinking water was distilled from the ocean, but the process needed coal.

And *Somali* was nowhere to be seen.

Two days later, as the sun ricocheted off the towering rocks and drilled through *Königsberg's* deck awnings, a dehydrated and almost comatose lookout signaled the approach of a British warship. It was *Somali*. *Königsberg's* crew came to life. Lines were swiftly thrown out as the collier hove alongside. For the next two days, without letup, officers and men worked side by side, speeding the transfer of fresh water and food—and nearly one thousand tons of good Ruhr coal. Even a total eclipse of the sun failed to interrupt the transfusion. On August 23, *Königsberg* was again operational as a raider.

By this time, however, it had become clear to Looff that pickings on the northern sea lanes were far too lean. He therefore decided to try his luck with the liners of the French Messageries Maritimes off Madagascar and in the Mozambique Channel. Luck ran against him. The French had diverted the big passenger ships to the Madagascar port of Diego-Suarez—and the protection of its harbor guns—until *Königsberg* could be hunted down. A few Arab dhows were sighted by the cruiser's lookouts, but otherwise the horizon was empty. Once again the coal supply began to shrink, and at the end of August Looff was left with no choice but another rendezvous with *Somali*. It took place in an unsheltered anchorage off Aldabra Island, a green speck in the Mozambique Channel. Here, strong winds and a titanic running groundswell threatened to bash the two vessels together and send them to the bottom. Looff was forced to discontinue coaling after he had taken barely two hundred tons aboard.

But fuel was no longer his most pressing problem. *Königsberg's* engines had begun to show the effects of the Bombay coal, and were crying out for a shipyard. There was only one open to German ships, in Dar es Salaam, and Looff was certain that the port by now must be under Royal Navy surveillance. Not only was this the case, but Dar's wireless facilities had been destroyed in the British attack of August 8. Without radio contact, Looff had no intention of risking entry. Instead, he set a course for the delta of the Rufiji river, far enough south of Dar es Salaam and sufficiently isolated to enable a try at the repairs which he hoped might somehow be improvised. And so ended the first phase of *Königsberg's* raiding voyage. Looff could not have considered it a conspicuous success.

The British may have thought otherwise. As of early September, Looff had taken only one enemy prize, but as far as the Royal Navy was concerned it might just as well have been ten dozen. The mere fact of *Königsberg* being at large was enough to throw convoy organization and scheduling into disarray. "No convoys of transports," minuted the First Lord of the Admiralty, Winston Churchill, on September 5, "are to go across the Indian Ocean or Red Sea unless escorted by at least two war vessels, one of which must be stronger than *Königsberg*."

And whatever warships could be spared from escort duty or the search for *Emden* had their hands full trying to hunt down Looff's cruiser. It might have seemed a hopeless task. Not fully aware of the extent to which coal shortages and engine malfunctions plagued Looff, the Royal Navy was even more in the dark as to his whereabouts. Some track at least could be kept of *Emden,* whose prizes were often able to get off SOS messages before being sunk. But *Königsberg* was a ghost ship. Since breaking out of Dar es Salaam on July 31, she had been sighted by the British exactly once, on the night of August 12, and had almost immediately been swallowed up by the storm which abetted her escape. And even that brief encounter had been a stroke of near-miraculous luck. Upwards of a dozen British warships sniffed for the spoor of a single enemy cruiser on a watery emptiness almost twice the size of Asia. Their assignment might not have been much more difficult if they had been hunting for a guppy.

During August and September, moreover, the search was complicated by two outside X-factors. One was von Spee's East Asia Squadron, which had been outwitting Royal Navy pursuit in the western Pacific and which, it was feared, might slip through the Dutch East Indies into the Indian Ocean and add *Königsberg* to its muscle. Even more unsettling was the possibility that Looff might join forces with *Emden's* skipper and broaden the path of that raider's depredations against Allied shipping in the Bay of Bengal. This in fact was what appeared to have happened on August 28, when *Königsberg* was reported off Sabang on the northern tip of Sumatra. Two days later, however, another sighting had her a few miles from the Madagascar coast. Such reports and rumors could only intensify the state of alarm created by the invisible bandit on the Indian Ocean routes.

Looff did his best to enhance the buccaneer image. While en route from Aldabra to the Rufiji delta, he began sending out wireless messages in the clear, arranging a rendezvous off southern Arabia as a prelude to a big foray on troop convoys bound from India to Europe. The British Admiralty took the bait nicely, getting off radio warnings to Aden, Bombay, Karachi and Colombo, and also diverting warships—which could have searched more profitably elsewhere—to the fictional rendezvous point.

The hunt also continued in East African waters, despite the loss to the British squadron of two-thirds of its strength. In mid-August, King-Hall was ordered back to the Cape with *Hyacinth* to reinforce South African sea defenses which, in his absence, consisted of two thirty-year-old torpedo boats. Several weeks later *Astraea* was also taken off station for convoy service to South West Africa. Only *Pegasus* remained—three knots slower than *Königsberg* and hopelessly outgunned. "I had represented this to the Admiralty," wrote King-Hall in his memoirs, "when I received orders to withdraw the *Astraea* . . . but was informed that the risk was slight and must be accepted." The Lords of Admiralty, of course, had no way of knowing that *Königsberg* was then lurking in the Rufiji delta, and that *Pegasus* was almost within range of the enemy cruiser's guns.

It was not long, moreover, before *Pegasus* began developing engine trouble. On September 19, after nearly two months of cruising with inferior coal, her captain, Commander J. A. Ingles, decided that he could no longer put off a badly needed boiler cleaning. This seemed reasonably safe, since wireless messages and other reports had given no recent indication of *Königsberg's* possible presence in East African waters. Accordingly, *Pegasus* entered the harbor of Zanzibar for the emergency surgery. As shipyard artisans went to work in the boiler room, gun crews commenced manning their stations on twenty-four-hour watch, even taking meals inside the oven-like turrets. As a further precaution, King-Hall had left direct orders that *Pegasus* keep steam up at all times in at least one engine.

But Ingles now disregarded that order, displaying "that contempt for the enemy," as King-Hall put it, "which is at once the strength and weakness of the British sailor and soldier." In this case it was weakness. Should Looff learn of *Pegasus'* temporary paralysis, the game would be up for the British cruiser.

Looff did learn. Late in the afternoon of September 19, *Königsberg's* radio shack intercepted a wireless report that a British warship with two funnels had anchored in Zanzibar harbor. The German cruiser by this time had again become operational after a fashion. *Somali* had joined her in the Rufiji delta and was now doing double duty as collier and mother ship. Under cover of night, lighters had been towed in with additional coal, and makeshift repairs had been carried out on the engines. Looff might not have been able to roam the Indian Ocean indefinitely, but his ship was more than capable of making the 150-mile run north to Zanzibar. He lost no time in ordering steam and anchor up.

The approaches to Zanzibar were poorly defended. Two ships patrolled the entrance to the harbor and the twenty-five-mile-wide channel dividing island and mainland. Neither of these craft could by any stretch of the imagination have been called a warship, although each mounted a toy cannon and a machine gun. One vessel, the nine-hundred-ton *Khalifa*, carried a brass plate on her upper deck with the legend: RESERVED FOR SECOND-CLASS PASSENGERS WHEN NOT OCCUPIED BY CATTLE. The other was a

German tugboat named *Helmuth* which had joined the Royal Navy in Zanzibar harbor the day before war was declared, when her Indian engineer, a British subject, "accidentally" broke an eccentric rod. Now commanded by Sub-Lieutenant Clement Charlewood—who had previously guarded the entrance to Mombasa—*Helmuth* was patrolling the channel at dawn on September 20 when the bulk of a huge ship loomed up out of the half-light. Charlewood thought it was a British Union Castle liner whose captain was unaware of a regulation barring the channel to merchant shipping. He bore down and signaled the vessel off, only to see the Imperial Eagle break out at foremasthead and gaff, and to hear the crash of a warning shot. Helpless, Charlewood then watched *Königsberg* swing round in a half-circle, turn the five guns of her port battery on the harbor and, at a range of eleven thousand yards, methodically begin pumping shells into the inert *Pegasus*.

It was over in less than half an hour. *Königsberg* quickly closed the range to seven thousand yards as the smoke and flame of her steady broadsides began to obscure the fixed target. At one point an officer shouted to Looff that *Pegasus* had surrendered, and pointed to a white flag in the inferno. Looff ignored it, assuming correctly that some British sailor had panicked and that Ingles would never strike his colors. Indeed, Ingles hit back with vigor, but even at seven thousand yards he was hopelessly outranged. Ten minutes after the action began, all of *Pegasus'* eight four-inch guns had been knocked out. But the White Ensign continued to snap above the dying ship, and Looff continued to pour it on until he was certain that *Pegasus* would never get up steam again.

With *Pegasus* accounted for, *Königsberg* made off down the channel at full speed. Within eight hours she had vanished once more into the maze of the Rufiji delta, where the chances of discovery were almost nil. Unaware that no other British ships were in the vicinity, Looff had not wished to risk interception by tarrying in the narrow Zanzibar channel. He had therefore passed up several other targets in the harbor, including an Admiralty collier and the town's wireless station (although he did knock out a dummy radio mast). He also made a point of covering his tracks by laying down a string of mines that kept large vessels out of the harbor until about a month later, when a minesweeper cleared the entrance of several dozen empty gasoline drums. And, while smashing up *Pegasus,* the raider had disabled *Helmuth* with a 47-mm. gun of her secondary armament. When two shells bracketed the tug, Charlewood had prudently ordered his crew to abandon ship. Only the Indian engineer disobeyed orders and remained at his post. He was boiled alive when the third shell sliced open *Helmuth's* main steam pipe.

The damage to the tug was quickly repaired, however, and early in the afternoon, as soon as thirty-one corpses and near-corpses had been removed from *Pegasus, Helmuth* began to tow the barely floating ruin toward shallow water. But at two o'clock, *Pegasus* turned slowly over on her side. Then she sank.

6

The Horse Marines

Not all of the british in East Africa seemed to have the right attitude toward the war. Many settlers resented it openly. Although they were certain that it could not last more than a few months, that was quite enough time, they felt, for their farms to revert to bush. Others looked on it as something of a joke. Not atypical was the inebriated farmer-volunteer who celebrated his short tour of army duty by standing everyone to drinks at the bar in Nairobi's New Stanley Hotel, proudly waving a discharge paper which read: "Length of service: two days . . . Reason for discharge: hopeless and incorrigible." No one dreamed of sending him a white feather.

But large numbers also joined up eagerly, even though they tended to think of the war as a great lark. Bands of settlers cantered into Nairobi on horses and mules and formed themselves into mini-regiments of irregular cavalry. Their weapons were fowling pieces and elephant guns, their uniforms tattered bush jackets and broad-brimmed terai hats with fish-eagle feathers protruding from leopard-skin puggarees. They went by such names as Bowker's Horse and Wessel's Scouts, after the fellow-colonists who more or less commanded them. One called itself the Lancer Squadron ("Lady Monica's Own," for the governor's daughter) and galloped through the streets of Nairobi brandishing steel-tipped bamboo spears that had been hastily fashioned by a local blacksmith. It was as if Nairobi had been overrun by vigilantes.

The members of this aristocratic rabble were expert riders, crack shots, wise in the ways of the bush. They also knew little and cared less about formal soldiering, and were somewhat taken aback when they found themselves being issued regulation uniforms and organized into what was grandiosely called the East Africa Mounted Rifles. But they quickly recovered, and enjoyed their training to the hilt by disregarding it. Hardly a night went by that did not see at least half the force absent over leave from its camp on the racetrack outside Nairobi. Privates and lance-corporals often escaped fatigue details by pleading invitations to dinner at Government House. No one ever paid any attention to the challenges of the sentries, since no one (least of all the sentries) troubled to remember passwords or countersigns. If the men learned anything about drill they were at pains not to show it. Their pride and joy was the regular army sergeant-major who was supposed to whip them into a crack outfit and did not. He spent most of his time with his troopers in Nairobi, performing the manual of arms and bayonet exercises with a broom, in front of applauding customers in the New Stanley or Norfolk Hotel bars.

Then, one day, the East Africa Mounted Rifles went to war.

About two hundred miles from Nairobi, on the eastern shore of Lake Victoria, was the British port of Kisumu. To the Germans it was an important although not quite vital strategic objective. The port itself had the facilities of a miniature naval base and would be useful to the German fleet on the lake—which consisted of a tugboat named *Muansa,* armed with two one-pound pom-poms and a brace of machine guns. Kisumu, moreover, was the western terminus of the Uganda Railway; as such it could give a sort of back-door access to British East Africa and threaten communications with Uganda. Therefore it came as no surprise when, early in September, a Schutztruppe column of about six hundred men was reported to have crossed the border near the lake and to have occupied a village called Kisii, only about forty miles south of Kisumu.

To meet this threat, three KAR companies and a few police, totaling about half the German strength, were rushed down from Kisumu. They were to be supported by a detachment of about one hundred troopers of the East Africa Mounted Rifles. This force would move by train from Nairobi to Kisumu and then board a steamer for a small lakeshore village called Karungu, some forty miles west of Kisii. (Their horses and mules would make the voyage in a separate steamer.) At Karungu, the troops were to disembark and launch a flanking cavalry attack on the German column. For the pub-crawling trainees in Nairobi, the fun and games had ended.

Or should have. As their transport, a shallow-draft steamer named *Winifred,* approached Karungu, a detail of troops took up battle stations at the twenty-six-year-old Hotchkiss gun mounted in the vessel's bow. The commander of the unauthorized gun crew impersonated Lord Nelson. He found a cocked hat somewhere, improvised a row of medals from cigarette tins and peered through an empty ginger-beer bottle while giving the commands to sink an imaginary German fleet. When the gun "missed," he ordered the gunners court-martialed and flogged. It was still a grand lark.

Then a shell screamed overhead, only inches from the wooden upper deck awning, as *Muansa* steamed out from concealment in the papyrus along the shore and began blasting *Winifred* with her pom-poms. A metallic thunderclap rang out when one shell tore a four-inch hole in the steamer's funnel. Within seconds, *Muansa's* machine guns were also in range, stitching *Winifred's* upper works. Taking precarious cover behind lifeboats and ventilators, the EAMR troopers returned the German fire with their rifles, temporarily deflecting the enemy gunners' aim as *Winifred's* captain changed course and headed for open water. At this moment, the Hotchkiss gun also came into action with a single round. Then it had to cease firing as the change of course put *Winifred's* bridge directly in its line of fire. Hastily, the gun crew hauled it over the bridge and mounted it aft, only to find the stern railing blocking its muzzle. After being elevated on some whisky cases and biscuit tins it was ready to fire again. Then the makeshift mount collapsed, the gun blasted a few rounds into the sky, and an exasperated lance corporal swiftly cut away a section of the stern railing with a hacksaw. Now the Hotchkiss could zero in on *Muansa*. But *Muansa* was no longer in sight. Having kept the British force from a daylight landing, she had vanished once more into the papyrus.

Night fell. *Winifred* blacked out and anchored near the shore. Presently a huge shape loomed out of the darkness: *Muansa* again. One of the German officers hailed *Winifred* in English. He said his ship was the British steamer *Kavirondo* and requested that *Winifred* identify herself. *Winifred's* captain refused to take the bait. A long exchange of challenges ensued. The British troopers put aside their rifles and prepared to repel boarders with unfixed bayonets, meat cleavers, pocket knives and the machetelike bush-cutters called *pangas*. Presently the captains agreed to lower ships' boats and inspect one another under flags of truce. *Muansa* turned out to be *Kavirondo*.

Next morning the EAMR finally went ashore. But they were no longer needed. On the previous day, the two KAR companies had deployed on high ground overlooking Kisii and had launched a surprise attack while the Schutztruppe askaris were drilling in the village market square. The Germans bounced back quickly and raked the small British force with a 1.5-ounce field piece and several machine guns that kept firing all day and far into the night. But the smoke puffs of the old Model 71 rifles provided the KAR with perfect targets and the Germans sustained heavy casualties. Shortly before dawn, with 25 percent of its officers killed, the force withdrew from Kisii and recrossed the border.

So there was nothing for the East Africa Mounted Rifles to do but return to Nairobi, where they marched directly into the New Stanley, stacked arms in the lounge and sat down to breakfast while an Italian string orchestra played "Tipperary."

The fighting at Kisii was the first major action in the East African theatre —although "major" is perhaps too strong a word. Despite the proportionately high casualties and the ferocity with which both sides went at each other, the battle could only have been minor because it took place in the wrong part of the arena. Neither the Allies nor the Germans were concentrated heavily in the west. At about the time of the Kisii action, some KAR units made a not very significant thrust across the Kagera river, which separated German East Africa and Uganda. Occasional skirmishes took place between handfuls of Schutztruppe and Belgian askaris in several spots on the Congo border. A small German force exchanged a few shots with an even smaller mixed bag of KAR and colonial police near Karonga in Nyasaland, far to the southwest. None of these fights had any bearing on the outcome of the campaign.

And for all its potential strategic value, the port of Kisumu was far less important in the overall planning of both commands than control of the rock and thorn wasteland that lay in the shadow of Kilimanjaro between Moshi in German East Africa and Voi on the Uganda Railway. Until and unless the Schutztruppe could be dislodged from that area, the Germans were in position to launch seriously damaging raids on the line. Indeed, small guerrilla parties had already started to blow up sections of track and ambush British detachments.

Furthermore, since this same area offered the least difficult land access to German East Africa and control of its Northern Railway, it was natural that the British should also concentrate there. By late October, the four thousand troops of Brigadier General James Stewart's Indian Expeditionary Force "C" were poised just north of Kilimanjaro for a swift drive on the Moshi positions. Their objective was to squeeze the Schutztruppe in the upper end of a two-hundred-mile pincer. The southern prong consisted of eight thousand men in two brigades. It was called Indian Expeditionary Force "B," and it was then about to land at Tanga. After capturing the port, Force "B" would advance north rapidly, join with Stewart's troops at Moshi and mop up what remained of von Lettow's broken command. To all practical purposes, this would end German resistance in East Africa.

The strategy was faultless on paper.

7

Adui Tayari

THE PORT OF TANGA lies about one hundred miles north of Dar es Salaam, the town itself being situated at the bottom and inner side of a large natural harbor. Its palm-dotted shoreline runs east for approximately two miles, then juts northward about half a mile in a thumblike peninsula called Ras Kasone, which forms the southern entrance of the bay itself. The Northern Railway had (and still has) its Indian Ocean terminus at Tanga. Trains arriving from the interior ran along the town's southern and eastern edges, coming to a stop at a large steamer wharf on the waterfront. Between Tanga proper and Ras Kasone, the Germans had several large rubber and coconut plantations. Much of the ground here was heavily overlaid with baobab trees, thorn and tall grass. Ras Kasone's beach was all but smothered in mangroves.

Under the Germans, Tanga was a busy and conspicuously tidy colonial seaport, with geometrically laid out streets and clean white houses nearly buried in bright tropical foliage. Because of its excellent natural anchorage and rail access to the Usambara highland region, Tanga was German East Africa's second most important coastal city. Its topographical and geographical assets also seemed, in British military eyes, to be tailor-made for the amphibious landing of Indian Expeditionary Force "B," whose troopships approached Tanga on the first of November in 1914.

The eight thousand men of the force were split into two commands: the 27th Bangalore Brigade led by Brigadier General Richard Wapshare, a somewhat Blimpish but respected officer; and an Imperial Service Brigade under a leather-faced brigadier general named Michael Tighe, tough as old boots and known as a scrapper. In overall command was Major General Arthur Edward Aitken, a burly, supremely confident soldier. All three generals, long-time veterans of Indian military service, expected that Tanga would be a walkover.

Indeed, on October 31, at a staff meeting in Mombasa attended by officers of Forces "B" and "C," the KAR and Royal Navy, it had been generally agreed that the assault amounted to little more than a landing exercise in the face of token opposition. Hope even existed that the enemy might respect the coastal truce terms and offer no resistance at all. In any case, the Germans were known to have fewer than four hundred troops defending Tanga. In effect, this meant that Aitken's force need only disembark and accept their surrender. This in turn would open the way for a rapid move north, linkup with Stewart near Moshi, and the swift capitulation of von Lettow's hopelessly outnumbered army. The capture of Tanga—not to mention the conquest of German East Africa—was going to be a piece of cake.

Only one officer dissented from this view. Despite his name and attitude, Captain Richard Meinertzhagen was not a German spy. The son of a prominent London banker (and a nephew of the Fabian Socialist Beatrice Webb, whom he detested), the 36-year-old Meinertzhagen had worn the Queen's and King's uniform since 1899, doing most of his service in the Indian army. He was attending the Staff College at Quetta when the war began, and had since become Force "B's" Intelligence Officer. Meinertzhagen was also the only member of the force with extensive African experience, having commanded a KAR company between 1902 and 1906 and gained a reputation as a wild man in bush warfare against two particularly belligerent tribes. During that hitch he had also made a point of visiting German military installations across the border, where he wrote the assessment of the Schutztruppe which is quoted earlier in this book. Meinertzhagen's opinion of the German askari's discipline and fighting qualities was only one reason why he did not feel sanguine about the prospects of the next day's assault on Tanga.

Both as a soldier and as a judge of other soldiers, Meinertzhagen was not a man to be disregarded. No conscientious study of the East African campaign can be considered complete without frequent reference to the diaries he kept during his two years' service in that theatre. Seasoned with peppery indignation and irreverent humor, these journals afford an almost unique glimpse into the workings of military common sense at its soundest.* Like all chronicles of the campaign, Meinertzhagen's contains inconsistencies and factual errors. Some of his character assessments seem harsh or even unfair: Meinertzhagen may have been the most outspoken officer ever to hold a commission in the British army, and his bluntness was not of the

---

* "The only factor common to my diaries and those of Field Marshals and Generals," wrote Meinertzhagen in 1960, "is that the keeping of a diary on active service is a contravention of military law."

sort designed to win friends. But the most striking thing that emerges from
the diaries is how often—and how clearly—he was right when everyone
else was wrong. In 1936, David Lloyd George (whom Meinertzhagen enjoyed reviling) remarked in his *War Memoirs:* "I met him during the
[Versailles] Peace Conference and he struck me as being one of the ablest
and most successful brains I had met in any Army. That was quite sufficient
to make him suspect and to hinder his promotion to the higher ranks of his
profession."

Meinertzhagen's brain did not have to work overtime to find flaws in
the Tanga operation. The landing, he felt, took little account of reality, in
great part because of the Royal Navy's coastal truce, "a foolish and un-
authorised agreement, unconfirmed by the Admiralty . . . which Aitken
should have repudiated." One of its provisions—that Tanga be warned of
British attack—struck Meinertzhagen as an open invitation to resistance
on the beach. At the Mombasa staff conference, he had conceded that Tanga
was probably lightly defended, but also pointed out that "there must be a
large [German] concentration in the Kilimanjaro area," and that if the
British tipped their hand, "troops could be rapidly transported by rail to
Tanga in thirty hours." The truce struck him as carrying sportsmanship too
far. "We do not yet seem to realise that we are at war and are no longer
playing at manoeuvres. Efficiency has been sacrificed to sentiment."

As an intelligence officer, Meinertzhagen was also distressed by Aitken's
failure to order a reconnaissance of the mangrove-choked beach where the
landing was to take place. In Mombasa, eleventh-hour local assistance had
been forthcoming when the commanding officer of the KAR's 3rd Battalion offered to bring in his own askaris as a covering force. "I was en-
thusiastic," wrote Meinertzhagen, "as it was my old battalion, I knew they
were first-class, accustomed to bush warfare and . . . would be a tremendous
asset." Then he added: "Aitken refused without a word of thanks. I was
disgusted."

Another aspect of the assault that troubled Meinertzhagen was the fitness
of the troops—"the worst in India," whose "senior officers are nearer to
fossils than active, energetic leaders of men." This could not be helped. The
cream of the Indian army had, naturally, been sent to France, while Force
"B's" ten regiments, battalions and miscellaneous detachments were a grab-
bag lot, hastily thrown together. A few of the units, to be sure, had spine.
The Kashmir Rifles, the 101st Bombay Grenadiers and the 2nd Battalion
of the Loyal North Lancashire Regiment—the only British contingent—
could be relied on to fight hard and fight well. The others could not. The
98th Infantry and 63rd Palamacottah Light Infantry battalions had seen no
active service for three decades. Meinertzhagen had once been attached to
the 13th Rajputs. "From what I saw of them then," he recalled on the eve
of Tanga, "they were hopeless." Few of the officers and men in any of the
units had ever served together, and many were about to hear guns fired in

anger for the first time. "I tremble to think what may happen," wrote Meinertzhagen, "if we meet with serious opposition."

Meinertzhagen also viewed the overall strategy as misguided. What the British should have done, he felt, was "concentrate . . . near Nairobi and advance by slow methodical steps toward Kilimanjaro where the enemy will certainly stand. We should defeat him there." Instead, by the proposed march north to join with Stewart's force near Moshi, "we lay ourselves open to defeat in detail, intercommunication between the two forces being quite impossible." This mistake, it seemed to Meinertzhagen, was compounded by what may have struck him as the most unsettling element of all: the cavalier attitude of the British commanders toward the Germans. "Aitken has a supreme contempt for them. . . . [He] means to thrash the German before Xmas. Fine words, but I know the German. His colonial troops are second to none, they are led by the best officers in the world, he knows the country and understands bush warfare and his troops are not so prone to malaria as ours are. And finally he will be operating in his own country and can choose the time and place for attacking our . . . forces."

When Meinertzhagen tried to point out some of these things to Aitken, the latter "said with some heat: 'The Indian Army will make short work of a lot of niggers.' "

A little after dawn on November 2, the British convoy hove to about fifteen miles off Tanga—just beyond sight of land—while the cruiser *Fox,* one of the two naval escorts, sailed directly into the port. A boat was lowered and *Fox's* captain, Commander F. W. Caulfield, went ashore to demand unconditional surrender of the town. Auracher, the district commissioner, was given one hour to haul down the German flag. Three hours later the flag was still flying. *Fox* steamed out of the harbor to bring in the transports.

There had never been any intention of complying with the navy's legally tenuous coast neutrality terms. Auracher had immediately telegraphed von Lettow in Moshi and informed him of the British presence. Meinertzhagen's fears were confirmed when he learned that Tanga had not caved in under *Fox's* guns. "This initial error," he wrote, as the transports approached Ras Kasone, "will have far-reaching results. . . . To give the Germans twenty-four hours' notice of attack seems criminal."

In fact, the landings could almost certainly have been carried out well inside of twenty-four hours. They were delayed for some time, however, when Caulfield insisted on sweeping the harbor for mines, a precaution which Meinertzhagen called "absurd." Assisted by two armed tugs, *Fox* diligently combed the harbor's approaches through the night of November 2 and well into the next day. One of the tugs was *Helmuth,* still commanded by the same Lieutenant Clement Charlewood who had fallen afoul of *Königsberg* off Zanzibar six weeks earlier. Charlewood found that sweeping

Tanga's inner channel had its own peculiar hazards. "Hardly had we begun," he later wrote, ". . . than we became aware that we had caught something in the sweep, and we endured some tense moments until we discovered that the catch was nothing more deadly than a sunken tree trunk. Several times this experience was repeated, and on each occasion we had to slip the sweep wire . . . and begin all over again." The riskiest moment of the sweeping exercise came when a German machine gun opened up on *Helmuth* from the shore. The tug's crew wasted some of its own machine gun ammunition firing back vainly at the muzzle flashes. There were no casualties on either side. And no mines were found.

Furthermore, since Aitken either shared Meinertzhagen's skepticism about mines or was simply impatient, the debarkation did begin before the harbor had been completely "swept." Aitken planned a night assault spearheaded by elements of Tighe's Imperial Service Brigade. Tighe's orders were to land near a red house on the southern side of Ras Kasone—the only spot on the headland which seemed relatively free of mangroves. The troops would then scale a low bluff, advance across the plantations and sieze Tanga without delay. It was hoped that the Germans would yield up the town before sunrise of November 3.

The landing did not proceed quite according to plan. At 4:30 P.M. on November 2, three transports steamed in close to Ras Kasone and lighters, towed by two tugs, began moving the troops in toward the red house. Within minutes they were hard aground on a reef, offering ideal target practice for a German machine gun which immediately opened fire from the bluff. The gun was silenced by a shell or two from *Fox,* but the men now had to wade ashore—through a mangrove barrier far more dense and tangled than anyone had expected. The first wave, such as it was, did not hit the beach swiftly. By 9:30 P.M., exactly two Indian companies and a handful of scouts had landed. "So here we are," wrote Meinertzhagen, "with only a small portion of our force, risking a landing in the face of an enemy of unknown strength and on a beach which has not been reconnoitred and which looks like a rank mangrove swamp."

As midnight approached, however, the force achieved something like strength on the beach, and well before sunrise on the morning of the 3rd, Tighe was able to order an advance on Tanga by the 13th Rajput and 61st Pioneer battalions. Uneasily, the sepoys began groping their way inland through the plantations, in a confusion of scrub which the scouts had been able to give only the most cursory reconnaissance. After a struggle of two or three hours, the Indians finally came within range of the German defenses. Although a bright moon occasionally slid out from a curtain of clouds to reveal the scruffy battlefield, the enemy—the Schutztruppe's veteran 17th Field Company—was invisible behind a line of well-dug and well-concealed entrenchments near the railway yard at the town's southern edge. Quickly, however, the 17th made its presence felt with scattered but continual rifle volleys and bursts of machine gun fire, concentrating on the attackers' left flank. The noise was fearful. The old Model 71 rifles alone made such a thundering racket that no one could even hear himself die.

Now the sun came up, and with it, a handful of armed Germans and a few police askaris led by Auracher—just enough reinforcement to stiffen the 17th. A little later on, the defenders were joined by one and a half more companies, and the two attacking battalions began to waver as British and Indian officers, exposing themselves as they tried to rally their men, were instantly chopped down by the enemy machine guns. After an hour of this, the Germans began a counterattack.

Both Indian battalions by now had suffered heavy casualties, particularly among their officers. The troops could barely be controlled; Meinertzhagen later reported that he had seen them "running like rabbits and jibbering like monkeys." Although they still outnumbered the Germans by at least three to one, there was every likelihood that they would break and scatter under a determined bayonet charge. Tighe saw no alternative but to disengage. At ten o'clock, under the cover of *Fox's* guns, the two battalions reached Ras Kasone and the relative safety of an outpost line held by the Lancs, who had just landed. "If the enemy had pressed the attack," wrote an outraged Meinertzhagen, "the whole force would have been captured or driven into the sea . . . I have never dreamed that such things could happen."

Force "B" spent the rest of November 3 continuing its debarkation and licking its wounds. There were many to lick. The floors of the red house, now converted into a field hospital, became slippery with the blood and bowels of nearly three hundred officers and sepoys who had stopped German bullets in the abortive attack that morning. But at Aitken's headquarters—a large white house on the northern tip of Ras Kasone—the atmosphere of high optimism prevailed. The defeat of the two battalions, however shameful, had been no more than a temporary setback. Next morning the entire force would be ashore, in position for the massed onslaught that could have only one outcome.

Meinertzhagen, of course, did not see it this way. Throughout the day he wallowed in gloom. At sunset, he watched the Rajputs and Pioneers flee to the beach in mass panic when a sepoy accidentally fired his rifle. "Jolly fellows to go fighting Germans with," he snorted to his diary, and then stalked off to catch a few hours' sleep on the lawn of the white house. Only momentarily could he take amused comfort in his improvised bedding. "My mattress consists of the underclothing of the lady of the house, nice soft bits of lingerie, and for the blankets I have a Union Jack and three German flags. My pillow is palm leaves stuffed into the corsets of a stout lady whose name I do not know."

Then he remembered where he was. "In front, the enemy, and behind, the sea. And in the midst a nervous array of unreliable men, ready to run at the slightest provocation. Thank God the Germans do not know our state. . . ."

All this while, von Lettow had not been idle in Moshi. His main force was already moving swiftly on Tanga. As far back as a month before the British landings, rumors and reports of such an offensive had been filtering into Schutztruppe headquarters. Von Lettow had therefore made a personal reconnaissance of the entire line of probable enemy advance between Tanga and Moshi, and had then deployed his field companies so that they would be in position to reach Tanga in the shortest possible time. Some would proceed by forced march. But the great bulk would move by train.

Not that the Northern Railway offered a Red Ball Express service. A single field company of 150 askaris and at least that many porters—not to mention its machine guns and all other equipment—filled every cubic inch of the six or seven tiny carriages in a troop train. And, since the narrow-gauge Northern line had only eight small locomotives to drag the heavily overloaded coaches, the shuttling of the Schutztruppe meant a round-the-clock, no-sleep operation for all railway personnel.

But the 190-mile movement was planned and executed with the efficiency one expected of the Germans. Hardly had von Lettow finished reading Auracher's telegram on November 2 than a troop train, packed almost beyond capacity with one and a half field companies, was chuffing out of Neu Moschi station. "The spirit of the troops was magnificent," noted von Lettow, citing as one reason that for the Schutztruppe askaris, "a trip on a railway train is at all times a great delight." Within eighteen hours, these troops were helping to launch the counterattack against Tighe's two demoralized battalions on the morning of November 3. And the trains continued to puff down the line. For two days without letup, the hollow-eyed officials of the Northern Railway shoveled upwards of one thousand Schutztruppe officers and askaris to the Tanga front.

Von Lettow himself was almost the last member of the force to reach Tanga. It was not until three o'clock in the morning on November 4 that he got off his headquarters train some four miles west of the town. Here, he met Captain Paul Baumstark, commander of the 17th Field Company, and learned that Tanga was hardly being held. Uncertain that his few hundred troops could hold off the British before the reinforcements arrived from Moshi, Baumstark had retired from the town, leaving only a handful of officers and askaris to patrol along the eastern perimeter. Of the newly arrived troops, only the 6th Field Company was in a forward position, near the railway station on Tanga's extreme southern outskirts. This naturally made von Lettow uneasy. With no way of knowing whether the British had seized the opportunity to enter Tanga unopposed, he decided to make a personal reconnaissance, and set off without delay on a bicycle.

He found Tanga deserted. "I rode . . . through the empty streets . . . the white houses of the Europeans reflected the brilliant rays of the moon. . . . A quarter of a mile out lay the transports, a blaze of lights, and full of noise." The sight of the transports made him regret that the Schutztruppe's two old Model 1873 field guns had not yet arrived. "Here, in the brilliant moonlight at such close range, their effect would have been annihilating, the hostile cruisers notwithstanding." Moving east toward Ras Kasone, von Lettow parked his bicycle outside the German government hospital and continued on foot along the beach. He was well within range of any alert marine or sailor aboard *Fox,* anchored only a few hundred feet from shore. But even in the moonlight he was unnoticed. Shortly afterwards, however, while cycling back into the town, he had less luck. An Indian sentry—inexplicably posted beyond the British perimeter—stepped from the shadow of a door and challenged him in Hindi. Von Lettow snapped out the Schutztruppe countersign: *"Stambuli."* The sentry fled.

By now it was almost dawn. Sporadic firing had broken out between a few opposing patrols near Ras Kasone. Von Lettow immediately sent a messenger to Baumstark with orders to bring the troops forward for deployment against the impending attack. At the same time, he moved the 6th Field Company from the railway station to a position along a half-mile front on the eastern edge of the town. This might have seemed a fragile screen to cover so long a line, but the defenses were bolstered by the sheer thirty-foot sides of the railway cutting. Besides which, von Lettow had a great deal of confidence in the 6th and its relatively high standard of marksmanship. Besides which, he did not have very many troops in the first place.

In any case, it seemed likely that the British would deliver their hardest punch in a flanking drive on the German right wing farther south. Here, near the railway workshops, the town would be defended by Baumstark, in command of an *abteilung,* or detachment, consisting of the 16th and 17th Field Companies and another company made up of miscellaneous units. To the rear of this position, von Lettow made his own headquarters, holding in reserve the seasoned 13th Field Company and two European *schützen* companies under Captain Tom von Prince—the legendary *"Bwana Sakarani."*

From a tactical standpoint, the defense of Tanga was very well planned. In the circumstances, however, this did not seem to mean a great deal. There was some doubt as to whether the 4th and 9th Field Companies—the remainder of the reinforcements—could reach the scene in time. Nor had the two ancient but all-important artillery pieces arrived. And even if every unit were in position, von Lettow would have barely one thousand rifles to hold off a pair of brigades whose total strength was not only eight times the Germans' but would be supported by far more modern field guns and *Fox's* devastating broadsides at almost point-blank range. As the morning wore on and the heat grew oppressive, von Lettow uneasily watched the completion of the British landings. "I estimated the total troops landed up to midday at 6,000. But even on this too low estimate I had to ask myself whether I dared risk a decisive engagement."

There were several pros and cons to weigh. Among the arguments favoring action was von Lettow's awareness that the British would probably run into trouble on the terrain which they must cross before trying the German defenses; in this "very close and completely unknown country . . . the slightest disorder was bound to have far reaching consequences." Furthermore, "With my own troops, of whom the Europeans were well acquainted with the country round Tanga, while the Askari were at home in the bush, I had a reasonable prospect of taking advantage of the enemy's weak points by skilful and rapid manoeuvre." Above all, it was simply "too important to prevent the enemy from gaining a firm footing in Tanga. Otherwise we should abandon to him the best base for operations against the Northern Territories."

There was also a very compelling reason for not fighting. "If the affair miscarried . . . my superiors would place insuperable difficulties in the way of my exercising command." By "superiors" von Lettow meant Schnee; "insuperable difficulties" was simply a polite way of saying removal from command. The governor had never forgiven von Lettow's near-insubordination. He never would.

"But," concluded von Lettow, "there was nothing for it: to gain all we must risk all."

The German troops took up their positions under a broiling sun. Soon they became intensely thirsty, but rather than waste the water in their canteens, the askaris split coconuts with bayonets and drank the milk, while the officers opened bottles of wine from the cellar of the Hotel Deutscher Kaiser. The men were also hungry. Master Butcher Grabow served out hot sausages along the line. No one's thirst was really quenched. Everyone fought off drowsiness in the sweltering heat.

At length, patrols reported that the British had completed their debarkation and had begun to advance on the town. Now the field companies came alive. Platoon commanders barked out orders to stand to. Weapons and ammunition were swiftly checked for readiness. Machine gunners went through last-minute traverses. Snipers, concealed in baobab trees, adjusted the sights on their rifles. Field telephonists blew tentatively into their mouthpieces. African NCOs laughingly encouraged the men in their squads with shouts of "*Tutaharibika Waingereza!*",We'll destroy the English, and "*Wahindi ni wadudu!*", The Indians are insects—"insect" being one of the most insulting terms in the Swahili language.

At headquarters, von Lettow waited for further reports on the British advance. There were few. Apart from an occasional rifle shot near Ras Kasone, the Tanga battlefield was silent. Von Lettow continually looked at his wristwatch. One o'clock in the afternoon came and went, then two o'clock. At two-thirty, heavier firing broke out as the snipers began to find targets, but there was still no sign of a general assault on the German positions. By three o'clock, von Lettow was beginning to doubt that the British would attack at all that day, when "an Askari reported to me in his simple, smart way: 'Adui tayari.' (The enemy is ready.) Those two short words I shall never forget."

The British order of battle on November 4 saw the two brigades advancing abreast along a thousand-yard front, Tighe's force on the right, Wapshare's on the left. This would bring Tighe into the north side of Tanga while Wapshare would penetrate the center of the line and deal with Baumstark's detachment on the German right flank. The drive began shortly after ten o'clock in the morning. It did not move on oiled wheels. "The day was intensely hot," wrote one battalion historian, "and in the dense, steamy rubber plantation . . . touch was hard to keep; consequently the advance was slow, in fact the whole force broke up into open order, or small columns . . . thus adding to the difficulty of control." Even the open order soon fell into a shambles. Some columns dropped far behind the line of advance. Communications between adjoining units became impossible except by runner.

The shabby procession seemed totally without spirit. Morale, never high, had plummeted earlier in the day when it was learned that there would be no artillery support to soften up the enemy. Apparently unwilling to destroy buildings which his own troops might later use, Aitken had given orders that Force "B's" crack 28th Mountain Battery was not to land, and that *Fox* was not to cover the advance or shell the German lines. The Schutztruppe, to be sure, would be unable to withstand the British assault, but its resistance would be stiffer, and Force "B" casualties higher, without the help of the big guns.

Still, there was nothing for it but to keep moving, or try to. The sun throbbed like a migraine headache; sepoys collapsed in little clusters from heat exhaustion. Abbreviated rain showers brought no relief in the Turkish bath through which the British line made its increasingly ragged way.

More than four hours of this. Finally, advance columns of Wapshare's brigade reached a wide dirt road running directly across the line of march. Much of the road was protected on the farther side by a maize field with stalks nearly eight feet high. Most of the force now halted, to rest briefly and try to reform lines. Then the advance was resumed through the tall maize. The dry stalks rattled like musketry, and the sound was soon replaced by the real thing as the German snipers opened up from the baobabs. In their wilderness of corn, the attackers had nothing to fire back at. All they could do was fall when the sniper bullets struck.

After about half an hour, the brigade began to emerge from the maize field, the Lancs in the van, with several hundred yards of open ground to

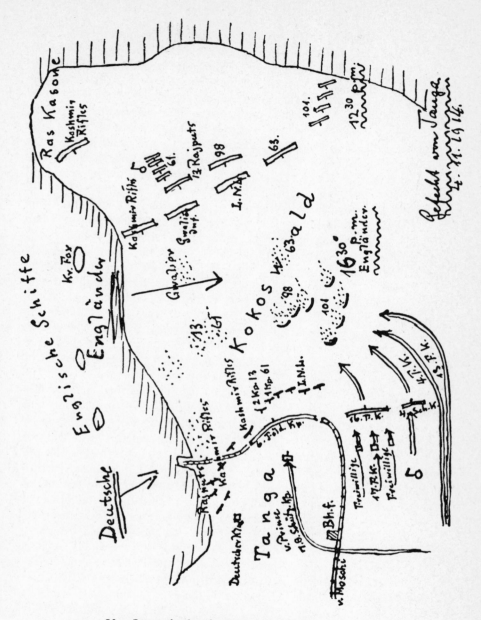

Von Lettow's sketch map of the Tanga action.

(From Mein Leben *by Lettow-Vorbeck published by Koelers Verlagsgesellschaft, 49 Herford, Federal Republic of Germany.)*

cross before reaching the railway cutting. Now the German machine guns went into action, and small black thunderheads blossomed along the entire enemy line as the 6th Field Company began pouring out massed volleys of rifle fire. This was where the men became separated from the boys. Among the latter were the sepoys of the 63rd Palamacottah Light Infantry. Hardly had they come under the German fire than they threw down their rifles and, as one man, fled back toward the beach. Their absence was to be felt later on. But the other units held fast; the Lancs even started to advance, crawling slowly across the open ground, trying vainly to take cover behind small bushes and smaller rocks. They paid an exorbitant price in dead and wounded to reach the cutting and fight their way across it.

At the same time, Tighe's brigade on the British right was also being cuffed about. "I could not believe my eyes," wrote Meinertzhagen, when "half the 13th Rajputs turned at once, broke into a rabble and bolted, carrying most of the 61st Pioneers with them . . . many men were deliberately firing at our advancing troops . . . I had to use my boots and pistol to stop it." Still, the brigade was also making visible progress. Along with two Rajput companies, the *kukri*-wielding Gurkhas of the Kashmir Rifles rapidly sliced their way into the northern end of Tanga, surrounding the Customs House and capturing the Hotel Deutscher Kaiser, where they hauled down the German flag and ran up a Union Jack. Soon they were joined on their left by elements of the Lancs that had forced a section of the cutting. The British now had their foot in the enemy door.

The next hour witnessed savage street fighting. German snipers laid down an unrelentingly accurate fire from rooftops. Askari machine gun crews moved their weapons rapidly from windows to doors to alleyways, often getting off bursts on the run. Black riflemen seemed to pop up from nowhere, fire a few quick rounds, vanish, pop up somewhere else. But the Germans presently began to falter. The Indians and Lancs dispersed into tiny improvised assault teams, slowly but steadily knocking out pockets of resistance and driving the defenders farther in toward the center of town. By four o'clock, the Lancs had occupied a large number of office buildings and were holding a small open square. Although the 6th Field Company fought back with fury, its askaris seemed outgunned by the attackers.

But then the advance was stopped dead in its tracks as the German riflemen and machine gunners of Prince's 7th and 8th Schützen Companies raced down the streets from the rear to fill the gaps in the askari line. The Lancs began to abandon some of the houses they had just captured. Firing from the hip, they moved back warily to take up stronger positions nearer to the cutting. The situation had not been reversed, but the center of the German line was now holding.

At his headquarters near the railway station, von Lettow chain-smoked furiously; this was his habit in battle, regardless of whether things were going well or badly. At the moment they were not going well. Although Prince had stiffened the left and center of the line, the extreme right was beginning to waver under the concentrated fire of assaulting troops that had crossed the cutting on a footbridge and had gained a foothold on the southern edge of the town. Baumstark had thrown two of his companies in to stem this advance, but many of the askaris, raw recruits who had never seen action, were now actually running from the fight and taking cover behind coco palms. At any moment the contagion of panic could sweep both companies into headlong flight. Trying to set an example, German company commanders and platoon leaders deliberately exposed themselves to the British fire. A cursing staff officer, Captain Alexander von Hammerstein, hurled an empty wine bottle at one of the fleeing askaris. Somehow these acts brought the men to their senses; a few could even be heard laughing and joking sheepishly as they returned to their positions in the line.

But the situation remained serious. Advancing just behind and slightly to the south of the Lancs were the eight hundred sepoys of the 101st Grenadiers, in position to roll up the entire German right flank and then launch a fresh attack on the German rear from inside the town. If this happened, the game would be up. Von Lettow now had virtually no reserves. The 4th and 9th Field Companies still had not arrived. Only the 13th Field Company could be thrown in against the enemy waves that were starting to pound on the thin wall of the Schutztruppe right flank.

And it was in this very sector of the attacking line that von Lettow recognized the spot where he might not only plug the leak but turn the tide. At the outbreak of the fighting, when the Palamacottahs fled, they had left a gaping hole in the British line between the Lancs and the 101st. To fill the gap, the 101st had been forced to move far to its right; this had the effect of shortening and exposing the British left wing. "Here, therefore," von Lettow decided, "the counter-stroke must prove annihilating."

It did. Shortly after 4:30, von Lettow ordered the 13th Field Company to swing round on its own right, then cut in and hit the highly vulnerable British left—and "no witness will forget the moment when the machineguns of the 13th Company opened a continuous fire at this point and completely reversed the situation."

That one move by von Lettow had indeed settled the fate of the British at Tanga. Almost before they knew what had happened, the Grenadiers found themselves caught in a typhoon of lead. The machine guns of the 13th had been reinforced with two more guns from less hard-pressed units; methodically, these four guns set about hacking the 101st to pieces. The Indians fought back savagely, but they could not fight long. Within minutes, their battalion had all but ceased to exist. And just about this time, the 13th Field Company was beefed up by the belated but timely arrival of the 4th Field Company. The whole British left flank became threatened with envelopment, and a general withdrawal was ordered. Now the Germans began launching bayonet attacks along the entire front, to a cacophony of bugle calls, whistle blasts and piercing tribal war cries. At least three Indian battalions would have been wiped out to a man by the cold steel if the sepoys had not already taken to their heels. All semblance of order and formation vanished as Force "B's" retirement degenerated into total rout.

Nothing could stop the headlong race to the beach. Even Aitken's decision to unleash *Fox's* six-inch guns came too late. *Fox* also proved useless, firing only two shells into Tanga. The first tore a hole in the roof of the German hospital on the waterfront. The second burst a few feet from Meinertzhagen, knocking him into the trunk of a coco palm and dazing him for a few minutes. But Meinertzhagen was even more stunned by the behavior of the troops. "It was too piteous to see the state of the men. Many were jibbering idiots, muttering prayers to their heathen gods, hiding behind bushes and palm trees and laying face down to earth in folds of the ground with their rifles lying useless beside them. I would never have believed that grown-up men of any race could have been reduced to such shamelessness." Not that all were totally paralyzed. Some units fired at the backs of the few Lancs and Kashmiris still holding desperately on the outskirts of Tanga. Meinertzhagen came across seven Rajput sepoys taking cover behind a bank. On being ordered to stand up and fight, one man seized his rifle and drew a bead on Meinertzhagen. "I shot the brute as he lay half-crazy with fear."

It did not seem possible that so demoralized a mob could fall into any greater disarray, but this was what happened. Suddenly, retreating men were seen to leap high in the air, caper about and perform grotesque contortions on the ground. Some unit or other had disturbed a hive of wild bees. These were to European bees what a leopard is to a tabby cat; a single sting from one of them was the deep thrust of an acid-tipped needle. Many of the troops were soon covered with stings; faces and arms swelled to twice their normal size. One officer, comatose from a bullet wound, was stung back into consciousness. For many years, it was believed that the bee attack was a fiendish German stratagem, that the hives had been upset by hidden trip wires. This was not so: the four machine guns of the 13th Field Company were also put out of action by the bees. But the British did bear the brunt of the assault. The entire force went almost literally insane trying to fight off the angry swarms.

Toward sunset, Force "B" had somehow managed to throw up a defense perimeter behind the Ras Kasone beachhead. Elements of Tighe's brigade also held a tenuous line closer to the town; Aitken, too, made a temporary headquarters here. And it was at Aitken's command post that German bugles were suddenly heard again. According to Meinertzhagen, "this caused a minor panic, even among Headquarters Staff, several of whom shouted out, 'My God, that's the charge!' " Vainly, Meinertzhagen told Aitken that it was just the reverse: that the bugles were sounding the recall, that for some incredible reason the Germans were withdrawing from Tanga.

Aitken would have none of this. But he did consent reluctantly to let Meinertzhagen lead two other volunteers on a reconnaissance of the town. On the outskirts, in the rapidly gathering darkness, the patrol exchanged a few shots with an indistinct group of Germans. No one on either side was hit.* Apart from that abbreviated skirmish, however, there was no other action, and further penetration into Tanga appeared to confirm Meinertzhagen's surmise that the Germans had indeed evacuated the town. Hastening back to Aitken with this news, he urged that as many troops as possible be collected to move in on the abandoned enemy positions. Aitken refused. "His one ambition seemed to be to get away."

This he did, ordering withdrawal to Ras Kasone with a view to launching a counterattack the next morning. But Aitken might well have heeded Meinertzhagen, who was simultaneously right and wrong about the German dispositions. It was later learned that the bugles had been sounded to rally the askaris for pursuit, but that either the buglers had blown the wrong calls or that some German officer had mistaken them for an order to disengage and consolidate. In any case, however, the vast bulk of the Schutztruppe had indeed withdrawn to its camp several miles west of Tanga. In the confusion, von Lettow himself did not learn of this at once, although when he did, the troops were ordered directly back to the line. But the move could not be completed until shortly before sunrise on November 5. For nearly all of the night, Tanga was Aitken's for the taking. It was the most stupendous irony of the battle.

Even so, Tanga's availability did not necessarily guarantee that Aitken's thoroughly cowed troops could—or would—have occupied the town. Meinertzhagen himself seemed to acknowledge this in an outpouring of enraged despondency in his diary: "Nearly the whole force is jumpy this evening. The dropping of a tin kettle or the shouting of an order is quite enough to send parties of men back to the sea in terror." But Meinertzhagen was less censurious of the rank and file than of a high command which dispatched "four battalions of no fighting value to face some of the best-trained native troops in the world. I do not blame the men, still less their officers. I blame the Indian government for enlisting such scum and placing them in the King's uniform." It did not seem to occur to Meinertzhagen that the scum, even though volunteers in the army, were members of an involuntarily subject race, and could not have had the slightest stake or interest in the outcome of a battle being fought for another white man's colony.

On the morning of November 5, Meinertzhagen approached the German lines under a flag of truce, carrying chloroform and bandages for the captured British wounded "and a letter of apology from Aitken to the German

* Meinertzhagen learned many years later, after he had become a close personal friend of von Lettow, that he had barely missed gunning down the commander of the Schutztruppe himself. Or, as von Lettow put it, "This was my first social contact with my friend Meinertzhagen."

commander for having put a six-inch shell into the hospital." The enemy
officers were "very communicative and let me see everything"; this enabled
Meinertzhagen to memorize—and later sketch—the Tanga defenses. At
the hospital, the Germans continued to be "kindness itself," sitting Meinertzhagen down to a breakfast, which he welcomed, having had nothing to
eat or drink since rising but some rum and water in a bucket. "We discussed
the fight freely as though it had been a football match. It seemed so odd
that I should be having a meal today with people whom I was trying to
kill yesterday. It seemed so wrong and made me wonder whether this
really was war or whether we had all made a ghastly mistake."

Returning to the British lines, however, there was no mistaking the German bullet that sliced through Meinertzhagen's sun helmet when an askari,
ignorant of flags of truce, took a pot shot at him from close range. Instantly
Meinertzhagen jammed the flag and its pole into the askari's stomach,
doubling him up. He then seized the man's rifle and impaled him on his
own bayonet. "I was furious with him. . . ."

Nor did his fury subside on arriving back at Aitken's command post.
Here, "I heard with the utmost dismay that orders had been issued for our
immediate embarkation . . . to 'sauve qui peut' back into the sea, a disgraceful scurry for safety." Although he could appreciate Aitken's second
thoughts on resuming the action—"another attack by our troops is out of
the question"—he was thunderstruck to learn that the force had also been
directed to abandon all its arms and equipment. When one of Aitken's
senior staff officers told Meinertzhagen to pass the information on to all
unit commanders, "I took it upon myself not to deliver this order."

But re-embarkation did commence that afternoon, and within three hours
all non-wounded troops were back aboard the transports—although few
had been put aboard the right ships and it required the better part of the
next day to sort them out. And, despite Meinertzhagen's efforts, a great
arsenal was left on the beach.

Also left behind were more than seven hundred bodies, at least three
hundred of them corpses. "The streets," von Lettow later recalled, "were
literally strewn with dead and wounded. In unknown tongues they begged
for help which, with the best will in the world, could not always be granted
at once." But the will was there. German field surgeons and African
dressers worked as swiftly as circumstances allowed—and with a fine disregard for their patients' uniforms. Not a few wounded Schutztruppe officers and askaris had to endure their pain while operations were performed
on more seriously injured British and Indian troops.

And, by the afternoon of November 5, negotiations were under way for
the removal of nearly all Force "B" wounded to the transports. Once again,
Meinertzhagen was chosen to represent Aitken under a flag of truce at the
German hospital, while the bottle-throwing Captain von Hammerstein acted
for von Lettow. The two men reached agreement without difficulty, although Meinertzhagen did not relish his role as the supplicant of a beaten

army. "I am dead beat this evening, thoroughly ashamed of my profession."

Early the next morning, however, Meinertzhagen was back on the mainland to supervise evacuation of the wounded and the handing over of abandoned material. (He called the latter a "revolting job.") At the hospital, Dr. Ludwig Deppe gave him a hearty breakfast: "good beer, ice, plenty of eggs and cream and asparagus." Meinertzhagen also had time to chat with Hammerstein about British and German war aims, neither of course convincing the other although by now the two had become quite friendly. Hammerstein gave Meinertzhagen his photograph, and both men exchanged addresses, agreeing to meet after the war "and to mutually help each other if either of us were taken prisoner." Not so agreeable to Meinertzhagen was his impression of the Schutztruppe officers and askaris whom he had a chance to study at close hand on the Ras Kasone beach. "They all looked fit, keen, determined and with good discipline. We must produce something better than the Indian Army before we beat what I saw today."

Just before Meinertzhagen returned to the convoy for the last time, Hammerstein took him aside and gave him a confidential message from von Lettow. The two German field guns, it appeared, were due to arrive at last from Moshi, and von Lettow wanted Aitken to know that the British transports would be fired on if they stayed within range. Meinertzhagen conveyed this warning to Aitken, who in turn lost no time ordering the convoy to depart.* "It was not a pleasant sight," wrote Meinertzhagen, ". . . to see the *Fox* leading our procession—a warship leaving an unprotected convoy. . . . I should imagine that such conduct on the part of the Navy is unique." Several hours later the ships anchored in Manza Bay, about ten miles north of Tanga—well out of harm's way.

Von Lettow observed the hasty exit with mixed feelings—first uncertainty, then elation. After bicycling north to Manza Bay, he became convinced that the British did not plan to land again but were only burying their dead. He was then able to return and have a closer look at his own victory. It had not been won without cost. The Schutztruppe lost sixteen Europeans ("among them the splendid Captain von Prince") and fifty-five askaris, while seventy-six Germans and Africans had been wounded. But this was a small price to pay alongside the staggering butcher bill run up by the invaders and the vast gains in materiel accruing to the Germans. Three field companies were completely rearmed with modern British rifles, and sixteen new machine guns were distributed throughout the force. No less welcome were half a million rounds of small arms ammunition, every one of Force "B's" field telephones and enough clothing to uniform the entire Schutztruppe for a year.

"Even greater," wrote von Lettow, "was the enemy's loss in *moral*";

---

* More than one date has been given for the arrival of the guns. Von Lettow writes that they had already opened up on the transports early in the morning of the previous day. In any case, few hits were scored and the damage, if any, was negligible.

after being so soundly thrashed by a force one-eighth their own strength, the British and Indians "almost began to believe in spirits and spooks."

This was not all. While Aitken's initial assault was being hurled back on November 3, Stewart's force, which was to act as the upper prong of the British pincers near Moshi, had also come a cropper. Having dispersed his troops too widely, Stewart found himself fair game for three German field companies and a mounted column which had little trouble scattering his troops even further during a brief but decisive action a few miles northwest of Kilimanjaro. That victory in itself assured the security of German East Africa for a long time to come. But this fight went all but unnoticed alongside the humiliation of the British at Tanga, which was to have an immeasurable effect on the conduct of the ensuing four-year campaign. As von Lettow put it, "Tanga was the birthday of the soldierly spirit of our troops."

The departing British did not attend the celebration. "Here we are now," wrote Meinertzhagen, "out of sight of land and steaming for Mombasa, a beaten and broken force. My confidence in the leadership and personnel of the force is badly shaken, and I am now suffering bad headaches from being blown into a palm tree by H. M. S. *Fox*."

It was the beginning of a long headache for all the Allied forces in East Africa. "Tanga," as one military historian has observed, "stands for a fruitful lesson on how not to start a colonial campaign."

PART III
BLACK YEAR

8

Die Wacht am Rufiji

THE ONLY ELEMENT LACKING in the Germans' victory at Tanga was the *coup de grace*. Despite the protection offered by H.M.S. *Fox*, the fleeing British transports could easily have been sent to the bottom of the Indian Ocean with a few well-directed 4.1-inch shells from *Königsberg*. Looff, however, had come nowhere near the convoy, let alone the battle. While von Lettow's riflemen and machine gunners were scything down Aitken's last hope of keeping even a foothold in Tanga, *Königsberg's* skipper and crew had their own plates full more than two hundred miles to the south, as the opening salvoes were fired in what was to become history's longest naval engagement.

Eight and a half months long, to be exact.

Hardly had H.M.S. *Pegasus* settled on the bottom of Zanzibar harbor on September 20 than the report of her sinking reached London by the cable which Looff had failed to cut. It was like the news of a cop killing. No longer would *Königsberg* be hunted by the mildewed semi-relics of the Cape Squadron. On September 21, wireless orders went out to Captain Sidney R. Drury-Lowe, commanding the British cruiser *Chatham*—which had just escorted a convoy up the Red Sea—to swing round and make full steam for East African waters. *Chatham* was not only newer and faster than *Königsberg* but mounted eight 6-inch guns against the German's 4.1-inch battery. And, as extra insurance, she was also to be joined by two equally new and muscular sister ships of the "town" class: H.M.S. *Dartmouth*, detached from Indian Ocean convoy duty, and H.M.S. *Weymouth* from the Mediterranean. Against this array of seagoing heavy artillery, *Königsberg's* chances of remaining afloat seemed only slightly better than an anchor's.

But only at first glance. The Admiralty had to assume that *Königsberg* had probably gone to cover in one of the innumerable tangled estuaries which formed a ragged two-thousand-mile hemline along the German and Portuguese East African coasts. If this were the case, it might take an entire navy to smoke her out, and no such fleet existed for that task. As it was, the loss of *Chatham* and *Dartmouth* to the East India Station placed a heavy strain on the already overworked warships which still had to seek out and destroy *Emden* while simultaneously trying to protect westbound troop convoys. Besides which, if the Admiralty's judgment was faulty and *Königsberg* had gone back to sea—waiting, perhaps, to pounce on inadequately guarded transports in the Gulf of Aden, or steaming eastward for the much-feared linkup with *Emden*—then the three cruisers in East African waters would simply be wasting valuable coal and even more precious time. By the mere fact of being at large, a single German cruiser which in seven weeks had sunk no more than two British ships was making a shambles of Britannia's rule over the western Indian Ocean waves.

Nonetheless, the three new cruisers sniffed diligently up and down the coast. Drury-Lowe, the squadron commander, divided the two-thousand-mile search area into three sectors. Two of these, covering the Portuguese East African coast and the Mozambique Channel, were patrolled by *Dartmouth* and *Weymouth*, while *Chatham* tracked down clues along the German coast. All three warships had a galaxy of leads at their disposal. As early as September 22, they had picked up wireless messages which continually repeated the letters AKO—*Königsberg's* radio call signal. Reports and rumors, some delivered by British agents, many planted by German spies, were duly relayed from Zanzibar and investigated: *Königsberg* had now made her base on the Comoro Islands in the Mozambique Channel . . . She was spotted firing rockets off Dar es Salaam . . . Her searchlights were seen outside Mombasa . . . She was sighted at anchor near a small island off the Portuguese East African coast, while almost simultaneously she was reported coaling at the port of Jeddah on the Red Sea. Drury-Lowe had his work cut out for him.

Mingled with all this ostensible intelligence were suspicious displays of red and white flags (and occasionally shirts), conspicuously placed and carefully arranged, on coastal islands and reefs, while mounted German patrols frequently trotted about on mainland beaches. At night, mysterious fires lit up the shoreline for miles; they "would accompany or precede us along the coast," wrote Drury-Lowe, "like a *feu de joie*."

But Drury-Lowe recognized the activity for what it was: "a most efficient intelligence system." The shirts, flags, fires and patrols were relaying *Chatham's* position and directions to mainland wireless stations. While an enemy cruiser's activities would certainly be of interest to von Lettow, a naval officer would benefit even more from the voluminous results of so painstaking a surveillance. Thus it seemed not only likely that the reports on *Chatham* and her sisters were being transmitted to Looff aboard *Königsberg*, but quite probable that the raider was indeed holed up somewhere in the neighborhood.

Even so, it was not until mid-October that the stalking squadron came on its first solid clue to *Königsberg's* hideout. Patrolling off Madagascar, *Dartmouth* captured the German tug *Adjutant* en route to Lindi, the southernmost port in German East Africa. This indicated the possibility, suspected for some time, that a three-thousand-ton DOA liner named *Präsident* might have taken refuge in Lindi. Since *Präsident* was ideally suited to serve as a mother ship for *Königsberg*, Drury-Lowe immediately ordered *Chatham* full steam southward to Lindi.

Sure enough, *Präsident* was anchored far inside Lindi harbor, with the white cross of a hospital ship painted on her hull. But all resemblance to missions of mercy ended there: not a single doctor, patient or bottle of medicine could be found by a Royal Navy boarding party. Accordingly, over the heated but vain protests of local German officials, Drury-Lowe sent a demolition team to disable *Präsident's* engines. When the party returned to *Chatham* it brought back a set of charts which showed the coast in far greater detail than did those of the Royal Navy. And, much more significantly, with the charts were a number of documents containing irrefutable proof that *Präsident* had been supplying lighters with coal and stores for *Königsberg* and her tender *Somali*. These papers, moreover, showed that the lighters offloaded their cargoes at a place on the German charts called Salale, four miles inside the delta of the Rufiji River. Unless Looff had already been alerted, the trap was closed at last.

Not quite. Even with the help of the new charts, entering the shallow, reef-laced Rufiji mouth was not going to be easy. For *Chatham*, in fact, the task proved impossible. The British cruiser drew two feet more than *Königsberg*, and those two feet made all the difference. They were just enough to permit Looff's entry into the delta and to keep Drury-Lowe five miles offshore, at least nine miles from Salale. And on October 30, when Drury-Lowe anchored *Chatham* as close to the river mouth as he dared, the masthead lookout reported no sign of the German raider.

But Drury-Lowe was not that easily put off. He had his steam cutter lowered and sent in through the reefs and shoals to a cluster of grass huts on the nearest beach. The cutter returned with a cooperative jumbe and two other Africans. After long questioning in bad Swahili by several of *Chatham's* officers, the three men finally understood what was being asked. Yes, they said, the *"manowari na bomba tatu"* was definitely inside. This could very well mean the end of Drury-Lowe's search. It could also mean nothing.

Then there was a shout from the lookout: far inside the delta, a tree had just moved several hundred yards. It was *Königsberg's* foremast, camouflaged with the fronds of a coco palm.

The delta of the four-hundred-mile Rufiji river, German East Africa's
mightiest waterway, encompasses an area roughly the size of metropolitan
New York. Lying in the sodden embrace of mud and mangrove trees, it is
a morass of serpentine creeks and brackish tidal channels, clogged with
sandbars, writhing with crocodiles, snarling with mosquitoes, trembling
with the crash of elephant herds in the matted rain forest around its banks.
The delta does not welcome man; one almost expects to find rubbery prehistoric animals wallowing about in its miasma. It breathes isolation and
spawns disease. Even a fugitive would hesitate before seeking asylum here.

But Looff had not hesitated on the day he sank *Pegasus*. If he were to
make desperately needed repairs on his ship—or at least try to make
them—he must have temporary refuge from the Royal Navy. The Rufiji
offered the nearest haven. And if its delta was a forbidding cesspool, so
much the better: few if any other spots on the coast could have been more
ideally suited as a hideout. The seaward side of the river mouth was guarded
by a line of reefs and islands. The delta itself had six main arms to the
ocean, at least four of which—the Kikunja, Simba Uranga, Suninga and
Kiomboni channels—were not only navigable for a light cruiser of *Königsberg's* relatively shallow draft but were also joined to each other by a net-
work of narrow creeks. Several of these, barely navigable at high tide, would
enable *Königsberg* to confound her pursuers by dodging about far inland,
well beyond range of British guns. Further protection was offered by the
tall and dense vegetation on the banks: with topmasts housed or camouflaged, *Königsberg* might well remain invisible for months.

But there was no question of stagnating in the delta that long; even if
this had been Looff's intention he could hardly afford to allow half his crew
to die of malaria. What he had in mind, specifically, was to take *Königsberg*
back to Germany.

No such voyage, to be sure, could be attempted while the cruiser's engines wheezed and retched on the brink of total collapse. There was not
even a chance of beginning the voyage so long as the Royal Navy kept
Königsberg from the shipyard in Dar es Salaam. But if *Königsberg* was
unable to reach Dar by sea, might not her engines go there by land? From
the Rufiji delta? Looff thought so. Reentering the delta on the afternoon of
September 20, he anchored off Salale in the Suninga channel and began
making preparations for an impossible journey.

Lieutenant Commander Werner Schönfeld was placed in charge of the
operation. Having farmed in German East Africa before the war, he was
now able to go ashore and enlist the services of several fellow-countrymen
who ran plantations not far from the delta. They had their African farm
workers build two immense wooden sledges, which were laboriously brought
alongside *Königsberg's* berth at Salale. Upwards of one thousand more
Africans were then recruited for the task of lifting one of the cruiser's now
dismantled boilers from the engine room and wrestling the tremendous

steel plates aboard the sledges. This done, the sledges were dragged off into the bush. Hopefully, they would somehow reach Dar es Salaam.

Meanwhile other preparations were under way. Allowing *Königsberg* to lie immobilized—up the creek, as it were, without a paddle—would entail enormous risk. Although the cruiser had not yet been discovered and was probably safe from effective shelling, detection, followed by attack of some sort, could not be ruled out. The British could easily launch suicide raids by fast, shallow-draft torpedo boats; they might try to block off the channel mouths; they might land troops in force, even field guns. Looff had to defend his ship against any or all of these tactics. He therefore set about transforming the delta into a swampy fortress.

First off, all the 47-mm. guns comprising *Königsberg's* secondary armament were taken ashore and mounted, behind well-comouflaged emplacements, in strategic spots commanding the approaches to the delta's navigable entrances. Machine gun nests and rifle pits, cloaked with mangroves and creepers, lined the banks of the channels emptying into these mouths. So that the cruiser's 4.1-inch guns could deliver their salvoes with maximum accuracy, telephone lines were run out several miles from her fire control stations to artillery spotting posts on land. There were shore watchers, connecting trenches, elaborate signaling systems. Having arranged the transfer of *Königsberg's* boiler, Schönfeld was now given command of the shore detachment. Every officer, petty officer and seaman who could be spared was assigned to duty in what soon came to be known as the Delta Force.

Looff naturally hoped that the Delta Force would never be called on to fire a shot, that as soon as *Königsberg's* engines were turning again, the cruiser could leave the Rufiji pesthouse and begin the long voyage home. Everything depended, of course, on whether the dismantled boiler could reach Dar es Salaam and return.

The question was iffy. An uneven road had to be hacked through one hundred miles of thorn, savanna and swamp that few men, white or black, had ever crossed. Several rivers had to be spanned with hastily improvised wooden bridges; rough rock fords enabled passage of smaller streams. *Königsberg's* damaged innards moved less swiftly than the ants and centipedes beneath the feet of the men who hauled the two sledges. A thousand sweating black shoulder muscles bulged and glistened in the white sun, a thousand deep voices roared "*Harambee!*" with every concerted heave on the towlines. Sometimes the lines parted like rifle shots in struggles with bogs or the slopes of hills. Trees would then be felled, their trunks or limbs used as levers to pry the stubborn masses of dead weight forward again. The procession was not unlike the moving of a pyramid block thirty centuries earlier. Nearly three weeks passed before the boiler could be carried into the shipyard foundry in Dar.

Here, however, work proceeded efficiently and swiftly. The African teamsters had hardly caught their collective breaths when they were back on the rutted bush track once more. By October 30, Looff was able to order a test run of *Königsberg's* engines. They hummed as if they had just been delivered from the navy yard at Kiel.

It must have seemed ironic to Looff that he did not have the engines twenty-four hours earlier, before his camouflaged foremast had been almost accidentally spotted. Henceforth, if *Königsberg* were to depart from the Rufiji delta, she would have to come out with all her guns blazing against an almost hopelessly superior British force.

With *Königsberg* tracked down at last, the Royal Navy hastened to place the delta under a well-organized siege, masterminded by King-Hall in Cape-town. Since King-Hall himself could not go to the Rufiji—being occupied with the sea transport of South African troops to German South West Africa —he placed Drury-Lowe in command of operations on the spot. That officer soon had a fearsome array of waterborne firepower at his disposal as *Dartmouth* and *Weymouth* joined *Chatham* on sentry duty outside the reefs.

Nor were the eighteen six-inch guns of the three cruisers Drury-Lowe's only weapons. At the entrance to the delta's main channels, a vest-pocket armada patrolled ceaselessly. Its ships were a jaunty little assortment of tugs, steam launches and converted whaling vessels, mounting popguns on their decks and sporting such names as *Echo, Fly, Salamander* and *Pickle.* Sometimes they almost seemed to be on a holiday cruise. Their officers and men went swimming in reef-sheltered lagoons, trolled for game fish and dined on turtle steak. But their work was vital to the quick inter-ception of the German raider: should she try to break out, rockets from the picket boats would instantly signal Drury-Lowe's cruisers to move in for the kill. And since this inshore spying entailed continual skirmishes with the much more muscular firepower of the Delta Force—not to men-tion the ever-present threat of being vaporized by *Königsberg* herself—no one serving on patrol was a good insurance risk.

Yet despite the staggering odds against the German cruiser, the months of November and December 1914 witnessed a stalemate. *Königsberg* might have been trapped, but Drury-Lowe seemed hard put to get at her. A stand-up gun duel inside the delta was out of the question. During the two or three hours at the top of a high spring tide, it was just conceivable that the British cruisers, with expert piloting and a modest miracle, might enter one of the main arms and at least bring *Königsberg* within range of their six-inchers. But more than two or three hours were needed if the cruisers were to reach open sea before the tide ebbed, and Drury-Lowe did not intend to risk an almost certain grounding. Not, at any rate, while he had other bolts in his quiver.

The first was a long-range artillery exercise. Early in November, *Dart-*

mouth managed to pick her way through the outer reefs and shoals to within two miles of the Simba Uranga mouth, while *Chatham* and *Weymouth* also moved in close enough for a joint bombardment. It was not close enough. Although the British salvoes threw up a wondrous display of waterspouts, *Königsberg* lay several hundred yards outside their maximum range of 14,500 yards, and the only result of the barrage was Looff's decision to move even farther upstream. A few days later, Drury-Lowe won a consolation prize of sorts when *Chatham* found *Somali's* range and turned the collier-tender into a floating torch that blazed for more than forty-eight hours. But it was small consolation.

Another plan called for the landing of several thousand troops near the Simba Uranga mouth to dislodge the Delta Force; this would enable light-draft torpedo boats to enter the channel undisturbed and move upstream to their target. But after the disaster at Tanga, a beachhead assault by Indian forces had to be shelved indefinitely.

Still, Drury-Lowe refused to abandon the idea of a quick kill. Just before dawn on November 7, a picket boat armed with a pair of torpedoes was towed into the Simba Uranga mouth by an old cable ship named *Duplex*. The attackers had an escort of three armed steam cutters and the ostensible cover of the British cruisers' guns. Hardly had they entered the channel, however, than the waters were churned into froth by a homicidal crossfire from the invisible Delta Force. Within seconds, the picket boat was staggering under the blow of a 47-mm. shell, which caused it to launch one of its torpedoes accidentally. No one saw where the missile struck, for the tiny task force was already withdrawing at *Duplex's* top speed of seven knots. The crews considered themselves lucky to reach open water unharmed. *Königsberg* had yet to sustain a near-miss.

The very fact of the raider's invulnerability, however, may have contributed to a growing climate of claustrophobia aboard ship. Hemmed in by the black mangroves, drenched in the fetid, malarial swamp air, often stuck fast on mud banks for hours at a time, *Königsberg's* crew would have been supermen of their esprit did not sag occasionally. November 9 was a particularly black day, as Radio Officer Niemyer intercepted a triumphant British communication proclaiming that H.M.S. *Sydney* had sent *Emden* to the bottom off Cocos Island in the eastern Indian Ocean. Nor could the crew have felt less alone in the world when Niemyer picked up another message *en clair*: orders to Drury-Lowe from the Admiralty to "sink or destroy *Königsberg* at any cost." Surely, remarked Niemyer, as he handed the message to Looff, this must be our death sentence. Looff smiled and reminded Niemyer of the medieval German folk tale about a posse of Nurembergers making plans to hang a bandit whom they had not yet caught. But the humor was forced; at that particular time, *Königsberg* was heeled over, hard aground, and Looff was feeling none too buoyant himself.

Shortly afterwards, however, the cruiser floated free, and Looff observed the crew's return to what he called "the old nonchalance."

And it was not long before morale skyrocketed with the interception of a third British wireless message: on November 8, off Coronel on the west coast of South America, Spee's peripatetic East Asia Squadron had annihilated a task force of British cruisers. Britannia was not having it all her way. It began to seem possible that Spee might take his warships across the South Atlantic and steam up the East African coast to extricate *Königsberg*. With luck, the bandit would still elude the scaffold.

This was not merely wishful thinking. If Drury-Lowe had thrown a noose around the mouth of the Rufiji, it did not necessarily follow that he could hold it there indefinitely. At regular intervals, each of the British cruisers had to sail north to Zanzibar and Mombasa for bunkering and engine overhaul; this alone left an opening. Further, the ships remaining on station were plagued by the thick mud which the Rufiji deposited in the shallows offshore. Stirred up by the cruisers' propellers, the mud quickly choked condensers; this caused *Chatham's* evaporators to seize up after only a few days on blockade. It took forty-eight hours to clean the machinery while *Chatham*, her fires out, lay immobilized and useless. A continuation of such breakdowns must increase *Königsberg's* chances of getting through the cordon. And if this happened—especially on the heels of the deep wound inflicted by Spee—a great deal more than Royal Navy prestige would be at stake.

Alarm over a possible breakout shaped Drury-Lowe's next move. The objective now was not to sink *Königsberg* but to cork her up in the delta forever, which amounted to the same thing. This would be done by scuttling a blockship in the channel of the Suninga outlet, which at that time was thought to be the German cruiser's only avenue of flight. The vessel chosen to act as the plug was a flat-bottomed thirty-eight-hundred-ton Admiralty collier named *Newbridge*. Her holds filled with dynamite charges and rubble, she would steam into the Suninga entrance and anchor bow and stern athwart the channel, at which point the crew would open her seacocks, board an escorting ship's boat and detonate the charges by remote-control firing circuits. It was that simple.

It was also suicide: anchoring in the Suninga channel would provide target practice for the Delta Force guns at point-blank range. But when Drury-Lowe called for volunteers, *Chatham's* entire ship's company stepped forward. Fourteen officers and men were chosen to man *Newbridge*. "I hardly ever expected to see them again," said Drury-Lowe.

The operation was scheduled for November 10. Some attempt to reduce the risk was made by putting up steel plates and sandbags around *Newbridge's* wheelhouse, afterdeck and forecastle. As in the abortive torpedo attack, three armed steam cutters and the old *Duplex* were assigned to escort the collier, while the cruisers would stand in as close as possible to provide at least token cover with their big guns. Drury-Lowe also tried for an element of secrecy by arranging to have the miniature convoy enter the channel just before dawn.

No one was caught napping. At exactly 5:25 A.M., as *Newbridge* crept past the Suninga entrance, the Delta Force, still unseen but very much in evidence, set the channel aboil with every gun it could bring to bear. For the next hour, the sodden air of the lower delta reverberated with the bark of 47-mm. guns and the clatter of machine guns, occasionally cried out when a shell burst against the steel plates of the blockship or the protected hull of one of the escorts. But *Newbridge's* crew behaved as if the whole thing were a dry run. At 5:50, almost hidden by the blossoms of exploding shells, the ex-collier was jockeyed into position astride the fairway. At a quiet order from the bridge, bow and stern anchor chains rumbled out while the volunteer skipper, Commander Raymond Fitzmaurice, signaled "Finished with engines." *Newbridge* might have been coming to anchor in Southampton roads.

At that very moment, a steam cutter glided alongside, took off *Newbridge's* crew, and the four escort craft steamed hastily—but still in formation—through the rain of steel toward open water. At 6:15, Fitzmaurice pushed the plunger that set off the charges in the blockship. There was a thundering belch as *Newbridge* gave a great shudder and then began to settle in the water. Within minutes, only her upper works could be seen.

By this time, the escort vessels had made good their escape through the channel mouth. Of the five dozen officers and men in the operation, two had been killed by shell fragments; nine others were badly sliced up but remained alive. By rights, all should have been feeding the crocodiles in the Suninga. Later that afternoon, a jubilant Admiralty announced to the world that *Königsberg* was "now imprisoned and unable to do any more damage."

It was a premature claim. Although the Suninga was indeed stoppered up, a nagging apprehension about the other channels began to mount swiftly. Drury-Lowe, in fact, did not rule out the possibility that Looff might still try a dash for freedom through the Simba Uranga or the Kiomboni mouth. If these arms proved to be navigable, *Königsberg* stood a not unreasonable chance of breaking out at night: slipping unseen past the small patrol craft at the entrances and steaming at least one hundred miles to sea before her escape was detected. And the likelihood of such a move might well become reality if any one of Drury-Lowe's cruisers, badly needed elsewhere, were to be ordered off the Rufiji station.

The latter happened sooner than anyone expected. Hardly had Spee struck his blow off Coronel than the report went out that the German squadron was now steaming east across the Atlantic to make short work of King-Hall's feeble cruisers on the Cape Station. It began to look as if Looff's hopes of assistance from outside might soon bear fruit. In mid-November, both *Dartmouth* and *Weymouth* were ordered south to reinforce King-Hall, leaving only *Chatham* to keep the watch on the Rufiji. The hole in the fence around the delta had become almost a yawning gap.

Almost but not quite. Escape may have been feasible at this time, but it was not the kind of feat that Looff could bring off at will. Tides hand-cuffed *Königsberg* not much less than they did the British cruisers. Even the delta's navigable channels could not always be relied on at low water, and while it was risky enough to run aground ten miles or more from the open sea, piling up on a sandbar within range of Drury-Lowe's six-inchers would mean the end. If the Royal Navy warships would not brave the delta's approaches without a high spring tide, Looff needed it just as badly to get out.

Nor would the tide do the trick alone. Escape under ideal conditions (and Looff could afford nothing less) also required that the tide reach flood between midnight and 3:00 A.M., and further, that the same full moon which raised the waters be hidden in clouds. It was not an easy combination to achieve, despite the southwest monsoon rains of the early winter months. At any rate, Looff did not see fit to exploit the absence of *Dartmouth* and *Weymouth*.

At least, however, Looff had by now made *Königsberg* all but invisible. Following Drury-Lowe's futile barrage in early November, he had taken the cruiser deep into the bowels of the delta, where the vegetation dropped an almost solid curtain over her upper works. Dhows occasionally brought in supplies, eluding the British by slipping in and out of tiny creeks that were unknown or risky even to the smallest patrol craft. The cruiser was now snug—to the extent that "snug" can be applied to so unlovely a hide-out.

The besiegers, to be sure, were reasonably confident that their prey had not flown the coop; from time to time a lookout at *Chatham's* masthead would glimpse a wisp of smoke that all agreed probably came from the German cruiser's funnels. Still, reasonable certainty was not enough—not when Drury-Lowe faced an adversary who had held the Royal Navy up to ridicule in the Indian Ocean for four months. There could be absolutely no margin for error.

Drury-Lowe therefore requested that aircraft be brought up to pinpoint *Königsberg* from overhead.

The proposal was unorthodox to say the least. In 1914, most Britons and Germans (Looff was one) had never even seen an airplane, and the concept of air reconnaissance had barely left the womb as an instrument of military or naval strategy. Besides which, the few Royal Navy planes in existence were busy in other theatres and could not be spared. But in Cape-town, King-Hall learned that a man named Cutler was making exhibition flights out of Durban in a single-engine Curtiss hydroplane. It was hardly a machine to reconnoiter an equatorial river mouth but it was the only machine available. No time was lost in twisting Cutler's arm with a naval

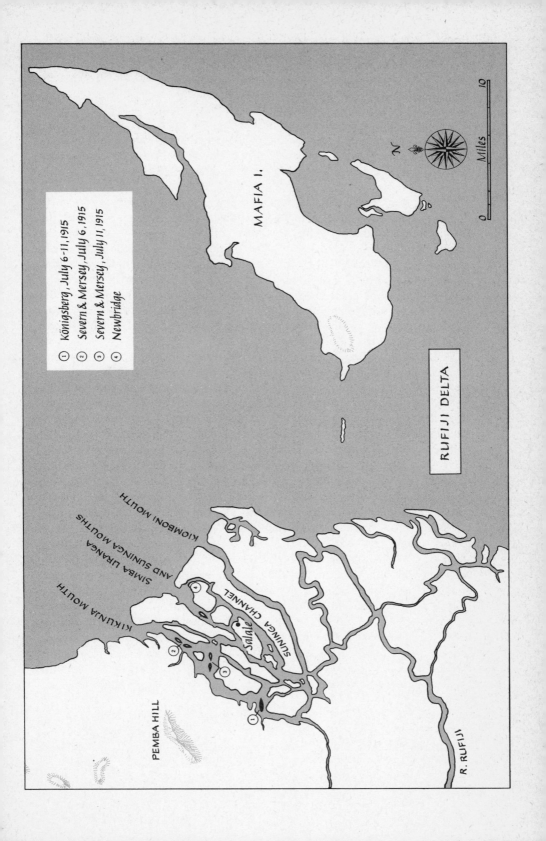

MAFIA I.

RUFIJI DELTA

① Königsberg, July 6–11, 1915
② Severn & Mersey, July 6, 1915
③ Severn & Mersey, July 11, 1915
④ Newbridge

Miles

0   10

N

KIKUNJA MOUTH

SIMBA URANGA
AND SUNINGA MOUTHS

KIOMBONI MOUTH

PEMBA HILL

Salale

SUNINGA CHANNEL

R. RUFIJI

ceed up the Kikunja and anchor behind a wooded island called Gengeni, some eight miles from *Königsberg*. Here, their six-inch guns would announce the beginning of the end for the German raider.

Unless Looff's 4.1-inchers had a statement of their own; no one underestimated their deadly accuracy and deadlier striking power. The final business of the briefing took place when Captain Fullerton and Commander Wilson handed the monitors' code books to King-Hall.

Shortly after five o'clock on the morning of July 6, the monitors, with *Severn* in the lead, crept like burglars toward the shallow water of the Kikunja entrance under the black woollen cape of a pre-dawn sky. Even the throbbing of their engines was muffled by the breakers on the outer reefs, and no one spoke except when necessary; the leadsman in *Severn's* bow chains whispered his soundings. At 5:20, the faint loom of the Simba Uranga headland was sensed more than discerned; within minutes, the monitors would have entered the Kikunja and the sun, shortly afterwards, would be climbing out of the Indian Ocean. Already, a barely visible thread of sulphur lined the eastern horizon.

Then three blinding flashes on shore sliced the darkness open. They were followed instantly by three stinging bangs. The monitors had been sighted and blank charges from a signal gun were alerting *Königsberg* and the Delta Force. Seconds later, from the British cruisers outside the entrance, came what Pretorius, aboard *Weymouth,* called "a thunderous roar that filled the world." For the next eleven hours the noise never abated.

The element of surprise had worked to the extent of allowing *Severn* and *Mersey* to cross the Kikunja bar and get inside the channel before being detected. But now that they were found out they must pass through the Delta Force's shooting gallery for nearly two miles. Every gun on both banks was trained on the monitors; big mountains of dead fish and mutilated crocodiles reared up all around the vessels with the bursts of near-misses. Fullerton and Wilson replied with their own three-pounders, silencing at least one German battery, and the defenders' aim was further deflected—as King-Hall had hoped—by the earthquakes from the salvoes of the British cruisers.

But the Germans, with the advantage of concealment, gave the monitors a hard time. So too did the tortuous channel; despite the accuracy of Pretorius' soundings, the thin ribbon of deep water twisted so crazily that it was impossible to steam ahead at more than seven and a half knots; this made *Severn* and *Mersey* doubly vulnerable. But they could hardly turn back. Their crews must simply stand up to the hammering and hope to get through.

It was also an anxious time for the men outside the delta. King-Hall felt cut off from the action. Although he was in wireless contact with the monitors, they were hidden from sight by the mangroves and the clouds of mud and dust thrown up over the shore by the cruisers' shells. And even if the ships had been visible, there would have been no way of knowing whether they could remain afloat under the concentrated German fire.

Looff was getting a slightly clearer picture of developments. "Finally, a relief," had been his initial reaction on hearing the three warning shots that signaled his 220 sick men to stumble to their action stations. From then on, an officer in the cruiser's main spotting post on an islet in the Kikunja had kept in constant touch by telephone, providing a play-by-play, or shot-by-shot, account of the monitors' duel with the shore batteries. There was a moment of tense anticipation as the officer reported *Severn* approaching a bend where a dugout, with an outboard motor and one of *Königsberg's* torpedoes, had been concealed. Then the telephone emitted a deafening blast of static: Fullerton had just spotted the torpedo and blown it out of the water with a six-inch shell.

Not long after this, the spotter's voice was heard again with an even less encouraging report: it appeared that the monitors would soon have steamed beyond the range of the Delta Force guns.

By about quarter past six they were clear. At 6:17, Cull appeared overhead in a Henry Farman and wirelessed that spotting could begin. At 6:23, *Severn* rounded up to her position behind Gengeni Island, let go bow and stern anchors at a range of slightly less than eleven thousand yards from *Königsberg* and prepared to open fire. At that moment, however, a trick current swung her stern around so that the forward six-incher could no longer bear on the target. It was not until 6:48 that *Severn* could be jockeyed back into broadside firing position. By then, *Mersey* was also anchored, about four hundred yards astern. But another ten minutes went by before the monitors finally opened up. And even then, they seemed to be wasting ammunition. Their shells fell so far astray of their target that Cull found it hard even to locate the bursts, let alone report whether they were "shorts" or "overs."

And *Königsberg's* gunners had not waited for the monitors to make themselves comfortable. Although the cruiser's cramped anchorage allowed Looff to fire only the five guns of his starboard battery, the German spotters made every broadside count. Five minutes before *Severn* was ready to fire, her decks were awash with the water thrown up by *Königsberg's* salvoes. Cull reported later that the German shooting, "obviously shore controlled, was magnificent, and the monitors were continually straddled, it appearing from the air that they had been hit many times, as the splash of the salvoes often hid the ships from observation."

Appearance soon became reality as Looff's spotters tightened the range. At 7:40, a great cheer went up from the cruiser when the telephone officer reported: "Hit bows of monitor lying to west." A 4.1-inch shell had burst squarely on *Mersey's* forward turret, tearing the gun and its four-man crew apart and mangling four other seamen. It also came within an ace of blowing the monitor sky-high by igniting a powder charge that threatened the magazine. But a quick-thinking chief petty officer saved the ship by throwing the charge overboard, frying his hands while doing so. Then *Mersey* reeled under a second hit, just below the waterline. The shell's impact, however, was cushioned by a ship's boat lying alongside. If it had not been where it was, *Mersey*—her empty petrol tins notwithstanding—might well have gone straight to the bottom.

The news of *Mersey's* plight continued to come in to Looff over the telephone: "Smoke issuing from bow and amidships" . . . "Her fire silenced" . . . "Monitor steaming away at slow speed." The cheers aboard *Königsberg* became deafening. Fever and isolation and hopelessness were forgotten. It began to look as if the disintegrating German cruiser and her crew of invalids were gaining the upper hand. Morale had never been higher since the sinking of *Pegasus* ten months earlier.

But although she bled badly, *Mersey* was not quite crippled. Commander Wilson had decided to shift anchorage a few hundred yards in the hope of throwing the German spotters off. The move saved her again. Hardly had she started downstream than her quarterdeck was flooded as a five-shell salvo plopped into the channel sixty feet astern—on the exact spot she had just vacated. It was her third miraculous reprieve in less than ten minutes.

Meanwhile, *Severn* continued to bang away wildly, then a little less wildly. At 7:55 she scored her first hit. It atomized *Königsberg's* forward 4.1-inch gun and killed two seamen. In the next fifteen minutes, Cull reported three more "ons" and a number of near-misses. One shell tore through the cruiser's bridge, cutting up Looff, his navigation officer and a signalman, although not seriously. Another smashed up the galley. The third drove hot steel into both of Lieutenant Richard Wenig's legs, nearly amputating his left foot. And *Königsberg* could now fire only four guns instead of five.

But her shooting remained steady and accurate. From Cull's Henry Farman, *Severn* was seen to continue her disappearing act in colossal fountains of spray. "It seemed only a matter of time," reported Cull, "before she was hit." The fact that she was not was due to incredible good luck rather than poor German spotting. But then her own shells began falling astray again, and at about 8:15 her forward gun was temporarily silenced as another surge of tide swung her out of broadside firing position. *Mersey's* undamaged after gun, now speaking once more, showed no better results.

At 8:40, both ships were deprived of their spotting directions: Cull's fuel tank was almost empty and he barely reached Mafia. For some reason, the relieving aircraft was delayed, and the monitors had to fire with blindfolds until it arrived. Their accuracy did not improve with the impact of the continual German near-misses.

By nine o'clock, things had become too hot for Fullerton aboard *Severn,* and he too decided to shift anchorage. What happened then could have made the German spotters weep: *Königsberg's* next salvo scored a direct hit on the spot that *Severn* had just that moment cleared. And whatever goblins were hexing *Königsberg* that day gave the Germans another setback when someone aboard *Severn* spied a few khaki-clad men on a camouflaged platform in a tree. They were knocked out of it at once by one of the monitor's three-pound guns. Looff's main spotting station had been destroyed. From then on, *Königsberg's* fire became visibly less accurate.

This by no means ended the threat from the cruiser, since there was a somewhat more distant observation post on Pemba Hill, about two miles west of the Kikunja. As the morning wore on, however, Looff began firing only one or two guns at a time, apparently in an effort to conserve ammunition, since the four remaining guns of the starboard battery were still intact. Yet the German's lower rate of fire did not help anyone's aim aboard the monitors, whose salvoes now started to wander farther and farther from their target without assistance from the air.

Even Cull's reappearance at noon brought no improvement. If anything, shooting became worse. Uncertainty arose as to which wireless signals were intended for which monitor. The confusion was compounded by the arrival overhead of a second spotter plane which threw more signals into the already tangled air. Soon, it was suspected that *Königsberg's* wireless had also butted in with a few misleading directions of its own. The net result of all this was that the three warships spent the better part of the early afternoon making a great deal of noise and wasting even more ammunition.

At 3:45 P.M. it was time for *Severn* and *Mersey* to go: the ebb tide had run more than half its course and the risk of grounding increased by the minute. But the fight had not yet ended: there was a brief but violent exchange of missiles as the monitors came back into the range of the Delta Force batteries. Two 47-mm. shells burst less than twenty feet from *Severn's* bridge and *Mersey* took her third direct hit of the day, while snipers on shore tried—successfully—to spoil the aim of the ships' three-pound guns. In due course, however, the gauntlet was run, and by sunset the monitors lay safely in the womb of the squadron anchorage.

Early the following morning, a spotter plane made a quick flight over the upper Kikunja to survey the damage which the monitors had inflicted on the German cruiser. The findings confirmed what everyone already knew: *Königsberg* was alive and fairly well. She had lived to fight another day.

There was much to be done before *Severn* and *Mersey* could renew the attack. The monitors had injured themselves far more than they had *Königsberg*. Firing 635 shells at extreme elevation for nearly nine hours, their guns had placed a fearful strain on bulkheads and frames, which had to be shored up and reinforced. New plating was riveted over the big puncture in *Mersey's* hull; her mangled forward gun and turret were extracted, and the gap left by the mounting plated over. For some reason, another gun could not be mounted; *Mersey* had become half a warship. Fire control also had to be remedied. In the next attack, it was decided, only one monitor would fire at a time, thus eliminating confusion as to whose aim was being corrected. This fit in well with the overall tactical plan, which called for *Mersey* to move up close as a decoy for *Königsberg's* guns, allowing *Severn* to get off her own salvoes undisturbed.

All these plans and repairs took four days to complete. On the evening of Saturday, July 10, the monitors were ready to move in next day for what they hoped, this time, would be the kill. Provided, of course, that they could get past the Delta Force. By now the combination of dawn and dead low water no longer existed to permit a surprise entry. There was no choice but to walk directly into the sea dragon's mouth in broad daylight.

An energetic greeting awaited the monitors as they approached the Kikunja entrance late in the morning of July 11. No sooner had they crossed the bar than the Delta Force batteries let loose and immediately plugged *Mersey* twice. One shell ploughed through Commander Wilson's cabin and burst near the after gun turret. No one was killed but pieces of flesh and bone splattered onto the deck with a few pints of blood. Sandbags kept the second shot from doing much damage, and the Germans' aim fell off as *Weymouth* and *Pyramus* commenced plastering the shore defenses from outside. But although the monitors got through again, the early hits showed that the watchdogs were alert as ever. They would be no less on the qui vive when the British ships returned down the river. If they returned.

For Looff was ready too. Although the forward gun of *Königsberg's* starboard battery was temporarily beyond repair, the all-important fire control system had been made serviceable again, with telephone lines now running from the cruiser to the new main spotting station on Pemba Hill. Looff also took the initiative, throwing the British tactical plan off stride when he ignored the bait offered by *Mersey* and opened up with all his guns on *Severn* as she came to anchor a few minutes after midday. But *Severn's* bow and stern anchor parties coolly disregarded the flying water and steel, and at 12:30 the monitor began to return the German fire, with Cull calling the shots from just beneath a low-lying quilt of black rain clouds.

The first salvo went wild. So, too, did the second. Cull's engine started to miss, but he stayed aloft, gradually coaxing the British shells toward *Königsberg*: "Four hundred yards down" . . . "Four hundred yards down, twenty yards left" . . . "One hundred yards down, twenty yards left" . . . At last, the British spotting seemed to be paying its way. Even one of *Severn's* misses was productive. It cut the telephone line between *Königsberg* and the Pemba Hill station. From then on, the cruiser's fire became increasingly erratic.

At 12:42 *Severn* sent off her eighth salvo and scored her first hit, kicking over another of *Königsberg's* guns and reducing the cruiser to three-gun broadsides. Two minutes later the German was down to two guns. By 12:53, only one turret was still in action.

At this moment, *Severn's* crew heard a mind-rending explosion aboard *Königsberg,* then watched a greasy column of black smoke begin to climb from her anchorage ten miles off. It was now only a matter of time.

But the dying sea monster could still spit fire. Seconds before *Severn's* next broadside obliterated the single remaining German gun, a signal came from Cull: "We are hit. Send a boat for us." *Königsberg's* last shot had not been wasted. It had blown a cylinder off the Henry Farman's pusher engine. The plane now began rocketing down toward the Kikunja like a bobsled out of control. Only at the last minute was Cull able to maneuver into a long glide and make an emergency landing not far from *Mersey,* which was steaming to the rescue. But when the wheels touched water the machine instantly flipped over on its back. Providentially, the noise of the guns had driven off the crocodiles, enabling Cull and his observer, Sub-Lieutenant Arnold, to free themselves and swim to one of *Mersey's* launches.

It had been a busy crash for Arnold. During the entire descent, he had continued sending corrections to *Severn* as if the plane were on a routine exercise.

Königsberg had now become a waterborne abbatoir. Her center funnel missing, the cruiser was ablaze from stem to stern. All gun crews and ammunition parties in the forward part of the ship were dead. "Blood flowed all over the deck," wrote Lieutenant Wenig; "only shovelfuls of sand made it passable. . . . Corpses lay in heaps near the forecastle. Two torn-off heads rested side by side beneath a locker." On the unprotected bridge, officers had been begging Looff to take cover. He had refused. Even when a shell fragment punctured him for the second time and turned his naval whites scarlet with his own blood, he had insisted that his presence on the bridge would buck up the crew. A few minutes later, however, he was forced to step down: another explosion studded him with shrapnel in a dozen places, one splinter slicing his stomach wide open. First Officer Georg Koch immediately took command of the cruiser from its dying captain.

This same explosion also neutralized *Königsberg's* last gun—now manned by two officers and a seaman who were not even in the gunnery department—but not before it got in the final shot that brought Cull down. Wenig remembered that moment: "There, the plane banked, remained motionless for a second, then went down like an arrow. Blackened with powder and blood, the gunners' faces lit up . . . only momentarily! They had triumphed and they disappeared, shreds of their flesh sticking to the bulkhead and deck."

Even without guns to fire back, *Königsberg* stayed alive for a while under *Severn's* merciless hammering. It no longer seemed to matter that the monitor had been deprived of its spotter: the gunners now had the range, and an oily obelisk of smoke, nearly a mile high, clearly marked the cruiser's position. Between 1:00 and 2:30 that afternoon, *Severn's* decks jumped continually to the recoil of forty-two more salvoes, the shells gradually crawling aft along *Königsberg's* entire length. *Mersey* soon joined the bombardment with twenty-eight broadsides, and after 1:40, with the arrival of the relief spotter plane, hardly a salvo failed to bring the signal "H.T."—hit target.

At 2:20, just as *Severn's* Fullerton decided that he had begun to waste shells, the spotter confirmed this with the message: "Target destroyed."

Looff had now resumed command of his floating heap of scrap metal. By rights he should have been dead, but the steel in his stomach had been stopped short of the abdominal wall by his heavy watch and a gold cigarette case. At 1:30, while bulkheads and deck plates screamed under the relentless blows of the falling six-inch shells, Looff—lying prone on a mattress which someone had brought to the bridge—gasped out four orders to First Officer Koch. They were swiftly obeyed. First, the breechblocks of all the guns were removed and thrown over the side, while a party felt its way below decks to flood the magazines. Then the wounded were placed aboard the ship's boats and rowed ashore, through continually exploding water, by the rest of the crew. Koch was the last man to leave the cruiser; Looff, too weak even to sit up, had been taken off with the other wounded. Koch joined him on the beach after carrying out the fourth order: to arm a torpedo and break *Königsberg's* back.

At two o'clock, Looff watched the torpedo do its work: "A muffled noise, weaker than we expected, hardly noticeable in the thunder of the enemy shells. . . . With a short jerk, the ship turns slightly on its side, and sinks slowly to its upper deck in the mud-colored water of the Rufiji. . . ."

That was as far down as she would ever go. Her battle flags still flew. At sunset, an officer went aboard and lowered them as a bugle sounded and the crew gave three cheers for the Emperor. Then the Imperial Eagle was carefully folded. Later, it would be presented to Looff.

Meanwhile, the British had to fight one more battle, for if *Königsberg* had been liquidated at last, the Delta Force had not, and its guns spoke with undiminished fury as the monitors approached the Kikunja mouth. This time, however, *Severn* and *Mersey* managed to steam past unscathed. Indeed, the battle of July 11 saw no British killed, although the observer of the spotting plane had a near thing when his machine somersaulted in another crash landing and trapped his head in the water. But he was pulled out in time and revived with champagne—as were the officers and men of both monitors, at a noisy victory dinner aboard *Hyacinth* that night.

A brief ceremony also took place the next morning, on the wet ground where the 188 surviving members of *Königsberg's* crew had made a temporary camp: thirty men were buried alongside the two seamen who had been killed in the action of July 6. Near the square of thirty-two white wooden crosses, a cairn was put up. On it was a plaque, hammered out of a muti-lated steam pipe, with the legend: *"Beim Untergang S.M.S. Königsberg am 11.7.15 gefallen . . ."* and the names of the cruiser's dead.

Of the officers and men still living, only twenty-three had not been wounded. Of the 165 others, 65 were on the critical list. Surgeon Eyerich and Bwana Mganga could do little for them except apply rough tourniquets and dressings made of torn uniforms, administer the ship's last supplies of morphine to the amputees and the worst burn cases. Wenig's left leg had to be taken off near the knee while he raved in an onslaught of malaria; it was a wonder that the stump did not go gangrenous in the corrupt swamp airs. Looff's condition was grave but he began to show signs of recovery in due course.

All made it, in fact. Presently, most were able to walk, even to work. There was much work to do. Lieutenant Commander Schönfeld, who had commanded the now disbanded Delta Force and also arranged the remark-able journey of *Königsberg's* dismantled boiler to Dar es Salaam, now told Looff that the guns too could be salvaged. Divers recovered the breech-blocks. Work parties removed the guns from their mountings and poled them on rafts to the shore. They were then lifted on to wagons and dragged through the bush, by four hundred sweating, chanting Africans, to Dar es Salaam. Here, the machinists at the naval shipyard and railway workshops improvised mobile gun carriages. It was not long before the German land forces boasted ten new field pieces—the heaviest artillery in East Africa. *Königsberg* might have been a gutted skeleton of buckled steel, but her guns had not been silenced.

The crew also remained a force in being. First abandoned by the Father-land, they now found themselves heroes; more than half of the officers and men, including Looff, were shortly to receive the Iron Cross. Looff was also promoted; wearing the seven stripes of a *Kapitän zur* See, he now outranked von Lettow—at least technically—which did not please the Schutztruppe commander. Relations between the two men, already strained by von Let-tow's earlier draft of *Königsberg* seamen, became even cooler as von Let-tow once again sought to bring the remainder of the ship's company under his own command. Looff appealed to Schnee with success, thus further widening the breach between Germany's senior soldier and sailor in East Africa.

But there was no question of Looff's importance in the theatre. He was placed in charge of defenses at Dar es Salaam, and his men began to train for land fighting. With Koch as a sort of battalion commander, they drilled, fired on a rifle range, marched ten to fifteen miles daily through the bush and studied Swahili. (It was not hard to learn, especially since each man had an African orderly who doubled as an informal language instructor.) By the autumn of 1915, they had become passable foot soldiers and were going through tactical maneuvers in the field. In one of their war games, Looff found himself a prisoner, but was freed when he pleaded to being an umpire and not a participant.

In the end, von Lettow had his way. One hundred and twenty men of Looff's crew were taken from him and enrolled in the Schutztruppe. But they remained together, as a unit known as the *Königsberg* Company. Looff had not gilded the lily in his official report on the sinking of the cruiser, when he wrote that "S.M.S. *Königsberg* is destroyed but not conquered."

Destroyed, then; that was no small thing. As long as *Königsberg* floated, she had imperiled the free movement of Allied shipping in the western Indian Ocean. Even the always-present possibility that she might leave the Rufiji had manacled upwards of two dozen British warships to the delta when they might have been more usefully employed elsewhere. What von Lettow was doing to divert enemy troops from more important land theatres had been paralleled by Looff—albeit on a smaller scale—with the instruments of British sea power. When *Königsberg* went down, so too did the last serious German naval threat on the East African sea frontier.

II

"A Small and Miserable Thing"

Althoughて BRITISH WAR OFFICE reluctance to sanction East African troop buildups in 1915 sometimes made it seem as if England wished to forget that East Africa was in the war, a few reinforcements did come in. March saw the arrival of the 2nd Rhodesian Regiment, five hundred strong, which might almost have looked like an army corps to the manpower-starved commanders in Nairobi. And in April, when the 25th Battalion of the Royal Fusiliers debarked at Mombasa, General Tighe found himself with no fewer than eleven hundred more fresh troops, raising his total armed strength to some ten thousand rifles. But—as Tanga had shown—this was nowhere nearly enough for anything like a crushing offensive against von Lettow. At least twice that number would be needed, and the War Office continued to make it plain that Tighe could consider himself lucky to be commanding even a patrol on his redundant battleground.

With the Fusiliers, however, Tighe did have the consolation, if that is the word, of claiming what may have been the most picaresque body of men to fight in East Africa or any other theatre of the war. Known quasi-officially as the Frontiersmen,* they had also acquired the sobriquet of "The Old and the Bold." Although the majority of the volunteers were in fact young men, quite a few whose khaki blouses sparkled with the ribbons of long-forgotten colonial campaigns would never see forty again—or pass any standard army physical examination. Captain William Northrup Macmillan, an American who owned a farm in British East Africa, wore a sixty-four-inch sword belt to encircle his 336-pound frame. Other Fusiliers included ex-bartenders, veteran big game hunters and arctic explorers, a

---

* Other Fusilier battalions (there were forty-eight all told) went by such names as the Stockbrokers, Bankers, Sportsmen and Public Schools. The roster of the Jewish Battalion, which fought in Palestine, included David Ben-Gurion, Itzak Ben-Zvi and Jacob Epstein.

number of Russians escaped from exile in Siberia, several circus clowns and acrobats, retired bandsmen, a few Texas cowpunchers, an opera singer, a Buckingham Palace footman, a lighthouse keeper and a general in the Honduras army. (He held the rank of sergeant.) But regardless of background, military experience or fitness, all had in common a schoolboy zest for adventure.

They also had unusual opportunities for advancement. Angus Buchanan, a naturalist who had left off collecting plants and animals around Hudson Bay to join up, found himself elevated from private to lance corporal to sergeant to subaltern to lieutenant to captain in barely eighteen months. Progress through the ranks could also be erratic. At a 6:30 morning parade one day, a certain insubordinate lance corporal was addressed by his commanding officer as a "bloody little bastard," then demoted to private and placed under arrest. At eleven o'clock he was promoted to full corporal and by two in the afternoon had been commissioned a lieutenant. Remarked Meinertzhagen: "He will probably end up where he started, a full private."

In addition to their eccentrics, the Fusiliers also boasted an authentic celebrity. Most Britons of the time looked on the sixty-four-year-old Lieutenant Frederick Courtenay Selous as a living legend. For nearly half a century his country's foremost big game hunter and naturalist, Selous was a sort of British Buffalo Bill and Davy Crockett rolled into one. He had been bagging record African game trophies and collecting specimens of African flora and fauna three decades before most of the men in his platoon were born. A veteran of the Matabele wars of the early 1890s, he was also something of a Renaissance Man: a prolific writer, a gifted musician, fluent in several languages. When he chose, he could be a champion of unpopular causes, and had jeopardized his hero status with fellow-Englishmen by spirited opposition to the Boer War. But it was a measure of Selous' great popular esteem that he never made personal enemies. "He was the easiest of all men to cheat," wrote one of his legion of friends, "but yet no one ever dared to do it. He was a moral antiseptic in a country where men are not saints." Another close friend, Theodore Roosevelt, said that "there was never a more welcome guest at the White House than Selous."

Meinertzhagen, himself a hunter and naturalist of modest repute, also claimed Selous' friendship. Their reunion took place at the Fusiliers' first formal inspection in Nairobi. "We recognized each other at once," wrote Meinertzhagen, "and were soon deep in the question of the validity of the Nakuru Hartebeeste and the breeding of the Harlequin Duck in Iceland. We both forgot we were on parade, much to the amusement of Selous' platoon, who still stood rigidly to attention throughout the discussion." The dialogue ended when Tighe came up and sharply reminded Meinertzhagen that "he was inspecting a battalion and not come to hear a debate of a Natural History Society."

The arrival of this battalion also pleased Meinertzhagen because he had once been a Fusilier officer himself. But even more to the point, the very fact of reinforcement—albeit hardly massive—rekindled his hopes that some kind of offensive action might be launched. About this time, the War Office reiterated its position that British East Africa must remain on the defensive until more troops could be spared, whenever that might be. "But," observed Meinertzhagen, "there are many minor operations we could undertake"; it was important to act, to end the stagnation: "anything to keep up the morale of the men."

Sharing this view, Tighe himself sought War Office approval of a concentrated assault on the port of Bukoba on the western shore of Lake Victoria, where a major wireless station gave the Germans their only reliable contact with Berlin. After two months, grudging consent was finally forthcoming and Tighe appointed General Stewart to lead the attack. On the morning of June 21, a force of about two thousand men, composed mainly of units from the Fusiliers, KAR, Lancs and the 29th Punjabis, packed their field pieces, their machine guns, their horses, their mules and themselves aboard four old lake steamers at Kisumu, and the second British amphibious operation of the East African campaign began.

Actually, it was little more than a glorified commando raid, and it nearly miscarried before a single soldier hit the beach. Stewart's plan called for a night landing three miles north of Bukoba, to be followed at once by a surprise attack on the town. At one o'clock on the morning of the 22nd, the steamers stood in close to the land while three volunteers prepared to slip ashore and strangle the sentry who was known to be stationed at the landing point. At that moment, five German rockets lit up the sky and shoreline for miles. As a precaution against ramming, Stewart had ordered the steamer captains not to black out their ships, thus eliminating the element of surprise—which may already have been ruled out by the light of the half-moon.

Stewart's only major change in tactics was to put off the assault until daylight, and no German fire greeted the British when they landed. Stewart had chosen the base of an almost sheer cliff, about three hundred feet high, as the spot at which his main striking force—the Lancs and the Fusiliers—would go ashore and launch the attack. The cliff was not defended because the Germans did not believe it could be scaled, and they were almost right. Even if the British troops had not been burdened with their rifles and machine guns, they would have faced a punishing climb. It said something about their eagerness for a fight that they reached the top.

Having overcome the heights, however, they soon found that their drive on Bukoba would be less than swift. The British order of battle saw a rough skirmish line etxending about two miles inland and moving south toward the summit of a gently sloping hill overlooking Bukoba. Supporting the advance were several machine guns and the field pieces of the Indian 28th Mountain Battery, one of the few crack artillery teams in the East

African theatre. The Germans were decidedly inferior in numbers but occupied decidedly superior defensive positions. They exploited the concealment of boulders, clumps of thorn, tree trunks and thick banana plantations, while the British troops could take no cover at all as they weaved and crawled toward the hill. Platoons, sometimes whole companies, had to hit the dirt continually under shell bursts from a pair of German 75-mm. field guns. "It was real guerrilla warfare," wrote the Fusiliers' Angus Buchanan. "From rock to rock one could see men dodge, while puffs of smoke puffed . . . from behind scores of rocks and from many a tree-clump bottom." Presently the two German 75s were knocked out by the 28th Mountain Battery, but the pace of the British advance did not quicken appreciably. By dusk, the troops were still more than a mile from Bukoba, and Stewart decided to forgo the final assault until the next morning.

The night bivouac was miserable. The men had been climbing, marching, wading, shooting and dodging bullets for more than twelve hours without rest. No one had eaten since debarkation, and no one ate that night. "Provisions were to have been sent on shore for us," wrote Selous in a personal account of the battle, "but if they were, we never got them. I had a hard biscuit and a lump of cheese in my pocket, but they were ruined in the swamp." At the same time, however, the sexagenarian lieutenant could not resist a gentle boast: "Most of our men were, I think, very much exhausted, but I, I think, was in as good shape as any of them. I really was not tired at all." But then it became cold, "so cold that we could not sleep. . . . We were wet through up to our chests." Someone set fire to several nearby grass huts, and Selous managed to dry his clothes, after which he joined Meinertzhagen seeking shelter under a rock. But it was still too cold to sleep. Both men spent the night talking about birds and shivering.

Bukoba fell on the 23rd, but not without resistance. Stewart ordered a general advance in the morning, covering his own troops with an artillery barrage, while the German companies in the town struck back with a single 75-mm. gun and a number of well-placed snipers. The latter pinged away with conspicuous effect. One officer-sharpshooter almost halted the Fusiliers by himself. Firing from a waist-deep position in a swamp, he could not be seen at close range, although he was visible from Stewart's command post, where a field piece, a machine gun and four dozen rifles hammered at him to no avail. An exasperated Meinertzhagen finally waded into the swamp with his own rifle and the sniper's work came to a sudden end.

The assault continued amid a terrible din. "Our ships had now crept into the Bay of Bukoba," wrote Selous, "and as they fired on the town . . . their shells came screaming and whistling over us. The machine-guns were going too with their wicked rattle, and bullets from the snipers' rifles came with an unpleasant sound . . . within a few inches of our bodies, which were just then pressed as close to the ground as possible. I thought, as I lay there only a yard away from the blood-stained corpse of poor Sergeant-

Major Bottomly, listening to the peculiar noise of each kind of projectile as it found its invisible course through the air above me and around me, that I could recall various half-hours of my life passed amidst pleasanter surroundings. And yet what a small and miserable thing this was, after all, in the way of battle compared with the Titanic contests which have been taking place in Europe."

By one o'clock in the afternoon, the German field gun had been silenced and the defending troops had melted away into the banana groves south of Bukoba. Under a great cloud of black powder left by the German Model 71s, the British entered the town, hauled the Imperial Eagle down from the small fort and ran up a Union Jack. Now the mission's main objective could be carried out. Sappers placed charges under the concrete base of the two-hundred-foot wireless installation (which looked to Selous "like a small Eiffel Tower") and blew it up. Some minutes later the whole town shuddered when the German arsenal went sky-high. All that remained was to bury the eight British dead.

Not quite all. Stewart was now approached by the Fusiliers' commander, Colonel Daniel Patrick Driscoll, requesting permission for the troops to loot the town. Consent was granted with the proviso that there be no drinking or violence; this, remarked Meinertzhagen, was like telling "a ferret that he can enter a rabbit hole but not touch rabbits." Although Selous recorded that he "saw no drunkenness amongst our men," he was probably being less objective than loyal. "All semblance of discipline had gone," wrote Meinertzhagen, "drunkenness was rife and women were being violated. . . . To see a battalion of my own regiment doing it was distressing to a degree. . . . It makes me ashamed to think of what von Lettow and his officers will say."

But Meinertzhagen also enjoyed the spectacle of "British soldiers in fancy dress wearing German officers' full-dress helmets, African porters clothed in European ladies' undergarments, savages smoking Henry Clay cigars and drinking champagne from the bottle and throwing stones at a huge picture of the Kaiser." Further entertainment was provided by a stuttering major named Turner when he liberated a parrot which continually squawked: *"Ach du schwein."* "Turner now says he is going to teach the bird to say all sorts of nice things about the Germans and the result should be interesting, for the bird will be sure to reproduce the stutter."

After this, there was nothing left to do but re-embark.

To whatever extent British morale may have been stiffened by the victory at Bukoba, it was dissipated swiftly in mid-July with the launching of another mini-offensive. This time the objective was a hillock called Mbuyuni, about ten miles east of Taveta astride the Voi-Taveta road beneath Kilimanjaro. The purpose of the attack was never made entirely clear: insufficient force—not to mention the War Office directive against large-scale operations—ruled out any possible follow-up to recapture Taveta itself. "Certainly had we been successful," wrote Lieutenant the Lord Cranworth of Cole's Scouts, "we must have returned to our starting-place."

Even so, General Malleson, under whose command the area fell, decided he was going to smite Mbuyuni. Some eight hundred Germans were dug in there with six machine guns, and Malleson planned an attack with about double that force. Meinertzhagen warned him that the Germans could throw in more than two thousand troops as reinforcements from within a radius of less than twenty miles, and would do so if the attackers revealed themselves by advancing in daylight. But Malleson "jeered at the information, remarking that my Intelligence Section was an amateur show unworthy of consideration." Accordingly, the force set off early in the afternoon of July 13, and finally bivouacked only a few miles from Mbuyuni. Next day, when Malleson attacked, he found that Meinertzhagen's amateurs were not all that amateur: instead of eight hundred Germans and six machine guns, the British now faced a force of at least equal strength with twenty machine guns.

But Malleson still held the initiative. He deployed a KAR and a Punjabi battalion for a frontal assault, while ordering two KAR companies, a Baluchi detachment and the Somalis of Cole's Scouts to skirt the Germans' right wing in a wide arc through the bush and then burst in on their weakly defended rear. The encirclement showed every promise of swift success. There was a brief exchange of ineffectual fire when flankers and defenders took each other by surprise in the screening thorn, but the British recovered first and let go with a pair of seven-pound screw guns which quickly emptied the outer trenches of the German rear lines. Now was the time to drive home the assault—right through to the back door of the main Schutztruppe defenses. Manning a machine gun, Cranworth "could see from my slight eminence considerable concentrations of men along the road, some indeed beginning to stream back towards Taveta, and I emptied several belts. . . . I heard the order to fix bayonets given, and the deep-chested grunting of the K.A.R. that prefaces a charge."

The Somals and the KAR askaris might just as well have kept their bayonets sheathed. "We waited with increasing bewilderment," wrote Cranworth, "for orders to advance," but they did not come, and "the . . . attack seemed to die down." By early afternoon, the flankers were ordered to retire. "The enemy followed us up for half a mile or so, but probably they were as mystified by our manoeuvres as we were and soon drew off." What had happened?

What had happened was that Malleson had simply bitten off more than he could chew. His frontal assault was stopped dead in its tracks by the German machine guns, and there was no way of dislodging them from their well-built rock and sand emplacements. He therefore had no choice but to break off the action and withdraw his entire force, flankers and all, later

covering the reverse—and its 10 percent losses in killed and wounded—
with an official communique calling the operation "a success . . . not out of
proportion to the casualties inflicted upon us." Remarked Cranworth: "It
was consoling therefore to know that someone besides the enemy was
satisfied."

There was more to come. In August, a strongly fortified British post at
Kasigau, an isolated hill south of Voi, was captured by a forty-man German
patrol in a surprise attack. Occupation of Kasigau now extended the railway danger zone by another thirty miles. "It is no longer a question," wrote
Meinertzhagen, "of invading German East Africa or of even undertaking
minor operations. We have lost the initiative." At this point Meinertzhagen could see nothing to keep the Germans from actually taking permanent positions along the line and bringing all rail traffic to a permanent
halt. "If only they would capture Malleson it might be an advantage."

Tighe may have seen the danger even more clearly. About this time, he
warned the War Office that owing to a probable German buildup through
an askari recruitment program, the British situation in Eastern Africa had
become grave: reinforcements simply must not be delayed any longer.
But there were no reinforcements to send. The cream of the British, Indian
and Canadian armies had been bled white at "Second Wipers." Every
available ANZAC soldier was pinned down by German and Turkish guns
at Suvla Bay. In South Africa, to be sure, some sixty thousand Union
troops under General Louis Botha had just completed the occupation of
German South West Africa, and might possibly be used now to beef up
Tighe's force. But strong anti-British sentiments existed in the Union's
Dutch-descended Afrikaner population. There seemed little prospect of
reinforcements from South Africa for a long time to come, if ever.

Not only troops were in short supply. The few actions fought thus far
had shown beyond question that the campaign was going to be predominantly a machine gun war, but Tighe's forces had yet to receive this decisive
instrument of bush fighting in anything like the necessary quantity. "We
want as many Maxims . . . as they can cram into the country," wrote one
officer in a letter home. "The Germans are simply bristling with Maxims,
and use them like artists, and Maxims do 90 per cent. of the damage we
suffer."

The same officer added: "If the Government think we can muddle
through this show, they'll find that we'll get badly mauled." But what the
War Office had for Tighe was sympathy and not much else.

And all the while, there was no letup in the grinding drudgery of trying
to protect the railway. Or rather the railways. With a view to supporting
a British offensive against the German colony at some time in the in-
determinate future, construction had begun on a light military line running
west from Voi toward the border. To von Lettow, this was "a glorious

objective for our patrols." To the British, it only meant that the railway defense operation became proportionately more cumbersome, wearying and frustrating. "It is very difficult, for those who have not seen the country," wrote the Fusiliers' Buchanan in his diary, "to conceive how terribly possible secretive work is in this virgin bushland. . . . A patrol, or an army, if it has sharp eyes everywhere, may escape, under cover of the screening bush . . . and be gone and hopelessly lost in a single night."

Buchanan's complaints were echoed by Selous. "This bush-work is very trying," he wrote to a friend in England, "as the German askaris are very much better at it than heavily equipped white men, many of whom have always lived in towns before coming out here. They are recruited from fighting tribes . . . and are not only very brave, but very well armed. . . . However, like everyone else here, I suppose I am despondent."

Selous at least found scraps of moral nourishment in his remarkable constitution, which he seldom lost an opportunity to mention: "The long marches do not tire me at all, and the men now say that when I fall out no one will be left standing in the battalion. This is, of course, nonsense, but as far as standing fatigue, sun, thirst, etc., I think that I am really better than most of them."

But good health alone could not compensate for Selous' deep-seated disenchantment with the way things were being done (or rather not done) in the East African theatre. The general climate of apathy had struck him immediately on returning to Nairobi from Bukoba. "One would have thought," he wrote, "that as our men had come out from England to fight for East Africa, and that as we had just returned from a successful attack on an enemy stronghold, and as our time of arrival in Nairobi had been telegraphed on ahead, that something might have been done by the townspeople on behalf of our tired and hungry men. . . . But not a bite of food for man or officer was to be had on our arrival. . . . Not even hot water could be obtained to make tea with."

A small oversight overblown, to be sure, but it typified the indifference to the war and the coolness toward the presence of "foreign" troops which prevailed among many British residents of the protectorate for the greater part of 1915. This attitude had been encouraged from the start by the governor, Sir Henry Belfield, who shared with his German counterpart, Schnee, the wish to keep his colonial fief out of the European conflict and thus be spared the inevitable setbacks to hard-won economic (and, to a lesser extent, social) gains. Unlike Schnee, Belfield did not stick his neck out for colonial neutrality, but he had spelled out his own position in January 1915 when he declared in a speech: "I wish to take this opportunity to make it abundantly clear that this colony has no interest in the present war except in so far as its unfortunate geographical position places it in such close proximity to German East Africa." Which prompted Meinertzhagen to comment that "somebody should shoot the man for such a treasonable statement."

But for some reason, the Colonial Office did not see fit to place Belfield in front of a firing squad or even remove him from office, and he pursued his hands-off policy without interference. It had to be contagious, not only among protectorate civil servants (who in any case were bound by their chief's rulings) but, more significantly, among the colonists. "Many settlers," wrote Meinertzhagen, ". . . have been only too willing to take their cue from [Belfield] and have preferred to sit on their farms whilst others protected them. It has been a disgrace to the British name and a considerable anxiety to us." At one point, even a large number of EAMR troopers dropped out of the conflict after having been granted indefinite leave of absence to harvest their crops. This was summer soldiering with a vengeance.

The settlers in fact felt caught in the middle. As pioneers who had tamed a raw wilderness they were physically brave men, and bitterly resented being labeled as slackers by an army whose most conspicuous achievement had been its speed record in leaving the field at Tanga. They felt that salt was being rubbed in the wound by a galaxy of petty regulations and restrictions imposed under the sanction of martial law. And insult, they believed, was being added to injury. The novelist Francis Brett Young, who served in East Africa as a medical officer with the 2nd Rhodesians, remarked on the settlers' ire at "the cavalier air with which the [army], which certainly, after the blunders of Tanga and Jasin, had nothing to shout about, had taken possession of their capital, their clubs and their womenfolk." One is reminded of the British reaction to the American occupation of London in the Second World War.

But while the colonists had a legitimate concern that their farms might revert to bush if they entered the army, they still passed the buck, blaming the protectorate government for encouraging them to continue their civilian work when in fact nearly all of them could have left at any time to join up. It was not an atmosphere conducive to the forging of a common front.

The spectacle of Briton turned against Briton rather than the enemy had its most ludicrous manifestation when one East African newspaper threw a not-too-subtle punch at Meinertzhagen, whose response was to be expected: "The *Leader*, a local rag printed in Nairobi, published an article pointing out the desirability of removing from the Army all those of foreign extraction and as a case in point went on to say: 'Even the head of our intelligence section boasts a German name. Is this to be tolerated when we have so many spies amongst us?' " Meinertzhagen promptly had the editor arrested and court-martialed "for bringing His Majesty's Forces into contempt, and meanwhile his rag is indefinitely suspended."

Eventually, local opposition to the war began to subside. In mid-August, the Colonial Office cabled a belated rebuke to Belfield, and forcibly recommended that he "try and induce every available settler to take his place in the local forces." Belfield received a further prod when a mass meeting of officials, merchants and farmers was harangued by a fire-eating young settler-soldier named Ewart Grogan, who called his audience "rabbits" for their lukewarm sentiments toward the war effort. The oration brought them to their feet, and a unanimous resolution, duly submitted to Belfield, demanded compulsory military service. Meinertzhagen, a behind-the-scenes organizer of the meeting, viewed it as "the turning point in the history of British East Africa." In a sense it was: seven months later, the protectorate became the first country in the British Empire to adopt conscription.

But that was seven months later. Meanwhile, East Africa remained an orphan theatre, with no prospect of War Office assistance in the foreseeable future, and Meinertzhagen continued to despair at the army's inept attempts to curb von Lettow's guerrilla bands: "Throughout my service I have always regarded a war with Germany as a certainty and as the climax of all training. . . . And here I am in the rottenest side-show imaginable, rotten troops and rotten leaders and in a colony where from the Governor downwards there is no feeling of patriotism."

Only an occasional quarrel or other nonmilitary diversion seemed to lift Meinertzhagen's spirits briefly. At a formal gathering of the Mombasa Club ("a pot-house dedicated to Bacchus and Dame Rumour"), "I sat down hoping for some amusing speeches. I was at once addressed by the chairman . . . as 'that officer in uniform' in a most offensive manner, and was requested to leave . . . as only members were permitted to attend. . . . As I had been on the books of the club since I first entered East Africa in 1902, I rose to my feet and told the chairman that I was an older member . . . than either him or any other member in the room, which on investigation proved correct. So I stuck to my chair, and made faces at the chairman for the rest of the meeting."

And there was always the running feud with Malleson, who evidently commanded little respect among his fellow officers, especially after the fiascos at Mbuyuni and Kasigau, which took place in his sector. "Malleson is beside himself with rage. He has received a postcard, purporting to come from von Lettow and with a good imitation of his signature, simply saying: 'Thank you.' Some young officer has a keen insight. . . . Malleson says my department is rotten if I cannot unearth the culprit. . . . I shall take no action beyond posting the card above my desk, for it makes me smile in these hard times."

It was a way to pass the time. It was hardly a way to fight a war. Indeed, it sometimes may have seemed as if the outside world had forgotten that there was such a thing as a campaign in East Africa—although perhaps one outsider was aware of it: "That was a first-class little fight at Bukoba," wrote Theodore Roosevelt to Selous.

The weeks went by and the contagion of inertia spread. Tighe, already suffering from gout, now took to drinking, "much more than is good for him," said Meinertzhagen. "I fear incipient delirium tremens. . . . The poor man told me that he could not resist his liquor and knew it was going to kill him in the end." It did not, but it produced some peculiar behavior. While crossing Lake Victoria after an inspection tour of Uganda, Tighe suddenly asked Meinertzhagen why the steamer had reversed its course. Meinertzhagen said that it had not. "[Tighe's] retort amazed me. 'If I say the ship is going back, it's going back; send for the captain.' " After that man and the chief engineer had been treated to the same declaration, Tighe then announced that the ship was on fire. On being told that he had merely smelled smoke from the galley stove, he roared: "Who's the best judge as to whether the ship's on fire or not . . . ? I'm in command here and if I say the ship's on fire it jolly well is and damn you all." Meinertzhagen finally persuaded Tighe to take to his bunk, where he continued to snap and sputter. "I nearly burst out laughing," wrote Meinertzhagen. "But it is really a crying matter, for he is such a good man. I felt nearer like tucking him up in bed and kissing him."

With the coming of the autumn rains, disease began to strike at the force. The Lancs' War Diary for October 31 recorded: "Of soldiers of the Battalion since the beginning of the war in East Africa, 836 have been admitted to hospital, and only 278 have not." Sickness cut the Fusiliers' active duty roster from eleven hundred to seven hundred. Malaria alone reduced the Indian battalions to a state bordering on mass coma. Only the KAR sick rolls did not seem inflated, and for some reason that force's white officers appeared far more resistant to fever than did those in other units. But there were no new proposals to expand the KAR.

The worst affliction of all, however, was the arthritis of apathetic gloom that crippled every limb and joint of the British East African military body throughout 1915.

No evidence of despondency could be found on the other side of the border: the grimly confident Germans were far too busy converting their colony into a war factory. *Kronborg's* running of the British blockade did not change the fact that supply lines from the Fatherland had been effectively severed by the Royal Navy. Officials and settlers knew that they would soon feel the pinch of shortages, and they spent all of 1915 preparing to meet them.

Food stood high on the priority list; nearly every arable acre in the colony came under intensive cultivation to feed both the Schutztruppe and the civilian populace. The European farms in the northern highland regions virtually became agricultural assembly lines as they stepped up their production of livestock, dairy produce and vegetables. This, however, was to be expected; the heartening surprise came in the volume of African farm output. Previously geared to little more than a subsistence economy, tribal growers and breeders now went on a war footing with official encouragement of large-scale planting and stock development even in the remotest districts. Wheat, rye and sugar fields began to blossom in communities that formerly grew small crops for their own consumption only. Depots were established along the Central Railway to expedite the purchase and movement of African grains. Livestock was bought by the herd from cattle-raising tribes. Dairy produce, once the near-monopoly of white farmers, now became a modest but thriving black man's industry.

Nineteen-fifteen was also the year in which everyone learned to improvise. The Amani laboratories retooled to turn out a wide range of products, most important of which was quinine for the army. Previously imported from the Dutch East Indies, the quinine was now made, after considerable experimentation, from cinchona bark. The supply met at least half the Schutztruppe's wartime needs. Among a diversity of other Amani manufactures were ten thousand pounds of chocolate and cocoa, twenty-six hundred parcels of tooth powder, ten thousand cakes of soap and three hundred bottles of castor oil. Amani even produced rubber nipples for infants' feeding bottles.

Individual enterprise flourished in behalf of the war effort. When supplies of cloth began to dwindle, indigenous cotton came into its own. Colonists' wives studied books on home spinning and weaving; missions built spinning wheels and hand looms for African women. The high attrition rate of boots in the Schutztruppe was met when the men learned to make their own, with cowhide and tanning materials extracted from mangrove bark. Ersatz abounded. Gasoline quickly ran out, but a settler came up almost at once with a copra distillate called trebol. Local rubber was vulcanized with sulphur to produce passable tires. A tallow shortage led to the making of candles from beeswax and coconut oil. Small distilleries turned out large quantities of palm wine, primitive brandy and a liquid-fire grain blend that was generously labeled whisky. German ingenuity, in short, made for what von Lettow described as "a curious existence . . . reminding one of the industry of the Swiss Family Robinson."

But defense had to be the overriding consideration of the German effort. Sooner or later the Allies must mount a real offensive, and von Lettow labored tirelessly to be ready for it. There were problems. Despite the arms captured at Tanga and those brought in by *Kronborg*, twentieth-century weapons remained in short supply; the old Model 71 noisemaker continued to be the standard rifle of the German foot soldier. Four of the five million rounds of small arms ammunition salvaged from *Kronborg* proved defective after their long sea water dunking; each round had to be opened individually, then cleaned and dried in the sun, a process that took months. Larger-caliber ammunition also caused headaches, as *Kronborg's* Nis Kock discovered when he was assigned to making fuses for 37-mm. Hotchkiss gun shells. "I could do about thirty in a day," he wrote, "which would keep a gun going for about half a minute. Still that was better than having nothing to fire at all." Ammunition stocks presently did reach a respectable quantity, but they were never overabundant.

The force itself was another matter. It underwent massive reorganization and expansion. Among other things, von Lettow created modern history's first integrated army. With a view to greater cohesion, he changed the complexion of all his units—literally—by placing Africans in the previously lily-white *schützen* companies and assigning European enlisted men to the ranks of the field companies, until both groups became virtually identical. Of even more immediate importance was the beefing up of each company's combat establishment from 160 to 200 men. Von Lettow was able to do this by tapping a bottomless reservoir of black manpower. At newly opened recruiting depots all over the colony, askari drill teams goose-stepped to the music of military bands, fired off blank-charge volleys, speared dummies with their bayonets—and enticed volunteers by the scores of hundreds. As 1915 drew to a close, the Schutztruppe's total enrollment had risen well above ten thousand officers and men. Numerically, the German army had become a match for the British.

But only for a brief time. Toward the end of December, the British high command in Nairobi was informed, almost without notice, that its force was about to be tripled in strength. After a year of officially imposed impotence and humiliation, the army at last would be able to move off its defensive square and fulfill the all but abandoned hope of delivering a death-thrust into the German colonial heartland.

What had brought about this more or less overnight change was a new attitude in South Africa toward the war in general and the East African campaign in particular. Thanks in great part to the Union's pro-British hero-premier Louis Botha and his equally anglophilic lieutenant Jan Christiaan Smuts, it had become possible to mobilize twenty thousand South African troops for service in the East African theatre. Command of the force was to be given to General Sir Horace Smith-Dorrien, who had led the British Second Army at Ypres.

Headquarters at Nairobi reacted to the news with something less than unbridled elation. "There has been a great flutter among generals and staffs," observed Meinertzhagen, "each only concerned about themselves and their jobs, wondering whether they will be replaced. . . . One hears very little about the future conduct of the campaign." Meinertzhagen himself did not seem to think that the infusion of new blood would work wonders, although he admitted to being "glad that something has happened" so that the army would "become a military machine instead of a rotting, undisciplined, weak, planless, gutless lot of buffoons in uniform." But he also voiced realistic pessimism over what the reinforcements would be up against: "If the War Office think that the campaign is going to be just polished off by two divisions they are hopelessly out in their calculations."

Only one officer looked forward unreservedly to the impending offensive: "It was important to encourage the [British] in this intention," wrote von Lettow, "in order that the South Africans should really come, and that in the greatest strength possible, and thus be diverted from other and more important theatres of war."

PART IV

DARK AND
BLOODY GROUND

12

Slim Janie's Plan

THE BRITISH ARMY in East Africa came out of its cold storage with a leap and a bound. The month of December 1915 saw a great river of infantry, artillery, armored vehicles, motor lorries and transport animals flow steadily from the troopships at Mombasa and sweep inland by rail. Pending Smith-Dorrien's arrival, Tighe remained in command of the force. By January 1916 he had two divisions, totaling upwards of thirty thousand Empire troops, poised to launch their big push and conclude the bothersome minor operation that should have been wrapped up at Tanga fourteen months earlier.

The force's main staging area was located only sixty miles from the German border, at Voi on the Uganda Railway. A city-sized camp was thrown up here. It was often blotted from sight in a billow of dust raised by the divisions and their supporting units as they readied themselves for the offensive in continual bush-fighting sham battles. The thorn winked for miles around in the mixed glint of bayonets and heliograph signals. Staff cars, armored machine gun carriers, supply lorries, ambulances and motorcycles jolted over potholes in frantic circles as if enacting some equatorial Keystone Cops chase. Frail BE2C biplanes described ungainly arcs overhead, darting like bees above Kilimanjaro's big white beret, occasionally vanishing into the dust bank as they dive-bombed imaginary German fortifications. The bump of their fifty-pound bombs could scarcely be heard amid a ceaseless crescendo of high-explosive shell bursts, with its counterpoint of yammering machine gun fire and frenetic bugle summonses to every manner of deployment and formation. It was a cyclorama of organized senselessness.

While the troops rehearsed, a steel carpet was being rolled out for their advance as army engineers pushed forward the tracks of the narrow-gauge Voi-Taveta supply railway with almost indecent haste. Rather than waste time blasting cuttings through rock or felling trees along the right of way, the engineers simply diverted the rails away from the obstructions, giving the line the appearance of an iron exercise in Spenserian doodling as it snaked its way around hillocks, boulders and even stands of acacia. The extra mileage was worth the days saved in construction refinements.

For speed was the keynote of the whole operation. A quick breach of the Taveta Gap—the narrow vestibule between the rugged Pare Hills and the colossal, brooding fortress of Kilimanjaro—was all the British needed to penetrate German territory and deliver the final crushing blow to von Lettow's army.

Although largely South African, the new force was a heterogeneous phalanx. Its regiments and battalions had been drawn from three continents and confused each other with a babel of national languages and obscure tribal dialects. The most seasoned units were the sepoys of the 129th and 130th Baluchis. Unlike the Indian troops who had given so sorry an account of themselves at Tanga, these warriors of the grim Afghan frontier were of a different stamp—"lean and lithe and of splendid physique," said Francis Brett Young of the 2nd Rhodesians—and they possessed both an instinct and an insatiable appetite for the battle royal. More to the point, they had already been blooded on the Western Front, and if their reassignment to East Africa seemed a bonus to von Lettow, it was no less a gift to the British. The Baluchis had been "trained," as one of their officers put it, "to a tradition of heavy gunfire, to being slaughtered patiently, and to the necessity of pushing home assaults." This education was to serve them well.

Although strangers to bush fighting, the Baluchis proved quick studies, and grew restless when denied the opportunity to slay. During a lull in the later fighting, a *havildar* (sergeant) of the 129th formed a band of sepoy volunteers whose services he offered for a night reconnaissance of the German lines. His commanding officer assented but reacted so skeptically to the havildar's subsequent report that the offended NCO asked to go out again. This time he brought back evidence of the Germans he had seen, and tossed it in front of the company commander. "Here," he said, "is the officer's revolver, the naik's [corporal's] stripes, the sentry's rifle and the bugler's bugle. So now you will perhaps believe my first story."

Even without that kind of panache, the Baluchis could not have gone unnoticed. Young soon learned that he "need not wish to be in a tight corner with better men"; his opinion was to be seconded by many other officers and men of the force.

Not necessarily, however, by the South Africans, who made up the vast bulk of the new army. They carried chips as well as rifles on their shoulders and complained bitterly at having to fight not only alongside the damned kaffirs of the KAR but the bloody coolies of the Baluchi and other Indian battalions. But despite or because of their prejudices, the South Africans were also very much to be reckoned with in a scrap, as the British had learned the hard way fifteen years earlier. Even those Union troops who had not yet seen action—and there were quite a few—were instinctive brawlers. They had the builds of piano movers and a national tradition of impatient bellicosity. Many had enlisted directly from the mine pits on the Rand. Others had been prospectors, big game hunters, farmers, ranchers. Few cared for drill, saluting, written reports and other niceties cherished by the British military mentality. But all were crack shots and had the commando feel for open warfare.

It could even be said that the South Africans had a special war aim, since there was some talk at that time of German East Africa becoming a South African colony after its conquest. South West Africa had already fallen into Pretoria's orbit, and many of the Union troops who had fought in that lightning campaign now spoke of polishing off von Lettow's army with equal dispatch. When Meinertzhagen suggested to several South African officers that von Lettow might be a tougher nut to crack, "they smiled and told me I did not understand the Boer."

The South Africans might have heeded Meinertzhagen. To break through the Taveta Gap, it was first necessary to sweep aside the German defenses on the slopes of a gentle rise known as Salaita Hill, about eight miles east of Taveta itself. Salaita in fact was the cork in the Taveta bottleneck, and no one knew this better than von Lettow, who had taken pains to dig a veritable labyrinth of trenches and earthworks on what was already a naturally commanding position. The British learned how solidly the Germans were dug in on February 3, 1916, when they hit Salaita with a pounding artillery barrage that hurled many tons of dirt into the air and failed to budge the defenders an inch. Clearly, Salaita could only be taken with machine guns and cold steel, and on February 12, a massed infantry assault was launched by two brigades under Malleson's command. By the end of the day, the British had brought off their most spectacular fiasco since Tanga.

The South African brigade had a lot to do with it. Many of its troops were seeing action for the first time, and, perhaps to their surprise, they quickly found themselves cowering under the well-directed shell bursts of a few German field guns. This was all the softening up they needed for a counterattack by two or three hundred Schutztruppe askaris who came hurtling down the slope screaming *"Piga!"* (Shoot.) It was too much for the green South Africans. After a few had been killed by bullets or clubbed to death by rifle butts or eviscerated by bayonets, the rest simply took to their heels—abandoning their machine guns while being mowed down. They were saved from total rout and annihilation when the 130th Baluchis moved into the gap and gradually hammered the Germans back up the hill. But the damage had been done and a general withdrawal was ordered, leaving Salaita littered with South African corpses. That night, the Baluchis returned the South African machine guns to their rightful owners. One now heard a little less talk of coolies among the Union troops.

And the Germans still held Salaita. Which meant that the Taveta Gap was still locked, bolted and sealed off to the British.

On February 23, 1916, the new commander of the British East African Expeditionary Force finally arrived in Nairobi. It was not Smith-Dorrien, who had come down with with pneumonia some weeks earlier, but one of England's most troublesome Boer War antagonists. Since that conflict, Jan Christiaan Smuts had undergone a conversion, becoming, with Botha, a bulwark of pro-British sentiment in the Afrikaner community, and the decision to give him the East African command had been at least as political as it was military. Smuts was not a career soldier but a career politician who had held important cabinet posts in the Union government; already, he was on the way to becoming a world statesman. But he had fought and he did possess the gift of command—perhaps the rarest commodity among the British East African forces at that time.

Smuts' physical energy was inexhaustible, his brain a memory bank, his personal courage a legend. The Bishop of Pretoria once remarked that Smuts "fears neither God nor man, and particularly the former." Patience was not one of his virtues; in manner he could often be distant if not rudely frigid. He also had what could almost be called a supernatural capacity for galvanizing troops into acts of uncommon bravery and prodigious endurance simply by his presence among them. "This man's personality," wrote Young, "remote, unsympathetic, cold, well-nigh inhuman as it seemed . . . impressed itself on the whole force as an incarnation of the will to conquer."

Above all, the spade-bearded, forty-six-year-old "Slim Janie"* was remembered by the British as a hell-for-leather Boer commando leader. In 1901, he had emulated Jeb Stuart and anticipated von Lettow by taking a force of 340 Transvaal horsemen on a ten-month, thousand-mile raiding expedition through the heart of the British Cape Province, eluding or cutting up regular British army units that should have made short work of the ragged band. Fifteen years later, Smuts' former enemies were still talking about that long-range sortie as one of the most daring acts of Boer initiative in the entire South African conflict. Smuts' boldness, his instinct for the tactics of mobility, seemed to qualify him uniquely as the man to outwit von Lettow and atomize the Schutztruppe in a swift final stroke. The War Office had therefore lost no time in making Smuts the youngest lieutenant general in the British army.

The reaction to Smuts' appointment was mixed. It delighted South Africans of British descent, who responded in great numbers to Kitchener-type recruiting posters that read JOHN SMUTS WANTS YOU. Unreconstructed

* Smuts was not at all thin, but many countrymen thought of him as sly—"slim" in Afrikaans.

Boers were unmoved, but others enlisted in droves to fight alongside an Afrikaner hero. "Now that you are at the head of affairs it is easy to get them," Botha wrote Smuts. This was just what the British War Cabinet had hoped for.

In East Africa, Smuts was warmly welcomed with reservations. Some high-ranking British officers grumbled, feeling it infra dig to serve under a "colonial" who spoke English in guttural tones. Lord Cranworth of the raffish-ritzy East Africa Mounted Rifles had no use for such snobberies, but felt that "this was essentially the time for a professional soldier." Meinertz-hagen voiced more explicit doubts. Although he took an instant personal liking to Smuts ("keen as mustard" . . . "grasps points at once and never wants telling a second time" . . . "we shall get on well together"), he naturally found flaws. One was the new commander's professed distaste for fighting in bush country, a far different proposition from the open veld of South Africa; Meinertzhagen thought that Smuts "will like [the bush] less in a year's time." He also worried over Smuts' contempt for the German askari: "I told him bluntly that before he leaves this country he will have a great respect for what he now terms 'damned kaffirs.' "

But the thing that troubled Meinertzhagen most was Smuts' tactical plan: to throw von Lettow off balance by maneuver rather than to crush the German force in a stand-up fight. "Manoeuvre," wrote Meinertzhagen, "is a peculiar form of war which I do not understand, and which I doubt will succeed except at great expense in time and money. A decisive action in the Kilimanjaro area might finish the campaign, but a series of manoeuvres will only drag operations on for years."

A word of explanation is in order. In hugely oversimplified terms, ma-neuver—or at least the kind of maneuver that Smuts had in mind—might be likened to the tactics of a street brawler who seizes his opponent's lapel with one hand to set him up for the blow that will put him out of the fight—whether it be an uppercut to the jaw, a kidney punch or a kick in the balls. When one uses troops instead of bare knuckles, the lapel becomes the enemy's main force, which the attacker seeks to pin down with a frontal assault or demonstration. Corresponding (very) roughly to the killer punch is an encircling movement around the enemy rear. If this encirclement suc-ceeds, retreat is cut off and the result must be either a donnybrook or the enemy's surrender.

Smuts was confident of the latter. He planned to take hold of von Let-tow's lapel with a drive on the main German force through the Taveta Gap while simultaneously throwing a strong enveloping column around the Schutztruppe rear to sever its line of retreat down the Northern Railway. Von Lettow, his army outnumbered by two to one and denied any avenue of swift withdrawal, would gain nothing from further resistance.

That was the rub as Meinertzhagen saw it. As in a fist fight, this kind of maneuver can work if the attacker is the bigger man, which Smuts certainly was, but only providing that the little fellow is not fast on his feet—and von Lettow's footwork had kept the British gasping on the ropes for more than a year. Meinertzhagen could not imagine the German commander ever allowing anyone to touch his lapel, much less get behind him: "Von Lettow is concentrated here and ready for a fight, but of course he is not going to risk a decisive action against vastly superior numbers. Smuts should bring him to battle and instead of manoeuvering him out of position should endeavour to surround and annihilate him, no matter what are our casualties."

In fact, Smuts' objective *was* to "surround and annihilate" von Lettow, and in the shortest possible time. He was so confident of doing so that on the day of his arrival in East Africa he had cabled the War Office of his intention to bring the Schutztruppe to its knees in the shadow of Kilimanjaro before the onset of the spring rains. But where he parted company with Meinertzhagen and other critics was in his preference for the rapier of maneuver, rather than the bludgeon of frontal assault, as the best weapon for quick victory. Any reservations he may have held about head-on attack could certainly have been more than justified by his awareness that the strategy of direct collision had met with consistent failure in East Africa.

There was also a political consideration. Smuts did not conceal his shock over the Salaita disaster, where a frontal assault lasting only a few hours had brought South African dead and wounded to nearly half the total casualty figure of the entire six-month campaign in South West Africa. To Smuts, a repeat performance of Salaita would have been political suicide. "He told me," wrote Meinertzhagen, "he could not afford to go back to South Africa with the nickname 'Butcher Smuts.' "

In any case, one can ask how Smuts expected to avoid a major battle and its inevitable high casualties once he had the Schutztruppe with its back to the wall. The obvious answer is that with his back to the wall von Lettow would accomplish nothing in a toe-to-toe slugfest; common sense would dictate running up the white flag. But, as Meinertzhagen noted, von Lettow was not planning to paint himself into a corner where surrender was his only logical option. The heart of his long-range strategy was to divert Allied troops from the Western Front; if his own force was beaten, his enemies would no longer need to squander their resources in East Africa. Therefore, he could never commit the Schutztruppe to a full-scale battle without being absolutely certain that he had an avenue of escape when his adversary's numerical superiority began to make itself felt. Smuts intended to deny von Lettow that avenue. To be sure, the mangled terrain of East Africa was anything but suited to the intricate movements and precise timing of an encirclement exercise, but there was no doubt in Smuts' mind that he could bring it off.

Actually, the blueprint for Smuts' initial move in the Kilimanjaro area was to some extent a refinement of an earlier plan drawn up by Tighe but which conformed to Smuts' own ideas of how von Lettow might be treed without further waste of time. The British army was to invade in two columns. The drive through the funnel of the Taveta Gap would be carried out by Tighe, commanding the newly formed 2nd Division and supported by auxiliary units giving him a strength of slightly less than fifteen thousand rifles. This was Smuts' bid to seize von Lettow's lapel, for the Schutztruppe would have to mass virtually all its own strength near Taveta to defend the only natural corridor into German East Africa.

Concurrent with Tighe's thrust at the main German front, the second British arm would be lunging out to clip von Lettow from behind. This force, the 1st Division under General Stewart, was to launch its encirclement from Longido, a dead volcano just a few miles northwest of Kilimanjaro, then burn up the bush for sixty miles in a wide turning movement that would bring it to positions astride the Northern Railway in the rear of the German lines below Schutztruppe headquarters at Moshi. Stewart commanded only four thousand troops but Smuts correctly anticipated that they would meet little resistance; von Lettow could spare only a handful of askaris from the main German force that must hold the pass at Taveta.

Stewart's drive around the Schutztruppe left flank and rear was in fact the key to Smuts' plan. Once the 1st Division had reached the Northern Railway, all conduits of orderly German withdrawal south would be stoppered up. Von Lettow would have no place to run. He must stand and fight, which would mean annihilation, or he must surrender with honor, which would be common sense. Here was a classic textbook maneuver: an unstoppable force hammering its way through the enemy's front gate and keeping his main columns occupied while another simultaneously slammed shut his back door.

Von Lettow had no illusions about what he was up against: "It was from the outset very doubtful whether we could in succession defeat the two main hostile groups." Although the two-to-one odds which he faced may have seemed negligible after the enemy's eight-to-one superiority at Tanga, the Germans were no longer confronting a frightened, seasick, ineptly led rabble. The British had finally brought a high-powered, well-oiled military machine to East Africa. True, some of the South Africans had bolted at Salaita, but that fight had been their first, and their performance was far from unknown among raw recruits. They were now blooded and would not bolt again. The rest of the force had also begun to learn the ways of the bush after Salaita. Its opulence of modern weapons, moreover, made the German arsenal look like a rusting scrap heap. There was Smuts, too: his courage, leadership and drop-forged steel resolve made him a commander worthy of von Lettow's respect. Kilimanjaro was going to be anything but a replay of Tanga.

But the British juggernaut, when all was said and done, was exactly what von Lettow had been hoping for. And if he could not hold it back, neither did he intend to cave in under its weight. The Schutztruppe positions in the Kilimanjaro area had been chosen with great shrewdness, situated not only for the most part on high ground but so expertly concealed as to be almost literally invisible. Even British planes, skimming the tops of the acacias less than fifty feet above the rumpled carpet of rock-strewn hillocks and tightly packed thorn, could detect nothing to indicate the presence of a single German askari. "This dense tropical bush," wrote the recently promoted Captain Selous, whose Fusiliers were preparing to advance with Stewart's division, ". . . lends itself at every yard to ambushes, and is everywhere in favour of the defending forces." Von Lettow could be relied on to make the most of these natural allies.

Smuts synchronized his offensive so that Stewart's 1st Division, with the greatest distance to cover, would begin its sixty-mile drive on Moshi three days ahead of Tighe's advance. Shortly before dawn on March 5, the division ground heavily into gear, as long, unwieldy columns of riflemen, mounted infantry, armored cars and mule-drawn artillery swung out of the Longido camp. With the pressure of boots, hooves and wheels, the division's forward units beat down a road through the semi-arid desert. They also raised a great thunderhead of chalky lava dust which cut visibility to only a few feet and reduced the pace of the march to a crawl. Every man in the division was soon coughing and gagging in the powdery blanket. Water had already been rationed and riflemen began to stagger out of ranks and collapse as the sun accelerated a mass dehydration process. But the columns stumbled forward. And the dust cloud plainly revealed their position and direction for many miles.

Not that von Lettow could do much to check Stewart's advance; he could only hope that the five askari companies which had been detached from the main Schutztruppe force might somehow contrive to delay it. And on March 8, an even more massive tower of dust rose in the east to capture his undivided attention: Tighe's fifteen-thousand-man battering ram had begun to hurl itself through the Taveta Gap.

Smuts had taken great pains to insure a rapid breach of the gap. Before giving Tighe the green light, he had to make certain that there were no German fortifications on Kilimanjaro—from which harassing attacks could be launched against the 2nd Division's rear. To get this information, he sent out a reconnaissance party under Major Pieter Pretorius, who had previously stalked *Königsberg* in the Rufiji delta and had since become Smuts' chief scout. Accompanied by five captured German askaris who had been persuaded to switch their allegiance, Pretorius prowled about the clammy, heavily forested foothills of the mountain for two days. It was stiff going. Much of the survey had to be carried out at night in below-freezing temperatures. German patrols were everywhere—one even came within a few yards of capturing Pretorius. But there were no forts. Pretorius was able to report that the coast was as clear as could be expected. Only then did Smuts order the advance to begin.

But still another precaution was considered necessary. To keep the 2nd Division from a further bruising by the Germans on Salaita Hill, Smuts ordered a swift flanking diversion by an independent South African mounted brigade under Brigadier General Jacobus ("Japie") van Deventer. A taciturn man-mountain who had been Smuts' good right arm in the Boer War Cape raid, van Deventer was to lead his troopers around the north of Salaita on a twenty-mile end run across the lower foothills of Kilimanjaro. This thrust was expected to draw the Germans out of Salaita or, at the very least, turn their attention away from the advance of the 2nd Division. Tighe would thus be enabled to move directly on Taveta and secure that vital position with minimal interference.

Actually, the dust that von Lettow saw on March 8 did not come from the 2nd Division; it was being kicked up by the four thousand hooves of van Deventer's brigade as the mounted force began its ride round the north of Salaita—a move which instantly revealed Smuts' intentions to the German commander: "The enemy . . . did not intend to get his head broken a second time on that mountain." But the knowledge did von Lettow little good. The Schutztruppe was then very low on artillery ammunition, and only big guns might slow up the British advance at this juncture. The shortage left von Lettow and his staff with no option but "to look on quietly while the enemy executed unskilful movements at no great distance from our front."

Unskilled or not, however, van Deventer's flanking thrust was working. With the German left wing exposed and an entire division poised to crash in on its front, any attempt to dispute Smuts' passage at this stage of the operation would almost certainly result in the stand-up showdown that might well jeopardize the very existence of the Schutztruppe. Von Lettow could only pull his entire force back to new defensive positions. And so it was that van Deventer's troopers rode through the dust into Salaita without firing a shot. The only sign of a German presence was an abandoned field telephone line, with empty beer-bottle insulators, strung on twenty-foot poles to protect it against giraffes.

Two days later, Tighe entered Taveta at the head of the 2nd Division. Facing him were elements of van Deventer's force which had already reoccupied the town without a fight. Tighe could have reached his objective unopposed at least a day earlier, but according to Meinertzhagen he had succumbed once more to alcohol and was "now completely under the thumb of the snake Malleson." Even so, the door of the Taveta Gap had been at least partially forced, and Taveta itself was back in British hands after nineteen months.

But the German army remained intact. "Manoeuvre number one," observed Meinertzhagen.

Von Lettow had now established his main defenses about five miles west of Taveta, on a northwest-southeast line astride and between two hillocks called Latema and Reata. He himself directed operations from a position closer to the Schutztruppe's Moshi headquarters, while charge of the Latema-Reata line was placed in the hands of his second in command, a major whose slit eyes and conspicuously high cheekbones gave him the look of a true "Hun"—and perhaps lent a little extra meaning to his name, which happened to be Georg Kraut. More to the point, Kraut was also—barring von Lettow himself—the wiliest bush tactician in von Lettow's army.

But Kraut's savvy promised to be of little use at Latema-Reata. Although the high ground here was advantageous to defense, there were not enough German troops to fill or hold the twelve-mile front dividing the hills. And since there had been no time to dig elaborate entrenchments, the Latema-Reata line was also vulnerable, for a change, to air attack. Smuts promptly launched one, confident that the mere sight of his half-dozen or so planes would strike abject terror into the black hearts of von Lettow's "natives."

Smuts should have known better: German rifle fire had already collected a reconnaissance crate over Salaita. And now, when a flimsy BE2C swooped down on Latema-Reata to unload a pair of fifty-pound bombs from only a few feet above a forward German entrenchment, the askaris ducked, laughed and told each other that "ndege fanya mayai"—the bird is laying her eggs. They also let go with a tearing rifle fusillade that forced the pilot to climb away so quickly that his engine stalled. He barely managed to stay aloft. The bombs themselves landed far off target and did no damage, although one German officer thought he had been hit by a steel fragment until he recognized the blood as a popular ersatz brandy which the troops called "hemorrhage." The bottle had broken in his pocket.

But this was about par for the course with aircraft in the East African campaign. The fact remained that the Latema-Reata line was pitifully fragile. Meinertzhagen saw it as offering "our chance to bring off a decisive action." Smuts thought so too. He prepared to strike the position hard and without delay.

Kraut and von Lettow could only wait and make their own plans. "It was a time of great tension," von Lettow later recalled, ". . . but, in view of the ground, which we knew, and the apparently not too skilful tactical leading on the part of the enemy, I did not think it impossible to give at least one of his detachments a thorough beating."

An eleventh-hour change in the British command took place as the attack began. "I could scarcely believe my eyes," wrote Meinertzhagen afterwards, "when I met Malleson in a car, reclining on a soft cushion and making good headway from the battlefield. . . . He said he was feeling very ill, [and] had handed over his brigade. . . . I felt like shooting the cur. . . .

He did not look in the least ill." Smuts later told Meinertzhagen that Malleson's defection showed him for what he was. "I had to agree, but I dislike a Dutchman calling an English general a coward."

The brigade which Malleson deserted had been chosen to spearhead the assault on Latema-Reata. It consisted of three battalions: the 3rd KAR, the 2nd Rhodesians and the 130th Baluchis. Along with his command of the 2nd Division, Tighe now took personal charge of this brigade, which commenced the attack, on the morning of March 11, with a frontal drive on the two high points. In extended order, the troops advanced across a broad stretch of open ground, dotted here and there with acacia trees, then entered a mini-forest of thorn at the base of the hills. One thousand yards from the German lines, the thorn began to spit flame as Kraut's machine guns opened up. The attackers threw themselves to the ground and lay there prone, unable to creep forward or inch backward, until their own artillery put down a jolting barrage which finally cleared paths for a renewed advance up both slopes.

But the going remained heavy for the troops in the man-high underbrush; their pace was further reduced by the pelting sun and scattered but sweeping rifle volleys from the askaris above them. It was too much, in fact, for the Baluchis, who presently had to dig shallow rifle pits and hold on desperately—well short of their objective atop Latema. After a while, however, the Rhodesians and the KAR approached the German positions near the crest of Reata, and drove in, bayonets fixed, at a crouching run. They did not stay long. Almost instantly, the KAR commander, Lieutenant Colonel Bertram Robert Graham, dropped dead with a bullet in his throat after standing upright to answer a German officer who had tricked him by calling out in English. Kraut's askaris now counterattacked, and after a brief hand-to-hand melee, swept the hill clear with their own bayonets. By nightfall, the Germans still held a firm grip on their position.

But their position remained precarious. Three miles to the north, at the extreme end of the German left flank at the bottom edge of Kilimanjaro, van Deventer's brigade was trotting west toward Moshi in the face of little opposition. The South African troopers were exhausted and half-starved—through his field glasses, von Lettow could see men dismount to pick unripe bananas—but their advance threatened to clip Kraut from the rear or cut him off from his own commander. And Tighe had not yet finished with Kraut's front. Shortly before midnight, just as von Lettow was issuing orders for a counterattack on van Deventer the next morning, he received a report by field telephone that the British had hurled another wave of troops at Latema-Reata.

This time the attackers were three South African battalions. They did not cringe as they had at Salaita, and their commander, Brigadier General Percival Scott Beves, was a puncher who did not seem to share Smuts' aversion to casualties—at least when the stakes were high. As the moon rose over the two hills in the early hours of March 12, two of the battalions scaled the crests at the run and knifed directly into the German lines with cold steel. At point-blank range, Kraut's machine gunners went to work. Stitching torsos, shearing off limbs, the guns swiftly shattered the spine of the assault. Bugles brayed above the hammering din as Beves threw in his third battalion to fill up the holes and overrun the position by the sheer weight of its mass and momentum.

But suddenly the attack came to a halt. The South African butcher bill had apparently become too high for Smuts: he had countermanded Beves' order and directed an immediate disengagement.

Carrying their wounded with them, the South Africans began backing warily down the slopes. Under continual rifle and machine gun fire, they took what scanty cover they could find on the moonlit ground, using the same light to pick off occasional German askaris. But the pickings were lean, and Kraut's concealed troops did far greater damage. The descent was proving far stiffer than the climb. At last, however, the moon set and the German fire dissolved as the hills blacked out. But the South Africans could not retreat any faster. They were now in total darkness and had no paths to guide them—and their screaming burdens—through the tangled thorn at the base of the hills. They could only grope blindly toward what they hoped was the rear and wait for the sun to come up.

When it did, a few men glanced back, like Lot's wife, at the scene of their dismemberment. What they saw had them cheering till their throats went hoarse. Incredibly, a handful of Beves' riflemen had somehow managed to hold on at the crests of both hills. At that moment, moreover, Smuts was reading a report from a scout that the Germans had evacuated Latema and Reata to stave off envelopment by van Deventer's mounted troops. Immediately he ordered the South African infantrymen to about face. Now in undisputed possession of the second German defense line, he had finally breached the Taveta Gap.

But the Schutztruppe had hardly been bruised, and its detachments were withdrawing in good order to a much stronger defensive position south of Moshi. "Manoeuvre number two," sighed Meinertzhagen, "and the enemy lives to fight another day. We score nothing but territory."

All this while, the key to Smuts' maneuver plan—Stewart's enveloping sweep around the German rear below Moshi—was stuck fast in the lock of its own route down the western foothills of Kilimanjaro. On March 11, just before the German withdrawal from Latema-Reata, the 1st Division was still twenty miles from Moshi, having averaged less than five miles per day in the six days since it left Longido. "The whole strategy of these operations depends on Stewart," fumed Meinertzhagen, "and here he is dawdling along and robbing us of success."

The crawling pace was not entirely Stewart's fault. Heat and dust had compelled him to order night marches, anything but conducive to speed in the volcanic slagheap over which his troops and their unwieldy baggage trains crept. Maps proved worthless; even with Pretorius guiding the columns, the division continually strayed from the faintly marked footpaths it tried to follow. Dust presently gave way to unseasonal rains which briefly churned the route of march into a gummy trap for motor and animal transport. Swollen rivers, their bridges previously destroyed by the Germans, caused further delay. "There is a certain amount of grim humour in such phrases as 'difficult but passable,' " wrote a 129th Baluchi officer of the division's attempts to get its ox-drawn wagons across raging mountain streams. "It was not only the animals which were exhausted on these occasions. Even the recording angel must have been considerably fatigued." Stewart hardly needed German troops to retard his advance.

Nor did he get them. "All are beginning to wonder where we are to 'bump' the enemy," wrote the Fusiliers' Buchanan after three days on the march. "Is there to be no resistance?" To all practical purposes there was none. Once a party of thirty-five Schutztruppe askaris fired from concealment on Stewart's advance scouts, only to be scattered immediately by a few shells from a mountain battery. Another scuffle saw the sowars of an Indian cavalry unit and some troopers of the East Africa Mounted Rifles exchanging potshots briefly with a small German detachment while guarding artillery and supply transport in the rear of the column. The stiffest opposition was encountered on March 14. As the division at last approached the outskirts of Moshi, the askaris of the KAR battalion in the van were caught in a charging ambush by several hundred horsemen. The attackers turned out to be troopers of van Deventer's mounted brigade, who mistook the KAR for Germans despite the outsize Union Jack at the head of the column.

And the linkup of the two British forces at Moshi had by now lost any tactical usefulness. Smuts' ring was closed, but the Germans had moved out of the trap two days earlier.

Although no one denied a formidable array of natural obstacles in Stewart's path, nearly all of the British staff agreed that this did not excuse his funereal pace. Terrain and weather notwithstanding, it was felt that the 1st Division could and should have made far better progress than five miles per day, particularly in the absence of any real German opposition. Stewart, apparently, had been loath to push forward without almost neurotically painstaking reconnaissance. He had called one halt lasting a full day, another for two days. He had disregarded irate and urgent wireless proddings from Smuts. Even a personally handwritten message, dropped from a low-flying BE2C into the 1st Division command post, brought no results. "Smuts is very depressed about Stewart," wrote Meinertzhagen.

Meinertzhagen was also on hand for the last straw when Stewart wired Smuts that the 1st Division would reach its objective four days behind schedule. "Smuts, poor little man, is livid with rage. . . . He told me . . . : 'Meinertzhagen, I am now beginning to understand how it was that we always outwitted your leaders in South Africa. Are they all like this?' What was I to say? I held my peace. I was very angry and ashamed."

Not everyone sided with Smuts. "In my judgment injustice was done," wrote Cranworth, noting that even if the envelopment had succeeded, "I venture to doubt whether . . . the result would have been all that the critics so definitely emphasized. Von Lettow . . . was far too astute to allow himself to be surrounded and captured in a vast broken country known intimately to him, but quite unknown to his opponents." (It was curious that Meinertzhagen neglected to say the same thing, having already criticized Smuts for underestimating von Lettow's talents as an escape artist.) Even so, Stewart's failure to get behind the Germans was generally seen as the blunder which cost Smuts his swift victory.

It also cost Stewart his command of the 1st Division. Apparently he knew this was coming; his confrontation with a fuming Smuts had the tone of "Fired, hell! I quit!"

Stewart was not the only casualty of the abortive envelopment. At about this time, the commander of the German detachment opposing the 1st Division, Major Erich Fischer, committed suicide. He appears to have become despondent over the feebleness of his effort to stop or at least delay Stewart's already faltering advance—although a rumor went out that he was virtually ordered to do himself in by von Lettow. No less infuriated than Smuts by a subordinate's incompetence, von Lettow is said to have handed Fischer one of his own revolvers and told him: "Let me hear some interesting news about you in a day or two."

The account of the suicide, it should be added, was given widest circulation by a British officer whose hatred of the "Hun" was pathological even for those times. It was probably no more or less true than the episode in which von Lettow was supposed to have shot one of his own officers in cold blood for cruelty to Allied POWs. That story made its way swiftly through the ranks of those members of the British force who were beginning to take the same kind of attitude toward the invisible enemy commander that they usually reserved for champion cricketers.

After von Lettow's seemingly effortless escapes from Taveta and Latema-Reata, Smuts spent more than a week building a better mousetrap. The Germans were now drawn up on a line defending the important Northern Railway station at Kahe, about fifteen miles south of Moshi, and although faultlessly deployed behind almost impenetrable cover, they also may have been more vulnerable to envelopment than ever before. For that encircling maneuver—on which the entire British plan hinged—Smuts pinned his hopes on the gargantuan van Deventer, whose hard-riding posse had never stopped hounding the Schutztruppe left flank since the drive on Salaita. Van Deventer was counted on to succeed where Stewart had failed. By continuing its end run in a wide arc south and east, the mounted brigade could not only roll up the German left wing but plunge like a scimitar into its unprotected rear below Kahe.

At the same time, von Lettow's main force was to be riveted down on its forward lines, with a staggering punch in the gut delivered by the 1st Division, now under the temporary command of Brigadier General Seymour Hulbert Sheppard. According to Cranworth, Sheppard "was . . . one of the few men I have met who really enjoyed fighting, and was generally known by the sobriquet of 'Ha Ha Splendid' from his habit of turning up at a crisis and remarking 'Ha, ha, splendid! Lots of fighting and lots of fun!' " After the dilatory Stewart, Sheppard may have seemed just what the doctor ordered.

Preparations for the offensive were thorough—sometimes too thorough. The British chief engineer officer "made a lovely trestle bridge," wrote Meinertzhagen, ". . . and has spent the last seven days looking for a river over which to place it. The bridge turns up at all sorts of places, blocks the roads, gets stuck in the mud, loses its way in the bush and visits every river in turn, seeking a home. . . . [The engineer] is very keen that I should procure for him the bank-to-bank measurements of every river between here and Tanga in the hopes that his bridge may fit one of them."

Meinertzhagen himself overdid things, setting out one night on a personal reconnaissance inside the German lines. This was work for a scout, not an army's chief of intelligence, but Meinertzhagen was in his element. "Several patrols passed me almost within touching distance. . . . Sometimes I felt inclined to scream just to tell the enemy I was there, sometimes I was giggling at my ludicrous position, sometimes I was petrified with terror when a sentry or patrol would look hard apparently straight at me." Undetected, he finally made his way back toward the British positions, but just after swimming a stream and eluding its crocodiles, he was challenged by a German sentry. Realizing that the askari could not see his uniform in the dark, he replied in Swahili, walked up to the man and bayoneted him— "a beastly job but vital." At length he reported to Smuts, who told him: "Meinertzhagen, you're mad, stark, staring. It's not your business to undertake this sort of risk, so please do not do so again."

But Meinertzhagen's reconnaissance had confirmed other reports of the German positions, and on March 20, Smuts ordered the advance to begin. He had good reason to believe that this attack would finally corner von Lettow and put paid to the German army in East Africa.

Behind their own defenses, the Germans waited calmly, not noticeably unsettled by the continual artillery barrages with which the British sought to soften them up. Schutztruppe headquarters were in a rough plantation building a mile or so from Kahe, and although shell bursts rattled the windows while field telephones jangled incessantly, the place had a domestic atmosphere. Von Lettow was able to catch an occasional hour or so of sleep on a sofa, using a tablecloth as a blanket, and saw to it that his line officers also lived in improvised opulence. "Even now, on active service," he wrote, "nearly everyone had two 'Boys,' who took charge of the cooking utensils and provisions . . . cooked excellently, baked bread, washed, and generally provided us with a good proportion of the comforts which in Europe are only to be found in dwelling houses."

But the plantation was no country club, and von Lettow could not remain there long. Nor did his troops merely sit passively in their entrenchments. Late in the afternoon of March 20, while Smuts' 1st Division moved up to its lines at a place called Store (so named, even by the Germans, for the Indian shop located there), a six-hundred-man Schutztruppe force also advanced for an attack.

The first hint of the Germans' intentions came when some Fusiliers were fired on while watering their horses and bathing in a shallow stream. Apart from the embarrassment of one naked private who ran headlong into the arms of his battalion and division commanders, little damage was done, and the British prepared to make camp. They were not given the opportunity. "At 8 p.m. at a suddenly given signal," wrote Buchanan, "tremendous fire swept the camp and . . . a deafening, close-grappling, vicious battle held forth." It raged for more than four hours, as the Schutztruppe askaris drove home no fewer than twenty bayonet charges and filled the air during the intervals with mind-numbing successions of massed rifle volleys. Not since Tanga had the Germans struck with such fury.

Ordinarily, the 1st Division might have been badly bruised by the surprise blow, for the troops had not been given time to dig in, and could only scoop out shallow depressions in the ground. But von Lettow's askaris, unable to see their targets too clearly, fired even higher than was their habit, while the attack itself, inexplicably, had no machine gun support. The British, on the other hand, had machine guns to spare, and they tore great shreds out of the assaulting force. "In the morning," wrote Selous, "the dead in front of our machine-gun commanding the road were collected and laid out in a row—like pheasants or hares after a drive."

The attack was one of von Lettow's rare blunders. Mistaking the 1st Division for a British screening column, he had sought to drive it back, and only after losing upwards of two hundred officers and askaris did he realize that his six hundred assaulting troops had collided with the main enemy force. The subsequent withdrawal was orderly, but the error did not bode well for the Germans on the morning of March 21, as Smuts set his own onslaught in motion.

It began with a whirlwind right cross at the exposed German left flank. On the night of the 20th, the troopers of van Deventer's mounted brigade, guided by some fitful moonlight, had cantered twenty-five miles through the thorn to reach a position well below Kahe station at sunrise on the 21st. Here they ran into their first real obstacle: the upper reaches of a river called the Pangani. Although only sixty feet wide at that point, the Pangani was without a bridge and approaching flood; its currents were so swift that van Deventer's horses and men came near to being swept away like leaves as they made the crossing.

Surprises awaited them on the opposite bank. Hardly had the squadrons re-formed than the horses began to buck and rear in a series of earth-jolting explosions all about them as a *Königsberg* gun opened up from eight miles away; von Lettow, apparently, had been husbanding his artillery ammunition for just such an occasion. Although the barrage was short-lived, it was followed almost at once by a swarm of rifle and machine gun bullets that swept the brigade's front from a nearby elevation called Baumann Hill. Holding well-concealed positions at the crest, a German field company was equally well placed to check van Deventer's further advance.

But it was only a company, and it proved no match for one thousand sharpshooting South Africans. The askaris were soon pried from their defense works and the hill was taken. With the high ground now secured, van Deventer could choose between two targets in the Germans' all but naked rear.

Only five miles to the north lay Kahe station, the pivot of the Schutztruppe's main defense line; a direct attack on the rear of this position could dilute the strength of von Lettow's army at the very moment when all that strength would be needed to withstand Smuts' assault on its front. Or van Deventer could simply wheel the brigade around and make for the tracks of the Northern Railway, which ran along the foot of Baumann Hill and then snaked southeast through the thorn as far as the eye could see. A crossing of the line at any point below Kahe would deprive the Germans of their only means of swift withdrawal when the weight of Smuts' frontal attack proved too heavy to be borne any further. The sole obstacle to either of van Deventer's objectives was the bush.

As soon as Smuts learned of van Deventer's position, he ordered Sheppard to smash in at the main German defenses with the 1st Division. Sheppard's plan was to drill a wide hole in the Schutztruppe line while the Germans were occupied with an enveloping thrust on their right wing, carried out by a South African brigade of Tighe's 2nd Division. Spearheading the 1st Division frontal assault would be two brigades, one South African, one mixed British and Indian, supported by four field and mountain batteries. Bugles sounded the advance at half past ten in the morning. At once, the artillery began thumping stolidly while the sun glinted on three thousand rifle barrels as the British infantrymen fanned out in extended order and moved forward, at a cautious but steady pace, to fight the last battle of the East African campaign.

It was not long before the entire advance had come to a grinding halt. The bush fronting the German right was so solidly packed that Tighe's South African flanking brigade never even got into the action, but the 1st Division troops plunged swiftly into the thick of things, which only made matters worse. Sheppard's two brigades had to cross about a mile of fairly open ground, bounded on each side by a stream that fairly spilled over with crocodiles. Dense thorn lining the banks of both streams provided total concealment for Schutztruppe snipers and machine gun emplacements, and effectively prevented the British artillery observers from finding ranges for their guns. By early afternoon, Sheppard's forward units were pinned down like butterfly specimens under a tightly woven curtain of rifle and machine gun crossfire—broken only by shell bursts from the *Königsberg* gun which had now been slewed round to stiffen the German front. Von Lettow could hardly have chosen a better line to hold.

If the deadlock were to be broken, a weak spot in the defenses must be found. The 129th Baluchis were sent forward, with one of their companies under orders to seek out—and if possible to turn—the German right flank. The sepoys made their advance on all fours, firing from the prone position at an enemy they could not see, while the thorn whipped and crackled from the fire of an enemy who saw them all too clearly. At last, however, a scout spotted a Schutztruppe machine gun nest about 150 yards off; its position seemed to mark the extreme right of the German line. As soon as a shattering rifle volley had exterminated its crew, the Baluchi company commander ordered his own machine gun to open up and cover a bayonet charge that would clear a path for a mass breakthrough. The Baluchis had raced to within fifty yards of the soft spot when their machine gun jammed. At that very moment, another askari crew put the German gun back into action, and the attacking company was nearly wiped out. The hole in von Lettow's dike had been plugged with seconds to spare.

But now the Fusiliers moved in. They accomplished even less. "We really could do nothing but lie very flat," wrote Selous, "trying to dig ourselves in with bayonets and fingers, being under the sweeping fire of three or four machine guns. The lie of the land just saved us . . . and the bullets just swept over us in bouquets." By five o'clock, it had become clear that the 1st Division's cutting edge was dulled if not hopelessly blunted. Orders went out to consolidate and dig in for the night, so that a fresh assault could be mounted early the next morning.

The next morning, however, the division found no Germans to attack. On the previous afternoon, while the Schutztruppe was holding fast against Sheppard's onslaught—indeed, at the very moment when one German detachment was readying a counterattack—von Lettow had received a message that van Deventer's brigade was moving on Kisangire station, fifteen miles south of Kahe. If the South African horsemen got there unopposed, they would jeopardize or more likely eradicate any chances of a

German retreat. Von Lettow had therefore been compelled to break off the action on the Kahe front and fall back on Kisangire with his entire force.

After the furious fighting of the morning and afternoon, it was too much to expect that the Germans could reach Kisangire before van Deventer— much less oust him from the place. But they had no other choice than to try. All night, the bone-weary askaris trudged southward through the scrub in a back-breaking forced march; not a few fell out as their legs gave under them. Incredibly, however, sunrise on March 22 saw the force on the outskirts of Kisangire, taking up positions for an attack.

Even more astonishingly, van Deventer's brigade was nowhere to be seen. The report of his advance had been erroneous. It was, von Lettow noted wryly, "remarkably striking proof of the extraordinary difficulty of observing the movements of troops in thick bush."

But the same bush had also mangled van Deventer's communications with Smuts, and, more to the point, had kept the mounted brigade from doing any real damage. The thorn south of Kahe was not only too dense for a swift cavalry advance on Kisangire but also held the horses to a slow walk in the move on Kahe. Although the German pullback did enable van Deventer to seize Kahe station without any real opposition, opposition had been the whole idea; what the South African troopers occupied was an empty barn. And while von Lettow's withdrawal had been an accident, it was a withdrawal nonetheless, and no one had stopped it. From a military standpoint, Smuts had won virtually nothing. And the Schutztruppe, like the African tribes from which it had learned so much, had lost virtually nothing.

"Virtually" was the operative word. Smuts' drive had been anything but a total failure. He had forced the gateway to German East Africa and removed the threat of further raids on the Uganda Railway, while his troops now occupied the richest region in the German colony. He had also scored a political coup; English newspapers in South Africa were to give the Kilimanjaro offensive bigger headlines than Verdun. "Your victories," Botha wrote Smuts, "have . . . contributed much to the development of a better spirit here."

The spirit in East Africa was another matter. Von Lettow remained at large; that was the main thing. And it was beginning to appear that Smuts might need something more than a fascination with maneuver to outwit the commander who seemed able to give him lessons in that art.

13

15 Rupees for the Bluddy Englisch

◁◇▷

A LULL NOW SETTLED DOWN over the lines below Kilimanjaro as Smuts prepared for his next shot at von Lettow. He could not push forward at once, as the spring rains of 1916 had set in with a vengeance that astonished him. "I have never in all my life dreamed," he wrote to a friend, "that rain could fall as it does here on the slopes of the Kilimanjaro. . . . The rivers are full, the country is one vast swamp." All transport was locked solidly in mud, all work on the Voi railway—crucial to the supply of a British advance—came to a halt in the deluge. "Nothing further can be done on our side until the rains are over," wrote Selous in a letter home. " . . . Horses, mules and men are all suffering terribly from the climate. . . . It is the constant unending wet and damp I think that gets into the mens' stomachs and bowels and gives them dysentery."

If nothing else, however, the weather gave the sixty-four-year-old Selous another chance to boast diffidently about his own endurance: "You will wonder how I stood it all at my age. . . . I have never been a day away from my company . . . and have never put my leg over a horse, but have done all the marching with the men . . . and am one of the very few in the battalion who has never had a day's illness." But not long afterwards, the indestructible old hunter-soldier discovered that where age, climate and the Germans had failed to leave their mark, a less dreaded foe had ambushed him. "I have seen a good doctor," he told the same friend, "as my trouble with piles is getting bad. . . . He advises me strongly to go home and have the operation there." Selous therefore left East Africa. But he was to return.

Illness and discomfort notwithstanding, the rains were not entirely unwelcome. For the first time in many weeks, the British troops could enjoy a little leisure. They caught up on badly needed sleep, washed and mended their reeking, tattered uniforms, wrote letters home. Football matches alternated with close-order drill on sodden improvised parade grounds. There was even a PX service of sorts. Long queues formed outside the YMCA store and at the entrance of a corrugated iron shop run by a dundreary-whiskered Goanese trader named Nazareth. This man soon monopolized the troops' business by selling soap and toilet paper, which for some reason the YMCA did not stock. Cranworth wrote a tongue-in-cheek official recommendation that Nazareth be gazetted to brigadier general.

While waiting for the skies to clear, Smuts made some shakeups in his force. Most immediate and conspicuous was the removal of the tough but lumbering Tighe from command of the 2nd Division. The puncher had become punch-drunk. "Though I am glad Tighe is going," wrote Meinertzhagen, "I am very sorry for him. He is a gallant soldier and a great gentleman. He failed because he allowed alcohol to ruin his health and because he had not the pluck to rid himself of Stewart or of Malleson who proved himself to be even more poisonous and treacherous than a viper." Smuts appeared to share these feelings, for he saw to it that Tighe—unlike Stewart and Malleson—did not leave under a cloud. Shortly before taking up a new command in India, Tighe was made a K.C.M.G.

The army itself was reshuffled, from two divisions into three, partly to keep the touchy South Africans together. The 1st Division became a mixed imperial bag of British, Indian, Rhodesian, KAR and EAMR units (although the troopers of the last were rapidly being absorbed into other regiments and battalions). Its new commander, Major General Reginald Hoskins, was no stranger to bush warfare, having previously served as the KAR's Inspector General. In the two South African divisions, van Deventer, now a major general, was elevated to command of the 2nd, while a 3rd Division, then in formation, would go to Major General Coenraad Brits, a six-foot-six-inch bruiser whose wife had embroidered purple forget-me-nots on his rank insignia. Each of the three divisions was made up of two brigades, with a brigade apiece of cavalry for the two South African divisions. Smuts expected that the mounted troops would make for greater mobility, which may or may not have been sound thinking in view of the very thick tsetse "fly belt" that lay ahead. All told, the British force numbered slightly less than thirty thousand.

The reorganization of his army completed, Smuts turned to the blueprint of the upcoming offensive. Still smarting from the failure to exploit the encirclement opportunities in the Kilimanjaro operations, Smuts by now had gained a healthy respect not only for von Lettow but—as Meinertzhagen had predicted—for the "kaffirs" whom he led. Writing to a colleague in South Africa, Smuts acknowledged that the Schutztruppe askaris "fight with great skill and bravery," and that "they are what our Zulus or Basutos would be if properly trained." None of this, however, had diminished Smuts' confidence that he would have von Lettow and his army in a net before the summer was out. Nor had his faith in the correctness of maneuver been shaken, and he accordingly drew up a plan for the most ambitious envelopment the campaign had yet seen.

It was based initially on the assumption that von Lettow, after an orderly but stubborn withdrawal south toward the Central Railway, would move his force some four hundred miles west along that line to Tabora, the largest German town in the interior and the colony's principal center of African recruitment. Intelligence received at Smuts' headquarters during April and May underscored the near-certainty that von Lettow would "fight out the last phase of the campaign in the Tabora area." To frustrate this intention, Smuts planned to have Hoskins' 1st Division engage the main German force, pushing it south but holding it to three more or less parallel lines in the east which were formed by the rugged Pare-Usambara mountain ranges, the savanna country of the Pangani river valley, and the Germans' Northern Railway.

While von Lettow was thus being contained in the east, van Deventer would already have taken his 2nd Division on a wide sweep west, far around the German left. His route would carry him 150 miles southwest of Moshi, across a waste of volcanic rubble and a rolling vacuum of bush, to the German military post at Kondoa Irangi, only 75 miles north of the Central Railway. This thrust would not just imperil von Lettow's left wing; Kondoa was the perfect springboard from which to pounce down on the Central line and block off the German route to Tabora.

Once von Lettow learned of van Deventer's threat, Smuts reasoned, he would be compelled to meet it, siphoning off troops from the main Schutztruppe force and freeing Hoskins to launch his own swift drive on the Central line with the 1st Division. It was anticipated that Hoskins and van Deventer, in due course, would approach each other along the railway, eventually to link up and trap von Lettow between them. The weakness of this plan lay in its splitting rather than concentrating the British columns, but its focus on the Central Railway was by no means unsound. Von Lettow could ill afford to abandon the principal artery of communications in German East Africa.

Nor was he likely to withdraw below the railway. To all practical purposes, the only part of the German colony that seemed worth occupying or defending lay north of the Central line. At this stage of the campaign, the British high command—both in London and East Africa—did not appear to appreciate fully that von Lettow might have other intentions than the mere holding of territory.

But even if von Lettow were to continue his retirement, other Allied armies, some under Smuts' command, would be moving in for the kill from more distant sectors of the theatre. A British striking force led by Brigadier General Edward Northey was then preparing to advance on the southwest corner of the German colony from Nyasaland and Northern Rhodesia. A Belgian army, eleven thousand strong, was poised to strike eastward from its bases in the Congo. Plans were being set in motion for a Portuguese column to punch across the Rovuma River on the Germans' southern border. The tentacles of a great military octopus were contracting.

The main German force at this time was concentrated only ten miles from the British lines, with its companies deployed in defensive positions on the wooded slopes of the Pare range. Work parties reinforced old entrenchments, dug new ones, hacked fields of fire for the Schutztruppe machine guns out of the dripping scrub. Headquarters at Kisangire was a scene of orderly bustle. From dawn to dusk in the hammering downpour, hundreds of newly recruited askaris drilled, lunged at bayonet dummies, banged away incessantly with defective ammunition at waterlogged rifle and machine gun targets. They were in a full-dress rehearsal for the stemming of the British tidal wave.

Nor was the real thing entirely absent. Supply trains rolled continually into Kisangire from the south while low-flying British aircraft swooped down from the north to bomb them—only to find the moving targets obscured in sheets of rain and blankets of mist. Sometimes a section of track might take a direct hit, but askari-supervised platelaying gangs quickly repaired the damage. Hardly anyone troubled to take shelter when the planes came over. "The spirit of the troops was good," wrote von Lettow, "and the Askaris were imbued with a justifiable pride in their achievements against an enemy so greatly superior." The Schutztruppe was not behaving like a beaten army because it had yet to be beaten.

But it was an army on the defensive. While Smuts polished his plan of attack, von Lettow, in the leaking Kisangire railway station that served as his headquarters, prepared for a phased withdrawal. He enjoyed certain advantages, not the least of which were familiar terrain, interior supply lines and the mobility offered by the Northern Railway. Particular reliance was also placed on a newly built rail shuttle which was expected to accelerate the movement of troops and supplies. There were two of these arteries. The longest ran about fifty miles south, from Mombo station on the Northern Railway to the village of Handeni. Still farther south, some ten more miles of track offered quick access to the Central line. Neither of these shortcuts could be called a railway in any purist sense of the word. Both in fact were toy trolleys, made of two-foot-gauge tracks that had been pulled up hastily from nearby plantations and laid down with little if any attention to embankments, cuttings or other refinements. Their "trains" were midget tramcars, previously used for hauling farm produce. They were driven by African manpower rather than locomotives. Yet both little tropical Toonervilles were to prove highly useful in greasing the skids for the German retirement.

Not that von Lettow was contemplating headlong flight—especially since the force had just received a new transfusion of energy with the second penetration of the British blockade. In mid-March, a four-thousand-ton German freighter named *Maria von Stettin* had slipped past two Royal Navy patrol vessels into Sudi Bay on the colony's southern coast, where she offloaded a cargo of supplies for the Schutztruppe. Although the navy plastered *Maria* until her upper works were a blazing tangle of steel and her hull a colander, the bombardment came too late; the cargo had already been taken off in record time and was being toted north, on the backs of several hundred porters, to depots along the Central Railway. The carrier loads included four field howitzers, a battery of mountain guns, five million more rounds of small-arms ammunition and several thousand 4.1-inch shells for the converted *Königsberg* guns. "So I shall have my work cut out for me as they say," wrote Smuts when he learned of the Schutztruppe's windfall.

Another item brought in by *Maria* was a quantity of medals for the German officers and askaris. Two were Iron Crosses, of the First and Second Class, for von Lettow. As for *Maria* herself, the ostensibly ruined blockade runner turned up a few weeks later in the harbor of Batavia, Java, not much the worse for her pounding.

One merit of van Deventer's enveloping drive on Kondoa Irangi was that it could be launched without waiting for the weather to clear. South African settlers living in the Kilimanjaro area had told Smuts that the spring rains held only along the line of the Pare-Usambara ranges and the Pangani valley, and that the high country of the Masai Steppe to the west was dry. Although this proved to be a sapphire of misinformation, the 2nd Division got off to a brisk enough start when it moved out on April 3, with the mounted brigade splashing smartly in the van. It was not long before the cavalry had far outdistanced the infantry, and the next day, after eating up forty miles in barely twenty-four hours, the troopers ran into their first opposition.

The scene of the action was a steep, rocky elevation called Lolkisale Hill. Although it was defended by only a single company, the German askaris held the crest and were dug in, as usual, like fillings in teeth, and their commander, Captain Paul Rothert, was a resourceful officer known to be good in tight spots. But the hill commanded the only water springs in the area, and by now, despite the rain, the horses of the mounted brigade were already suffering from thirst. Lolkisale had to be taken.

It was. Dismounting, the troopers advanced cautiously but swiftly up the hill in commando style, taking cover behind the boulders that littered the slopes, firing with telling effect at the black puffballs of the German Model 71 rifles. Before they reached the crest they saw a white flag. With Rothert seriously wounded, the Schutztruppe's crack 28th Field Company had surrendered.

Not quite to a man: a number of the askaris managed to make off down the reverse slope and escape south to fight again. But the Lolkisale action was the first real defeat sustained by the Germans in the East African campaign. They had lost a wireless station at Bukoba in 1915; they had been outwitted from time to time in minor skirmishes; they had abandoned a vast tract of their colony in the withdrawal from the Kilimanjaro sector; many Schutztruppe officers and askaris had fallen in combat and others had been taken prisoner. But never before had a single one of von Lettow's units capitulated. It was a small but welcome shot of adrenalin for the British.

Nor could success have come at a more opportune moment for the mounted brigade, which soon needed all the moral uplift it could get. To reach Kondoa Irangi from Lolkisale, the troopers had to negotiate more than one hundred miles of gummy soup which became increasingly sodden with each day the rain continued to smash down. It was not long before the force was all but imprisoned in the ooze. If the horses had slaked their thirst at Lolkisale, they now began dying by the scores from hunger and horse sickness. The men were not any better off. Lions continually interrupted their sleep at night. Each trooper plodded through the gunk inside his own private cloud of mosquitoes. The brigade's original strength of twelve hundred was swiftly halved by malaria and dysentery.

In outracing the infantry, the mounted force had also cut its own supply lines, and its wireless instruments went out of commission in the unceasing deluge. Neither remounts nor fresh stores could be brought up. The men supplemented their quarter-rations with nuts, berries and scrawny ears of maize which had to be eaten raw, since the rain quickly doused all fires. What had begun with a victory at Lolkisale had degenerated into an immobilizing mud bath.

And yet, somehow, the brigade—or what was left of it—ploughed through the liquid clay and finally took up positions outside Kondoa Irangi on April 18. Next day they attacked. Apparently impressed by the South African marksmanship, the four hundred German defenders fired off a few token volleys from their whitewashed mud-walled fort and retired. In less than three weeks, the mounted brigade had covered nearly two hundred miles. Considering the weather, the advance should not have been completed inside of two months. One military writer has called van Deventer's push "one of the outstanding cavalry feats of the First World War."

The maneuver also threw von Lettow off balance. "I ask the reader," he once wrote, "to imagine himself in the position of a Commander, with insufficient means, exposed to attack by superior numbers, who has continually to ask himself: What must I do in order to retain freedom of movement and hope?" Seldom did this question perplex him more than at the end of April 1916, when he learned that van Deventer was threatening the Central Railway from Kondoa while his main force was occupied with Smuts' and Hoskins' steel juggernaut 150 miles to the northeast. If von Lettow moved to check van Deventer at Kondoa, Smuts could order Hoskins to launch his own drive on the Central line unopposed. But if van Deventer's division were disregarded . . . It was Hobson's choice.

In fact, van Deventer at that time could not have threatened a trolley line, his troops being at the brink of total collapse from hunger and sickness on the march to Kondoa. But von Lettow did not know this. Further, since Smuts appeared unlikely to move down the Pangani until the end of the rains, von Lettow concluded that the Schutztruppe's main effort must be directed at Kondoa. He therefore ordered fifteen field companies and two mounted companies—nearly four thousand rifles all told, supported by two artillery pieces—to march on that objective at once. Major Kraut was placed in charge of the badly weakened Pangani force, and von Lettow followed his own troops to take personal command at Kondoa.

While the German columns could cover part of their route by train, thus reaching Kondoa in only a few days, they may have found the going at least as stiff as did the South Africans. Despite an effort to avoid confusion by keeping a one-day interval between detachments along the narrow military road through the bush, units soon began jamming into each other like taxis on a one-way street in a rush hour. The rain did not improve matters. Wallowing thigh-deep in mud, some companies strayed well off the route of march, some became hopelessly entangled with other detachments. Many units also lost their porters but solved that problem by kidnapping the bearers regularly assigned to the line of communications. It was a wonder that the officers and African NCOs were able to unsnarl their squads, platoons and companies, extricate the mired-down field guns and continue to bash forward.

Von Lettow's own journey was not much easier—although he and his staff at least got off to a good start when the widow of a Northern Railway official pressed upon them the last bottles from her wine cellar. On the first leg of the trip, made in a staff car, von Lettow noted that "there were only a few bad places, and twenty or more carriers managed to get us through them." Soon, however, the weather began to make itself felt, and it was not long before von Lettow had been cut off from telephone contact with the force, "on account of earths caused by the heavy rain and breakages caused by columns of carriers, wagons and giraffes."

In due course, the staff car was brought up short by a swollen river whose bridge had been swept away. A tree was felled as a makeshift foot crossing but the current carried it off like a discarded toothpick. Von Lettow's adjutant tried to swim the river and followed the tree downstream. Another officer took off his uniform and barely managed to reach the opposite bank, but no one could get a line to him. "And so there we were, Captain Tafel without any clothes on the far side, and we on this one. The prospect of having to wait for the river to fall was not enticing, for I could not afford to waste a minute in reaching the head of the marching troops." Eventually, a tribesman led the party to a ford. Even then the crossing took nearly an hour.

Continuing on mules, von Lettow and his staff rode into the night, often saddle-deep in water. At length they reached the southernmost of the two narrow-gauge tramways, where a "train" and its two-legged black locomotives were standing by, ready to roll. "In their endeavour to do the job really well, the good people took several curves rather too fast, and the trucks, with everything on them—including us—repeatedly flew off into the ditch alongside, or beyond it." But the tramway did connect with the Central line, and by early morning von Lettow reached a station where, after discarding his drenched uniform and donning askari garb, he finally boarded a westbound troop train. Within two days he was deploying advance units of his force into position for an assault on Kondoa Irangi.

Had he known the state of the South Africans, von Lettow might have attacked at once. Van Deventer's troops were almost comatose from disease and near-starvation. There was no reliable way of moving bulk food or medical supplies across the ocean of mud that isolated Kondoa from the rear bases. (Van Deventer tried to build an airfield but succeeded only in making the world's largest swimming pool.) The hospital tents overflowed with patients and rainwater. The men were subsisting on pawpaws, bananas and occasional maize cobs. Uniforms had turned into torn blotting paper; grass and leaves patched the holes in boots. To all practical purposes, the mounted troops had now become foot soldiers, for their horses were dropping dead almost in regiments. At this time, the South African government offered to send one thousand remounts to East Africa every month, but the request was for twice that number. A daily ceremony at Kondoa was the piling up and burning of putrescent horse cadavers. When the infantry brigade finally struggled in, it had already been poleaxed by fever. Swiftly, the 2nd Division shrank to half-strength, and the hollow-eyed troops who could stand looked like an army of concentration camp inmates.

Vainly, van Deventer called for reinforcements. Beves' 2nd South African Infantry Brigade was being held in reserve near Moshi; could not Smuts spare two of its battalions? Smuts could not. To release them would deplete his own strength in the east. And all the while, the German force outside Kondoa continued to build up. By early May, the 2nd Division was outnumbered by von Lettow's troops. German rifle fire continually harried South African patrols and outposts. One party was disposed of by a Schutztruppe African officer named Juma Mursal, who picked off six mounted troopers with his Model 71 from concealment near a waterhole. A few reinforcements did reach van Deventer at this time, but their numbers were not significant. And a German attack was clearly imminent.

Smuts' reluctance to strengthen Kondoa did not sit well with Meinertzhagen, who by now had joined van Deventer as an observer and was urging that Smuts send out not two battalions but a division. It was clear to Meinertzhagen that von Lettow had drained his own eastern force of all but about two thousand rifles—thus leaving the Pangani line virtually unprotected—so as to overwhelm the South African positions at Kondoa. "It is the Germans' only chance," he wrote, "and von Lettow is no fool. He can be relied on to do the right thing. Kondoa is now the decisive point and the present is the decisive time, so here he will concentrate and try to annihilate van Deventer's detachment. Attack it he must before the rains finish."

Meinertzhagen also fretted over van Deventer's apparently cavalier attitude toward the coming onslaught. "I asked him what his plans were. 'Let them attack,' said the taciturn Dutchman. 'Are you dug in?' I asked. No reply. 'For God's sake do not despise the enemy,' I said. 'Damned kaffirs,' says he. . . . I suspect that the troops are not dug in." But, added Meinertzhagen, "we shall know in a day or two. Von Lettow is rarely late for an appointment."

Von Lettow kept it, teeing off during the afternoon of May 9 with his pair of four-inch field guns in a heavy bombardment of the South African positions on a line of hills about three miles east of Kóndoa. This was followed shortly after dark by a determined infantry assault on the hills. It came suddenly. "The whole camp blazed," wrote Meinertzhagen, "and we could see the spiteful little flashes of rifles and hear the cheering of troops on the ridge." The German askaris drove home their attacks with fury, and the battle quickly became a hand-to-hand melee. For seven hours, the adversaries shot and stabbed and clubbed each other with primitive and almost gleeful abandon. As one German charge was hurled back by South African bayonets, Meinertzhagen could look up momentarily from his own dirty work and enjoy "the fine sight in the glare of star shell and flares."

Meinertzhagen, of course, had lost no time getting into the thick of it. When a Schutztruppe machine gun opened up at thirty yards from behind a rock, he helped a platoon wipe out the crew with bayonets. "I ended up by using my rifle as a club—with disastrous results for the stock broke, but it was great." Another free-for-all followed, and Meinertzhagen found himself unarmed except for "my fists and boots," which he used to effect when a German officer nearly shattered his shoulder blade with an African war club called a knobkerrie. "I finally wrenched [it] out of his hand, got my knee well into his stomach and then set to on his head with the knobkerrie until he was silent. I was furious with him for hitting me on the shoulder."

For all the wrestling, however, the fight remained first and foremost a shooting match, and presently the South African marksmanship began to tell. Von Lettow himself stopped a shell splinter, although this did not keep him from tongue-lashing a medical officer who had dragged his feet in aiding seriously wounded askaris. At about three o'clock in the morning, von Lettow's field commander, Lieutenant Colonel von Bock, was gravely wounded by a bullet and Captain Friedrich von Kornatzki took over, only to be slain almost instantly when he made the mistake of going for Meinertzhagen with his knobkerrie. Command now devolved on Captain Friedrich Lincke, who soon realized that what von Lettow called "the dominating fire of the enemy" would deprive his force of any mobility once the sun rose. "As, therefore, no success appeared attainable," wrote von Lettow, "[Lincke] cautiously broke off the action while it was still dark."

Strictly speaking, it was less a South African victory than a German tactical setback. Von Lettow had not only failed to bring his full strength to bear but, owing to faulty intelligence reports, had chosen the most firmly held sector of the South African lines as the target of his attack. "Van Deventer is a very lucky man and I told him so," wrote Meinertzhagen, observing that if the Germans had struck at the proper spot, "we should now all be prisoners of war." Even so, the men of the 2nd Division felt no need to apologize for anything. Meinertzhagen himself acknowledged that "it is a first real knock von Lettow has had," and freely offered "all credit to old van Deventer and his South Africans."

All that lacked was a positive result. Van Deventer had succeeded only in beating off an attack by an enemy who was supposed to be always on the defensive. Although 2nd Division casualties were light, the ferocity of the battle—not to mention the attrition of weather and fever over the previous month—left the South Africans even less capable of moving on the Central Railway than they had been when they had first staggered into Kondoa Irangi three weeks earlier. More than two months would pass before van Deventer could resume his drive on the line. Smuts' bold end run was paralyzed.

Returning to the scene of the action after sunrise, Meinertzhagen learned the identity of the officer whom he had hammered to death with the knobkerrie. "My God, I should have liked to have caught old von Lettow instead of poor Kornatsky."

On May 21, 1916, in a minor action on the Western Front, German troops stormed Vimy Ridge and recaptured it from the British. On the same day, almost as if in retaliation, Smuts set in motion his long-awaited push down the Pangani river. The spring rains had ended. So too had the waiting game. "I hope [it] will be the last phase of the campaign," wrote Meinertzhagen, adding that it probably would be if Smuts rid himself of his compulsion to maneuver and struck a hard blow. "We have ample troops to force a decision, but if this is not done, there will be the danger and expense of bush warfare and flying columns and at that game von Lettow will beat us every time. . . . It remains to be seen whether Smuts can smash up von Lettow before that wily man drags us all over Africa."

At that moment, in fact, Smuts was not facing von Lettow at all, for the Schutztruppe commander had yet to bring the bulk of the German force east from Kondoa Irangi. Only Kraut blocked the path of the British advance, with barely two thousand rifles to guard the passes of the Pare Mountains and key points on the Northern Railway. To clear the Germans from these positions and to keep his own casualties down, Smuts organized the southward thrust of Hoskins' 1st Division into three columns. One detachment, composed mainly of KAR units, would slice along the heavily wooded eastern flank of the Pare range to press in on the German right wing. A center column, under Brigadier General John Arthur Hannyngton of the Indian army, was to lunge directly down the Northern Railway, while Sheppard, with the main force, would follow the acacia-lined banks of the Pangani River and contain the German left. Unless he wished to abandon all his positions—not to mention the Northern Railway—Kraut would be completely boxed in.

The columns got under way in a cloud of dust—literally. Country that had lain under water only a few days earlier had now been dehydrated by the equatorial sun. Quickly, the parched earth was churned up into towering, powdery nimbus clouds by the marching battalions, by the hooves of their horses, mules and oxen, by the wheels of their staff cars, supply lorries, motor ambulances, armored cars, artillery caissons and limbers, by their ammunition wagons and mule-drawn field hospitals. The man-made fogbank was a mass strangler. "The head of the column," wrote an officer of the 129th Baluchis, "[was] a position coveted not so much as being the place of danger and honour as for its comparatively fresh air."

Other discomforts soon made themselves felt. The columns were advancing across unknown country whose few wagon roads and bridges had been torn or blown up by the retreating Germans. The end of a day's march was not a time for rest but for road repair work. The hungry, thirsty, wilted, dust-caked troops were seldom given more than fifteen or twenty minutes to bolt down their rancid bully beef, gulp down their tins of lukewarm tea, roll a few grains of coarse South African tobacco into scraps of paper for a quick smoke. Then the NCOs had them back on their feet to take up picks, shovels and axes. Boulders must be removed, potholes filled, corduroy strips laid down, trees felled, paths hacked through the thorn, so that the wheeled transport might keep up its lumbering pace in the rear.

Even after repairs, however, the roads were hardly recognizable as such, and transport soon began to come apart at the seams. It was physically impossible to extract every rock or fill in every ant-bear pit, and thus to prevent the continual shattering of wheels, axles and undercarriages. Scores upon scores of motor vehicles and wagons had to be dragged to the sides of the rough tracks and abandoned to natural burial in the ever-growing vegetation. Animal depreciation was no less severe; at times it almost seemed as if the wagon tracks had been designed to snap the ankles and fracture the legs of oxen and mules. Several dozen of these casualties might be shot in a day.

But the uniformed road gangs kept at it, often toiling until far after midnight. When they finally laid down their tools, the men were ready to sleep for at least twelve hours. They were lucky if they got three. Orders to break camp and move out were usually given long before the sun rose. The Pangani force became an army of somnambulists. "Commonly you will see a man dozing on his feet, but marching unsteadily on," wrote Buchanan, "and if the man in front of him should have occasion to halt, the sleeping man behind him will walk forcibly into him."

When the troops were not digging, sleepwalking or shooting, they were raving and dying from disease. What they endured on the march was not actually a great deal worse than anything experienced by a later generation of British and American soldiers in the southwest Pacific, Malaya and Vietnam. The only difference was that army doctors in those more recent wars could call on a galaxy of antibiotics and other wonder drugs to cope with the invisible living things that racked the body and scrambled the mind. It was the difference between purgatory and hell.

The most widespread sickness on the drive down the Pangani was malaria, of whose symptoms death was not necessarily the most violent, although it was common enough and sometimes welcomed. Other manifestations included chills, heat stroke, epileptic seizures, delirium tremens, cardiac failure and insanity. The British suffered much more from malaria than did the Germans, partly because their relative newness to the tropics made them less resistant, partly because their knee-length shorts and short-sleeved shirts were a standing invitation to the anopheles mosquito. (The Schutztruppe's more sensible long sleeves, ankle-length trousers and puttees did a great deal to hold malaria at bay.) Quinine was a helpful prophylactic but it could do only so much, and stocks were often in short supply owing to transport snarls. Mosquito netting, which ripped like tissue paper, was slightly better than worthless, but could never be used when most needed: on night sentry or patrol duty. The British soldier in East Africa who escaped malaria in some form was almost a freak.

Everyone also caught dysentery—amoebic or bacillary or both—from contaminated food or the waters of the Pangani and other rivers; East Africa had the highest dysentery rate of any theatre in the First World War. The most noticeable symptom was uncommonly virulent diarrhea: more than one British unit could be followed by its miles-long trail of bloody feces. Also common was blackwater fever, so called because it turned one's urine black, although the advanced cases vomited themselves to death. There was also relapsing fever caused by ticks; its symptoms could resemble malaria. Small cuts often expanded quickly into livid, suppurating jungle sores as big as a fist. The afflicted airs were almost enough to make a man welcome a bullet.

Other ailments, caused by insects, seldom killed but were troublesome enough. The jigger flea burrowed into a man's toe and laid several million eggs. If the eggs were not extracted with a knife or a safety pin, the toe would presently rot. Literally thousands of British, Indian and African toes were amputated on the march to the Central Railway. The bott fly laid its

eggs in a soldier's arms or back. The eggs soon grew into large white maggots; unless removed, they would die and form festering abcesses. Army
surgeons often pulled out as many as four dozen of these things from a
single patient. The bite of the sand fly caused a fever lasting about three
days—mild alongside the maddening itch that persisted for weeks after-
ward. There were also the black soldier ants called *siafu*, which traveled in
great armies and bit like white hot skewers; scorpions whose stings made
their victims witless with agony for at least twelve hours; harmless centipedes that crawled in great numbers beneath soldiers' blankets for warmth
at night. The soldiers did not welcome their guests.

Perhaps the worst thing about the nightmare world through which the
British columns moved was its beauty. Young of the 2nd Rhodesians later
wrote a novel in which his protagonist recalled the drive down the Pangani:
"The background, ever changing yet ever the same, of golden grasslands
and silvery bush; of a winding, impetuous river, now near, now far, yet
ever present to the parched imagination in a vision of greener trees in whose
shadow temptation and death were always lurking . . . of suns that rose on
new landscapes of an incredible, golden calm . . . a calm which, like as not,
would be suddenly broken by the boom of the invisible enemy's naval guns
and the shriek of shells that ripped the blue tissue of sky like tearing silk,
or the whip-crack of snipers' bullets snapping in the air, or a rattle of
maxim-fire simultaneous with shots that smote . . . like a sudden hailstorm
launched from the cloudless heaven."

For the enemy was never absent. The Germans had to retreat—they
could do nothing else—but they did not turn tail and flee, any more than
had the tribes who had coached the Schutztruppe in the finer points of hit-
and-run. Kraut was a grandmaster of that tactic; if he could not halt the
British advance he could delay it, and his troops did a great deal more than
just tear up roads. A *Königsberg* gun was mounted on a railway truck and
harried Smuts' supply columns with high-explosive shells until the advancing British troops forced the gun train to reverse down the line a few miles—
at which point it commenced pounding away again. Snipers took a healthy
toll of forward and flanking patrols. Ambushes seldom gave one a chance
to fire back.

Above all, the Germans relied on their machine guns. "Even in this bush
warfare, where man, one would think, is matched against single man,"
wrote Young in a letter, "the machine-gun has become the most important
weapon. That is partly the reason why the Germans in this campaign have
been able to put up so splendid a resistance." The fields of fire which the
Schutztruppe askaris had hacked out of the thorn in anticipation of Smuts'
advance were now paying dividends. Even the ranges had been marked out,
and the British quickly learned to keep a wide berth of the tempting open
spaces which promised greater speed but produced sheets of machine gun

fire. A single machine gun team could, at the very least, hold up a platoon or company for the time it took to get its own Maxim or Vickers gun off its mule and return the fire. By then, the Germans would have put their weapon on a wooden carrying frame and moved it off to open up from another position. The emplacements were always invisible. "I hope you'll see something to aim at," said one of Young's fictional officers to another. "I never have."

But German resistance, its artfulness and ferocity notwithstanding, did little more than scratch the hides of the three military rhinos that charged down the Pangani. The British even picked up momentum. Smuts continually called for speed and more speed. He got it—often by the strength of his personality alone. It did not seem quite natural that so outwardly icy a man could win so warm a response from his troops, but that was the way it was. At one time the Rhodesians spent fifteen hours trying to cut a passage through an uncommonly deep and stubborn wall of thorn. Their officers finally told them to give over the attempt. Just then Smuts rode up, cantered ahead, returned in five minutes and ordered the work resumed at once. The Rhodesians were almost blind with exhaustion, "and yet," wrote Young, "I do not think there was a man in the brigade who was not cheered and stimulated by this order. . . . By [Smuts'] swift passage one realized with an extraordinary clearness the driving force that was behind all this dusty pageantry of our plodding through the centre of Africa."

And so it went. For ten days with hardly a pause, the lumbering British force ploughed ahead, racking up distances of ten, fifteen and even twenty miles daily. Young could check the troops' progress by looking back at Kilimanjaro, which "rose . . . like a gigantic ghost . . . away to the northward, utterly dominating, as we had never suspected, all the country which we had traversed. It was almost as though the great mountain smiled: 'Look what you have been fighting for.' "

Then, suddenly, on May 30, as the army approached a village called Buiko, it was brought to a jarring halt. At Buiko the Pangani took a sharp turn to the east beneath the foothills of the southern Pare range, forming a narrow neck through which the railway also ran. The position did not lend itself well to a Smuts-type maneuver but it was ideally suited to a punching rearguard action. Kraut made the most of it, posting artillery observers on the Pare slopes to get the range of the British supply columns far to the rear. The immense dust clouds kicked up by the lines of lorries and wagons offered an easy target to the *Königsberg* gun, which began making clouds of its own as it hurled out shell after shell, scoring few direct hits but causing great confusion among the transport drivers and pandemonium among the animals. The Germans were going to have to be pried from their defenses before the British advance could be resumed.

To dislodge them, Sheppard was sent ahead in a frontal assault with the Rhodesians in the van. Not a single Schutztruppe askari could be seen as the attacking infantry picked its way forward through the scrub, but a sudden eruption of rifle and machine-gun fire had the Rhodesians hitting the dirt as one man. The advance was reduced literally to a crawl on all fours—until the intensity of the German fire abated when Kraut began his withdrawal. The time had come to drive the attack home with cold steel, to surround the *Königsberg* gun before it could be rolled beyond the British grasp. The Rhodesians rose to their feet, fixed bayonets, waited for Sheppard to order the charge.

Besides enjoying a reputation for bellicosity, Sheppard was also known—paradoxically—as a man of almost saintly courtesy and patience. Both those qualities now underwent a trial by ordeal as an inexplicable order winked out over the British heliograph: Break off the action.

It was a gift on a platter for Kraut: twelve hours' grace to pull his own troops back and move the gun down the line once again. Smuts was eating up the enemy's land but he had yet to make much of a dent in the enemy.

The first week of June 1916 saw the British Pangani force resting at Buiko. The columns by this time were almost foodless, having outraced their transport, whose main supply base had not yet been advanced from Mombasa, three hundred miles away as the worm crawled. Stores might have been brought down with relative ease along the captured Northern Railway if the Germans had not blown up every yard of track with their every yard of retreat. Weeks would pass before British army engineers got the line in working order again. Meanwhile, supplies had to come down the Pangani Valley in lurching ox-wagons that could never creep faster than three miles an hour flat out, or in motor lorries whose engines threatened to stall if they went out of low gear. And even if the troops had been fed, they still teetered on the brink of mass physical prostration from malaria, dysentery, blackwater and lack of sleep. The army simply had to stop. A week was not nearly long enough.

But a week was all that Smuts allowed. The enemy never rested. Or at least he never seemed to rest.

Smuts' next objective took the main force off the Northern Railway. Some seventy-five miles due south was Handeni, terminus of the narrow-gauge shuttle tramway which connected with the Northern line at Mombo station, a few miles below Buiko. Like Kondoa Irangi to the west, Handeni was strategically important as a jumping-off place for the Central Railway, and Kraut in fact was already deploying to make for that position. Smuts planned to get there first, so as to drive a wedge between Kraut's force and von Lettow's main army. Von Lettow at this time was still outside Kondoa, watching the 2nd Division, uncertain of van Deventer's strength and plans. But he could not indefinitely disregard Smut's columns as they pushed down in the east. Sooner or later he must move to support Kraut. Handeni, or the country just south of it, seemed to Smuts likely ground for the confrontation that could bring von Lettow to account.

The new drive got off to an inauspicious start. Its only upbeat moment came with the daring capture of an important bridge by a KAR force which made an enveloping thrust some miles down the railway. But this accomplishment was nullified by the KAR's failure to catch the German detachment whose presence at the bridgehead was the sole object of the attack. The main British column had even less luck. Smuts' almost desperate resolve to overtake Kraut only caused Kraut to strike back with greater fury while continuing to withdraw—pulling up the tracks of the trolley line as he did so. As always, the scabrous bush and tall grass favored snipers, hidden machine guns and ambushes. And as always, everything conspired against attack. Beneath a triphammer sun in a sea of thorn and mosquitoes, their aim spoiled by the innumerable small things that crawled about in nostrils, armpits and crotches, so weakened by fever that they could barely lift their rifles, the British troops were something less than fit to deliver devastating blows. But they never stopped trying. Sometimes they almost succeeded.

Typical of their efforts at this time was a nasty little rearguard action outside the village of Mkalamo, where Sheppard hurled a flanking column of Baluchis and Punjabis round one German wing and beefed up the attack with the guns of half a mountain battery. The blistering shell fire turned the grass huts of Mkalamo into a raging bonfire and minced up a number of Kraut's askaris, but the assault ran head-on into what Young called "the usual trap—a tempting open space, with the ranges all marked, and massed machine-guns sweeping it almost point-blank." After a double company of Baluchis had nearly been wiped out to a man, Kraut kept his guns hammering away until nightfall covered a characteristically neat vanishing act into the undergrowth. Mkalamo was only one of many such frustrations.

Apart from its lagging pace, however, the drive on Handeni was a repeat performance of the push down the Northern Railway, only more so. Transport's limp became increasing noticeable as the "roads" pounded vehicles to death while disease took an almost genocidal toll of animals. The columns had entered one of the more lethal "fly belts" of eastern Africa, and the air shimmered with whining banks of tsetse flies, whose stingers drilled effortlessly and endlessly through the hardest hides, introducing unseen armies of trypanosomes into the animals' bloodstreams. When a horse or mule or bullock began to show a swelling in the chest, or when an air bubble enlarged the beast's jugular vein, the end was at hand. Frothing muzzles and nostrils heralded the presence of another killer called horse sickness. Both afflictions worked overtime. "One may say with truth," wrote a medical officer of this phase of the offensive, "that the commonest and most frequently prescribed veterinary medicine is the revolver." The 1st Division's route of march was embroidered with the bloated, noisome cadavers of transport animals. The army's busiest camp followers were the hyenas and vultures.

And as transport dragged its feet, the men's rations shrank proportionately. "Bare flour without bacon or fat to cook it with," wrote Buchanan, "is almost a 'straw' ration, for flour and water dropped into a dry canteen doesn't make anything digestible or palatable. But if one is hungry it is eaten." Disease continued to grow like a boil among the troops and became aggravated by an epidemic of thirst as the sun shriveled rivers and streams; armed sentries were posted at shallow, stagnant pools to assure equal portions of slime for all. Debilitating fatigue returned with a vengeance; sleep became the British soldier's most precious commodity. He got very little of it as Smuts drove the army forward pitilessly.

Smuts shared the troops' hardships and risks. He ate their maggoty biscuits and drank their tainted water. He got as sick as any private but seldom bothered with doctors, for whom he appeared to have little use. The only distinguishing feature of his moldy, tattered headquarters tent was the Union Jack outside its entrance. He showed no interest in the special creature comforts permitted by his rank—except for the gray Vauxhall staff car which drove him to the front lines nearly every day. When the car could go no further, Smuts got out and walked to the outpost closest to the German positions, where bullets spanged around him while he wrote orders in a pocket notebook and got a first-hand look at the progress of his advance.

That he was taking a fearful risk never seemed to occur to him. At one time, he even put himself—unknowingly—in the crosshairs of a rifle carried by von Lettow, another commander who felt most at ease in the thick of it. Von Lettow did not squeeze off the round, deciding at the last moment that it would be unsporting to gun down the head of the British army. Smuts somehow learned of this later and grunted that von Lettow was a damned fool but a gentleman.

Not everyone appreciated this quiet daring. "Smuts has made a mistake in mixing himself up with local conditions," wrote Meinertzhagen, who was guilty of the same offense. "During an action he is often in the firing line and loses control of the fight." Smuts felt otherwise: the front line was where one could best see what was happening. Besides which, he knew that his presence in the middle of the shooting had the effect of adrenalin on his troops. But his staff officers deplored his total disregard for his personal safety and continually tried to keep him beyond range of Schutztruppe machine guns. They continually failed.

In his infrequent moments of leisure, Smuts expended a prodigious amount of intellectual energy, swallowing in great gulps the voluminous egghead literature sent to him regularly by friends in South Africa and England. He chafed when the latest issue of the *Philosophical Review* or *The New Republic* was late in reaching his headquarters. Walter Lippmann's *Drift and Mastery* (which Smuts called "an extraordinary book for so young a man to write") was devoured in barely one sitting. Smuts could not seem to get enough. Thanking a friend for Croce's *Philosophy of the Practical* and *Hegel's Philosophy*, he added hungrily that "I believe there is another volume or two translated which you might send me. Send me also Balfour's lectures on *Humanism* and Baldwin's *Genetic Theory of Reality*." While waiting, he had to live off the land. "Some of my dear old German philosophers I have found in this country," he told the same friend, "and I can therefore reread them at odd times."

Smuts was also an almost compulsive letter writer, particularly to his wife, to whom he showed his less frigid side, addressing her always as "Dearest Mamma" and signing himself "Pappa." While he did not conceal the rigors of the campaign from her, he sometimes tried to sugar-coat the pill with anecdotes which he may have thought amusing: "Last week three mules tethered together went to drink; a crocodile seized one by the nose and was strong enough to drag all three under the water and drown them. What a feast for him and his friends!" And he never forgot to close with something like "sweet kisses for Mamma" and "all the little ones."

As the dreary advance on Handeni continued, the news from the major theatres of war did not bring much comfort. When a Reuters dispatch on the Battle of Jutland was passed among the troops, "our minds," said Young, "were filled with a torturing uncertainty which shadowed the whole of that day. . . . And yet, in a way, the news . . . made us anxious to be done with this side-show . . . so that we might help to get to the root of the whole tragedy, at home in Europe."

The Fusiliers were becoming surly. Always reliable whenever there was shooting, they chafed more than ever at military protocol even during the briefest lulls. Their battalion adjutant went to Cranworth with a problem. He had given an order to one officer who in turn "had responded by telling him to go to hell and commit a peculiar and indecent offence with spiders. 'As if I could,' he pathetically added."

And the German machine guns never let up. They were "like an errand boy," wrote Young, "trailing his stick along a line of wooden palings, sometimes running, sometimes walking, sometimes forgetting what he was about."

At last, on June 19, elements of Sheppard's column burst wearily into Handeni. Kraut had departed only hours earlier from the cluster of fly-blown grass-roofed hovels. But he had left behind several hundred porters for the British. They were all dying of typhus.

Scarcely pausing for breath, the British columns left Handeni behind and pressed on after Kraut in high gear, only to be brought up short about twenty miles to the south at a place called Kangata. Here, Beves' brigade took a terrible mauling when it walked straight into a German trap. Kraut had concealed his riflemen and machine guns to cover a road along which he had expected the attack to come. When Beves refused to take the bait, a German patrol drew the South African fire toward the prepared positions.

Then the slaughter commenced. Before they could extricate themselves, upwards of two hundred South Africans lost their lives or parts of their bodies. Nearly half the casualties were sustained by troops trying to man a single machine gun which kept firing until its water jacket began to steam—and which wasted endless belts of ammunition against the invisible German emplacements. When he decided he had caused enough damage, Kraut ordered the customary lightning dispersal into the bush and the British resumed their advance, a little less swiftly.

Thus far, the trail of pursuit had crossed country which for the most part was fairly level, coated only with the familiar layer of grass and uncountable quintillions of steel toothbrushes, dotted here and there with stands of flat-topped acacia trees or occasional bloated baobabs, scarred with the dried-up stream beds called *nullahs*. But below Kangata, the rivers began to flow again, the terrain became bumpier and the trees thicker as hunters and hunted approached the Nguru Mountains. It was imperative that Kraut be stopped before he could snuggle inextricably into the maze of serpentine valleys, passes and solidly forested slopes of that sub-Alpine hideout. Dismayed not in the slightest by his consistent record of failing to make maneuver work for him, Smuts planned another.

Its prospects looked more hopeful than usual. By June 24, Kraut had retired about twelve miles below Kangata and was firmly entrenched at a bridgehead on a river called the Lukigura. If British troops could move upstream, swing far around the German left flank and then strike in its rear while the main force was being held down by a frontal attack on the bridgehead, an attempted retreat across the river itself might just mean a withdrawal into annihilation.

To envelop the German left, Smuts sent out a strong flying column made up of Lancs, Fusiliers, Kashmir Rifles and two South African battalions. They would be led personally by Hoskins, the 1st Division commander. The assault on the bridgehead was to be delivered by Sheppard with an infantry brigade. Success depended on timing and secrecy. Kraut must not learn of the envelopment before it was completed, which in turn meant that Sheppard could not press his own attack too energetically until the Germans found their line of retreat closed off. At the same time, however, Sheppard had to strike hard enough to keep Kraut busy on the defensive. For this task, he did not rely on his infantry and artillery alone. A new and formidable instrument of war was to join in the assault on the Lukigura.

The British armored car detachment was commanded by Major Sir John Willoughby, who had gone to jail a decade and a half earlier for his complicity in the Jameson Raid, but whose advancing years had not diminished his appetite for the aggressive surprise. Disqualified by age from serving in France, Willoughby had personally organized and paid for the East African armored force. Up to now, the detachment had been little more than a noisy nuisance—to the British. Looking for all the world like wheeled strongboxes mounting machine guns, the vehicles weighed three and a half tons each and often needed more than their 50-hp. Rolls-Royce engines to drag them from the mud, sand and cavernous potholes that never stopped trapping them. Smuts' troops invariably dove for cover at the farting blast of the cars' exhausts, which sounded almost exactly like German machine guns firing at point-blank range. Willoughby was understandably eager to demonstrate that his armor could also discompose the enemy.

Their Maxim guns ablaze, the cars roared out in front of the infantry as Sheppard launched his attack on the Lukigura bridgehead. They had scarcely advanced two hundred yards before the lead car, containing Willoughby himself, snorted to a halt only inches from a wide trench as an armor-piercing pom-pom shell tore its radiator apart. The trench also stopped the other vehicles, whose crews had to jump out and fill it in while German bullets punctured their shovels and sometimes their bodies. But when the steel-plated heaps lurched forward again, they seemed to be justifying their presence at last. British armor never did very much again in the campaign, but now, with their well-protected Maxims firing down from a 45-degree angle, the cars cut a path of sorts for the infantry and helped the troops rivet Kraut's askaris to their positions. The Germans were nicely set up for the flying column's right cross.

That envelopment, meanwhile, was racing along on surprisingly well-oiled wheels. Getting into position had been the stiffest job. To reach the Germans' relatively exposed left flank undetected, the troops of Hoskins' flying column had been expected to march for twenty-four hours without making a single halt and then hit the Germans at once. Perhaps to their own surprise they did just that. "I have never seen men more utterly tired and woebegone than [the Fusiliers] at the time of their approach to Lukigura river," Buchanan recalled, ". . . and yet, when they went into battle all fatigue was forgotten, or they were careless of further physical trial; and they fought like madmen." In fact, the Fusiliers borrowed a page from the Schutztruppe in this action, storming the German positions in one of the wildest bayonet charges yet seen in the campaign, while the Gurkhas of the Kashmir Rifles swung their kukris like berserk vivisectionists on another sector of the line. It was over in a matter of minutes. At long last, a Smuts envelopment had been brought off without a hitch.

Except that the Germans got away again.

To be sure, they had been forced to leave the bridge intact, but still they got away. Nothing, it seemed, could keep the Kaiser's bush-wise black soldiers from being swallowed up by the country that was tailor-made for mobile defense and which conspired with such consummate artistry against sophisticated western maneuver.

Once more, Smuts had to call a halt. After covering nearly 250 miles in four weeks, the army's life juices were drying up and the men verged on physical and mental breakdown. Only the KAR seemed fairly hale, although it still had not yet occurred to anyone that the black force might be expanded—and although every other unit was shrinking almost visibly. Climate, disease and—to a much lesser extent—battle casualties had all but broken the back of the South Africans. The Rhodesians were down to one-fourth their strength. Of the Fusiliers' original eleven hundred troops, two hundred could stand up for roll call. The Lancs consisted of a single machine gun company. The Indians, reduced in numbers by two-thirds, were even worse off psychologically. Having proved themselves incomparable fighting men, they now showed an almost total incapacity to cope with sickness, succumbing to a peculiar—perhaps oriental—lethargy and fatalism which sabotaged recovery and confounded medical officers. "They had no more interest in life," wrote Young. "Their souls were as sick as their bodies." And, he added, why not? After all, "it mattered nothing to them whether this detestable country, the scene of their exile and purgatory, were ruled by German or British."

Thus drained by the attrition of nature, Smuts may also have been outnumbered at this point by the enemy, for von Lettow by now had brought the main German force back from Kondoa Irangi. And, unlike the sick, dispirited British troops, the Schutztruppe's black soldiery was physically in the pink and psychologically ten feet tall. "I had expected [Kraut's] Askari to be depressed by their retreat," wrote von Lettow, "but found them in excellent spirits and full of confidence." By its very presence, indeed, the army seemed able to buck up the whole civil populace, white or black. On the march to rejoin Kraut, von Lettow's columns passed through the Central Railway town of Morogoro, where a large community of German residents was in a blue funk over Smuts' advance. But, said von Lettow, "when the Europeans there saw the splendid bearing of the Askari they lost the last traces of their depression; every man and woman had comprehended . . . that our force was, from its whole quality and nature, capable of carrying on for a long time to come."

Logistically, the Germans certainly enjoyed a vital edge. Most of their food supplies came from the country through which they retired: maize fields and other cultivation were stripped bare; not so much as a bean or a stalk of millet was left for the pursuers. The Schutztruppe's transport system also left the British far behind. For the haulage of ammunition, medical supplies and other stores, porters were relied on almost exclusively; as prime movers, the lumbering ox wagon and the malfunctioning lorry engine were proving hopelessly inferior to human back and leg power. Above all, since the Germans occupied interior lines, every step of their withdrawal brought them that much closer to their main supply bases along the Central Railway, while the British columns put an ever-increasing mileage between themselves and their own depots in Mombasa.

Indeed, if fresh troops and fresh (or not so fresh) food were now to reach him, Smuts must stop.

The place he chose was a scrofulous little clearing in the bush and grass called Msiha. The men looked forward eagerly to resting there for at least four or five days. A month later, when ordered out again, they took up their rifles joyfully. Msiha could hardly have been better suited to German artillery practice. Directly above the camp loomed Kanga mountain, a six-thousand-foot elbow of the Nguru range, and von Lettow had positioned two *Königsberg* guns near its summit. At first, their crews fired off infrequent, desultory shots which had little effect except to make the British wonder what had happened to the Germans' aim. The British should have known better: the Germans were simply getting the range. When they found it, they put the guns to work with a homicidal—if less than pinpoint accurate—vengeance, walloping the Msiha positions literally around the clock every day. Only at dinnertime did the gunners take a brief cease-fire. It was not long before Msiha became known as Shell Camp.

Living at Msiha was like living in an earthquake. And not a thing, it seemed, could be done to stop or even reduce the bombardment. Temporarily without artillery to answer the Germans, Smuts' troops eagerly awaited the deadly retaliation that would be wrought as soon as the "Peggy guns" were brought into position. These guns had been taken off the cruiser *Pegasus* after *Königsberg* sank her in Zanzibar harbor, and it seemed poetic justice that like Looff's guns, they too had been mounted on carriages as if to avenge their earlier defeat. Eventually, they rumbled into Msiha and commenced thundering at the *Königsberg* guns in a landlocked repeat performance of the Zanzibar battle. But it was a reenactment in every way, for the "Peggy guns" did not have anything approaching the range to throw their shells even within a mile of the German emplacements.

Aircraft fared somewhat better; they could get above the German positions, and always put on a good show when attacking. The pilots of Royal Flying Corps Squadron No. 26, which supported Smuts' advance, were the army's daredevil elite, and earned that distinction the hard way. The squadron's eight obsolete BE2C biplanes were patched-up castoffs from the Western Front. Their design made them look more like butterflies than heavier-than-air machines and gave grim new meaning to the word "crate." Although not quite helpless when airborne, BE2Cs were notoriously hard to maneuver, and had been brought down like flies by German pursuit planes and anti-aircraft guns over the Somme. It was fortunate for Smuts that von Lettow had no aircraft.

Even so, flying in the East African campaign was a hairy proposition. Because of the atmospheric conditions, the planes could seldom even get off the ground during daylight hours; flights took place almost exclusively at dawn or dusk—which made it that much easier for a pilot to stray off course and risk being forced down behind the German lines. In low-level bombing attacks, a BE2C's flat-out speed of sixty miles per hour invited shell, machine gun, rifle and even pistol fire. A pilot never knew when his plane's sniffling 70-hp. engine would cut out. But he could usually rely on this to happen at least half a dozen times in a ninety-minute mission.

Such hazards made flying all the more fun, and some of the airmen in East Africa added handicaps of their own. Not being required to drill or stand formation, they had ample time to make themselves unfit for air duels by treating their malaria with whisky and champagne. One pilot dosed himself at the rate of a quart daily; "the only time I had flown with him sober," wrote the novelist Leo Walmsley, who served with the squadron as an observer, ". . . I'd been terrified because I could actually feel the trembling of his hands on the joystick." Flight Lieutenant W. D. M. ("Karamoja") Bell, who had ranked with Selous and Pretorius as a prewar elephant hunter, never went up with an observer; anyone sitting in the front cockpit would block Bell's field of fire as he shaved the top of the bush to pepper away at German askaris with a repeating rifle.

It was natural that this picaresque band should have welcomed the opportunity to have a go at the *Königsberg* gun emplacements on Kanga mountain. Just before sunset every day, their BE2Cs performed gracefully perilous ballet steps amid violent storms of German machine gun bullets only a few feet above the mountain crest while letting fly with their fifty-pound high-explosive bombs or the incendiary charges known as "Clarke's Bombs." All the troops turned out to watch the missiles land. "Their explosions were as balm to our spirits," said Young, "for the mountains began to play with their echoing sound so that each bomb made a detonation which sounded like the bouncing of a gigantic metal football."

The only trouble was that the pilots never hit anything, for the simple reason that they never saw anything to aim at, so snugly were the German guns tucked into the forests that quilted the slopes and peaks like bushels of cauliflower. As von Lettow understated it, "we had learned to make ourselves invisible." And the guns pounded away undisturbed.

The endless blasting upheavals of the ground beneath them were particularly trying on Msiha's sick and wounded—who comprised more than half the force at that place. Although the Germans were not seeking deliberately to hit the camp's so-called hospital, that was the way it often worked out. Young, now down with malaria, recalled that "in the ordinary way I had not so far minded shell fire, but in this case the effect was really . . . terrifying, because I was not a whole man . . . but sick and badly off for nerves, lying alone with no more than a flimsy tent in darkness only lit by the tremendous flashes of the bursting shell, and shaken by the reports which echoed through all that forest." When it was realized that the "hospital" may have been the most vulnerable spot in the camp, it was moved behind a steep declivity which sappers said could not be touched and where a 4.1-inch shell immediately exploded. The Germans had emplaced their guns in deep pits, enabling them to throw their missiles, howitzerlike, in high looping trajectories that made a mockery of natural cover.

Clearly, the patients had to be evacuated, a move that was easier planned than carried out. To reach the nearest casualty clearing station, fifty miles north at Handeni, ambulances ran a gauntlet of potholes and rocks which smashed up axles, springs and already shattered bones with impartiality. The narrow dirt motor track was clogged with southbound troop and supply convoys which created hopeless traffic jams and attracted ambushes by infiltrating German patrols. Land mines were an ever-present hazard—although perhaps not as fearsome as the smell of dead animals. The mounted brigade of Coen Brits' 3rd Division was then losing fifty horses a day to tsetse and horse sickness; there was no time to bury the cadavers and they lay on the side of the road in bloated heaps, swarming with flies, crawling with maggots, raising a stench that struck like the blow of a maul. The troops called them "Brits' violets," and they may have made the sick men sicker. The thorn flanking the road gave concealment to lions, who preyed not only on the noisome animal carcasses but on more than one living or half-living soldier whose worn-out ambulance had packed up or blown up.

On arrival at Handeni, the blood-soaked, fever-flayed men who survived the jolting nightmare journey may have wondered whether their destination had been worth getting to. The casualty clearing station—a converted German jailhouse with the legend GOTT STRAFE ENGLAND painted on one wall—could accommodate about fifty patients, but the two British doctors there (one was Young, still partly out of his mind with malaria) had to treat literally thousands. Owing to the crippled supply lines and the even more mangled condition of the army's red tape, there was sometimes nothing to treat them with except morphia, which generally killed pain effectively and caused not a few incurable addictions. Nearly all hospital equipment had to be improvised or liberated. Metal braces for casts were made from corrugated iron roofs, as were cradles for putting smashed limbs in traction. Bed sores (when a patient was lucky enough to have a bed) could sometimes be prevented with "ring pillows" woven from elephant grass. Sheets were torn into bandages. One of the doctors toured neighboring German plantation houses to commandeer bedsteads, blankets, pillows, mattresses and silk cushions; the last were used as rests for amputated stumps. No British soldier would soon forget his Handeni convalescence.

Back at Msiha, the "healthy" troops did not seem all that robust. South Africa's Premier Botha visited Smuts' headquarters at this time, and men toppled over in scores while trying to stand at attention during a formal inspection of what remained of the force. But there were few such ceremonies. For the most part, the troops simply huddled in their frail entrenchments and hoped that the next 4.1-inch shell would pass harmlessly over-head. "It was very marked," wrote Cranworth, "how the drawn out shelling without opportunity of reply told on everyone's nerves to a far greater extent than an engagement." Even Smuts could not treat the ordeal lightly for his wife's benefit, although he tried. "The camp is full of holes," he wrote her, "and the thousands of troops here have been living practically underground. A piece of shell fell into my tent while I lay reading on my bed; another burst near our mess tent. I am bringing for the children pieces of this last shell."

For all the noise they made and for all the earth they moved, the *Königs-berg* guns in fact scored relatively few direct hits, and British casualties during the month-long barrage were not high. But this did not lessen the impact of the "whistling Willies" on the frayed nerve-ends of men who had dragged themselves across 250 miles of fever-soaked African scrub in pur-suit of an enemy they seldom saw but who always saw them—and who always knew how to hit where it hurt most. Msiha was not the Somme or Verdun. It was enough.

Probably the only merit of the enforced holiday at Msiha was the oppor-tunity it gave the British to reconnoiter the route of march ahead. British intelligence operations may have been the sharpest thorn in the Schutz-truppe's tough hide—by now, Pretorius had a price on his head, dead or alive—which meant that it took as much moxie as brains to prowl about in enemy country. One of the most daring probes behind the German lines at this time was carried out by three former EAMR troopers who had joined Smuts' field intelligence apparatus. With four askaris, five mules and no rations, the scouts groped their way across the Nguru Mountains. It took them three weeks to make a round trip of barely thirty miles, but the trek brought them to within whistling distance of von Lettow's headquarters camp and put the entire intervening country into focus for the next British advance. Von Lettow himself later remarked that "we could none of us help honestly admiring [the scouts'] excellent work."

Nearly every step of the journey offered cliff-hanger suspense. Schutz-truppe patrols continually passed by only a few feet from the rock or scrub concealments behind which the party literally held its collective breath. On entering African villages to barter for food, the scouts never knew whether they would be fed or handed over to the Germans or both. But at least one close shave was turned to their advantage. Coming across a German supply column not far from von Lettow's camp, the scouts masqueraded as Schutz-truppe officers and ordered the bewildered porters to burn their loads. More than six tons of stores—including large quantities of sausages, cases of schnapps and several thousand pairs of pants—went up in smoke.

The party's luck almost gave out when an African guide deliberately led it into an ambush. Two of the scouts got away; the third, Lieutenant Arnold

Wienholt, was captured after taking a bullet in the hip. At German army headquarters, he became one of the first British prisoners to meet von Lettow personally. The plainly dressed Schutztruppe commander, Wienholt recalled, "impressed me favorably. . . . His manner [was] not at all overbearing; his face the face of a strong man."

But then came the third degree. "Von Lettow spoke to me . . . for a few minutes, asking me what nationality I was. 'I am an Australian, sir.'

" 'But your name is German.'

" 'Yes, the family is of German extraction, though not for the last three centuries.'

" 'But the name is German.'

" 'Yes, certainly, sir; originally, I believe, from near Bremen.'

"Again he asked me, 'Have you had fever?'

" 'No, sir, I have no fever.'

" 'Oh, it is wounded then that you are?'

" 'Yes, just slightly.'

" 'Ah,' said he, 'we have known all about you.' Then he asked me if I was the leader of the scouts, and I told him I was the oldest."

End of grilling.

From his scouts, Smuts got a good picture of what he would be up against as he prepared to move out of Msiha early in August. His objective now was Morogoro, one of the most important German communications and supply centers on the Central Railway. Morogoro lay some sixty miles to the south, but the British path was blocked by von Lettow, who now had his headquarters at a place called Turiani, about twelve miles below Msiha. If Smuts tried to ram his force into Turiani by the main road—which was to say the only road—he would run head-on into a formidable concentration of German soldiery and hardware. The length of the road itself was pocked with land mines and hemmed with snipers, while machine gun nests and artillery emplacements commanded the Nguru heights. The positions could be forced, but only at a high price in British casualties, so Smuts decided on another avenue of advance. The scouts had told him that the seemingly impassable Ngurus could be negotiated if troops were to march several miles west and then south, following the valleys of two rivers which ran down the entire length of the range. The routes not only seemed practicable; they also offered the opportunity for still another of those turning movements which so intrigued the British commander.

This time, moreover, there would not be one envelopment but two. While Sheppard's 1st Brigade held the main German force to its positions about four miles south of Msiha—near a spur of the Ngurus called Ruhungu—the 2nd Brigade under General Hannyngton would be driving down the center of the mountains, some ten miles to the west. And, at the same time, still ten miles further west, Coen Brits and his 3rd Division would be delivering the flanking haymaker. On emerging from the southern foothills, Brits would stand astride the main road directly behind the Schutztruppe's Turiani headquarters. Even von Lettow would be hard put to break south through an entire division.

As usual, speed was of the essence, and the British were given a spectacularly encouraging omen when the 3rd KAR moved down from Handeni to join Hannyngton's brigade. It took the battalion less than twenty-four hours to march through forty-four miles of shoulder-high bush, causing Smuts to remark with grudging approval that the black soldiers could eat up ground even faster than South African cavalry.

This was the last swift move his force was to make in the entire operation. As Buchanan put it, "the extremely awkward nature of the country proved again the enemy's disconcerting ally and for him his saving." Within two days, the transport of both Smuts' flanking columns had become stuck fast in a great trash heap of boulders, swamps and forests, all hemmed in by a madman's jigsaw puzzle of towering escarpments and black valleys. Most of the troops were turned to felling trees, throwing corduroy log-strips across morasses, trying to coax supply wagons—each dragged by as many as forty-eight bullocks—over vertiginous bush-choked hills. In due course, all transport was pulled back or simply abandoned. The Germans, too, interfered with progress. Hannyngton's brigade came under a drenching rain of steel from Schutztruppe detachments concealed on higher ground; they harrassed the column to such effect that the infantry of Brits' 3rd Division had to back out of its own valley and move to Hannyngton's support. This left Brits with only his mounted brigade; it was not enough to keep the Germans from carrying out an orderly withdrawal south.

And meanwhile, Sheppard's holding action beneath the eastern slopes of the Ngurus was swiftly getting nowhere. Sheppard and the men of the 1st East African Brigade spent two days floundering blindly about in the elephant grass before they finally located the German defenses at Ruhungu. The position had been abandoned.

Perhaps it was just as well. Cranworth called Ruhungu "the most elaborately fortified of any position I saw during the campaign." To storm and capture the works, the British would have had to cross a 150-yard field of fire that had been cleared in advance by the Germans, then negotiate a complex of pitfalls and several dozen rows of sharpened stakes—all the while under the fire of hidden machine guns and snipers. Buchanan was even more impressed with the fortifications on the overhanging hills, where "regular subterranean caves, and pits, had been excavated everywhere . . . some of them even hewn out of the solid rock by the industry of many hands."

But the Germans had seen no point in holding Ruhungu. Their objective now was to reach Morogoro in the shortest possible time. Thus, when the three British columns finally linked up at Turiani in mid-August, they found another empty fort. One more Smuts envelopment had enveloped one more pocket of thin air.

Pursuit continued southward. The British advance picked up speed; occasionally the Germans came within an ace of being overtaken. About twenty miles north of Morogoro, there was a blistering fight outside the village of Dakawa, where the Gurkhas once again ran amok with their kukris; by now, Young noted, "the enemy had reason to fear those blades more than any bayonet." But the Schutztruppe askaris had a curious way of showing fear: their rifles and machine guns hacked down nearly 20 percent of the attacking column before the Germans withdrew to fight another day. The British might have been closing in on Morogoro, but the real quarry was no more in their grasp than it had been when "surrounded" in the shadow of Kilimanjaro five months earlier.

One reason for the Germans' haste to reach Morogoro was the pressure now being exerted on the Central Railway by van Deventer in the west. When von Lettow had removed his main force from Kondoa Irangi at the end of July, only a few Schutztruppe companies stood between the 2nd Division and the railway. Van Deventer resumed the advance at once, splitting the division into five columns which fanned out in various southerly directions to converge on the line. None of the routes was a parade ground. The men had to pick their way across a grim scar tissue of steep hogbacks which were further gashed by dried-up river beds and strewn everywhere with church-size boulders and cheveaux-de-frise thorn. Thirst stalked the land. Patrols of the mounted brigade rode for long hours in search of water pans, and often found that wild game had already drained the supply. Lions were a particular nuisance. Lieutenant Deneys Reitz, an Orange Free State lawyer who had joined the mounted force, wrote that much of the troopers' time was spent "pacifying our frightened horses, who threatened to stampede every time a lion roared."

The Germans did not make things easier. Although retreating, they were hardly bolting. They chose their points of resistance well; as often as not these commanded the only waterholes in an area, and the ingeniously laid-out defenses enabled the askaris to keep the South Africans very thirsty. Sooner or later, of course, the positions would be taken, but the Germans would not be. "When our cordon tightened," said Reitz, "they . . . filtered away like water through a sieve."

And even while on the run, the Schutztruppe, as usual, was able to sting badly. For mounted troops, following paths or tracks rather than keeping to the bush was to invite trouble. "The enemy custom," wrote Reitz, "was to lie in wait at a bend, fire a volley, and then decamp along some pathway, to repeat the process further on." Sometimes the askaris even counterattacked. One South African cavalry detachment was saved from being cut to pieces by the timely arrival of two armored cars. But such assistance was rare, armor for the most part being about as useful as aircraft in East Africa. Van Deventer's men had to clear the Germans out on their own.

That this would happen was a foregone conclusion. What was remarkable was the speed with which the 2nd Division accelerated the German withdrawal. Terrain, thirst, wild animals and the stiffest Schutztruppe resistance failed to halt an almost record-breaking march. Van Deventer had moved out of Kondoa Irangi on July 24; by the 29th, his advance units were astride the Central Railway, having rolled up an average of twenty miles a day. By early August, the South Africans had begun driving east along the line to effect the linkup with Smuts, Hoskins and Brits at Morogoro. Mounted patrols were everywhere, nipping at the heels of German detachments, forcing the pace of their retreat. "It's just hell," said one Schutztruppe officer at this time. "We can't race their cavalry."

But the retreat never became a rout. The South Africans could not occupy a single German position without grappling for it. When captured, moreover, a former stronghold yielded up little to the occupants. A South African officer once liberated a case of ersatz whisky and planned a celebration with some friends, only to open the box and find it crammed with receipt blanks—which turned out to be counterfeit. Reitz remarked on the skill with which von Lettow used the railway to shuttle his troops "up and down from one threatened point to another, in a manner that was to cause us a great deal of trouble before we finally shouldered him off." Artillery had to be brought up to dislodge Schutztruppe detachments from the larger towns along the line.

And the Germans always hit back with their own guns. A particularly troublesome field piece was a little six-pounder which van Deventer's men called "Big Bertha." Reitz said that it was "daringly handled by an officer whom we learned to know by sight, so often did he appear from behind boulder or thicket, with his field-piece carried on a wooden frame by its askari crew. In a moment, half a dozen rounds would come screeching at us, after which the gun was taken off to reappear at some other spot." Mounted troops tried vainly to capture this gun. The closest they ever came was when a patrol stormed its bush "emplacement," only to find a few coins and a note reading 15 RUPEES FOR THE BLUDDY ENGLISCH—"a joke at which we were not amused," said Reitz, "after our long crawl in the heat." The Germans enjoyed leaving such messages in their wake.

Resistance to Smuts' advance in the east continued no less spirited or imaginative. As von Lettow drew back on Morogoro, that town came within range of the RFC squadron, and to discourage the British pilots, the Germans improvised an anti-aircraft gun by mounting a venerable 1873 Hotchkiss field piece on a railway turntable. Although the thing nearly jumped the tracks every time it was fired, its shells screamed dramatically and their bursts threw out authentic flak. No British planes were brought down, but the British bombs did little if any damage to Morogoro. In all likelihood they would have missed their targets even without the anti-aircraft gun, but its presence symbolized the cussedness of the Germans' fighting retreat.

The land mines were more than a symbol. By not defending Turiani, von Lettow had saved a good deal of artillery ammunition. Several hundred 4.1-inch shells, re-fused and timed to detonate on contact, were now seeded on the main road to Morogoro and other paths of the British southward drive. So many advance guards were sent sky-high that Smuts' columns presently began making long time-consuming detours—and no one could be certain that the new routes had not been tampered with. Denied the luxury of mine detectors, the British were like blindfolded men crossing a field of bear traps. "So far as I could see," wrote an intelligence scout, "the only way to find a mine was to walk into it and be blown up." Some battalion commanders tried to clear their routes by driving slaughter oxen ahead of the forward companies; one South African officer seriously suggested that local tribesmen be put to the same task. No method, however, was foolproof; the mines continued to blow and slow things up.

But the doors of the British encirclement were gradually and inexorably swinging shut. As August of 1916 drew to a close, von Lettow's troop trains could run only twenty miles west of Morogoro as van Deventer stepped up the pace of his eastward drive. Smuts' columns were now less than ten miles north of Morogoro itself. Smuts was certain that von Lettow must make his last stand here. To abandon Morogoro would mean a great deal more than simply yielding up control of nearly half the Central Railway. South of the line sprawled more than 200,000 square miles of sterile wilderness. Virtually everything worth holding in German East Africa lay north of the railway. The fall of Morogoro would mean the end of effective German resistance in the colony.

From the British standpoint, the site of the final showdown could not have been more strategically advantageous. It was in fact the perfect cul-de-sac. Morogoro had no back door. Its southern outskirts lay directly beneath the mile-high Uluguru Mountains, which reared up almost vertically and did not seem even to trouble with foothills. While Smuts shattered the German front and right and van Deventer crashed in from the left, von Lettow would be forced to defend Morogoro with his back to a wall. After six months in which every British encircling movement had been eluded neatly—indeed, almost casually—Smuts was about to see his faith in maneuver vindicated in the grandest envelopment of all.

Von Lettow thought Smuts was out of his mind. He looked on the British commander's assumption that the Schutztruppe would fight without any avenue of retreat as "never altogether intelligible." With his own force hopelessly outnumbered, "it was surely madness to await at this place the junction of the hostile columns . . . and then fight with our back to the steep and rocky mountains." Von Lettow in fact was about to do what Smuts least expected.

Actually, "Slim Janie" was not totally blind to von Lettow's intentions. From Turiani, he had written his wife that von Lettow might choose to sacrifice Morogoro and the railway to keep the German force intact. Another hint of this had come when Kraut slipped through the narrowing gap between the two British armies, leading a large column across the railway almost within sight of van Deventer's advance patrols, and then vanishing into the blue to the southwest. Both Smuts and van Deventer, moreover, had already sent mounted brigades below the line to intercept another German detachment that was obviously making its way south into the Ulugurus. And the closer the British came to Morogoro, the clearer became the evidence of evacuation. Barely six miles from the town, wrote Cranworth, "we lay through the night . . . and heard the crashes and saw the flames as the Germans ran their engines and rolling stock from both sides of a destroyed bridge over a steep gorge." But despite all this, there appeared to be little doubt in Smuts' mind that the main body of von Lettow's force would defend Morogoro or be trapped there before it could escape encirclement. Either way, the only result must be the annihilation of the Schutztruppe.

Certainly it was touch and go whether von Lettow could get out in time. On August 25, with the dust of British columns rising in the north, orders were given to clear Morogoro in two hours. "Every bearer in the district was summoned by drum," wrote Nis Kock; "loads were handed out in all possible haste." But not in panic: "When all the bearers had got their loads . . . the endless length of the safari moved off, striking up one of the customary songs of the march . . .

> " 'Let all men stay home
> " 'Who are jealous of their wives . . .' "

Most of the loads were artillery shells and small-arms ammunition, but vast tonnages of ammunition also had to be left behind. They were not left intact, though, and if Smuts had not yet realized that Morogoro was being evacuated, he must surely have known that something was afoot when the town's main ammunition dump went up. "Never in my wildest imaginings had I conceived such violence of explosion," Kock recalled. "And it went on and on. . . . We lay pressed flat to the earth, as if under the heaviest shelling." The sacrifice of the munition stocks was painful and would be felt later, but the Germans had been given no other choice. "If the English should come now," said Kock, "they would not find much to capture."

Nor did they. On August 26, the 130th Baluchis and the 2nd Rhodesians marched into Morogoro at the head of Smuts' army. The tidy, sand-paved streets fronting the town's palm-shaded colonial bungalows were crowded with Africans in gaily printed cotton robes, but not an askari could be seen.

In the Bahnhof Hotel, officers found a sausage machine and a coin-in-the-slot piano plonking out *"Deutschland Über Alles,"* but they saw no German soldiers. The only sign of the enemy's presence inspired Cranworth to a play on words as he inspected an empty Schutztruppe barracks: "The troops had left under pressure and in a great hurry, but they had had time to issue their evacuation orders and on every piece of furniture was laid an exhibit of human excreta."

Smuts had been supremely confident that he would round up the German army at Morogoro. He had rounded up something else.

14

Hornblower Landlocked

WHILE SMUTS was consistently failing to pin the tail on the donkey of von Lettow's main force, Allied armies were not inactive on other East African fronts. In the summer of 1916, the offensive against the Germans' western territories was making visible if not spectacular progress. It had got off to a very slow start well over a year earlier, when Britannia launched a campaign to rule waves which rolled nearly a thousand miles from any ocean.

On a map, the Central African lakes appear deceptively tiny, not unlike a chain of puddles splashing unevenly north and south between the lower Sudan and upper Mozambique. But they are really fresh water seas. If their total area were combined into a single body of water, the state of Washington could be dropped in and sunk without a trace. Lake Victoria, the largest, could easily accommodate the islands of Sicily and Sardinia and still have ample room for long ocean voyages; a steamer trip between the Lake Victoria ports of Kisumu and Bukoba is half the distance between New York and Bermuda. Due not only to their size, and to their position as the natural inland frontiers of eastern Africa, but to their value in the swift movement of troops, domination of all the lakes was a central strategic objective of the German and Allied forces fighting for control of the entire western region.

On the lovely, four-hundred-mile-long Lake Nyasa, southernmost of the chain, the Royal Navy had little trouble gaining the upper hand, even though its 350-ton armed lake steamer *Gwendolen* and the German *Hermann von Wissmann* were more or less evenly matched. Neither vessel looked in the least warlike. Both in fact had been built to carry cargo and a few passengers, but their graceful, yachty hulls made even that role seem infra dig. In peacetime, their respective captains had made a practice of hoisting a few together whenever they happened to meet at the same port, but someone apparently forgot to tell *Wissmann's* skipper that there was a war on. On August 8, 1914, *Gwendolen* steamed into the harbor of Sphinxhaven at the northern end of the lake, found the German vessel on a slipway and put her out of commission with a few well-placed three-pound shells. "Gott for damn, Rhoades!" screamed the unhurt but dumfounded loser at the British captain. "Was you drunk?"

British mastery of Lake Victoria, farthest north, did not come quite so easily. During the early months of the war, a sizable fleet of moderately large British passenger and cargo vessels on the lake was thoroughly cowed by a single eighty-ton German tugboat. This was the *Muansa*, whose ambush of the East Africa Mounted Rifles has already been recorded. *Muansa* terrorized simply because for many weeks she was the only ship on Lake Victoria with guns (a pair of pom-poms) worth mentioning. Her very appearance on the horizon was enough to send all visible British craft scurrying for the safety of their nearest port, thus throwing troop and supply movements into considerable disarray. Obviously, something had to be done about *Muansa*.

In October 1914, four British lake steamers were hastily armed with a grab-bag of light guns, gathered from the sunken *Pegasus* and other real warships, and sent out to hunt down the raider. The squadron looked like the old Fall River Line going to war, and the chief result of the search was that the senior vessel, a six-hundred-ton dowager named *Sybil*, was abandoned after becoming stuck fast on an uncharted rock off German territory on the western shore. (Her captain's assertion that she had struck a mine was amended later by an inspecting officer who reported: "*Sybil* holed by an uncharted mine laid by Almighty 4,000 B.C.") *Muansa* was not even sighted. The Germans had devised a rudimentary but smoothly working system of signals—smoke by day, beacons by night, African coast watchers on duty at all times—which gave ample warning of the British "fleet's" approach. Until and unless *Muansa* was destroyed, she would be a miniature *Königsberg*.

It was not until early March 1915 that the British finally caught up with *Muansa*—when the steamers *Winifred* and *Kavirondo* literally trapped the tug by blocking both ends of a narrow channel between an island and the southern shore. Although outgunned, *Muansa* returned the British fire with spirit while making full steam for shallow water. But there was no escape, and the German skipper, anticipating Looff by four months, opened the tug's seacocks, sank her at a depth of nine feet and then made for shore with his crew. After their guns had transformed *Muansa* into a sieve, *Winifred* and *Kavirondo* turned around and steamed north, whereupon the Germans began salvaging the wreck. A few weeks later, *Muansa* was operational once more. Although she never mounted a gun again, she did continue to serve the German forces as a supply tow for more than a year. But with *Muansa's* teeth removed, British command of Lake Victoria was no longer in dispute.

The Germans, however, still controlled twelve thousand square miles of deep water between Lake Nyasa and Lake Victoria. This was the most important inland ocean of all.

Lake Tanganyika suggests a Norwegian fjord with a pituitary condition. Four hundred miles long, never wider than fifty miles, its shores are girdled by the almost sheer slopes of mountains rising to heights of six thousand feet and more. A steamer voyage on this lake offers scenic experiences surpassing in their majesty—seasoned with a certain amount of risk. The furious windstorms which often pounce down from the mountains without warning have long been known locally, and not altogether extravagantly, as typhoons. In the First World War, however, Lake Tanganyika's most conspicuous feature was strategic.

Even while the British War Office was imposing its defensive policies on its East African forces in 1915, the long-range Allied strategy called for a large-scale invasion of the German colony. Offensives were to be mounted not only in the Kilimanjaro area but also across the German border in the southwest and west, with British columns moving up from Rhodesia and Nyasaland while a Belgian army thrust eastward from the Congo. However, because of its central position in these theatres of operations, Lake Tanganyika loomed large as a roadblock against any British or Belgian drives. Large Schutztruppe detachments could be moved rapidly by steamer to either end of the lake to strike the invaders in their rear, slice their communications and reduce the pace of their advance—perhaps halt it in its tracks. During 1915, in fact, the lake was even being used as an avenue for minor raids against weakly held British and Belgian posts on the southern and western shores. So long as the Germans controlled Lake Tanganyika, they would hold the high cards on the western side of the arena.

Dislodging them would be difficult, perhaps impossible. With a strongly defended base at the port of Kigoma, Tanganyika was the only Central African lake on which the Germans had anything like real naval muscle. Their flagship, the brand-new fifteen-hundred-ton *Götzen*, did double duty. As a troop transport, she was capable of moving nine hundred fully equipped askaris between the northern and southern ends of the lake in two days. (It would take at least a fortnight to cover the same distance on land.) As an armed cruiser, *Götzen* commanded even more respect, especially after the summer of 1915, when a 4.1-inch *Königsberg* gun was mounted on her bow. No other inland warship packed so lethal a wallop.

Two smaller craft supported *Götzen* as vest-pocket destroyers. The 150-ton *Hedwig von Wissmann*, according to one German naval officer, "rolls in such a way that it is no pleasure to voyage in it," but the little steamer compensated for that shortcoming with the bite of two six-pounders which threw their shells more than two miles, and a Hotchkiss gun which discouraged stern chases. There was also the fifty-three-ton tugboat *Kingani*, sporting a six-pound gun which Max Looff had removed from the *City of Winchester* in the Gulf of Aden. Besides helping *Götzen* to hold Lake Tanganyika, both of the small craft were also well suited for hit-and-run raids on Allied ports.

British and Belgian naval forces on the lake had been disposed of with ease by this tiny flotilla. Late in August 1914, *Hedwig* had trapped the ninety-ton Belgian steamer *Alexandre Delcommune* and pelted her with steel for two hours; this put paid to the Belgian "navy." Polishing off the British fleet took even less effort. The Royal Navy on Lake Tanganyika consisted of two beached steamer hulls, without engines or boilers, lying all but forgotten on the south shore. To make certain that they would never become operational, *Hedwig* and *Kingani* steamed south late in 1914 and shelled them into rubbish. For the Germans, Lake Tanganyika had now become "*mare nostrum*"—or, more correctly, "*unser see*."

To the Allied high command, this was unthinkable, and in the spring of 1915, the British Admiralty found an opportunity to oust the Germans from Lake Tanganyika when a white hunter named John R. Lee approached Sir Henry Jackson, the First Sea Lord, with a plan that might have been concocted by Jules Verne.

At first glance, Lee's idea hardly seemed exciting or even original. He simply proposed that a small armed motorboat be launched on the lake to seek out and destroy the German squadron—exploiting the elements of surprise, speed and mobility. Jackson responded enthusiastically. It did not seem to matter that the only available route to the lake was three thousand miles overland, that it traversed five hundred miles of virtually unexplored bush country, forest and desert, without roads or even paths, that the boat must somehow be manhandled over a large range of mountains more than six thousand feet high. As far as Jackson was concerned, "it is both the duty and the tradition of the Royal Navy to engage the enemy wherever there is water to float a ship." His only major modification of the plan was to order two boats instead of one.

It was also decided that Lee should leave for Africa at once, to supervise advance preparations, and that overall charge of the expedition should be placed in the hands of a regular naval officer. This man, Lieutenant Commander Geoffrey B. Spicer-Simson, was a sort of Hornblower and Queeg rolled into one: simultaneously intrepid and hypercautious, almost pathologically jealous of his own authority and possessed of an inborn feel for the dramatic gesture. He sported a goatee, his body from the neck down was covered with garish tattoos of snakes, birds and butterflies, and he enjoyed embellishing accounts of his naval career with hair-curling episodes which he tended to believe.

In fact, Spicer-Simson's service record was rather drab, consisting almost exclusively of desk work. Early in the war he had been given command of a gunboat flotilla, but when one of these vessels was torpedoed at anchor, the Admiralty concluded that Spicer-Simson would serve his country better in an office than on a warship's bridge. And here, almost certainly, he would have spent the rest of his naval career, but for the fact that at one time he had carried out a survey on the Gambia River in West Africa. This gave the fickle Admiralty second thoughts when Spicer-Simson volunteered for the Lake Tanganyika expedition, which was duly placed in his charge along with a temporary promotion to commander. Spicer-Simson knew an opportunity when he saw one: so quixotic an adventure could carry him far in the navy. He meant to make the most of it.

Preparations were appropriately hush-hush: the Germans must not learn of the boats' overland approach; every member of the party took an oath of secrecy, whatever that may have been worth. Besides Spicer-Simson and Lee, there were seven reserve officers and ten enlisted men. Several had previous African experience, while the surgeon, Dr. H. M. Hanschell, had been commissioned from his post as Assistant Director of the London School of Tropical Medicine. No difficulty was encountered in finding the right boats: a pair of motor launches, recently completed at the Thornycroft yards on the Thames, seemed just right for the operation. They had been built as tenders for the Greek Air Force but the Admiralty gave Lake Tanganyika priority and commandeered them.

Each was forty feet long, with twin screws and two 100-hp. engines which drove it ahead at a very good nineteen knots—much faster than anything the Germans had on the lake. Conversion for combat was simple enough: each launch had a three-pound gun mounted forward and a Maxim aft, while the gasoline tanks were protected against rifle and machine gun fire by steel plating. Thornycroft built special rubber-tired trailers to carry the boats overland and also furnished a big lorry for the party's supplies. Traction engines to haul the trailers would be obtained in Africa.

On June 8, 1915, the launches had their shakedown cruise—complete with engine trials and test firing—on the Thames. When the three-pounders were tried out, the first shot saw one of the guns and its gun layer hurled into the river: someone had forgotten to secure the weapon's locking ring. It was also discovered that the guns could fire only dead ahead, as the deck planking was not strong enough to take the strain of lateral recoil. But this problem was canceled out by the boats' impressive speed and maneuverability.

Less simple was the business of naming the craft. Spicer-Simson christened them *Dog* and *Cat*, which shocked the Admiralty, although one might have expected no reaction from a board which sanctioned names like *Salamander* and *Pickle*. Spicer-Simson therefore put his inventiveness to work and came up with *Mimi* and *Toutou*—which for some reason scandalized his officers and men. But the names stood, and on June 15, 1915, *Mimi*, *Toutou* and the members of the expedition boarded a Union Castle liner bound for Capetown and the first leg of the journey halfway across Africa.

All was bustle and efficiency when the party reached Capetown on July 2. The boats were hoisted immediately on to the goods wagons of a special train that would carry them north to Elisabethville, capital of the Belgian Congo's Katanga province. The twenty-five-hundred-mile rail journey was without incident, the crew riding comfortably in a passenger coach and standing alternate watches on the tarpaulins which covered the boats, to put out any fires that might be started by embers from the wood-burning locomotive. Arriving at Elisabethville on July 26, Spicer-Simson took the opportunity to have Lee sent back to Capetown, after examining charges that the man who conceived the expedition had failed to prepare the route properly, violated security and got drunk. None of the accusations (except possibly the last) had any basis in fact.

The next stop was a village called Fungurume, about 140 miles to the northwest and 4,200 feet above sea level. It was also the end of the railway line and the beginning of the expedition's real work. Arrangements had been made here for teams of oxen to help the supply lorry and the traction engines move boats and stores through the bush, while four hundred African laborers had been contracted to hack out a path of sorts, build bridges and otherwise clear the way. On August 6, after being lifted by crane from the goods wagons to their trailers, *Mimi* and *Toutou* were ready to roll.

But the traction engines and the oxen were not; they had yet to arrive and there was no sign of them. Spicer-Simson therefore ordered the supply lorry to take the boats in tow. With the entire British party pushing, the four hundred Africans pulling and everyone shouting or complying with contradictory orders, the lorry managed to move *Toutou* forward about five hundred feet. Next day *Mimi* was brought alongside and the lorry dragged *Toutou* another five hundred feet ahead—to the first of the 150 shaky wooden bridges that had been built for the expedition. Then both trailers began to buckle. Repairs took several days, but were completed just as a train arrived at Fungurume with the two traction engines.

These ungainly machines were really miniature wood-burning locomotives. Each weighed about ten tons, raised a terrible snorting and clanking din, vomited asphyxiating clouds of dense black smoke from its pipestem smokestack, and could cover nearly one hundred miles a day on good roads. Spicer-Simson and his men were prepared to accept less than one-tenth that daily average. At dawn on August 18, with the noisy traction engines in the van, the ponderous cavalcade began to rumble across the bridge.

Halfway over, everything banged and shuddered to a halt when one of the bridge's supporting beams gave way under the weight of the leading engine, which leaned over precariously and threatened to plunge into the river below, taking *Mimi* with it. After much yelling in Bantu and Anglo-Saxon, launch and engine were dragged back to safety by the first engine. Now time had to be called for the building of a stronger bridge. This took nearly half a day, but it allowed *Mimi* to be towed across without difficulty. Then the slope on the opposite bank proved too much for *Mimi's* traction engine. There was nothing for it but to build a third bridge further upstream, permitting the second engine to cross with *Toutou*, then return to haul *Mimi* and the first engine up the bank. Toward the end of the afternoon, the expedition had advanced a full quarter of a mile. And only 149 more bridges remained to be crossed.

In the next ten days, the caravan lumbered thirty miles forward through crackling bush and leafless forest. The country was almost bone-dry, and the lorry had to move out far in advance to find water for men and machines. The traction engines continually lost their grip in the dust that lay on the ground in thick greasy layers; bundles of faggots were placed beneath the wheels to give them purchase. Engines and trailers lurched as if in a heavy sea, threatening to snap rudders and propellers against boulders or the lower limbs of trees. The sun was so hot that the launches' bottoms were filled with precious drinking water to keep the seams from opening up. On August 28, when the party reached a small village called Mwenda Makosi (meaning roughly "the end of bad luck"), the trailers fell to pieces. They were now beyond repair, so the big carts which carried fuel for the traction engines had to take their place. This meant replacing the wheels, which in turn meant a week's delay some hundred miles or so south of the middle of no-where.

On September 3, the expedition ground into gear again. It had now been joined by the ox teams—forty-eight beasts pulling three wagons—and an escort of Belgian askaris. (The latter had been furnished partly as protec-tion, partly because the Belgians worried that Spicer-Simson might decide to annex Katanga.) The procession stretched out for three miles, raising a column of white dust nearly the same height. An even larger cloud came close to wiping out wagons, men and boats when a grass fire swept down on them without warning—only to veer off at the last minute with a shift in the wind as the flames roared less than two hundred yards from the nearest traction engine.

On September 4, there was a stop at a small cluster of huts called Mobile Kabantu (Two People) at the edge of a nearly dry river bed. Here, one of the party had spent the previous week supervising construction of the big-gest bridge the launches must cross. It was 108 feet long and 32 feet high and 500 tons of timber, covering two square miles, had been felled to build it. *Mimi* was towed across first and then up a gentle incline on the opposite bank. Near the crest, the tow cable parted and *Mimi's* improvised trailer took her on a roller-coaster dive back into the bridge, where it crashed to a splintering stop with its front wheels suspended well over the river. A new cable finally got launch and trailer back across. *Toutou* followed and the men breathed easily once more.

Not for long. Barely a mile ahead loomed the upper escarpments of the six-thousand-foot Mitumba mountain range. By climbers' standards the slopes did not intimidate, but they promised to be a sheer wall for the traction engines. The drivers began working up colossal heads of steam in the engines' boilers, all the while staring glumly at the mountain crest and shaking their heads. They knew their machines' limitations.

These became evident as soon as the first traction engine grunted a few yards uphill with *Mimi* and then wheezed to a halt. The second engine was brought up and coupled to the first, but the gradient proved too much even for the pair. Finally, with both engines, 32 oxen and 420 men straining on cables, chains and tow-ropes, *Mimi* began to inch upwards. A few hundred yards were conquered before muscles, lungs and engines gave out entirely. The ascent had to be abandoned for the day.

Next morning a new lifting technique was tried out. One end of a block and tackle was rigged to *Mimi's* trailer, the other to a tree trunk about fifty yards up the slope, and the free end of the rope was fastened to the oxen's draw chain. Now the oxen pulled downhill and *Mimi* crept slowly up toward the tree. The block and tackle was then rigged to another tree farther up the escarpment and the process was repeated all day. By sundown, *Mimi* had been dragged over the hump. The same method brought *Toutou* alongside *Mimi* the next day. Now all that remained was to get down again.

The descent proved much stiffer than the climb. Even in reverse gear and with brakes clamped down tight, *Mimi's* traction engine gathered momentum quickly, snapped the towline and went careening down the escarpment until a tree brought it up short in a noisy shower of splinters and metal fittings. The men spent the rest of the day blaspheming, sweating and hauling their stubborn contraption upright. This done, they turned back to the more reliable block and tackle. Tree by tree, the boats were gradually lowered onto the valley floor.

It was now mid-September. Since leaving railhead at Fungurume a month earlier, the expedition had covered ninety miles—about three miles a day. Spicer-Simson had never expected to make such good time.

Traversing the valley floor made the mountain look easy. The caravan staggered along a sun-drilled moonscape of alternating baked earth and soft sand, furrowed by ravines and gullies so deep that the block and tackle rigs were in continual use. Ant-bear holes proliferated, trapping engine and trailer wheels for hours at a time. Daily progress was sometimes measured in yards rather than miles. The heat shriveled everything. The oxen lived on scraps of sun-cracked grass; the men were permitted a few tablespoons of water daily, since the traction engine boilers had first call on the scanty water supply. This consisited of sandy moisture scooped from the ground; the boilers soon became ulcerated with silt. One day the engines simply stopped running. Only the lucky discovery of a fresh stream nearby kept the Lake Tanganyika naval expedition from foundering in a desert, five hundred miles from its destination.

At last, on September 22, the wanderers came out of the wilderness at the village of Sankisia. This was the southern terminus of a fifteen-mile narrow-gauge railway that would take the boats to the "port" of Bukama on the Lualaba River—really the uppermost waters of the Congo. At Bukama, a shallow-draft steamer waited to carry the party three hundred miles downstream to Kabalo, the railhead of another line running directly to Lake Tanganyika. The worst was over.

Or so Spicer-Simson thought, until he arrived at Bukama, where he found an empty wharf. The river was too low for the steamer, which lay at anchor fifty miles downstream. The launches would have to risk the Lualaba's snags under their own power. But the water proved too shallow even for their few inches of draft, so they were raised on empty gasoline drums and poled downstream by teams of African paddlers. In twelve miles they ran aground fourteen times. Frequently they had to be portaged for hundreds of yards before enough water could be found to float them. At length, the river became slightly deeper and very swampy—and so thick with clouds of tsetse flies that at one point the gasoline drums were removed and the party took its chances with sandbars by running the engines to escape.

After four days, the steamer was sighted. Getting the launches aboard took four more days. Then the steamer ran aground and could not be floated. Eventually a stern-wheeler of lesser draft came up-river and the boats were laboriously transferred. It was not until October 22 that they reached Kabalo, where a steam crane swung them on to goods wagons for the final two hundred miles to the lake.

Even this last lap had its moments. The narrow-gauge railway line crossed a series of frail wooden trestles and the Belgian engine driver refused to take both launches in a single train. Two trips had to be made. But on October 26, four and a half months after leaving England, Spicer-Simson at last gazed out over the choppy waters of Lake Tanganyika. The occasion called for a formal parade. As the men stood to attention, Spicer-Simson hoisted a vice admiral's flag. He had made it during the journey.

Lukuja, where the expedition made temporary headquarters, was the Belgians' principal naval base on the western shore of the lake. Since *Alexandre Delcommune* had been put out of action, the Belgian fleet had consisted of a self-propelled ten-ton river barge named *Ten Ton*, which mounted a 47- and a 57-mm. gun but could turtle along at no more than six knots. There were also two auxiliary craft: *Netta*, a little speedboat with a machine gun, and an open motor launch, generally known as "Vedette," which was used mainly for patrols. The men of this squadron took their orders from Lukuja's Belgian commandant, an army major who refused to acknowledge Spicer-Simson's superior rank. None of the Belgians, in fact, quite knew what to make of Spicer-Simson, who had now taken to wearing a skirt which his wife had designed for him and which won him the amused sobriquet,

"Le Commandant à la Jupe." But despite this eccentricity and numerous squabbles with the Belgians over the proposed site of an artificial harbor for *Mimi* and *Toutou*, friction was kept to a minimum and work on the British base soon began.

Spicer-Simson chose the mouth of a small river called the Kalemie, about two miles south of Lukuja. The launches would be protected here by a breakwater made of stones from a nearby quarry, and the entire British force—including its commander—pitched in to assist several hundred African workmen move the stones. Everyone toiled a fourteen-hour day. There was no rest, the only diversion, aside from Spicer-Simson's costume, being provided by a baby chimpanzee mascot named Josephine, who took her meals with the men and stood to attention during morning parade. By mid-December, the harbor had been completed.

All this while, the work on the western shore had been under covert enemy observation—although, oddly enough, Belgian rather than British activities were the point of focus. While the Germans did know of Spicer-Simson's expedition (a secret like that could hardly remain under wraps indefinitely), they were completely unaware that the party was dragging a pair of armed fighting ships across Africa, and might not have believed this anyway unless they saw the craft—which by now were too well hidden in the undergrowth to be detected. What excited their interest was not Kalemie but Lukuja, where well-founded rumor had it that the Belgians had started building a new warship to replace *Alexandre Delcommune,* and Lieutenant Commander Gustav Zimmer, the senior German naval officer on the lake, sought specific data on the vessel.

In the autumn of 1915, therefore, Zimmer sent *Hedwig's* commander, Lieutenant Job Odebrecht, on a night mission to learn what he could. Odebrecht sailed south from Kigoma, waited for darkness and brought *Hedwig* as close to Lukuja harbor as he dared. He then boarded a dinghy and rowed in even closer until he came to what was obviously a shipyard—big enough for a vessel 250 feet long, larger even that *Götzen.* Although no ship could be seen, the yard itself sufficed at least to corroborate the rumors. Zimmer ordered further surveillance.

Now begun a series of daring probes by Odebrecht and *Kingani's* skipper, Lieutenant Rosenthal. Night after night, the two men took turns stealing within range of Lukuja's harbor defense guns under cover of darkness. Disguising themselves as Africans with burnt cork and long blankets, they went ashore and sometimes even managed to walk past Belgian picket lines unchallenged. They learned little, however, until one night at the end of November when Rosenthal captured a small patrol skiff manned by Belgian askaris who told him that the vessel was already under construction in the yard. Rosenthal decided to take its picture. Toward dawn on December 1, he brought *Kingani* to within two hundred yards of Lukuja and made several time exposures of the construction while Belgian shore defense guns banged away at him vainly in the dim light. The latter also spoiled the photographs.

Rosenthal therefore made his boldest move. The following night he returned to Lukuja for a personal closeup look. After swimming ashore through a heavy surf which kept the crocodiles away, he sprinted for the shipyard—only to be frustrated at the approach of a sentry. But he was back again the next night, and this time he made it all the way to the yard. No large vessel was there, but the two armed launches were, having just been taken from their concealment preparatory to launching.

They were enough for Rosenthal. He plunged back into the lake and swam out to *Kingani*. She was gone; Rosenthal had been given up for lost. There was nothing he could do but swim back to shore, where he was soon captured by a Belgian askari patrol. The Belgians allowed him to inform Zimmer of his POW status and nothing else, but on the back of the letter Rosenthal wrote an invisible message in his own urine, warning Zimmer of the British motor launches.

The letter reached Kigoma two months later. If it had arrived before Christmas, the battle for Lake Tanganyika might have had a different outcome.

Toward the end of December, *Mimi* and *Toutou* were launched, sliding one hundred yards out into the harbor on specially laid tracks. On Christmas Eve, they made their first trials on the lake. This time the guns were fired without mishap. It was just as well. Early in the morning of Sunday, December 26, after a quiet and somewhat cheerless Christmas, Spicer-Simson was awakened by a Belgian officer who told him that lookouts, some twenty miles to the north, had sighted a German warship approaching.

Spicer-Simson acknowledged the news without visible interest. At 9:30, all hands fell in for church parade. Spicer-Simson read the service, then ordered his chief petty officer to dismiss, adding, almost as an afterthought, "and man the launches for immediate action." Hornblower and Drake together could not have handled it with more aplomb.

By now, the German vessel had been identified as *Kingani*, steaming southward from Kigoma at at an easy cruising speed of five knots. Spicer-Simson waited for her to pass Kalemie so that his own craft could cut off her retreat to the north. Since it was known that *Kingani's* single six-pounder was mounted forward and could only fire over her bow, a stern chase was planned, with *Toutou* and *Mimi* attacking from port and starboard quarters respectively. Shortly after ten o'clock, the Allied naval "force" weighed anchor and headed for open water in line-ahead formation. *Ten Ton* was in the lead, followed by Spicer-Simson aboard *Mimi*, then by *Toutou*, *Netta* and "Vedette" in that order. The procession was cheered by several hundred Africans who lined the bluffs above Kalemie as if they were spectators at a football match. The sky was cloudless and the calm waters of the lake sparkled gently in the morning sun. It was a perfect day to watch anything.

In a few minutes, *Ten Ton* was overhauled and left far astern. *Mimi* and *Toutou*, now sailing abreast, rapidly closed with *Kingani*. Lieutenant Jung, the new German captain, did not realize that he was being pursued until about 11:30, when it was too late. He now swung ninety degrees to port, brought *Kingani* to her full speed of seven knots and opened fire on *Mimi*, the closest of the two attackers.

At this point, both launches were outranged by *Kingani's* six-pounder and *Mimi* could only duck and weave as the shells tore up the water all about her. Spicer-Simson appeared oblivious to the German fire. With a long cigarette holder protruding from his jaws at a jaunty angle, a pair of binoculars glued to his eyes, he stood erect in *Mimi's* bow, a completely exposed target for *Kingani's* gunner. By now, the wind had picked up and all three vessels had begun to leap wildly in a short, steep chop. *Kingani* had continued her wide swing to port, and the change of course presently brought her six-pounder to bear on *Toutou*, while rifles and machine guns threw the water around *Mimi* into a boiling lather. By about 11:40, however, *Kingani* was heading almost due north and her gun could no longer bear on either of the British craft. At 11:47, the launches came to within two thousand yards of the German and their three-pounders commenced barking. *Kingani's* number was up.

But now, Spicer-Simson began to lose his cool, shouting incoherent firing orders to his gunner and wigwagging indecipherable arm signals at *Toutou*. All of this, along with the increasingly heavy seas, did not improve marksmanship aboard either boat. For ten minutes, three-pound shells screamed continually around *Kingani*. One or two seemed to strike the ship. None stopped her.

Then, suddenly, a ripping explosion, accompanied by a gout of crimson flame and oily black smoke, burst from *Kingani's* forward deck. Immediately she went out of control, wallowing clumsily as she lay broadside to the seas. Down went the German colors. Someone on deck was seen waving a white handkerchief. Almost beside himself with jubilation, Spicer-Simson ordered *Mimi* alongside. In that weather it was not a prudent move. *Mimi* rammed *Kingani* head-on, throwing Spicer-Simson to the deck, and then began to sink. She was brought into Kalemie and run ashore only minutes before foundering.

Kingani followed, limping into Kalemie under *Toutou's* escort. The German ship was also sinking. A three-pound shell had drilled a jagged hole in her port side below the waterline. On deck, the British boarding party found a butcher shop, littered with the meat of the two sailors who had caught the full force of the explosion. The entire forward part of the ship was drenched in blood. The dead Lieutenant Jung leaned grotesquely over the gun shield, his thigh gouged away at the hip. *Kingani* gave a slow lurch and the corpse tipped over gently toward the deck, as if making a bow. A British petty officer fainted.

One down, two to go.

The dead Germans were buried that night, and a guard of British naval ratings was posted over the graves to keep Belgian askaris from digging up the corpses and eating them. Next morning, two British seamen visited Dr. Hanschell to get a preservative for small bottles of blood clots which they were keeping as souvenirs of the battle. They had taken the blood, along with half a finger, from Lieutenant Jung's cadaver. Spicer-Simson also had a memento of the action; he wore the dead German skipper's ring.

Spicer-Simson was now a hero. The local African population even looked on him as a demigod. Magical significance was attached to the tattooed bestiary covering his torso, and he became known as *Bwana Chifunga Tumbo*, Lord and Master of the Loincloth—to the great discomfiture of a Belgian missionary who saw his evangelizing labors going down the drain. Spicer-Simson did not object. But he was naturally more pleased with England's reaction to the victory. The Admiralty lost no time in confirming his permanent promotion to commander, and even Buckingham Palace took note of the feat, in a telegram offering "His Majesty's congratulations to his remotest expedition." At long last, Spicer-Simson was winning the recognition which had eluded him throughout his career.

The victory also gained the expedition a new member, when *Kingani's* African stoker, Fundi, begged his captors not to turn him over to the Belgians—far more dreaded than Germans for their treatment of blacks—as a prisoner of war. Always glad to put one over on his allies, Spicer-Simson had Fundi enrolled as a Royal Navy stoker. *Kingani* joined the fleet too. With the hole in her side patched up and a twelve-pound quick-firing gun mounted in her bow, she became H.M.S. *Fifi*. On her maiden cruise under the White Ensign she was fired on by British and Belgian shore batteries along the south coast. No one had been told of the transfer.

For more than six weeks, the squadron lay inactive as "typhoons" flayed Kalemie and kept all hands busy repairing the ships which were torn, one by one, from their moorings and driven ashore. On at least two occasions it was impossible to go out and fight the second German warship, *Hedwig*, as she steamed past during abbreviated periods of calm weather, searching for survivors of *Kingani*—which was still believed to have been sunk by Belgian shore guns. But on the morning of February 9, 1916, only *Toutou* remained out of commission when spotters reported *Hedwig* approaching once more from the north.

Spicer-Simson again reacted with a show of imperturbability, ordering the crews to breakfast and, oh yes, action stations. He also made swift plans for the engagement. They were simple enough. Instead of waiting for *Hedwig* to get south of Kalemie so that he could cut off her retreat, he would close with her straightaway. *Fifi's* new twelve-pounder should make matchwood of her ex-sister in short order.

At 7:45 A.M., the Anglo-Belgian flotilla left the harbor. Spicer-Simson had command of *Fifi* in the lead, followed by *Mimi* under Sub-Lieutenant A. E. Wainwright, with *Ten Ton* and "Vedette" panting along astern. Once again the weather was tranquil, but unnaturally so. The sun peered faintly through a gray membrane of haze, creating a curious optical effect that made it almost impossible to distinguish the sky from the glassy surface of the lake. As *Fifi* and *Mimi* left the Belgian craft in their wake and moved in on *Hedwig*, the spectators on the banks saw a sight that challenged their reason. The two British vessels and their quarry, each magnified about ten times actual size, were suspended motionless a thousand feet up in the air.

This phenomenon may have fooled *Hedwig's* captain, for he continued on his course even with the British in sight. It was not until 9:30, when *Fifi* and *Mimi* were only six miles away, that he saw them. Instantly, *Hedwig* swung to port and began churning northward at her flanking speed of eight knots. Spicer-Simson, who had been cruising at half-speed to conserve the wood-burning *Fifi's* fuel, now ordered full steam up and gave chase, instructing Wainwright to hold *Mimi* on station just astern. *Fifi* was known to have a one-knot edge over *Hedwig*: the German should come within range in half an hour.

She did. At ten o'clock sharp, Spicer-Simson gave the order to commence firing. His gunner saw only a shimmering object dangling just above the horizon, but he took aim at it and jerked the twelve-pounder's lanyard. The gun crashed out and *Fifi* stopped dead in her tracks with the recoil. Before she could gather way again, *Hedwig* had picked up a few hundred yards. The chase continued, now at a shuffling gait. *Fifi* kept flinging shells at *Hedwig*, but the mirage on the horizon spoiled the gunner's aim, while the braking effect of the recoil from every shot helped widen the distance between the two ships. By now, both Fundi and *Hedwig's* stoker were pouring oil on their firewood to increase speed, but the absence of any wind failed to give *Fifi*, at least, the draft she needed in her stack. Her boiler pressure dropped steadily—although the engine room had become a cremation chamber and the heat in the smokestack was so intense that the man at the wheel had to be relieved every five minutes. And all the while, *Hedwig* was getting away.

Then, without warning, *Mimi* thundered past, her gasoline engines wide open. Almost hysterically, Spicer-Simson tried to wave her back to her station. Wainwright ignored the hand signals, drove down to within three thousand yards of *Hedwig* and let go with his three-pounder. The German could not return the fire: bringing to bear the brace of six-pound guns in her bow would mean changing course and losing ground. All she could do was reply with the Hotchkiss on her after deck. It was well outranged. *Mimi's* shells howled past, each one bursting closer to the target.

One finally struck. *Hedwig* swung sharply to port and both the six-pounders roared as *Mimi* veered off to starboard. Again *Hedwig* changed course and fired. Again *Mimi* sidestepped. For thirty minutes, the cat-and-mouse game went on, the more maneuverable British vessel easily evading the German salvoes and occasionally scoring a hit. The damage appeared slight but this did not matter. Wainwright was buying time for Spicer-Simson to get back into action.

But as *Fifi* began to close the gap again, the lake's optical aberration continued to confound her gunner, and the twelve-pound shells consistently landed far beyond *Hedwig*. Noting this, Wainwright turned back to inform Spicer-Simson, who let loose a broadside of curses—at Wainwright for disobeying orders, at the lake for spoiling his aim. *Fifi's* ammunition was now down to three shells. If they failed to stop *Hedwig*, the German would be free to fight again and Spicer-Simson's hard-won hero image would be badly tarnished.

The first shot jammed. *Fifi's* crew had to sweat for twenty minutes before they dared open the breech and gingerly toss the shell overboard. With two rounds remaining, the next landed squarely. *Hedwig* reeled as the explosion tore her side open. In a blanket of smoke and flames, she turned slowly to starboard and her bow began settling in the water. A few sailors could be seen leaping over the side; others lowered the shell-pocked ship's boat which promptly sank.

Fifi hastened to pick up the survivors, who were dumbfounded to find themselves aboard the old *Kingani*. The German prisoners also had a last look at the vessel which had just been destroyed by her sister. At 11:15, an hour and a quarter after the action had begun, an immense bubble erupted from *Hedwig's* engine room, her stern lifted almost vertically, hung motionless for a few seconds, then vanished without a sound beneath the waters of the lake.

Two down, one to go.

Having won demigod status among the local Africans for his earlier victory over Kingani, Spicer-Simson now found himself promoted to full deity. When he came ashore after sinking *Hedwig*, tribesmen met him on the beach and poured sand over his head to signify that the land belonged to him—a gesture which the Belgians could not have applauded. Small, squat clay figurines—each complete with skirt, tattoos, goatee, sun helmet and binoculars—begun appearing in villages along the lake shore. The Belgian missionary despaired. Spicer-Simson took it in stride and awaited further homage from his own government. It was not long in coming: the Distinguished Service Order.

Others in the party were also decorated. Wainwright, whose disobedience had been conveniently forgotten, received the Distinguished Service Cross, while *Fifi's* two engine room artificers, Lamont and Berry, got the Distinguished Service Medal. Lamont did not seem to think this was enough. He went into the workshop at Kalemie and struck another medal. On one side was engraved the inscription: "H.M.S. *Fifi,* 9 February, 1916." The other side read "Fundi, R.N." The medal was hung round Fundi's neck at a formal parade, while all officers and men stood to attention.

One of the German prisoners was *Hedwig's* captain, the daring Lieutenant Odebrecht. He felt that he had been disgraced in having lost his ship to amateur sailors—as he regarded reserve officers—but his self-respect returned when he learned of Spicer-Simson's regular navy commission. He also became talkative, telling Spicer-Simson that the Germans were still completely in the dark as to the presence of Royal Navy warships on Lake Tanganyika. While aware of the expedition itself, they had no idea of its purpose—although one of their African spies had reported that a railway bridge was being built across the lake when he first saw the tracks which had launched the motorboats in December.

But the Germans' continuing ignorance could mean only one thing: their dreadnought, *Götzen*, must search for survivors of *Hedwig* along the Belgian coastline. Spicer-Simson's third—and biggest—opportunity should not be far off.

It arrived, in fact, much sooner than he expected. On the very morning after *Hedwig* had been sunk, *Götzen* steamed into plain sight barely two miles off Kalemie. Eagerly, the men awaited the now familiar casual order to battle stations. The order did not come. The men looked at each other. One officer went up to Spicer-Simson and asked if they were going to fight. Spicer-Simson shook his head. The officer started to plead with him. Spicer-Simson cut the man off. What had happened to Hornblower?

Shortly after this, Spicer-Simson announced that he was going down the Congo River to pick up another vessel which would augment his squadron. The idea made little sense. Not only were all three British craft back in commission but the Belgians had repaired and rechristened *Alexandre Delcommune* (now the *Vengeur*), and were completing a fifteen-hundred-ton armed steamer named *Baron Dhanis*. Even *Götzen's Königsberg* gun would be no match for the combined metal and speed of these five little warships. But Spicer-Simson went off all the same, leaving Wainwright in command with explicit orders not to fight *Götzen* unless she actually attacked Kalemie. He stayed away eleven weeks. *Götzen* reappeared twice and did not attack. Wainwright obeyed orders. The expedition's morale began to sag.

During Spicer-Simson's absence, Kalemie came in for much attention. The British offensive on the Kilimanjaro front had already begun, and the Allied high command in East Africa was now ready to launch the long-hoped-for drive against the Germans' western borders. General Tombeur, commanding the Belgian forces in the Congo, was pressing his own commandant at Lukuja for action on Lake Tanganyika. But that officer could do nothing without Spicer-Simson's fast launches, which in effect had been ordered out of the war.

In mid-May, when Spicer-Simson returned to Kalemie—without a boat—he did little to ease the situation, becoming embroiled almost at once in a complex and acrimonious dispute with the Belgian commandant over strategy and final authority. Toward the end of the month, however, the confusion began to dissipate when Spicer-Simson received orders to support a British advance on Bismarckburg, the principal German base on the south shore. The squadron was to proceed to that port and cut off any possible German withdrawal by ship.

At dawn on June 5, the squadron stood off Bismarckburg. There was no sign of British or German troops. But a massive white fort overlooked the town, and five large dhows could be seen inside the harbor. Since the dhows were used by the Germans as troop and supply transports, Spicer-Simson's obvious move was to go in and sink them before the British land attack was launched. But he held back, declaring that the guns in the fort were far too powerful for his trio of cockleshells. One officer volunteered to dash in with *Toutou* and destroy the dhows before the batteries could find the range. Spicer-Simson refused to let him go. The squadron weighed anchor and made for the port of Kituta, about twenty miles to the south.

Arriving there, Spicer-Simson found new orders. He was to return to Bismarckburg forthwith. The British advance had finally begun, and the squadron was counted on to block any German getaway by ship. Spicer-Simson waited four days before leaving Kituta.

On June 9, when the ships approached Bismarckburg for the second time, a Union Jack was seen flying over the fort. The town had been taken without a shot being fired in its defense. No Germans had been there to man the guns: the entire garrison had boarded the dhows and cleared out while the British squadron was dawdling in Kituta. Spicer-Simson now went ashore to explain his absence to the commander of the British column. Having no explanation, he therefore submitted to an almost apoplectic tongue-lashing. In its own small way, his firm irresolution had duplicated General Stewart's earlier failure to net a larger German force beneath Kilimanjaro.

No one could put Spicer-Simson's behavior down to physical cowardice: in two consecutive hard-fought actions he had demonstrated just the reverse. But for this very reason he had probably become afraid. By beating the Germans twice, he had finally won the Admiralty's favor and and salvaged a career which had previously seemed headed for a dead end. It was not altogether unnatural that he should suddenly become reluctant to jeopardize his long-sought professional security. What would happen if for some reason he should fail to sink or capture *Götzen*? How would the Lords of the Admiralty react should a naval assault on Bismarckburg miscarry? Two victories in a row seemed, to Spicer-Simson, quite enough to keep him safe in the navy's good graces and out of any further desk assignments.

And that was where his reasoning went astray. By not even trying, he had committed an offense almost on a par with poltroonery.

After the Bismarckburg fiasco, Spicer-Simson seemed to lose interest in the campaign. He welcomed Dr. Hanschell's recommendation that he be invalided home on grounds of physical exhaustion, and the British command in East Africa appeared just as eager to see the last of him. This did not quite end his troubles, however. Back in England, he found himself in even hotter water over his conduct during the quarrel with the Belgians at Lukuja. Only Hanschell's medical report saved him from a fate worse than a desk— which was where the Admiralty finally reassigned thim.

As for *Götzen*, the Allies eventually went after her from the air. In mid-June, Belgian planes carried out a raid on Kigoma and reported the German warship destroyed by bombs. She was not, but shortly afterwards she had her teeth pulled when von Lettow ordered the *Königsberg* gun removed and railed down to the main fighting front. At the end of July, General Tombeur's forces entered Kigoma and saw *Götzen's* masts protruding from the water just outside the harbor. The Germans had scuttled the ship, first taking care to oil all her machinery with a view to raising her after the war. *Götzen* eventually did go back into service, sailing up and down Lake Tanganyika for forty years as the British passenger steamer *Liemba*. She continues to ply the same waters today under the Tanzanian flag.

And in the long run, Spicer-Simson had the last laugh on the Admiralty. His sense of the dramatic never deserted him, nor did a press and public with an unquenchable thirst for heroes. And a hero was what he soon became. It could hardly have been otherwise, with such headlines as "Nelson Touch on African Lake," "The Jules Verne Expedition," "Commander Spicer-Simson's Exploits on Lake Tanganyika," "The Hero of the Gunboats." This sort of thing did no harm in greasing the skids for eventual promotion to captain. And even twenty years later, Spicer-Simson's feat had not been entirely forgotten. It sparked the idea for a book called *The African Queen*.

15

Sidetracks

WHATEVER ERRORS OF JUDGMENT may have been committed by Spicer-Simson in his Lake Tanganyika adventure, there could be no denying that the British speedboat squadron had done basically what it set out to do. Even with *Götzen* still afloat, the capture of *Kingani* and the sinking of *Hedwig* had broken the German grip on the lake. By the spring of 1916 the path had been cleared, at long last, for both the Anglo-Belgian drive from the west and Brigadier General Edward Northey's British advance in the southwest.

At times, however, the Anglo-Belgian offensive seemed to be less a military than a political campaign. It was hardly a secret that Belgium wished to annex the Germans' western provinces of Ruanda and Urundi to the Congo on which they bordered, that the whole eastern shore of Lake Tanganyika and a huge tract of country running south from Lake Victoria to Tabora were also being eyed by Brussels. At the very least, this potential Belgian real estate might prove useful as a bargaining chip in some future peace negotiations. Certainly the commander of the eleven-thousand-man Belgian army in the Congo, General Tombeur, was no stranger to the dynamics of empire, having previously been governor of the Congo's Katanga province.

But Belgium's British allies, as managers of the most massive imperial institution ever known to man, were not necessarily going to applaud their partner's designs on territory that might just as easily come under the Union Jack. Perhaps for this reason, Smuts' choice to lead the nineteen hundred troops of the British Lake Force—which was to advance in tandem with the Belgians after moving south from Lake Victoria—was Brigadier General Sir Charles Crewe, better known in South Africa as a politician than as a soldier. Not surprisingly, Crewe and Tombeur never really hit it off, and the entire western offensive was conspicuous for bickering, petty jealousy and

Lull before the storm: von
Lettow (second from right)
relaxes with friends at Moshi,
early 1914. (*Imperial War
Museum*)

The tribal irregulars known as *ruga-ruga* were valuable adjuncts to Schutztruppe field units. (*Bilderdienst Süddeutscher Verlag*)

A contigent of East Africa Mounted Rifles marches down Government Road, Nairobi, 1914. (*Radio Times Hulton Picture Library*)

German troops display a Union Jack hauled down after the recapture of the Deutscher Kaiser Hotel, Tanga, November 4, 1914. (*Bundesarchiv Koblenz*)

Creeping in for the kill:
H.M.S. *Severn* makes her
way up the Rufiji delta
prior to an attack on
Königsberg, July 6, 1915.
(*Imperial War Museum*)

British officers, captured at Tanga, conceal their faces from a German photograper. (*Ullstein Verlag*)

"Manowari na Bomba Tatu": S.M.S. *Königsberg*.
(*Bundesarchiv Koblenz*)

Loof surveys damage to his ship after the first attack on July 6, 1915. (*Ullstein Verlag*)

Königsberg's corpse. (*Bundesarchiv Koblenz*)

A Schutztruppe patrol sets off for a raid on the Uganda Railway, 1915. (*Ullstein Verlag*)

Smuts. (*Ullstein Verlag*)

Meinerzhagen as KAR officer, 1906.
(*Dr. Theresa Clay*)

Dug in: Schutztruppe machine gun nest at Latema-Reata,
March 1916. (*Bundesarchiv Koblenz*)

South African artillerymen haul a field piece into position near Kondoa Irangi, May 1916. (*Pictorial Press*)

Partly hidden by smoke from its M-71 rifles, a Schutztruppe field company gets off a volley during the retreat from Kilimanjaro to the Central Railway, summer 1916. (*Bundesarchiv Koblenz*)

In an obviously posed
photograph, sailors of
Schutztruppe's *"Königsberg
Company"* man a machine
gun against imaginary British
aircraft. (*Bundesarchiv
Koblenz*)

Indian troops find a smooth
stretch of road near the
Mgeta front, autumn 1916.
(*Imperial War Museum*)

"The General's gone to hell": von Lettow leads his unbeaten army through Portugese East Africa, 1918. (*Bundesarchiv Koblenz*)

Men of the Nigerian Brigade
on the north bank of the
Rufiji River, December 1916.

"Haya Safari": Schutztruppe
askaris on the march in
Portugese East Africa, 1918.
(*Bundesarchiv Kolbenz*)

lack of coordination. The British refused to help the Belgians when they ran short of porters. Tombeur turned a deaf ear to Crewe's plea for reinforcements. Each ally disregarded the other's strategic plans. Possibly the only constructive thing the British and Belgians did together was refrain from opening fire on each other.

Allied rivalry, as its push began in May, might have been intensified by the weakness of the small German border force under Captain Max Wintgens, who could do little more than retire eastward, in relatively good order, on the Schutztruppe's principal inland base at Tabora. Although Wintgens' askaris pulled up the tracks of the Central Railway as they withdrew and caused further inconvenience for the pursuers by dumping barbed wire and garbage into wells and waterholes, the force simply did not have the muscle to hold back—even seriously delay—the invading columns. Thus the Anglo-Belgian drive on Tabora became in effect a race for a prize.

The Belgians won. While the contending partners had about the same distance to cover—slightly over two hundred miles—the Belgian column under Colonel Molitor got off to a commanding head start, rolling due east along comparatively easy terrain. Not so Crewe's Lake Force, which became badly bogged down almost at once. After capturing the German port of Mwanza on the south shore of Lake Victoria, Crewe drove headlong in pursuit of the Mwanza garrison at such a clip that he soon outdistanced his supply columns and had to call a long halt. An outbreak of cerebro-spinal meningitis among the British troops also retarded the advance, and what with one thing and another, the Lake Force lay idle for nearly two months in a camp about 150 miles north of Tabora.

The retreating Schutztruppe companies failed to exploit this delay by widening the gap. Instead, they halted their own southward retirement and dug in only a mile or so from Crewe's camp. Possibly they planned to counterattack but they never got around to it. Askaris of the 4th KAR and Uganda Rifles held daily football matches within German sniper range. Once, the Germans did open up with a small field gun whose shells landed so far off target that the British gunners did not even trouble to return the fire, while the Lake Force askaris simply stood up and cheered. Finally a projectile burst a few feet from Crewe's tent. The cheers became deafening.

At the end of August, when Crewe ordered the advance resumed, his troops were still at least three weeks' marching distance from Tabora, while forward units of Molitor's Belgian force had almost come to within sight of the town. In the last week of September, as the Lake Force finally neared its objective, the thunder of artillery could be heard just over the horizon. Although communications with Molitor had broken down almost completely, it had to be assumed that a real battle was raging outside Tabora. As German East Africa's principal inland administrative, commercial and transportation center, this town was only less important to the Germans than Dar es Salaam. It was defended by at least four thousand askaris under

Major General Kurt Wahle, who in 1914 had removed the kinks from von Lettow's supply machinery and had since demonstrated that he could fight as well as organize. Clearly, the Belgians were not just strolling into Tabora.

At the same time, however, there could be no question of Wahle's holding Tabora indefinitely, and Crewe prepared to cross the railway just east of the town, to cut off the German retreat. He never got the chance. On September 25, he received a message that the Belgians had entered Tabora six days earlier and that Wahle's force was already eating up the bush in a swift withdrawal to the southeast. Had there been something like a climate of cooperation in the Allied drive, Wahle and his askaris might have been POWs and not a vest-pocket army very much to be reckoned with.

One reason for the swiftness of the Belgian advance on Tabora may very well have been the Belgian askaris' unique image among noncombatant tribesmen along the route of march. Although nearly all African troops in the campaign were accused at one time or another of cannibalism, there could not have been more than a hundred or so man-eaters in the total strength of both sides. As it happened, however, most of these came from cannibal communities in the Congo, and they gave the rest of the Belgian army a reputation which always preceded its advance. Many Africans actually believed that the Belgians economized on pay and food by serving their porters to the troops when the loads carried by the former had been eaten. One tribe working on German defenses at Tabora even had its own song about the cannibals:

> Dig, O Bin Makoma, trenches in Tabora.
> Others will arrive, the Belgians,
> Who eat men.

But cannibals were of only peripheral concern to the Germans. With the worldwide publicity given to the atrocities in Belgium, it was natural that the German civil population of Tabora should have been apprehensive at the approach of Molitor's columns. Indeed, it was generally believed that the Germans hoped the town would be taken by British rather than Belgian troops—just as British and American conquerors were preferred to Russians in 1945. Certainly Tabora of all places seemed a fitting locale for vengeance. Once an important caravan stop on the great Arab slave routes of the mid-nineteenth century, Tabora was now the site of one of German East Africa's two main POW camps.

This prison accommodated several hundred Allied noncombatant internees: engineers, doctors, missionaries and others, along with their wives and children; most of the military prisoners were housed at a village called Kilimatinde, some miles down the Central Railway. But if the Allies expected to find precursors of Dachau and Buchenwald they were disappointed—although not completely so. Conditions in the camps left much to be desired, which was hardly surprising considering German East Africa's shortages of food, medicine and sanitary facilities. A few genuinely dark deeds were also uncovered. Probably the worst was perpetrated by a prison officer who tried to recreate the Black Hole of Calcutta by forcing about fifty internees (mostly women, some with babies in their arms) to spend twenty-four hours without food in a small and almost airless iron goods shed. This sort of thing was all the more shocking because it was so rare an exception to a rule of not necessarily friendly but certainly humane treatment.

Inconsistency was the keynote of prison life. At Kilimatinde (Buttermilk Hill), the camp commandant greeted each newly arrived POW with a grim recital of draconian rules, followed by a personal handshake. Going to their quarters, the prisoners found beds, dressers, cane chairs, wash stands and basins—all kept tidy by African servants. Before food began to run out, meals were plain but ample, consisting mainly of meat, bread and cheese served by African waiters in a roomy mess hall. The prison cook was a hausfrau whose habit of boiling all meat caused continual complaints; she also touched off a wave of consternation among the British prisoners by making a Christmas pudding in cold slices. Tea (or rather coffee or milk) was served punctually at four o'clock every afternoon, although for one period the commandant had the ritual suspended to punish the prisoners for cheering some new arrivals.

Ennui could be offset to some degree by various types of recreation. Exercise was permitted in the form of hour-long afternoon strolls outside the camp. A marathon poker game went on for the duration of the men's captivity. The prisoners also started language classes, teaching each other German, French, Italian, English, Swahili, Latin and Greek; specialists gave lectures on geology, entomology, physiology and even drier topics. The Germans encouraged these classrooms to the point where the POWs were given the choice of going to class or making wooden hobnails for askari boots.

If it was a disagreeable life it was not intolerable. Apart from hunger, the worst hardship may have been a tobacco shortage which drove many prisoners to a crude African product that almost asphyxiated the smoker and anyone else near him. The Germans usually expressed their inhumanity in exasperatingly unreasonable regulations and restrictions, along with a great deal of taunting about ostensible Allied reverses on the Western Front. Solitary confinement was the severest punishment for attempted escape (although only a few tried, since there was really no place to which one could flee in safety). Gestapo methods had yet to be invented. "It is only fair to mention that from von Lettow downwards no one ever appeared to have any idea of attempting to ask for information," wrote Lieutenant Arnold Wienholt, who, as a captured British intelligence scout, could have told the enemy a great deal.

The most unspeakable bestialities in the prison camps were perhaps those that were "calculated," as one British officer put it, "to lower the prestige of the British race in the eyes of the natives." Prisoners were often made to remove manure from streets and roads with their hands, clean out askari latrines and perform other chores involving ordure. But that was not all. "Imagine the picture!" wrote a Royal Navy POW. "White men, barefoot, and clad only in ragged vest and trousers, pulling a truckload of stores, or some German officer's luggage, under a *native* guard!"

Throughout the campaign, Hun-haters also had a field day with other displays of Teutonic decadence. Outrage was not always unjustified; one can appreciate the British reaction to the Schutztruppe's practice of mass defecation on the floors and furniture of houses before abandoning a town. But perfectly harmless eccentricities could cause even greater shock among those Germanophobes for whom (the paradoxically Germanophile) Queen Victoria was still alive and well. After the sack of Bukoba in 1915, there was much gasping among the primmer types over the German commandant's family album, which included a photograph of that officer in full regimentals seated next to his naked wife (another picture had the wife in formal evening dress and the commandant in his birthday uniform). Even Meinertzhagen occasionally allowed himself to be caught up in the hysteria, speaking of "the most revolting letters and photographs" found among captured German papers.

If Meinertzhagen, who was no prude by anyone's standards, and who also admired the Germans both as soldiers and people, could succumb to this sort of sanctimoniousness, his attitude was forbearing alongside the full-time haters. "We have often been amazed," wrote Captain Robert V. Dolbey, an army doctor and a person of vast compassion except when discussing the enemy, "at the disclosures from German officers' pocket-books. In the same oiled silk wrapping we find photographs of his wife and children, and cheek by jowl with them, the photographs of abandoned women and filthy pictures, such as can be bought in low quarters of big European cities. . . . When we have taxed them with it, they are unashamed. 'It is you who are hypocrites,' they reply; 'you like looking at forbidden pictures, if no one is about to see, but you don't carry them in your pocket-books. We, however, are natural, we like to look at such things.' "

Dolbey was unmoved. "If this this be hypocrisy," he declared, "I prefer the company of hypocrites."

It is only fair to add that Dolbey, who helped circulate the story of von Lettow's role in Major Fischer's suicide, who called German women "Hunesses" and referred to Ehrlich as "that excellent Hun bacteriologist," was an extreme case. Thanks in part to the shared hardships of tropical warfare, even more to the British soldier's ever-growing admiration of von Lettow, Germanophobia never really became an epidemic in East Africa. (Nor, by the same token, were the "bluddy Englisch" seen by the Schutztruppe as much more evil than an adversary to be checked.) Even Dolbey was capable of tempering or at least restraining his bigotry to the point of engaging two German nurses to assist him in his hospital at Morogoro. Not, to be sure, without reservations. He at first suspected that Sister Elizabeth had offered her services to obtain information on British casualty rates for von Lettow, but "soon I had reason to know that she played the game." Dolbey went so far as to acknowledge that Sister Elizabeth's husband, a Schutztruppe company commander, "must have been quite a good fellow for a Hun." The other nurse, Sister Hildegarde, "proved to be just as kind to our men as she was to her own people." From Dolbey that was no small compliment.

Dolbey even implied strongly that most of the British patients became infatuated in one way or another with the enemy nurses. This would have been hardly surprising, especially since the few Englishwomen in the East African theatre tended to be planklike missionary types who could not have inspired much in the way of romantic or randy thinking when placed alongside their *zaftick* teutonic cousins.

But Dolbey was prepared to go only so far. He never got over his disgusted bafflement "that the German, who consistently drinks beer in huge quantities, takes little or no exercise, and cohabits with the black women of the country extensively, should have performed such prodigies of endurance on trek in this campaign. One would have thought that the Englishman, who keeps his body fitter for games, eschews beer for his liver's sake, and finds that intimacy with the native population lowers his prestige, would have done far better in this war than the German."

The Belgian army came to a halt at Tabora. The occupation of Ruanda-Urundi, the securing of Lake Tanganyika's eastern shore and a claim to the region below Lake Victoria had been Belgium's only principal objectives in East Africa. A few of General Tombeur's troops would later assist the British in operations to the east and southeast, but to all practical purposes Tabora was the end of the Belgian line.

The investment of Tabora followed the pattern of all other Allied conquests in East Africa thus far: the defenders yielded up everything but their troops. Even before Colonel Molitor's Belgian columns entered Tabora, General Wahle's retirement to the southeast had gone into high gear, ploughing through the bush in three columns with a strength of nearly four thousand rifles. Barely a month later, Wahle seemed on a collision course with the British flanking drive from the southwest corner of the colony.

That movement, already well under way, was led by Brigadier General Edward Northey, who had previously commanded a brigade on the Western Front, where he had been wounded twice. Northey was no stranger, either, to guerrilla tactics, having fought Pathans in the Khyber Pass as a young officer. He was to discover that his earlier Indian frontier experience would serve him well when he finally came to grips with the Schutztruppe.

Northey's force numbered about twenty-five hundred men, more or less equally divided into South African rifle companies and a KAR battalion, plus a smattering of miscellaneous police units. These troops had begun their advance into German territory at the end of May, splaying out from Nyasaland and Northern Rhodesia in four columns and swiftly occupying all the major German posts along the southwest border. Schutztruppe opposition was not very intimidating at first, but Northey soon learned, like all other British commanders, that the terrain was foe enough and more. His mile-high front was a wind-whipped and rain-lashed labyrinth of jagged peaks, gorges and passes that soared and tumbled over an area the size of South Korea. It was not long before the advancing British troops had left their cumbersome supply columns far behind and consequently had to reduce their own pace. By July, however, they had punched forward to positions more than one hundred miles from their frontier bases.

German resistance now began to stiffen as Northey approached the town of Iringa. This place consisted of a stone fort, a few white-walled European residences and the usual sprawl of grass-roofed African hovels, but it had lost none of its strategic importance to the Germans since Captain Tom von Prince had taken it from the Wahehe nation twenty years earlier. Iringa lay on one of the main lines of possible withdrawal from Tabora and the Central Railway, and the Germans knew they must hold it at all costs.

By the end of August, Smuts was prodding Northey to lose no further time in occupying Iringa. Although Smuts and van Deventer were then squeezing in on the Central Railway, Kraut had just slipped through their converging columns and was descending south on Iringa with all the speed that his twelve hundred askaris could muster. Northey himself had come to within only three or four days' marching distance of the same place, but it was not at all certain that he would get there in time to block Kraut's retreat—or prevent him from stiffening Iringa's defenses. For at this stage of the campaign, Northey's supply lines had become stretched to the breaking point.

They were not only the longest but the most fragile lines in the East African theatre. Stores and ammunition had to be carried more than five hundred miles from bases in Rhodesia and southern Nyasaland. They traveled on a shaky multiple conveyor belt of rough motor tracks, footpaths and rivers—alternately swollen and shriveled—which meandered through choked vastnesses of bush that could have engulfed Ireland or Wales. There were even howling ocean storms on that leg of the route which crossed Lake Nyasa. Moreover, it was only in the southwestern theatre that the British employed African carriers on a large scale, and this added to Northey's problems, since the porters must be fed, which in turn meant long files of bearers for the bearers. And as if that were not enough, porters approaching the combat zone also had to be armed, so that they could fight off—or try to fight off—behind-the-lines ambushes by German askari patrols. It was not the most suitable method for supplying an army on a forced march.

Northey's flanks, too, had become dangerously exposed. He had to halt his advance for several days when a 350-man Schutztruppe flying column struck hard at his rear far below Iringa in a bid to occupy a large region of grain fields which it was hoped would feed Kraut's askaris. It took a force of six hundred South African and KAR troops, backed up by twelve machine guns and a 75-mm. mountain-gun section, to evict the Germans from that area. Only then could the push on Iringa be resumed.

Northey got there in time, too late. On August 29, a company of Northern Rhodesia Police advanced cautiously into Iringa at the head of the British column, only to find that the garrison had already evacuated the town. Then it was learned that Kraut, too, had swerved off: rather than waste time and troops in a direct clash with Northey's superior force, he was now heading away from Iringa in a southerly direction. At last momentarily, Iringa had been sacrificed as the whole pattern of German movement in the southwestern theatre began to shift.

Northey threw a detachment after Kraut, but his main force could advance no further for the time being. Scattered Schutztruppe companies threatened the over-extended British supply lines in the rear, and Northey could spare no seasoned troops to protect them: the only men available were a handful of freshly recruited KAR askaris who took drill and rifle instruction while guarding mountain passes and river crossings.

And it was not long before Northey found himself preoccupied with a much more worrisome task than securing his communications or overtaking the elusive Kraut: he must block the retreat of Wahle's three columns as that anything but beaten army swept southeast from Tabora.

Wahle's objective, actually, was not Iringa but Mahenge, a large administrative center on a high plateau about 180 miles from the coast—ideally situated as a springboard from which his force could move east or southeast to effect a linkup with von Lettow's main army as it, too, drifted southward. To reach Mahenge, however, Wahle must first get past Northey's twenty-five hundred troops, and he did not lose sleep over the prospect. Indeed he welcomed it.

For one thing, the terrain was tailor-made for the kind of dodging at which the Schutztruppe excelled and on which the British seemed continually to trip over their feet. Furthermore, Northey's own force—then exhausted and short of supplies—was hardly in a position to stop a gypsy caravan. But most significantly, this was one of the rare instances of the campaign in which a British commander found himself heavily outnumbered by the enemy. The odds against Northey, in fact, were nearly two to one, and offered Wahle an opportunity which he could scarcely refuse: the chance to transform his retirement into an offensive.

As October approached, it began to look very much as if the Imperial Eagle would soon be flying over Iringa again. Northey found himself riding out what amounted to a siege as Wahle's three columns converged on the town. With four thousand askaris and several big field guns that had run the Royal Navy blockade aboard *Maria,* Wahle was very much in position to call the shots. Indeed, if Smuts had not ordered elements of van Deventer's 2nd Division—along with a KAR battalion—to Iringa from the Central Railway, the place would almost certainly have reverted to its earlier status of German stronghold.

But van Deventer's relief of Iringa—while it did force Wahle to veer off—was a defensive move, leaving Wahle free to roam more or less at will. And, although Wahle had not forgotten his principal objective, the eventual link-up via Mahenge with von Lettow's main force, he did not move east at once. Instead, his columns plunged farther southward on a route that would take them through the heavily forested valley of the Kilombero River, one of the larger tributaries of the Rufiji.

While Wahle's main reason for making this detour was to gain control, if possible, of rich grain-producing regions, he also recognized a golden opportunity to bruise—perhaps even to cripple—Northey's lines of communication. Near the head of the Kilombero Valley, in the village of Lupembe, was an important but lightly defended British supply depot. Early in November, Wahle assigned Lupembe to his largest column, a 750-man detachment under Captain Max Wintgens.

After having led the Germans' western force in retreat from the Belgians during the summer, an attack would be a welcome change for Wintgens—especially since Lupembe's capitulation was a certainty. The town's 250-man KAR garrison had barely begun its basic training and could defend the supply depot with only three prehistoric muzzle-loading field pieces. Wintgens moved in swiftly, deploying his askaris in a huge arc around Lupembe and ordering them to take the place by storm.

A four-day battle in the clouds ensued. The British askaris might have been raw recruits but Wintgens did not know that their wives and children were in the village. That was all the incentive they needed to fight like wounded lions. Although many of them were skewered on Schutztruppe bayonets as the first German wave swept over Lupembe's outer defenses, the line somehow held. More screaming, head-on attacks followed the next day. Again the outer perimeter was breached; again the Germans were hurled back. That night, Wintgens' askaris carried their own wounded off the field under a white flag.

Wintgens now changed his tactics. Instead of trying to bayonet Lupembe into submission, he sprayed it for two days with machine gun fire. But by this time he was less concerned with taking the town than with diverting attention from Wahle's main force as it passed by several miles away, with one of Northey's detachments in hot pursuit. As soon as Wahle's askaris seemed safely out of British reach, Wintgens' own column promptly vanished into the hills.

The failure to take Lupembe was a serious reverse for Wahle, and an even more smarting setback came at the end of November, when a British column cut off his rear guard and forced its surrender. It was a substantial bag for Northey: 54 German officers and NCOs, 250 askaris, one of the Schutztruppe's irreplaceable 4.5-inch howitzers and Wahle's senior commander, Lieutenant Colonel Huebner. Although Wahle's other detachments were able to slip off down an escarpment, the British had made their biggest haul since van Deventer's horsemen had rounded up the 28th Field Company in April. In fact, the British at last seemed to be scoring all the points in the southwest.

Their only real failure was with their only real objective: to halt the retirement of Wahle's main army—or even to check Wahle's freedom of movement.

Northey's tribulations in the southwest at this time—not to mention Smuts' frustrations on the main front—did not have counterparts in British efforts to control the German East African coast. Here indeed was the only theatre where it could be said that von Lettow's forces were losing important battles. In their campaign to seize the principal German seaports, the British had at least two strategic objectives, one being the establishment of supply bases closer to the advancing land armies. The main goal, however, was to acquire launching pads for major flanking drives to coordinate with the Allied offensives in the north, west and southwest. When these inland armies linked up with the columns moving westward from the coast, von Lettow would at last be cut off from further retreat, and thus forced into the showdown battle which he had so adroitly ducked for so many months.

The coastal ports toppled like ninepins under the sledgehammer blows of combined British naval and military might. Perhaps symbolically, Tanga was the first to fall; hardly had the Union Jack gone up over the town on July 7, 1916, than Royal Navy bluejackets "avenged" their country's earlier humiliation by pulling down and beheading a statute of Bismarck. Three weeks later, the navy occupied Pangani and Sadani opposite Zanzibar, and in mid-August an amphibious force descended on the ancient slave port of Bagamoyo. Here some resistance was encountered in the form of a *Königsberg* gun which had the harbor boiling with shell-burst geysers for a while. But the demonstration was no more than that. Bagamoyo's toy garrison could only withdraw before a battleship, a cruiser, two monitors and a landing force of three hundred marines and askaris. By the end of August, all of German East Africa's northern coastline, except for Dar es Salaam, was in British hands.

It was expected that Dar would be a tougher nut to crack. As the capital of the colony and the Indian Ocean terminus of the Central Railway, the port must surely be all but impregnably fortified. It was not. Captain Max Looff, commanding the garrison, had only 125 *Königsberg* seamen and a corporal's guard of Schutztruppe askaris to hold off the British, but the

British did not know this. They did know, on the other hand, that at least two *Königsberg* guns were mounted somewhere in or near Dar es Salaam, and they knew even more about Looff's capacity for resistance in the face of impossible odds. So they prepared to beat the town to death.

As part of the softening-up process during the summer of 1916, the Royal Navy expended vast tonnages of ammunition on long-range bombardments of Dar. Direct hits caused a good deal of consternation and aroused even more ire. When one shell, intended for a line of trenches, struck the town's cathedral instead, the Bishop of Bagamoyo ordered the excommunication of Rear Admiral Edward Francis Benedict Charlton, the commander of the offshore squadron. After seeing the top floor of the Governor's Palace blown into toothpicks, Frau Ada Schnee boarded a train for Tabora, taking an oath never to speak to an Englishman again—which may have been something of a sacrifice since Frau Schnee herself was a New Zealander. For a long time, however, the rain of shells did its most frightful damage to the palm trees, enabling the German troops to have hearts-of-palm salad with dinner.

Reluctant to reveal the positions of their two *Königsberg* guns at once, Looff's men initially confined their return fire to a few small field pieces and a huge monstrosity which they nicknamed "*Dicke* Bertha." This was an ancient naval cannon which for years had squatted outside the cathedral as a decoration while a local blacksmith used its breechblock for an anvil. In fact, "*Dicke* Bertha" fired only one shot at the British, but it went off with an earth-rending bang and caused the gun crew great merriment. The Germans spent far more time seeking to lure Royal Navy fire toward an immense coco palm trunk which had been mounted on a pair of tractor wheels and dragged to the crest of a sand dune. Hundreds of British shells were wasted on this dummy.

But in due course, the navy began reaching more valid targets—helped by spotter aircraft which also showered the German positions with bayonetlike steel "arrows." And in mid-August, one of the *Königsberg* guns was finally knocked out when Lieutenant Richard Wenig—who had now learned to hop about nimbly on an artificial leg—ordered his crew to open up against an attempted landing. The British hit back with everything they had. So thick were the sandstorms thrown up by bursting Royal Navy shells that the barrel of the *Königsberg* gun had to be cleaned out between every round, seriously reducing its rate of fire. Presently a direct hit put the gun permanently out of action and wiped out half its crew in the process. But the landing was hurled back.

Repulsing the next assault would be another matter. By the end of August, Dar es Salaam had become a refugee town, its streets and houses crammed almost to bursting with German and African women and children who had fled from Morogoro and neighboring farms, plantations and villages as the British juggernaut rolled south toward the Central Railway.

There were far too many noncombatants, and nowhere nearly enough troops, to defend the port when a British column, two thousand strong, approached from the north on September 3. Caught between this force and the naval squadron standing offshore, Looff could only order his own men to retire.

As usual, however, no one cut and run. Demolition crews methodically blew up all the dock installations. Wenig fired the remaining *Königsberg* gun all day, continually moving it to different positions so that the British would think they were up against at least a battery. When darkness fell, Looff turned on every searchlight in town, handed out lanterns to askaris and seamen with orders to flash signals at each other all night. Looff later remarked that the British "were always taken in by the clumsiest of ruses," and indeed these deceptions delayed the capture of Dar es Salaam long enough to allow an orderly evacuation and withdrawal down the coast. There was even time to recruit several hundred Africans to drag the *Königsberg* gun through the bush with the retreating force. And when the British finally entered Dar the next day, they were unable to run up the Union Jack for several hours: Looff had had the halyards removed from every flagstaff in the town.

Even worse, there was no beer for the troops, although this was not Looff's doing. A Royal Navy salvo had atomized the Schulz-Brauerei.

These inconveniences were a small price to pay: with Dar es Salaam cleared of the enemy, the British not only had a more convenient supply base for Smuts' (and later Northey's) forces but also a perfect springboard for amphibious attacks on the ports farther south. By the end of 1916, in fact, virtually the entire coast of the German colony had fallen, and Dar itself had become the command nerve center for all the British forces in East Africa.

It was also inevitable that Dar should instantly become a bustling hub of less than military enterprise. "I never saw such a disgraceful stampede for loot," wrote Meinertzhagen as the British entered the port. "Major-Generals were to the fore in their greed. . . . Even the Provost Marshal . . . took the chairs and the picture of the Kaiser from my prospective office." So busily were these officers liberating enemy property that at least a day went by before they learned that their own kits had been looted by their own servants.

This sort of thing was contagious. For front-line troops on convalescent leave in Dar, the city became a love-hate object. The men were enamored of the port's lush tropical beauty, its creature comforts, its distance from the sound of the guns. They loathed and despised its black market prices, its bunko artists and other wheeler-dealers who were out to relieve every fighting man of his meager pay in the shortest possible time. Dar's narrow streets spilled over with furtive peddlers of fake African curios, adulterated whisky, stolen army supplies. No part of the city—or for that matter of the army—

seemed immune to some sort of slick operation. Even the inviolate postal system had been tapped; more than one soldier, visiting an Indian shop in Dar, found himself buying a parcel of tinned foods or other delicacies that had originally been mailed to him by relatives in England or South Africa.

A few of the swindles were harmless enough. The celebrated "Tabora Sovereign," to mention one, was in fact a real German coin—perhaps the most beautiful wartime currency ever minted. Designed by a Singhalese engraver, it was a fifteen-rupee gold piece bearing the German coat of arms on the obverse side and an elephant with trunk raised beneath a mountain on the reverse. Although the production of such a piece of craftsmanship was a prohibitive indulgence for a country under siege, about two thousand of these coins were struck in Tabora's railway workshops. However, the "Tabora Sovereign" soon became so highly prized as a souvenir among British troops that local money traders in Dar es Salaam did a land-office business in counterfeits.

What the combat soldier found most odious about Dar es Salaam, however, was not its fast-buck climate but its rookery of rear-echelon "base wallahs"—the administrative personnel whose paperwork kept them well out of the action. One intelligence scout, during a furlough in Dar, observed that "the number of officers one saw was in remarkable proportion to the men, and many of them seemed to have military cars or motor bikes, while our transport at the front was mighty short of vehicles. . . . There seemed more able-bodied men in khaki pottering about here at the base, I suppose organizing our rations, than there were fighting at the front. Yet still we seemed to get very little to eat in the firing line."

It was the age-old lament. To a fighting soldier, a "base wallah" was only slightly less unworthy than a slacker. That same fighting soldier would have given a year's pay to become a "base wallah."

Back at Morogoro, the main British force had reached another state of mass collapse. Smuts now commanded an army that was decomposing on its feet, which had been all but eaten alive by sun, rain, insects and exotic microrganisms. Hardly a man in the force did not have some festering corruption on at least one part of his body; few did not feel their blood freeze, their brains boil, their bowels explode. Transport was in a shambles; food and medical supplies were running dangerously low. The troops had come to look on their half-rations of putrid beef and crawling bisquits as banquets. Fatigue was almost an epidemic; the men had become zombies. In barely three months, they had marched and fought their way across a diabolical obstacle course. Their two extended halts had brought not respite but purgatory. Somehow, though, they had stood up to everything the tropics could throw at them. But at Morogoro they had finally reached the end of their tether. If they were to remain a force in being, they must rest and recuperate here for a long time.

Smuts drove them forward without a pause.

"It may be said that I expected too much of my men," he later wrote, "and that I imposed too hard a task on them under the awful conditions of this tropical campaigning. I do not think so. I am sure it was not possible to conduct this campaign successfully in any other way. Hesitation to take risks, slower moves . . . would only have meant the same disappearance of my men from fever and other tropical diseases, without any corresponding compensation to show in the defeat of the enemy and the occupation of his country."

And, irrespective of his tactical errors (if errors indeed they were), Smuts could look back on the summer of 1916 with a feeling that his tenacity had been vindicated. It was no small thing to have conquered nearly half of German East Africa, to have gained command of both German railways, to have driven the enemy from the only economically viable part of his country. And now, as Smuts pushed his near-prostrate columns out of Morogoro with a view to encircling the Schutztruppe in the tangled fastnesses of the Uluguru Mountains, he could voice "the strong hope that this supreme effort might end the campaign."

Not everyone shared this optimism. "I think we are in for an expensive game of hide-and-seek," wrote Meinertzhagen, "and von Lettow will still be cuckooing somewhere in tropical Africa when the cease-fire goes."

16

Lib for Die Today

Eᴀʀʟʏ ɪɴ ꜱᴇᴘᴛᴇᴍʙᴇʀ of 1916, when French armies under Pétain and Nivelle were starting to lift the six-month siege of Verdun, Smuts was placing his German East African foe under a different kind of siege in a vastly different kind of fortress. The Uluguru mountain range ran some fifty miles south of Morogoro. Although its beetling slopes, dense forests and hidden passes could conceal ten armies ten times the size of the Schutztruppe, its very labyrinthine character seemed also to make it a dead end for the German retreat. Smuts therefore choreographed another envelopment.

It was the standard model. While Coen Brits' 3rd Division raced down the western flanks of the Ulugurus, Hoskins and his 1st Division would be advancing along the eastern slopes. The two columns were expected to get ahead of the German line of withdrawal; their junction at the southern end of the range should at last compel von Lettow to make the stand—or more likely the surrender—which he had avoided at Taveta, Latema-Reata, Kahe, the Nguru Mountains and Morogoro. If Smuts had begun to entertain doubts—and by this time he had—about bagging the Germans in a lightning stroke, he was able to banish or at least disregard them.

In fact, von Lettow was to make a stand. But it was not the sort that the British had in mind. Having by this time acquired the ability to anticipate his enemy's intentions—no great feat considering that Smuts' tactics never changed—von Lettow also knew that the topography of the Ulugurus would conspire mightily against the speed and coordination so vital to encirclement. That factor, he was certain, would enable him to deal with each of Smuts' columns separately when the time came. Meanwhile, he planned to hold up the British advance by strewing its path with every possible inconvenience. Like Smuts, von Lettow was not trying anything new. He had been employing this tactic ever since the beginning of the war. Its virtue was that it always seemed to work.

The chase began smoothly enough. After three months of pursuing the Germans through almost nothing but arid, shriveled thorn, the British found the Ulugurus like a park. "Fine tropical trees, on either side of the road, were tall and dark-foliaged and majestic," wrote Buchanan of the march down the eastern flank with the 1st Division; ". . . the undergrowth [was] luxuriant and flowerlit, while through the trees, every now and then, one glimpsed the fair valley and hills below and beyond." The vista would have been even more beckoning but for the presence of a large Schutztruppe column which played the nuisance by conducting a fighting retreat. Forward units of the 1st Division had to duck continually beneath the locomotive chugging of shells from a howitzer battery and a *Königsberg* gun, which seemed to be firing even while being dragged away over the plunging slopes.

The division also found itself caught up in endless numbers of hot scraps with German rear guards, but could never quite come to grips with the main body. After one bloody set-to for possession of a hillock, KAR askaris found a mockingly courteous note inside a champagne bottle; written by Captain Stemmermann, the Schutztruppe detachment commander, it informed the British of the exact time the Germans had evacuated the position. Rain began to fall as KAR officers read the note. "Colonel furious, I furious, all of us wet and filthy," wrote a lieutenant in his diary.

On September 4, after a week of failure to get behind his quarry, the 1st Division was brought to a sudden halt when Stemmermann's column stopped retreating and opened up in earnest with its artillery from a ridge six miles distant. With half that range, the British mountain batteries were impotent. And even after the Fusiliers managed to locate and destroy the main German artillery observation post, Stemmermann's askaris continued to hold the ridge in strength. It took two days before the KAR, the newly arrived Gold Coast Regiment and several other units could work round the Schutztruppe flank and take the position. But they did not take Stemmermann or his troops or his guns; all vanished into other hills, and by September 7, the 1st Division's front had become silent. It was so silent that heavy firing could be heard twenty miles to the southwest.

That was where the real action was.

Having guessed correctly that Smuts would deliver his hardest blow on the western flank of the Ulugurus, von Lettow had concentrated the bulk of his own retreating detachments in that sector, and the chase rapidly degenerated into confusion—for the pursuers. Brits split his 3rd Division into two columns, the main body keeping to the western slopes while Colonel Albert H. M. Nussey's 1st Mounted Brigade—borrowed from van Deventer, who was then pursuing Kraut much farther west—plunged directly into the mountains. The troopers found the going much stiffer than did the Germans. "For two days," wrote Deneys Reitz, "we ascended and descended endless parallel heights, dragging our weary animals behind us. A great many of them were beginning to show the effects of tsetse bite . . .

and it was easy to see . . . that our own existence as a mounted force was drawing to a close."

At the end of the third day, Nussey's force finally caught up with the Germans—"up" being the right word, as the Schutztruppe field companies were bivouacked at the bottom of a valley, two thousand feet almost directly below the ridge which the South Africans had just gained. "In the clear mountain atmosphere," said Reitz, "it looked as if one could drop a bullet among them," which was not very helpful. When the brigade finally entered the valley the next morning, the Germans had cleared out, and the dismounted troopers continued to stumble over more beetling hills in pursuit. Presently they came on a thunderous fireworks display: the site of an ammunition dump which the retreating force had set alight. "We estimated the destruction of a million rounds," wrote Reitz, "and the men began to say the campaign was over. We were soon to be disillusioned on this head."

That was putting it mildly. The trap which Smuts had set for von Lettow came within an ace of snaring the wrong army.

By September 7, Brits' main columns had reached the southern foothills of the Ulugurus. But Hoskins' 1st Division still had at least a two days' march before it could effect a linkup with Brits. And even Brits' force remained divided. Nussey's brigade was floundering about somewhere in the mountains—less than ten miles to the north, to be sure, but it might just as well have been a hundred miles, for the brigade's wireless had broken down and neither Nussey nor Brits had any idea where the other was. The Ulugurus had done their work better than von Lettow had hoped in throwing Smuts' move out of synch. There were now not just two but three British columns which the German commander could deal with almost at his leisure.

To his pleased surprise, the number suddenly became four. On September 7, sixteen Schutztruppe field companies were deployed a few miles outside the village of Kisaki, on both banks of a stream called the Mgeta. (There was a fort in Kisaki itself, but von Lettow had decided it would be too easy a target for the British.) From his own positions several miles to the west, Brits attacked, sending Beves' 2nd South African Infantry Brigade in a direct assault along the Mgeta's north bank while the 2nd Mounted Brigade under Brigadier General Barend (Barney) Enslin crossed the river and moved east to strike the German left flank. If Brits had been acting on orders of the General Staff in Berlin, he could not have served von Lettow's purposes more efficiently. Separated by the river, the two brigades lost contact almost at once. Beves' head-on infantry attack quickly ran head-on into a series of stone walls, in the form of skillfully camouflaged and stoutly fortified entrenchments held by a detachment under Captain Ernst Otto. From these positions, German rifles and machine guns lashed out with such withering effect that Beves was presently forced to dig in himself. He could now advance only to the rear. In due course he did.

At the same time, Enslin's formations were rapidly breaking up into dis-organized bands of threes and fours as the South African troopers led their horses through the dark and steaming confusion of a rubber plantation. But they advanced without meeting any resistance until they had worked behind the Schutztruppe lines, enabling Enslin to reform the brigade for a shattering blow at Otto's rear. It was to be the first all-out cavalry charge by British forces since Kitchener's 21st Lancers had routed a horde of Fuzzy-Wuzzies at the battle of Omdurman eighteen years earlier.

It never came off. Succinctly, von Lettow later explained why: "Evidently the enemy did not expect German reserves to be posted under cover still further back." Before the troopers could even remount, the under-growth had erupted in the screaming madness of an askari bayonet charge. Thrown completely off balance by the jolt in their exposed rear, unable to rally in the tangled vegetation, the South Africans could only scatter, or try to. Quite a few were taken prisoner. Not a few were spitted on German bayonets. The flankers had allowed themselves to be outflanked.

By evening, the tattered remnants of Beves' and Enslin's brigades had managed to extricate themselves from any immediate danger. But any immediate renewal of the British attack was out of the question.

Now it was Nussey's turn. His position was better known to von Lettow than to Brits, since one of the African grooms in the 1st Mounted Brigade was in reality a Schutztruppe askari named Ali Hassan who, according to Reitz, "helped to cut grass for the horses, carried water and fuel, and took such careful stock of everything that he had us down almost to a man." When Reitz and his fellow cavalrymen learned this, the spy had flown the coop, and "we promised Ali Hassan a warm reception should he come again, but in the meanwhile we admitted his courage and resource."

But in the meanwhile it was too late. Von Lettow had placed one of his most seasoned officers, Captain Theodor Tafel, in charge of a five-company detachment which marched north to face Nussey. It says something about the acoustics of bush warfare that the sounds of the September 7 action at Kisaki were clearly audible to the men of the 1st Division, at least twenty miles to the northeast, but not to the 1st Mounted Brigade, less than half that distance from the fight. And early in the morning of September 8, un-aware of what had happened the previous day, Nussey's troopers rode, equally unsuspecting, into a wall of German fire.

At once they leaped from their horses, but so solidly matted was the undergrowth that for some time they could see nothing to fire back at. All they could do was stamp down rough paths in the elephant grass and chop shallow slit trenches in the earth with their bayonets while bullets from the unseen enemy droned and occasionally smacked. There was no water. The high grass seemed almost airless. The sun smote the men with personal malice. "We were committed to an unpleasant day," said Reitz.

It was all of that. As the morning wore on, Tafel drove in at the South

Africans with wave after wave of bayonet charges. "For the first time in the campaign," wrote Reitz, "I saw the Askari in action at close quarters, and I even heard them shouting their 'piga, piga' as they came. It was confused fighting, for the jungle was so thick that one never saw more than twenty or thirty of the enemy at the same time. . . . We hung on. With repeated attacks threatening us we could not advance . . . and to retire under these conditions was impracticable, so we fought in the steaming heat." By nightfall they were on their last legs. Four officers and two dozen troopers lay dead in the elephant grass. Nearly half the men in the force wore gaping bullet or bayonet wounds. All were croaking with thirst. In the gathering darkness, a ragged South African infantryman crept up to Nussey's command post with the first message from Brits in a week. It was an order to withdraw. Somehow, Nussey managed to obey it.

Next day, when the brigade finally made contact with Brits, Reitz observed that "the old fellow was surly as a bear over the setback he had received." This may have been a diplomatic way of putting it. In his jovial moods, Brits was known to sit down with his enlisted men and put away glass after glass of the napalm-laced South African brandy called *dop*. But when his Boer Irish was up, the man-mountain general was just as likely to flog the same men senseless with his *sjambok*. Subordinates may well have kept a wide berth of Brits on the day after the thrashing he had taken from von Lettow's bloody kaffirs.

There is no telling how Hoskins' 1st Division might have fared had it come to bat next, but after what Smuts himself called "a double retirement and a regrettable recovery of enemy morale" a third successive humiliation for the British might have been a safe bet. However, the 1st Division did not get into the Kisaki melee because the tide of the fighting swiftly moved eastward along the Mgeta River as von Lettow resumed his own inevitable withdrawal. For the rest of the month, Smuts' two eastern divisions concentrated on trying to hold the Schutztruppe to the river's north bank.

They had their hands full. "Truly the enemy chooses his positions well," wrote Buchanan of the Mgeta operation, "and it is the country, not he, well though he fights, that robs us again and again of decisive battle. Their positions are, with rare exceptions, chosen where they and their movements cannot be seen, and thus their strength, at the many points of battle, may be either a handful of men or a dozen companies. Moreover, under cover of the bush, they have sure and safe lines of retreat . . . in a dozen directions, to meet again at a given point when their flight is over." Buchanan might have been writing for the Schutztruppe's early field manual on tribal warfare.

By the end of September, these tactics proved too much for the British. Under heavy fire, the Germans finally crossed the Mgeta and threw up a strong defensive line below the river's southern bank, on a front extending nearly fifty miles eastward from Kisaki. "The two armies were now comparatively at rest," wrote a 1st Division officer, "only snarling at each other across the river, like two dogs still angry, but too weary to fight."

Von Lettow's men, actually, may not have been all that spent, for they soon began withdrawing again, this time southward toward the Rufiji river. And even on the Mgeta they seemed energetic enough. "We could hear them felling trees," wrote Reitz, "and sometimes, after dark, they sang 'Deutschland über Alles' and other songs, which the men declared was on 'rum nights,' for they were enviously convinced that the Germans received a rum ration twice a week."

On September 30, Smuts addressed a formal communication to Governor Schnee. He said that after talking with many interned German civilians, he had reached the conclusion that "in spite of [the Schutztruppe's] conspicuous ability and bravery," German prolongation of the war could only mean "terrible losses and suffering to the population." Accordingly, he suggested that both Schnee and von Lettow "might consider very seriously whether this useless resistance should not now close in a manner honourable to yourselves." He added: "If any discussion with me could assist Your Excellency and Colonel v. Lettow in coming to a conclusion, I am prepared to meet you and him at a time and place to be agreed on."

A copy of the proposal was forwarded to von Lettow. It delighted him: "General Smuts realized that his blow had failed. He sent me a letter calling on me to surrender, by which he showed that . . . he had reached the end of his resources."

Smuts had reached no such thing; if he had, von Lettow's task of diverting Allied energy from the Western Front and other theatres would have been finished. Britain had hardly begun to dip into the till of money, materiel and manpower for East Africa. But there could be no getting round the fact that Smuts had temporarily run out of gas, that whether he wished it or not, his force must come to a halt once again.

Smuts himself seemed to acknowledge this just before the autumn rains broke. "An old missionary informs me," he wrote his wife late in September, "that the 40-mile plain between Kissaki and the Rufiji River becomes one continuous sea of water in the rainy season. How am I to pursue the enemy thence? And if I do so . . . how do we get food and what will become of us, cut off from the world on the Rufiji?" His customary buoyance returned, however, as he added: "But everything will come right."

Then the skies opened and everything came to pieces. The army was almost literally submerged as a biblical deluge transformed the front lines into an ocean of jellied consomme. Fighting, to the extent that there was any, consisted largely of patrols that wallowed blindly about in knee-deep swamps and seldom reached their objectives. Desultory exchanges of rifle and machine gun fire found few targets in the near-zero visibility. Artillery observation was a waste of time. Worst of all, Smuts' anxieties about being cut off from the world became very real as the rains inundated roads, swept away bridges and otherwise threatened to obliterate the force's already slender supply lines. "All motor transport is at a standstill," reported the army's War Diary. "It was hoped to . . . feed [the troops] well for the next two weeks, as they are all very weak from fever, lack of food, and continuous fighting. These rains have, however, put this out of the question, and the best that can be hoped for . . . is to prevent them from starving."

Famine was in fact staved off, but only just. The army's 1.5-ton lorries had already proved of little use in dry weather, churning dirt "roads" into fine dust that robbed their wheels of traction. In the rains these big trucks became a total liability, simply settling deep into the mud where they had to be abandoned. Lighter vehicles were brought in; their capacity was one-fifth that of the 1.5-tonners, which meant a need for five times as many drivers. But the drivers were succumbing to fever by the hundreds. And animal transport was hard put to fill the gap. During this period, twenty-eight thousand oxen were slain by the tsetse fly. Horse mortality was even greater; "more than thirty thousand of these dumb gentle brutes died here," wrote Reitz, "and that part of me which loved and understood horses somewhat died too."

The routes themselves had become longer and, with the rains, more precarious than ever before. Despite the capture of the Central Railway, bulk supplies could not be moved on that line at once, the Germans having blown up all the bridges and destroyed nearly all the rolling stock. Although makeshift repairs were quickly carried out on the bridges while small fleets of Ford trucks and tractors were converted to run on the rails, this did not suffice to feed the entire British force on a daily basis. Until the first real train reached Morogoro from Dar es Salaam at the end of November, Mombasa remained the principal supply base, which meant a journey of more than five hundred miles and nearly two months for a soldier's beef, biscuits, jam and tea—assuming that he received such a banquet, which he almost never did. The only virtue of gnawing on tainted half- and quarter-rations—or sometimes on a few undersize maize cobs—was that the men had come to expect no more. The energy expended on simple survival left the troops with practically no resistance to disease, and the army gradually became a slab of gasping, suppurating flesh. Although the rains presently abated somewhat, the Mgeta line remained a squishy abbatoir of nature. "Really," wrote Smuts to a colleague, "this is not a country into which to bring a force of white men."

That was a breathtaking understatement: between October and December of 1916, fifteen thousand British troops were invalided home. (Their numbers would shortly be enlarged by a mass departure of Indians.) Hardly a single unit had not had its heart cut out by malaria, dysentery and blackwater. Despite having just been beefed up with a draft of four hundred new recruits, the Fusiliers' roster numbered five hundred of all ranks, less than half its strength on leaving England. The Lancs had not benefited much from a long recuperation in South Africa and relatively little action since their return: originally eight hundred strong, they now had barely three hundred men fit for duty. Fewer than seventy men could answer roll call among the 2nd Rhodesians, although more than one thousand troops had passed through their ranks in various drafts.

But the South Africans were by far the worst off. They had been pole-axed. A year earlier, twenty thousand strapping outdoorsmen had descended on East Africa from the bracing air of the veld; now, twelve thousand of them, broken in body, uncertain in mind, were being taken aboard hospital ships. Reitz was greeted by one of these living cadavers, "but disease had so emaciated him, that I did not recognize my own cousin, Will Schreiner from Capetown."

Those who did not go home simply rotted on the Mgeta line. Despite the absence of German shelling, it was an even more dismal ghetto than the Msiha camp and the Handeni "hospital" combined. "It is terrible country," wrote a South African officer; "there are no names, save such names as we gave it, no roads. . . . Hardly any natives live here, as it is too poisonous." A favorite joke among the troops at this time was: "Von Lettow's surrendering! He's made only one condition: we've got to keep his colony."

Selous was back again, showing no effects either of his operation or of the miasma into which the army had dunked him once more. He spent his off-duty hours splashing through miles of bush, hunting down rare butterfly specimens with a brand-new net.

Smuts did some collecting too, sending souvenirs of the campaign to his wife and children. In one package were a German flag, a rocket gun, an Arab dagger, an ivory elephant paperweight, a jackal skin and some African basketry. Smuts apologized for not being able to deliver the gifts personally, "but Mamma must wait patiently. Pappa will come himself one day and bring something else for dearest Mamma."

The attrition of stalemate left its mark on Meinertzhagen, who began to lose appetite and sleep until he "found my mind wandering and brooding over plans of a lunatic." Smuts sent him to Nairobi to rest, but he enjoyed little peace of mind. Before being invalided out of the theatre in December,* he buried himself in his diary, letting the cup of his disgust with the conduct of the campaign spill over in a flood: "Discipline does not exist, bush warfare is not understood, looting is rife" . . . "Gross carelessness and slackness has been overlooked, and favouritism, the arch-enemy of discipline, has been allowed to creep in." Meinertzhagen also deplored the "fantastic cables" which Smuts sent to England, creating the "entirely false impression" that his generals were "budding Napoleons" when in fact (or

---

* Six months later, Meinertzhagen was assigned to the Middle East as chief of intelligence on the staff of General Sir Edmund Allenby, who afterwards wrote that "this officer has been largely responsible for my successes in Palestine."

at least in Meinertzhagen's opinion) they were "incompetent gasbags, their reports amounting to mere flatulence."

Smuts in fact was Meinertzhagen's special whipping boy, mainly because of his continuing unwillingness to abandon maneuver "from political motives. . . . It is a poor reason for his strategy and tactics when some thousand officers who are badly needed at home are anchored out here, and it is a standing disgrace that the campaign drags on and on when it might have been finished some months ago by any ordinary British general with half the troops. . . . I asked a captured German officer the other day why they did not surrender now that we occupied most of their colony. He replied: 'Why do you not give us the chance of surrendering? We cannot surrender with a fight and so far every time we have offered you battle you manoeuvre us out of position and will not fight. Give us a good fight and if you win we may surrender, but surrender is impossible without a battle.' " To which Meinertzhagen added: "All very true."

As far as Meinertzhagen was concerned, the "ordinary British general" who would have polished off the Germans beneath Kilimanjaro was the originally designated commander, Smith-Dorrien; this man, said Meinertzhagen, would simply have broken the Schutztruppe's back in a massive head-on assault. "Our strategy was simple, our numbers vastly superior. . . . Smith-Dorrien would not have shrunk from a decisive action." This was not one of Meinertzhagen's soundest judgments: he must surely have known by this time that Smith-Dorrien had been removed from command of the British 2nd Army at Ypres for the very caution which Smuts' chief of intelligence found so deplorable in his own commander. But Meinertzhagen stood on firmer ground when he expressed "no hesitation in saying that if we had had a general of the calibre of . . . von Lettow Vorbeck . . . the East African campaign would have been over by the end of 1914."

The mass exodus of white contingents (which was to go on for the rest of the war) from the British forces was no small feather in von Lettow's cap; very few of those disease-shattered troops would ever be fit to serve on the Western Front or anywhere else. And still more Allied soldiery became unavailable for the fighting in Europe as Britain hastened to fill the gap in East Africa with other Empire contingents. Black units from the Caribbean and West Africa had first begun to make their presence felt in September—the 2nd West India Regiment taking part in the assault on Dar es Salaam and the Gold Coast Regiment bashing down through the Ulugurus with the 1st Division. And early in December, the largest reinforcement of all, the Nigerian Brigade, thirty-two hundred strong, took up positions on the Mgeta front. Along with the KAR, the new arrivals were starting to give the British East African Expeditionary Force a darker complexion.

Unlike the Lancs and the Fusiliers—and even some of the Indians,

Rhodesians and South Africans—the fresh troops did not enter the campaign as strangers to tropical African warfare. Both the Gold Coasters and the Nigerians had served for two years in the Cameroons, where a steaming climate, rugged terrain and not much less stiff enemy resistance gave them an extensive education in bush fighting—and made them something of a windfall for the British army in East Africa. That the Germans were quick to note this savvy became evident when a captured Schutztruppe officer remarked that while his askaris had never been much impressed by Smuts' white forces, "we respect the men in the green caps and take no liberties with them." Green headgear being standard issue for the Nigerians and Gold Coasters alike, both units claimed credit for the tribute. Both deserved it.

Their arrival injected not only new blood and color into the campaign but new flavor. The Gold Coasters, with their pagoda-shaped straw helmets, were the jauntiest-looking troops in the theatre. The Nigerians, who wore drooping slouch hats and fought barefooted (which made them unique among British and German forces), conjured up hillbillies in blackface. Both units considered themselves the most worldly of all the African contingents, having seen Charlie Chaplin movies and visited the zoo when their troopships stopped at Durban. As West Africans with three centuries of contact with Europe, they looked down on the KAR as hayseeds, and enjoyed mocking their comical language. The Nigerians called the KAR askaris "Jambos" and "Hapanas" ("hello" and "no" being practically the first Swahili words they learned), while the KAR reciprocated by rubbing their stomachs and shouting "yum yum." This was taken as a huge joke or a huge compliment or both. Although the West Africans were no more cannibals than were their white officers, the myth persisted. Porters assigned to the Nigerians when they entrained for the interior at Mombasa sat on the roofs of the railway carriages rather than inside, where they were certain that the new troops would cook them.

With their priceless bush fighting experience, the Gold Coasters and Nigerians received a conspicuously warm welcome from the remaining white troops of Smuts' force. Or from nearly all of them. The South Africans, wrote one Nigerian Brigade officer, "really must not call soldiers of His Majesty . . . by the term 'boy.' "

While Smuts' troops stumbled in sickness and wallowed in misery on the Mgeta front, the German army's remarkable capacity for survival was also undergoing a severe test. Up to now, the Schutztruppe had enjoyed a much more comfortable war than had its foes. As a predominantly African force, it was far less prone to the malaria and other tropical scourges that broke the bodies and bent the minds of the British whites and Indians. Even the German officers, with long service in the colony, were in large measure "salted." Further, the Schutztruppe's enforced reliance on porters rather than wheeled transport gave the Germans an immensely important edge over the British not only in respect of supply but mobility. If von Lettow had had unlimited numbers of trucks, oxen and mules at his disposal, his columns might have been as badly mired down as were his pursuers'.

Even more to the point, the German troops had seldom if ever gone hungry. Interior lines enabled the Schutztruppe to fall back, with almost rhythmic regularity, on food supply depots which had been established weeks and even months earlier at strategic locations along various possible routes of withdrawal throughout the colony. In many areas below the Central Railway, local populations had been set to growing maize in anticipation of the army's approach. Maize was the staple not only of the German askari but of the entire country: the area crossed in a day's march might support a dozen companies for a week or even longer. If the neighboring villagers starved as a result, that was a misfortune of war, while the denuding of the countryside for the pursuing British was an incalculable strategic plus for von Lettow. The Schutztruppe's self-sufficiency may have been its most potent not-so-secret weapon.

But along the Mgeta, the improvised cornucopia began to spring a large leak. During the fighting that followed on the heels of the Kisaki actions, the Germans had been forced to abandon one of their richest cultivated areas, and on the Mgeta front they found themselves unable for a change to live off the land—the land, such as it was, yielding nothing more nutritive than swamp grass. Furthermore, this was one of the few areas where the Schutztruppe got its supplies from the rear on the backs of donkeys instead of porters, and the donkeys were soon massacred by the tsetse fly. An attempt to recruit local porters also fell on its face: "even presents of clothing, which were ordinarily so highly valued, failed to hold them," wrote von Lettow. "It seemed as if all the evil spirits had conspired together to deprive us of transport." If the force did not take its leave of the Mgeta's sodden boneyard, it might just possibly lose the war—not to the British but to famine.

Owing partly to the weather, von Lettow was unable to carry out the withdrawal as swiftly as he might have wished. Schnee's administrative red tape also blocked his path; at one point, he had to commandeer a river steamer from civil officials who would not hand over the vessel without the governor's authorization. Still, most of his columns did move out by stages, and in due course the main body of the Schutztruppe had taken up positions along the middle and lower reaches of the Rufiji, some thirty or so miles south of the Mgeta. And once the men were ensconced in their new sector, the country again supported them in the manner to which they had become accustomed. Maize abounded in the Rufiji area, and a prewar sisal plantation was converted into what became virtually a flour factory, its old steam engines clanking day and night to grind up corn for the army. Von Lettow even ordered that the makeshift mill be evacuated only when the maize ran out. The region was that crucial to the force's survival.

But long-run strategy as well as hunger dictated von Lettow's new dispositions, and no one was quicker to recognize this than Smuts. "The campaign is dragging on far beyond the period I had expected," he wrote to a friend in October. "Every portion of any value of this colony is lost to the enemy who is now confined to the deadly malaria region of the great southern river systems. . . . But the word has gone forth from Germany that they must hold out here to the uttermost, and in the swamps and jungles where the enemy is now it is most difficult to get at him. . . . So you can see what a dismal prospect there is in front of me."

Smuts, of course, did not flinch from the prospect. To check von Lettow's withdrawal even farther beyond the British reach, he lost no time in launching another herculean end run around the German rear. This one, however, differed from its abortive predecessors in that its objective was not the Schutztruppe at all but the Schutztruppe's food supply.

Or at least that was the way it started out.

Early in September, after a torpid exchange of shells with a German shore battery, a British amphibious task force had occupied the ancient slave port of Kilwa, about 120 miles south of Dar es Salaam, giving Smuts a major base from which, at an opportune moment, he could thrust elements of his army far inland behind the enemy lines. In October, when von Lettow made his own move to the Rufiji, the time seemed ripe and Smuts acted. His plan was to send a strong column one hundred miles southwest of Kilwa to the vicinity of the German post at Liwale, where vast maize fields were already being cultivated in preparation for the Schutztruppe's eventual—and inevitable—withdrawal to that district. With the British in control of Liwale, von Lettow might well be starved into submission.

There was only one hitch. Before the drive could begin, it was considered necessary to keep von Lettow from interfering by holding him to his positions along the Rufiji in the north. This would be accomplished with the capture of a key German fort at Kibata, which lay in a cluster of hills some fifty miles northwest of Kilwa. Accordingly, the greater part of a 1st Division brigade—composed mainly of KAR units and the 129th Baluchis—marched out of Kilwa in October to seize the strongpoint. Had Smuts known what awaited this force, he might have sent out the whole division.

Things started to go badly at once. The route to Kibata took the troops through country which, according to Cranworth, "harboured more and worse examples of nature's obstacles to man than any other district I have traversed." Among the inconveniences, Cranworth ticked off tsetse flies which slew six hundred mules in two weeks, lions which devoured thirteen sepoys and askaris before being dispatched by a machine gun, black cotton soil which literally swallowed a wagon and its team of six mules, burrowing grubs which had to be extracted from the body with razors, the usual fogbanks of malarial mosquitoes and "a plague of rats innumerable." Rations, said a Baluchi officer, were "so green with rottenness and so full of weevils and maggots that they could only be eaten with the eyes closed." Thirst stalked the column at every step. Unlike the soupy Mgeta front, the approach to Kibata was bone dry; the temperature locked in at 100°F., and everyone breathed thick dust rather than air. During one halt, several companies came near to a bayonet duel in a scramble for a few coconuts.

After all this, Kibata was a breath of mountain air—literally. The fort stood at the crest of an immense hill, ringed by a multitude of other beetling elevations, several thousand feet above sea level in a bracing climate. The prevailing cool breezes quickly erased sweat and grime; streams of clear, icy water chuckled everywhere. It was not even necessary to capture the fort. A German flag flew over its battlements but the place had been evacuated. Therefore, General Hannyngton, the column commander, sent half the force back to Kilwa while the remaining units settled down to patrolling.

These reconnaissances were actually more like journeys of discovery. Kibata and its environs were terra incognita to the British, whose maps bore no discernible relation to the chaos of humpbacks and scrub which they purportedly clarified. Even the new maps made by the patrols were not much of an improvement, being mired down in a bewildering anarchy of place names. "Everybody," reported the Brigade Diary, ". . . has been trying to solve the great question, where is Mtumbei Chini? The 2/2nd K.A.R. have found three possible Mtumbei Chinis. The 1/2nd K.A.R. have a special one of their own. Lewis has gone to our Mtumbei. . . . A composite map made up of three sketch-maps superimposed . . . fairly bristles with Mtumbei Chinis. This, however, is only half the trouble, as there is a Mtumbei Juu, which also seems to wander at will round the country-side. This has got mixed up with the Chinis so that the maps simply dance with Mtumbeis, some Chini and some Juu."

In due course the confusion was cleared up: "It is settled beyond a doubt that the Brigade has been misinformed, and that the Mtumbei Chini they mean, and which they wish to be held, is not an Mtumbei at all but an Abdullah Kitambi."

Patrols also began to keep an eye out for the Germans: the British presence around Kibata could not remain a secret long. Nor could von Lettow be expected to let Smuts prepare for a strike undisturbed, although he had mixed feelings about diverting troops from the Rufiji positions. While it was obviously necessary to discourage a British southward move on Liwale, von Lettow felt that "a prolonged operation in the mountains of Kibata . . . offered but little prospect of leading to a decision." All the same the thing had to be done, and von Lettow took personal command of the counter-thrust. In November, a steady flow of British intelligence reports indicated that at least five Schutztruppe field companies—perhaps one thousand rifles or more—were moving south through the hills toward Kibata, and patrols became increasingly vigilant as the reports became increasingly specific.

The search for the Germans was more fruitful than the map-making,

although not much more. One urgent message had a large Schutztruppe
column bivouacked near a mission not far from Kibata itself. A Baluchi
detachment converged on the position, surrounded it and moved in with
bayonets fixed. The men found a gramophone playing German military
marches. But such near-misses were storm signals which left no doubt that
the Germans were infiltrating the Kibata region in strength, and energetic
measures were taken to stiffen the defenses of Kibata fort. Trenches were
dug, barbed wire entanglements laid down, the bush on the crests and slopes
of Kibata and nearby hills shaved clean to give machine guns unobstructed
fields of fire. Von Lettow's askaris would need more than their usual quo-
tient of pugnacious daring to recapture the position.

They would also need artillery, and big guns were out of the question.
The British had not even tried to manhandle a single cumbersome field piece
over the unending succession of swooping furrows around Kibata. Nor,
obviously, would the Germans.

The Germans did not bring up a gun. They brought up four: two mountain artillery pieces, a 4.5-inch howitzer and a *Königsberg* gun. Their journey was a prodigy of road-building know-how and elbow grease and it
nearly failed at least half a dozen times each day. "A wheel slips," wrote
Richard Wenig, "two tree-trunks shift. Muzzle down, the gun sinks to its
axles. . . . The carriage groans. . . . The gun will not budge! . . . Men are
sent back to bring up the gangs of another gun. . . . The lines are now so
long that one command can no longer direct them. Almost eight hundred
men stand waiting. . . . Then, 'Pull!' The bodies lie almost horizontally. A
resounding twang, and the black masses are flung to the ground, shouting,
rolling about in a tangle: the tow cable has parted! With much difficulty,
arms and legs are unsnarled, injured men are unharnessed. The cable is
spliced. . . . Again the eight hundred haul. Suddenly the gun heaves upwards, rolls noisily across the splintering tree-trunks. . . ."

And so it went. By early December, the guns were in position and unseen, concealed in the vegetation just beyond the open spaces that the
British had cleared around Kibata to hurl back infantry attacks. All that
bare ground offered the juiciest of targets to von Lettow's artillery observers.

On December 6, at one o'clock in the afternoon, the crest of Kibata and
its surrounding hills suddenly began blossoming with explosions as the four
big guns announced the commencement of what was to be a three-week
siege. Covered by the barrages, waves of Schutztruppe askaris swarmed up
the slopes of several elevations where the British held forward positions.
Surprise was all but total in the madness of bursting shells, flying dirt, rasp-
ing bugles, gleaming bayonets, shrilling whistles and ululating war cries
that swept like flash floods into the defenders' trenches. By the end of the
day, the Germans were holding two strongpoints within a mile of Kibata
fort.

Both sides dug in for the night. But next day, the German artillery went
to work again, concentrating its fire on a strongly held advance point called

Picquet Hill, barely five hundred yards northwest of Kibata. Control of Picquet Hill was the key to the door of the fort. To clear the way for an askari assault, missiles rained down on Picquet Hill for a good part of the day. By Western Front standards the bombardment was not heavy—probably fewer than four hundred shells were fired all told—but nothing like its intensity had ever been seen in East African ground combat. Even the barrage-wise Baluchi veterans who hung on grimly were accustomed to the protection of man-deep trenches in Flanders. The comparatively shallow ruts they had scooped out on Picquet Hill proved next to useless, and were soon littered with chunks of screaming raw blubber. Showers of dirt buried many officers and sepoys alive. It was a reeling, punch-drunk handful of survivors that barely managed, with their machine guns and rifles, to beat back the German infantry attack when it was launched at sunset.

But the assault had not failed completely. A sizable Schutztruppe force now held the appropriately named Lodgement, a well-protected fold in the earth a few yards from the crest of Picquet Hill. Just as Picquet Hill provided easy entree to Kibata fort, so too was the Lodgement a back door to Picquet Hill. A domino situation had now been set up by the Germans. Unless they could be pried loose from the Lodgement and the position retaken, Picquet Hill and then Kibata must fall. It would be only a matter of time.

Meanwhile, von Lettow also had other detachments working through the hills round the British flanks, until the converging German lines almost met behind Kibata. Only two rough bush trails connected the beleaguered fort with the outside world. It became practically impossible to bring in food, and the Germans controlled most of the water. The siege settled down to the static grimness of trench warfare. Heavy shelling and well-directed machine gun fire inhibited counterattacks in strength, and reduced the fighting to continual patrol actions in an ever-shifting no-man's-land. Scouts were impaled on poisoned-stake lion traps; reconnaissance parties of both sides were sometimes machine-gunned by their own troops while returning from probes of enemy lines. The British did have time to strengthen and deepen their fortifications, but they were never invulnerable to the Schutztruppe's big guns. KAR and Baluchi companies took regular turns cringing under shell bursts in forward positions. Star shells at night guided the howitzer's high-trajectory missiles to posts that had been dug in on reverse slopes. Kibata had become the Somme in microcosm. Even the names of strategic points—Platform Hill, Observation Hill, Ambush Hill, the Lodgement—helped lend a Western Front flavor to the battleground. All that lacked was gas.

Things got worse for the British almost by the hour. A steadily growing casualty list was beefed up by a proportionate rise in disease and an alarming drop in medical supplies. "On the whole," remarked a Baluchi officer, "it was better to be shot dead in the Kibata area than to be badly wounded."

Dressings, caked with dried blood, oozing with pus, crawling with flies, could be changed only once a week, and only if Kibata's single doctor and nis half-dozen orderlies could take time off from amputations. These latter were performed by the score every day, on a wooden door that had been removed from the crude grass-roofed shack which served as a hospital. The "operating table" was always occupied, either by shredded bodies or by officers who dined off it; "If not wanted," wrote one of them, "the ejected guests would sit outside eating and watching."

The hospital itself was not immune to attack. The Germans opened up on it one day with a machine gun which they had carried to a hillock a few hundred yards off. Fire ceased only when the medical officer rushed directly at the bursts, cursing and waving a Red Cross flag.

One took consolations where one could find them. A severe clothing shortage, caused by the wear and tear of bush and shell fragments, was alleviated slightly in auctions of dead soldiers' uniforms. The proceeds were credited to the estates of the deceased, while men who lost out in the bidding had the satisfaction, as one officer put it, "of hinting to the fortunate purchaser that there might be another auction in the near future."

Reinforcements presently began to fill the holes left by the dead and wounded. A KAR battalion marched in from a post forty miles away, covering the distance in less than thirty-six hours. With the fresh troops was a section of a mountain battery, enabling the British to talk back to the German guns. More sinew was added with the arrival of the Gold Coast Regiment, and on December 13, the force was ready to flex its new muscles when Brigadier General Henry de Courcy O'Grady took over from Hannyngton, who had just been given another command. O'Grady was an eye-gouger who disliked sitting still, and two days after taking charge at Kibata he had a counteroffensive under way.

It was launched by the Gold Coasters, from positions beneath a hill two miles west of Kibata. The Germans were strongly entrenched at the crest, and the Gold Coasters' objective was not only to dislodge them but to get around their rear. By thus weakening von Lettow's right wing, the pressure on Kibata itself would be greatly relieved if not entirely removed.

There was only one problem here: von Lettow had been expecting such an attack all along. Hardly had the Gold Coasters begun climbing the spine of a steep hogback that led to the crest than the Germans' long-range artillery commenced beating down on them like mallets, while the defending askaris hacked at them with a merciless machine gun and rifle crossfire. Within minutes, any chance of storming the heights had become academic; it was all the Gold Coasters could do to hang on to their own positions. But neither could they retire: the lower slopes of the hogback were almost bare of cover, and the slightest movement to the rear brought down a torrent of lead and steel that cut short any thoughts of withdrawal. For six hours, the Gold Coasters could only sit there and take their pasting.

But there was no talk of surrender. At one point in the action, Cranworth crept up to a Gold Coast sergeant and asked how things were going. "With a cavernous grin he answered: 'Going splendid, sar! All Gold Coast lib for die today!' " They did not quite, but when the regiment was relieved as the barrage lifted at sundown, its dead and wounded numbered 15 percent of the enlisted men and 50 percent of the officers. The hogback became known as Gold Coast Hill.

And despite the ordeal by artillery, the Gold Coasters lost none of their high spirits. Not long afterwards, a handful of captured German officers found themselves surrounded by a howling band of black madmen who performed a war dance, brandished their bush knives and chomped their jaws in a realistic pantomime of eating raw flesh. The Germans breathed a collective sigh of relief as an amused British officer led the laughing West Africans off.

The attack on Gold Coast Hill was not the only bolt in O'Grady's quiver. If von Lettow had anticipated the thrust at his right flank, he was completely unprepared for what he called "a manoeuvre then unknown to us" —which was launched only hours after the Gold Coasters had been stopped. This was a counterattack against the all-important Lodgement beneath Picquet Hill. It had been meticulously timed to take place just before moonrise at eleven o'clock, when an assault party would break through the German position—and occupy it with a new secret weapon.

The Kibata force had just received one hundred Mills grenades. They had never been used in East Africa. Even the Baluchis were unfamiliar with them, and the time element ruled out any kind of real practice. Instructions consisted of an officer holding up one of the grenades and explaining to eighty Baluchi volunteers: "This is a Mills bomb. You pull out the ring and throw it." That lecture, it was hoped, would suffice. It had to.

At half-past ten, the assaulting troops began to creep forward, barefoot, toward the Lodgement. Minutes before eleven, the advance line of bombers crouched beneath a barbed-wire entanglement less than three yards from a German machine gun. Its askari crew was sharing a cigarette but alert. The wind, however, favored the Baluchis and their approach went undetected. At a signal from the jemadar in command, the sepoys hurled their grenades. Not all exploded but the Lodgement nearly did.

The moon rose on a scene of pandemonium. The German askaris who had not been killed by the blasts were badly stunned, but only for a moment. Their ears and noses spouting blood from the concussions, they lashed back in grim fury with rifles, bayonets, fists, fingernails and even teeth, as the Baluchi assault wave hacked and shot and bombed its way through the barbed-wire and pointed-stake defenses. The Lodgement became a maelstrom of ricocheting bullets, plunging steel, whining metal fragments. The jemadar leading the charge had his face blown off. A grenade shard grooved the skull of a British officer and went on to decapitate a Schutztruppe askari ten feet away. The ground reeled as the British artillery battened down German support troops to the rear of the position. For fifteen minutes the air throbbed with explosions, war cries, cheers of pain.

Then the firing sputtered out. There was no one left for the Baluchis to fire at. Forty German officers and askaris were dead or partly dead, another dozen had been captured, and the rest of the defending force was in full retreat down the reverse slope of Picquet Hill. The secret weapon had done its work well. With the Lodgement back in British hands, the Kibata operation had become a new ball game.

Their energies momentarily spent, the adversaries now settled down for a while to desultory patrols and occasional shellings. The German artillery concentrated on Kibata fort, the gunners taking their range from a small Union Jack that flew over one of the battlements. Although the fort itself was reduced almost to rubble, the shells caused few casualties and the Union Jack snapped defiantly through the dust and smoke. The British retaliated with aircraft that flew out from Kilwa, but von Lettow's positions were so well concealed, as usual, by bush and forest that the bombs made an impressive racket and did little else. Certainly neither German shells nor British bombs kept the troops of either side from catching up on badly needed sleep.

The recess also allowed von Lettow to deal with a problem of African jurisprudence. A local tribesman's grandfather, it appeared, had recently been eaten by a fellow villager, and the grandson lodged a formal complaint with the Germans. Mindful of the community's relative permissiveness toward cannibalism, von Lettow decreed a fine of a dozen hens, after which, he said, plaintiff and defendant "went off as good friends, the one with the grandfather of the other in his stomach."

The British, too, exploited the pause to bring up fresh supplies and even a few luxuries. Baluchi and KAR officers celebrated Christmas with *pâté de foie gras* and two bottles of champagne. On that same day, the Germans cheered lustily when a British plane went off course and accidentally bombed Kibata fort. The cheering stopped after a Schutztruppe officer had a look through his field glasses and discovered that the bombs were cartons of cigarettes for the troops.

Von Lettow received a Christmas present from Smuts: a letter congratulating him on having been awarded the *Pour le Mérite*, Germany's highest military honor. The letter may have pleased von Lettow almost as much as did the decoration; he saw it as "proof of the mutual personal esteem and chivalry" that existed between himself and the British commander.

Certainly he could afford to be magnanimous at this stage of the fighting at Kibata. Although the Germans had gone back on the defensive after losing the Lodgement, the British had taken so severe a mauling that they were momentarily in no position to exploit their advantage. If indeed they held any edge at all, for the original intention of driving southwest to Liwale had yet to be realized. Nor would it be for a long time to come. Von Lettow attributed the setback for Smuts to "our vigorous action at Kibata," which compelled the British "to leave the rest of the country and the whole of our supply and transport apparatus in peace." Smuts was in no position to disagree.

But there were more ways to get at the Germans than by sabotaging their logistics machinery. At the end of December 1916, nearly four months had gone by since Smuts had dealt a final crushing blow to von Lettow's army. Another death stroke was long overdue and Smuts prepared to deliver it.

Actually, after eleven months of East Africa's climate and terrain, Smuts knew all too well what he was up against; eleven months of almost unnaturally dogged German resistance had snuffed out his earlier confidence in lightning victory. But these things had also stiffened his resolve. In his obsession with catching von Lettow, Smuts could be likened in a sense to a persistent youth courting a girl who is playing hard to get. Von Lettow, of course, was playing impossible to get, but Smuts would have none of that. Never had he been more determined to break the back of Germany's East African army for once and for all.

By now, the main body of the Schutztruppe was south of the Rufiji River, most of its companies, under von Lettow's personal command, being concentrated in or near the Kibata sector. To oppose them, Smuts had beefed up his Kilwa force by sending nearly the entire 1st Division to that port. On the Mgeta front there remained only about one thousand German askaris. They had a good commander in Captain Ernst Otto, whose detachment had stopped Beves and Enslin dead in their tracks at Kisaki in September. But Otto's companies were ridiculously outnumbered. Facing them across the river was a combined British–Nigerian–South African force of sixty-two hundred rifles, fifty-one machine guns and two dozen field pieces. This phalanx was to descend on Otto in four columns, three of which (the main detachment under Sheppard) would drive him south toward the Rufiji. In the meanwhile, the fourth column, led by Beves, would have made a wide southwest turning movement across the river. This would block the German retreat and bring Otto to a fight he could not possibly win.

With Otto out of the way, the second and last phase of the drive would commence, as the four British columns continued south for a linkup with the 1st Division, which by that time would have punched far inland from Kilwa. The juncture of the two British forces was expected to close the ring around von Lettow's main body in the vicinity of Kibata. That encirclement was the crowning and final objective of the British offensive.

On New Year's Day of 1917, Smuts' bulldozer began lumbering forward along the Mgeta line, and Otto, with no other option, prepared to evacuate his positions on the south bank. But the five-day retreat toward the Rufiji was orderly and stubborn. Advance units of Sheppard's main column found themselves locked in continual hand-to-hand fights with Schutztruppe rear guards. In one action the Fusiliers were almost overwhelmed by three successive bayonet counterattacks. Rare was the tree or boulder that did not conceal a German sniper. *Kronborg's* Nis Kock, now a Schutztruppe ordnance specialist, had seeded the path of pursuit with mines, improvised from whatever he could lay his hands on: 4.1-inch *Königsberg* shells, captured Mills grenades, even explosive charges packed into discarded British bully beef tins. Enough of these things went off so that Smuts' columns were not only delayed but badly confused. One convoy of wounded Nigerians was seriously cut up by the fire of an Indian battalion which mistook it for a German patrol.

Still, the Germans had to keep falling back before overwhelming pressure on their rear and flanks. Halfway to the Rufiji, near the village of Behobeho, they faced total annihilation when strong elements of Sheppard's force worked round Otto's forward lines in an effort to arrest his further withdrawal. In the fire fight that ensued, Behobeho won a small measure of immortality as the place where Selous got his. While leading his Fusilier company against the vanguard of the retreating force, he took a sniper bullet in the mouth and died instantly. The killing of the aged folk hero may have maddened the rest of the British troops,* for after several hours they managed to take up strong positions directly astride the road leading to the Rufiji. Otto had finally been trapped.

For approximately ten minutes. "The wily foe," wrote Buchanan, ". . . would, and did, avoid the danger in their path by taking to the wide area of vacant bush . . . and scattered there to meet at some prearranged rendezvous."

That rendezvous was the Rufiji itself, and Otto led a battered but unbowed force across the river. Nis Kock was there to watch the grinning askaris go by, their rifles carried butt-backwards at jaunty angles as they "came marching over the long bridge, in their torn, faded uniforms. They looked rather the worse for wear, but they stepped out well, and sang their monotonous songs in strong voices." Even the noncombatants seemed buoyed up: "The bearers sang as they went. First the leader: 'The bearers are coming . . . Great is the safari!' and the bearers answered, 'The bearers

---

* Selous' old African servant and gun bearer, Ramazan, is said to have gone berserk at this moment, charging directly into the German lines and killing several officers and askaris, as well as the sniper who had shot his master. Selous' death was also an occasion for mourning throughout the whole force; there is hardly a single written work about the East African campaign which fails to record the event with some tribute or other. Not surprisingly, von Lettow paid his respects by noting that Selous "was well known among the Germans, on account of his charming manner and his exciting stories."

are coming!' The songs were improvised, they arose from joy in movement, from the sense of unity. From time to time came a rallying call: 'Are ye there? Are ye there?' from the leaders, and then the chorus of bearers: 'We are here . . . We are here.' "

Once across the Rufiji, Otto had the bridge blown up, halting the British pursuit until boats could be made ready. Even then, the crossing did not proceed smoothly, being carried out under continual sniper fire. The Rufiji itself, nearly in flood, caused further delay as currents flowing as fast as a horse could gallop swept many flatboats far downstream. The river's natural inhabitants also worked for Otto; one Nigerian company had its boat bitten in half by what a British newspaper later called a "pro-German hippopotamus." On reaching the south bank, advance British units were sent sprawling by massed rifle volleys and concentrated machine-gun fire. By the time the pursuers were ready to take up the chase again, Otto's force was vanishing below the southern horizon.

How could this have happened? Beves' fourteen-hundred-man flanking column had already forded the river without opposition some thirty miles upstream, and was expected by now to have moved down to the positions which would halt Otto's further retreat below the south bank. But Beves had not reached those positions. Even before his troops began their forty-mile forced march to the Rufiji, their last reserves of energy had all but given out. It was a wonder that they were even able to get to the river and stumble into their collapsible boats for the crossing, but they were simply not up to winning the race across the final thirty miles that would have placed them on the German line of withdrawal ahead of Otto. So much for that encirclement.

True, Otto was small potatoes alongside von Lettow, whose main force would still be rounded up when the four British columns now below the Rufiji joined with the 1st Division somewhere to the southwest of Kibata. But Otto should never have been allowed to escape; at the very least, his detachment would do a great deal to hamper the final mopping-up. As von Lettow put it: "The unity of General Smuts' otherwise quite well-planned operation was wrecked."

This was not all. As a coordinated by-product of the Rufiji offensive, Smuts had ordered a double-barreled strike at Wahle's elusive askaris who were continuing to lead British troops a merry chase in the shaggy mountain country of the southwest. For some reason, Wahle had not yet chosen to withdraw eastward to Mahenge for his eventual linkup with von Lettow, and it remained important to keep him from doing so. Northey by now had most of his force concentrated some eighty miles south of Iringa, near Lupembe, where the bulk of Wahle's army was believed to be dug in, with Kraut somewhere in the neighborhood. At Iringa itself, van Deventer was in command, facing five hundred of Wahle's askaris under Captain Friedrich Lincke, whose attack at Kondoa Irangi he had beaten off nearly eight months earlier. On Christmas Day of 1916, both Northey and van Deventer were to seek out and destroy their respective opponents, or failing that, to place themselves between the Germans and their avenues of eastward escape into the Kilombero Valley. If the latter alone could be brought off, the Schutztruppe's western forces would be hard put to reach Mahenge, and Smuts would have received a welcome Christmas gift.

The fighting—to the extent that any took place—was terribly confused. Both British thrusts relied on encirclement and were made doubly complicated by the crumpled ground on which they had to be carried out. In the vast hideaway of trolls that comprised the southwestern front, neither side could ever be certain of where the enemy was, or in what strength, from one hour to the next. Clearly, however, the terrain, as always, worked to the great advantage of the pursued rather than the pursuers, and they made the most of their edge.

In Northey's sector, some twelve hundred of Wahle's askaris had been at work for several weeks, digging entrenchments at the crest of a beetling escarpment. Northey planned to take it, with his own nineteen hundred rifles, by diverting the Germans in a frontal attack while two other detachments simultaneously lunged in—or rather up—on the flanks. It took several days of bashing about the heights in blinding, icy rainstorms before the columns could get into position, but on Christmas morning they were ready for the assault. So too were the Germans, who had abandoned their entrenchments and were now dug in on another ridge about six miles away.

Undismayed, Northey performed the envelopment ritual again, and again Wahle's troops skipped off to another crest. Three more days went by as Northey's KAR askaris picked their way up the escarpment trying to locate the German flanks. They failed to find them. They also failed to find the Germans. This time, Wahle's force had tucked itself into some fold of the mountain where it could no longer be reached or even seen. If Wahle was finally beginning his eastward withdrawal toward Mahenge, it appeared that Northey would be the last to know of it.

Van Deventer's prospects of snaring Lincke near Iringa did not appear much brighter, although he outnumbered the five-hundred-man German force by nearly three to one with a mixed command of South African and KAR infantry, part of an Indian mountain battery and a composite mounted brigade. The last, led by Brigadier General Nussey, was mounted in name only. In November, it had ridden to the relief of Iringa with eight hundred horses and sixty mules; it had arrived, in Nussey's terse words, "with 32 horses and 6 mules and these were dead within a week."

But van Deventer, who had bumped down to Iringa in a staff car to direct the operation, was satisfied that his manpower and firepower were more than enough to carry out a three-armed encirclement that would leave Lincke with nowhere to go but a British POW camp. The details of the plan were spelled out at a staff conference, and "before the meeting was over," wrote Deneys Reitz, "van Deventer had the enemy surrounded on the map, within a ring of indelible ink."

Reitz, now a colonel commanding a "mounted" regiment, suspected that Lincke might come up with an ink eraser, but he had his orders and the regiment marched off into the hills. "As we progressed, the forest grew denser and the climbing more steep. We had generally to go in single file along game paths, led by natives, and it rained much of the time. I was under strict injunction to reach my point in the drive by a given date, and as the distance proved to be nearly twice that shown on the map, I had to push the men unmercifully." The going was even stiffer for the Indian mountain battery, which lost seventeen mules, nine of them tumbling off precipices. But all the troops managed to gain their positions by Christmas morning, and Reitz's men celebrated by dining off a herd of goats. It was their first food in thirty-six hours.

Van Deventer ordered the attack to begin. The South African infantry were to close in on Lincke from the northwest and the KAR from the northeast, forcing him to retreat south, where Nussey's brigade stood directly astride his path. Reitz was part of the blocking force and soon saw his earlier doubts confirmed. "On paper, our opponents were encircled. In practice, it worked out differently, for the cordon we had established was full of loopholes . . . through which men with knowledge of woodcraft could escape." Which was what they did, slipping off like ghosts into the Kilombero Valley to the east. All the British could do was take cold comfort in the scenic beauty of the German exit route. Although Wahle, Lincke and Kraut had yet to join von Lettow, the British had yet to keep them from doing so. It was becoming increasingly clear that the Schutztruppe's western columns were free to move eastward at their leisure and in their own good time.

Otto's escape across the Rufiji, along with the failure to trap the German western army, while maddeningly frustrating to Smuts, were setbacks of relatively marginal importance. Smuts could still wrap up the campaign before the end of January 1917 by gaining his primary objective: to effect the linkup of the Rufiji columns and the 1st Division, as the latter drove inland from Kilwa, and encircle von Lettow, whose main force was still concentrated just north of Kibata fort.

There was only one problem. As long as von Lettow held on at Kibata he was in a position to strike and delay the 1st Division columns on their right flank as they pushed inland from the coast. It therefore became necessary for the now-reinforced British Kibata garrison to drive the Germans a little farther north in an all-out counterattack. It began on January 7 with a concentrated artillery barrage, followed up for the next several days by large KAR and Baluchi detachments which swarmed over the hills in a drilling rain and occupied several strong German positions without meeting any resistance to speak of. It was almost as if the Germans had cleared out.

At the end of the week, "almost" proved to be an understatement. With no intention of sitting idly at Kibata and waiting to be surrounded, von Lettow had carried out a childishly elementary tactic. What he had done, quite simply, was vacate the area, stealing a march of at least two days on the British and moving his whole force west to join hands with Otto again. The rendezvous point was an oversized pond called Lake Utungi, about forty miles northwest of Kibata and far beyond the jaws of the trap that Smuts had set. It was the same old story. The Schutztruppe's escape from encirclement and annihilation had been almost comically easy.

It also helped von Lettow take a sanguine view of what other commanders might have considered dire straits. "I regarded the military situation in the colony as remarkably favourable," he wrote, "for I knew that the South African troops were for the most part worn out. . . . Prisoners had repeatedly assured us that they had had enough of the 'picnic' in East Africa. The Indian troops also . . . were reduced in numbers, while the late arrivals . . . might not be expected to stand the fatigues of African warfare for a very prolonged period. The enemy's Askari were, generally speaking, new troops, and only a small proportion of them had at that time been in the field. So we could continue calmly to contemplate the continuation of the war for a considerable time."

Late in December of 1916, Smuts had asked his wife to tell their little son Jannie that "Pappa is now going to fight against the terrible monster Rufiji who . . . has drunk so much water that his snout is now terribly big and his belly is full of hippos and crocodiles!" On January 20, 1917, the struggle with the monster came to an abrupt end when command of the British East African Expeditionary Force was handed over to Major General Reginald Hoskins, then leading the 1st Division. Smuts had been invited to represent the South African government at the Imperial Conference in London.

This was anything but a kick upstairs. In early 1917, the armed forces of the British Empire could claim only one authentically victorious general. Smuts had occupied more than three-quarters of German East Africa, gaining control of its railway system, its harbor installations and all its richest land. He was the only Allied commander at this time who had the Hun in full retreat—no minor achievement after the charnel-house stalemates of Verdun and the Somme. Smuts, in short, had become a hero, and his presence at the Imperial Conference seemed a fitting honor.

Somehow, it seemed less fitting to ask why he had not defeated his fleeing enemy.

17

Gasping Spell

Five days after smuts' departure, the skies opened. To be sure, they had been opening and closing intermittently since the abatement of 1916's heavy autumn rains, but those showers proved to be no more than a rehearsal. The early rains of 1917 not only set in sooner than anyone had expected but also heralded the wettest season in East Africa's recorded history. Between January and May, the fighting fronts were a shallow ocean, studded with little islands where companies, battalions and regiments found themselves marooned for days and weeks at a time. Although shots were continually exchanged by what would only be slightly extravagantly described as submarine patrols, fighting of any real consequence became impossible. To all practical purposes, the rains imposed a four-month cease-fire on the opposing forces in East Africa.

For the British, this phase of the campaign was a struggle not so much to remain operational as to remain alive in ten thousand square miles of molasses. What was left of the invading armies was splayed out along a four-mundred-mile front, with supply routes—groping as far back as one hundred miles to the Central Railway—now largely impassable and for long stretches literally invisible. Even in the mountainous western sector, Northey's scattered KAR units were usually hobbled to their camps because only a trickle of food, ammunition and medicine could get through to them. One campaign historian summed up the British plight when he wrote that the army "went lamentably short of everything save water, of which there was an odious superfluity."

The experience of Nigerian units, temporarily holding most of the forward positions below the Rufiji, typified what the rest of the force had to put up with. The Nigerians were occupied mainly with bridge building, "road" repair and digging trenches and latrines in ground not yet submerged. They also went on patrols in canoes, often tying up to the grass roofs of houses which the floods had not carried away. In one of its more ambitious actions, a Nigerian battalion waded through twenty-five miles of swamp and half-drowned elephant grass to fire a few rounds at a German detachment, after which the men marched back to camp by a different route—up to their necks in water.

Ordinarily, this sort of thing might have been no more than an occupational discomfort of war. Thanks to the inundated supply lines, hunger made it something else. "February, March and April 1917 were all black months for the Nigerian Brigade," wrote its historian. "Our condition could not have been worse if we had been in a siege." The Nigerian officers received a daily food ration weighing five and one half ounces. It consisted of a half-ounce of bacon, one ounce of jam, one ounce of condensed milk, three quarters of an ounce of onions, and two and two-thirds ounces of "fresh" meat. Breakfast, lunch and supper for each enlisted man was eight ounces of rice.

Such banquets were enjoyed when food was relatively plentiful. At other times, one sampled whatever the sunken land would yield. "I doubt," wrote the brigade historian, "if the reader has ever tasted monkey's brains on ration biscuit, bush rat pie, or stewed hippo's sweetbreads, but all three were consumed . . . and thoroughly enjoyed." Not so delectable were the poisonous roots and herbs which killed a fair number of troops, although this failed to discourage other eating habits. The carcasses of mules, condemned after being slain by the tsetse fly or horse sickness, were dug up and eaten until it became necessary to burn them instead. One company ate part of a bridge. Its spars had been lashed together with strips of rawhide, which were stolen one night to make stock for a soup. The remains of the bridge were swept one hundred miles out to sea.

Under such conditions it was also natural that inflation should have made itself felt when an occasional luxury item became available at auctions of dead officers' effects. A bottle of Hennessey Three Star brandy was knocked down for fifty dollars, a toothbrush for six dollars.

As the waters continued to rise, the flow of supplies shrank proportionately. On the ninety-mile road connecting the Nigerian positions with the Central Railway, nearly every bridge was washed out. Most of the road itself lay under three or four feet of water. Even the stretches on higher ground swarmed with crocodiles, and had been so churned up by the rains as to become traps for all wheeled vehicles and animals. The army's few available porters, as often as not, were brought to a halt at the banks of the Rufiji, where a mill-race current continually snapped the overhead cables of flat-bottomed ferries and flicked the craft downstream as if they were paper boats. Carrier loads grew into small mountains on the river's northern bank.

Understandably, the famine-stalked Nigerians could not always appreciate such logistic problems, and bitter complaints were lodged (after long and arduous journeys) with supply officers in the rear; it was universally believed that these "base wallahs" were too immersed in the comforts and pleasures of Dar es Salaam to exert any real effort for famished combat soldiers. That attitude did not begin to change until one of the brigade's regiments was evacuated to the railway. After a two-week trek that would ordinarily have been completed in five days or less, one of the officers entrained for Dar, where he formally withdrew all his charges of incompetence. The wonder, he said, was that any supplies had reached the brigade at all.

For a change, the Germans also suffered. Apart from the brief threat of hunger along the Mgeta, the Schutztruppe had undergone no serious hardships from climate or weather, but the new deluge quickly made its presence felt. For a while, contact between von Lettow's headquarters and other units could be maintained only by boats which had to be paddled through a forest. Some companies were forced to make temporary bivouacs on tree limbs. Marches and patrols came to be known as "water pantomimes." A fair number of officers and askaris were drowned in the swiftly rising waters. At least one field hospital sank.

These relatively minor difficulties were compounded by an acute food shortage. By January of 1917, nearly all the maize grown in the Rufiji region had been consumed. The large fields that were being cultivated farther south near Liwale could not be harvested for several months. A few hundred acres remained to be picked in the Rufiji area, but they also needed long weeks before ripening. Drastic steps were necessary to stave off famine.

Von Lettow took them. First, the force itself was pared down by the release of all expendable personnel—mainly several thousand porters. Although confident that other bearers could be recruited when the time came to move again, von Lettow also knew that most of the discharged men lived inside the British lines and would be a useful source of information to the enemy. It could not be helped. A different kind of problem arose when a large number of "*bibis*"—the soldiers wives, whom the Germans sometimes called *askarifrauen*—were also told to go until the food shortage was relieved. They protested vociferously but were sent off to the south, escorted by a German NCO. After a day's march, the women halted, beat the noncom senseless and returned to their husbands. It took some time before they could be prevailed on to leave again.

Further trouble was not long in coming with the directive that no officer could have more than five servants. "That sounds a generous allowance to European ears," wrote von Lettow, "but under African conditions native attendance is really indispensable. . . . When one considers that in peacetime a travelling official on a long *safari* . . . took with him from eleven to thirteen bearers, in addition to two or three personal servants, it will be understood how drastic this order was and what a storm of indignation it aroused." Providentially, von Lettow himself had been setting an example all along with only three bearers and a cook. Besides which, his officers had no choice but to obey.

Then von Lettow cut the troops' maize flour ration. Originally it had been one kilogram per day, subsequently reduced to 750 grams. Now, a further paring-down to 600 grams (or 400 grams of rice) touched off another explosion of protest throughout the force. Company and detachment commanders deluged von Lettow's headquarters with telegrams, field telephone calls and runners carrying messages which warned that under the new regulations, the Schutztruppe would soon perish from malnutrition. "Many did not scruple," wrote von Lettow, "to lay the whole blame . . . at the door of the wicked commander-in-chief."

At this time, in fact, von Lettow was on the receiving end of considerable bad-mouthing—which sometimes fell just short of insubordination—by more than one German in the force. Although the unrest might have been a natural reaction to the hardships of rationing and the inactivity imposed by the rains, it was not a healthy sign in an army whose greatest strength lay in its morale. Worse, it was the kind of thing that could spread swiftly and reflect itself in a weakening of the will to further resistance. But von Lettow was not unduly troubled, for he also believed that the majority of the Schutztruppe's Europeans "had enough soldierly spirit to shut up the grousers pretty bluntly." The real measure of his troops' esprit, he felt, could be gauged in a wounded corporal's rejoinder to the complaints of a particularly strident barrack-room lawyer: "I tell you what: Colonel von Lettow is the brains of this force. You're its asshole."

And the army did manage to survive, bolstering its skeleton rations with game brought down by officer and askari hunting parties. "Owing to the demand for fat," wrote von Lettow, "hippopotamus shooting became a matter of existence," and detachment cooks soon learned the somewhat tricky art of extracting the animal's white succulent fat. Elephants were no less sought after for the same reason; "Ordinarily," von Lettow noted, "the elephant hunter gauges the length and weight of the tusk before firing; now the pressing question was: how much fat will the beast supply? For elephant fat is very good, and possibly tastes even better than that of the hippo."

Even this protein supplement, however, was hardly enough: a field company could reduce a four-ton elephant to its bare bones inside of twenty-four hours. What may have kept the troops from real starvation was a combination of ingenuity and plain good luck. One day, von Lettow visited an outlying camp and was served what he first thought to be asparagus but which proved to be unripe maize—normally not only inedible but poisonous. An officer, it appeared, had almost accidentally learned how to accelerate the ripening process by artificial drying. In this way, a substantial quantity of maize became available to the force; by early March, von Lettow could even raise the maize flour ration to 750 grams. Any immediate danger of famine had been eliminated.

And it was at about this time that the Schutztruppe also began a gradual withdrawal from the area below the Rufiji to the hopefully more fertile regions farther south. While the move witnessed little serious fighting, it did give von Lettow an opportunity to inconvenience the enemy. In retiring, the force abandoned not only its positions but all its sick and wounded to the British, "who took pity on their need"—von Lettow's way of saying that he had dumped a large and unwanted responsibility on already overburdened shoulders.

Hoskins, a man with a formidable Roman nose and a preference for wearing a sweater instead of his ribbon-bedecked tunic, had taken over from Smuts at record-breaking speed. When he received his new orders on January 20, he had just finished breakfast at his headquarters near Kibata, where he was still commanding the 1st Division. Mounting a horse at 10:30 A.M., he rode for twenty miles over the hills until he reached a rough dirt track where a Ford staff car picked him up, to bounce another forty miles into Kilwa. Here, a BE2C awaited him at the "aerodrome," and after a 160-mile flight over the Rufiji basin, he bumped down at the British army's forward command post at four o'clock in the afternoon, having covered some 220 miles in barely six hours.

There was need for this almost indecent haste. While the East African theatre may have been socked in by the shattering rains, a new offensive had to be readied swiftly, and at that stage of the campaign, the British army was hardly in a position to mount a punitive expedition against a leper colony. Apart from the attrition of the wet season, other factors had helped bring the force to new heights of impotence. Like Samson shorn of his hair, the army had lost nearly all of its fighting potential. Most of the South Africans —the bulk of British manpower in East Africa—and many of the Indians had been invalided home, and the huge gaps they left had been filled only partially by the Nigerians and Gold Coasters. Thousands of other troops lay in field and base hospitals; few would be certified fit to fight again. Disease had even begun to eat away at the indestructible KAR askaris. Thanks to starvation diets at the front, not many men in the field were capable of more strenuous action than tottering or splashing about on sentry duty.

And even if twenty thousand fresh troops were to arrive overnight, Hoskins would still have no means of supplying them: rain, terrain and tsetse had snapped the spine of British motor and animal transport. The Germans, to be sure, could not take the initiative, but in the early months of 1917, the British force was giving a good imitation of a beaten army.

The army, in fact, was back to square one, and Hoskins had to rebuild it from the ground up.

Hoskins' appointment was popular not only because it put a British officer back in the driver's seat but because he was very much the man to take charge of the army's reorganization. Like Eisenhower, albeit on a far smaller scale, his experience was largely administrative, and like all good desk men he knew how to get things done swiftly despite the booby traps of red tape that would often defeat the best of combat soldiers. But hardly had Hoskins waded into the task of putting the East African force back on its feet then he ran into a serious and totally unexpected snag.

It seemed that there was no longer any war to fight in East Africa.

No less a figure than Smuts had said so. "Regarding East Africa," he declared in a speech shortly after arriving in London, "the campaign . . . may be said to be over. . . . What is delaying the absolute end is the fact that March and April are the heavy rainy season." The Schutztruppe, Smuts added, was "merely the remnant of an army . . . and not a formidable fighting force."

Hoskins was flabbergasted. He was not alone. Smuts' pronouncement touched off a wave of astonished indignation that swept the British army. What was the man up to? How could the former commander-in-chief, of all people, even imply that the Schutztruppe had been trounced when it had yet to be caught? Smuts had built a large reservoir of good will and esteem among his troops, but it sprang a leak when his reports of the campaign's sudden conclusion began reaching East Africa. One is reminded of American generals in a later war who continually assured the home front that they could see the light at the end of the tunnel.

Bitterness grew with mail from home, congratulating or reproaching officers and men for having found a "safe" theatre. "It was a poor consolation to those of us left in the field," wrote the scout Arnold Wienholt, "to read that [Smuts] had been acclaimed as the conqueror of German East, and . . . that the German forces were now nothing but scattered fugitives amongst their fever swamps and jungles. . . . I remember being distinctly annoyed by a letter from a friend, who asked me why I stayed on in East Africa, on a 'black veld police patrolling job,' now that the campaign was finished here." Having just brought off a daring escape from a German POW camp, Wienholt was in an almost unique position to observe with first-hand authority that the Schutztruppe, "though much reduced in numbers, was still in the field and undefeated, with the *moral* of both whites and blacks probably higher than ever, and with a great stretch of country most suitable for a defensive and bush warfare still in enemy hands."

But this mattered little to the high command in London, for Smuts had become an oracle. He was now a member of the War Cabinet. Admiral

Lord Fisher, former First Sea Lord, was urging that Smuts lead the British army in France. Lloyd George was considering him for the command in Palestine.* As early as November 1916, Smuts had written to a friend that "in a few months the campaign will become a purely police matter." Now, if Smuts said the war in East Africa was over, the war in East Africa was over.

Thus the Imperial General Staff could only have been caught completely by surprise when Hoskins, like Oliver Twist, began asking for more: more artillery, more machine guns, more rifles, more bayonets, more ammunition, more medical supplies—more, in fact, of everything. And every item that Hoskins requested was urgently, indeed desperately, needed if the British force was to be overhauled and made ready for a fresh offensive when the rains ended. Hoskins eventually did receive all that he asked for, or nearly all, but after Smuts' declaration of peace, the business of requisitioning was almost like cracking a safe.

Meanwhile, the army's underpinnings needed to be reinforced with a workable means of moving supplies to the front. Poor roads, incredibly frightful weather, continual engine breakdowns and staggering animal casualties had shown the previous system of wheeled hooved transport to be a serious liability. Now, as the force prepared to penetrate a region whose few roads were known to be immeasurably worse than any yet encountered, it was clear that the old method must give way to something else. In March, Hoskins telegraphed the governor of British East Africa with a request that large-scale recruitment of African porters be initiated without delay.

In effect, Hoskins was proclaiming a revolution. Although the British had already been using some porters, they had never—for practical as well as humane reasons—considered the human black a suitable vehicle for the movement of supplies. But now, what was literally an army of bearers entered the service as the East Africa Carrier Corps. Its growth was phenomenal. Previously, the army had about 7,500 porters on its rolls; in the early part of 1917, that figure swelled to 135,000, subsequently reaching a grand total just short of 175,000—more than four times the size of the armed force in the field.

Not that other forms of transport were abandoned entirely. Light lorries, carrying loads of four hundred to six hundred pounds, were to be used in fairly large numbers, along a few roads running inland from coastal ports. But the roads, such as they were, seldom extended farther than twenty or thirty miles. When they came to an end, the porters would take over. From 1917 on, the army's ammunition, food, medicine and all other stores were moved almost exclusively by two-legged beasts of burden.

Every single porter volunteered, whether he wished to or not. Recruiting for the Carrier Corps had to be done on an assembly-line basis. District

* An apocryphal story has it that Botha urged Smuts to refuse, cabling: "Don't do it, Jannie. You and I know you are no general."

officers in British East Africa were expected to meet wartime emergency manpower quotas to keep the troops at the front alive; the swiftest and most efficient way to do this was to use press-gang methods in Kikuyu, Kavirondo and other tribal reserves. Not to put too fine a point on it, a large percentage of the Carrier Corps was shanghaied. For men who had seldom traveled more than ten or fifteen miles from their homes, the experience was emotionally shattering. Many a bearer would literally die of homesicknesss before the war ended.

To be sure, the porters were clothed and paid and fed and given good medical care. It was freely acknowledged that the British army could not have advanced a single yard against the Schutztruppe in 1917 and 1918 without the Carrier Corps. "I was most particular," wrote Wienholt, "not to allow an askari in any way to order or bully my porters. . . . My askaris were often told that I might manage without *them,* but never without my porters." The British troops even paid their respects to the carrier as a poor man's Gunga Din, with a bit of doggerel called "Omera":

> Oh! The Lindi road was dusty
> And the Lindi road was long
> But the chap wot did the hardest graft,
> And the chap wot did most wrong,
> Was the Kavirondo porter with 'is Kavirondo song.
> It was "Porter, njoo hapa!" *
> It was "Omera, hya! Git!"
> And Omera didn't grumble,
> He simply did his bit.

Still and all, for unlettered black tribesmen who knew little or cared less about the superiority of "civilization" over *"kultur,"* there was small reward in being kidnapped and forced to play the role of mule in an alien and deadly land. A porter's-eye-view of life in the Carrier Corps has been depicted vividly by the novelist Elspeth Huxley. It deserves quotation at some length.

There were four soldiers to take us, armed with rifles, and they marched us together down the road. The road was dry and the dust strong in our throats, and as we marched the noise that our feet made was ru-tu-tu-tu-tu-tu-tu on the road.

At Thika we were put into the train and taken to Nairobi, where we were given food and blankets, and then put into another train. Here we slept together in a wagon like cattle, on the hard floor; and the noise of the wheels was tee-chee-chee-chee-chee-chee-chee on the rails.

We stayed two days at Mombasa, and . . . were put into this wagon on the sea. We were locked into a small room with iron walls. Then the room began to move about beneath our feet: it was as if we had been in the belly of an animal. We were so frightened that we could not speak. . . .

* Come here.

But we saw land again at a place called Dar-es-Salaam, and came out of the ship. . . . We went by train to Dodoma, and there we were told to walk for ten days to Iringa. No European went with us, and no soldiers, only guides; but we could not run away, for everywhere there was nothing but bush. . . . We marched for many days. The sun made our heads like pots of gruel boiling on the fire, and our feet went ru-tu-tu-tu-tu-tu-tu through the bush. On the way many people got diarrhoea, but lay down and were left behind, and the hyenas ate them. . . . Soon we came to a camp of soldiers and I went with my brother and another man to see a European. Many people were dying under the same roof without being taken away; that building had a dreadful curse; there was death in it, and an evil smell. So I ran away and went to cut firewood; but when I inquired for my brother I was told that he had died.

We left that place and went on to a big river like a lake, where men took us across in boats. On the other side was a camp. Here a sickness fell upon men again and I was taken to another hospital; but people were dying all around me, and after two days I escaped in the night. Next day I went to work digging ditches, although my limbs were weak.

A month later we marched on again; we reached some mountains. . . . We stayed at a place called the camp of bullets. It was on the top of a hill. We carried bullets down to the bottom, where wounded men were taken, and we carried wounded men back to the top. Sometimes they died on the way, but we still had to carry them, and to defile ourselves with corpses; and at night we were too tired to cook food.

From the camp of bullets we were taken to a place where we had to dig graves and bury those who had been killed. We had to lay our hands on corpses. There were two flags, a red one and a white. When the red flag was hoisted we were told to stop work and lie down. When the white flag was put up we had again to bury corpses. . . .

I was no longer afraid to touch corpses. I wished to die, and therefore no danger could come to me from thahu [a curse]. I walked about seeking a bullet that would kill me, but I could not find one. I did not think that I should ever see my home again. Sometimes I dreamt of home, but we did not speak of our own country at all in the camp, because we tried to keep our minds empty of such thoughts that hurt us more than hunger or wounds. . . .

Those of us who returned agreed that we would never speak of the things that had occurred, because they are too evil to be mentioned; and even now I have not told you all of what I saw, for words do not exist to describe such things. Sometimes these things return to me in dreams, and then I wake and I cannot asleep again. Sometimes, when I see a European, they come back to me also, because it was the Europeans who captured me and the evils that swallowed me when they took me for the war were caused by them. But now I have a wife and children, and I do not often think of such things any more.

Hoskins also needed fresh blood to spill. A year earlier, when Smuts forced his way through the Taveta Gap, British strength in the East African theatre had reached a peak of thirty thousand officers and men. Now, with nearly all the South Africans and Indians gone, the army had been whittled down to half that figure. In fact, if one subtracted the men in hospital, it was just possible that the British at this stage of the game were actually outnumbered by the Schutztruppe's eleven hundred Germans and seventy-three hundred Africans. To change those odds, Hoskins ordered a speedup in the expansion of the KAR.

If the army had been slow in utilizing porters rather than vehicles and animals as the backbone of its transport, so too had it dragged its feet in exploiting African manpower as an invaluable—and inexhaustible—reservoir of soldiery. To be sure, the arrival of the Nigerian, Gold Coast and West Indies contingents in 1916 had indicated some awareness of what might be accomplished with black troops. Shortly before his departure, Smuts himself had initiated a buildup of the KAR to a strength of about eight thousand. Nonetheless, before Hoskins took over, it was quasi-official policy to disregard East Africa as a source of recruitment.

The two principal reasons for this neglect contradicted each other. Although the KAR, in a hundred obscure but vicious actions, had showed themselves beyond question to be the best bush fighters in the British army, more than one high-ranking officer stoutly maintained that African troops could be of little use in modern warfare. But many dissenters from this view also opposed the recruitment of blacks—because they seemed *too* good. One of Francis Brett Young's fictional officers spoke for a substantial number of other whites when he called African participation in the war "one of the damned dangerous things about this campaign—for the future of Africa, I mean. Up till now the white man in Africa's been a sort of God. Now black men, on both sides, have seen the pretty spectacle of white men running away from them. Our Askaris, as well as the Germanis', are devils to fight; they don't know what danger is, and they don't feel pain like we do. It's been a hell of a mistake, in my opinion, bringing them into it. There'll be the devil and all to pay for it sooner or later."

That was the way white men thought in those days. While one cannot estimate the degree to which fear of the black ogre retarded British military progress in the East African campaign, that fear was anything but a British monopoly. The time had only just passed when an African tribesman was considered no more than a sort of super-intelligent animal, but another half-century would have to go before he would be deemed fit—albeit grudgingly—to share equally with Caucasians in the mismanagement of human affairs. Meanwhile, although there remained little doubt of the African's credentials as a bona fide *homo sapiens,* he was still consigned to that half-world called "native." This meant that while you could like him and admire him and even respect him you also had to be on your guard against him. After all, it was common knowledge that the native mind was unfathomable; who could tell when he might succumb to some atavistic impulse and revert to his savage ways, smashing up the lofty but frail edifice of virtue and cheap manufactures which so nicely sugar-coated the pill of white mastery? The era of punitive expeditions—whether by British, German, French, Belgian or Portuguese authorities—against fractious African tribes had not yet ended. Any European could still push the panic button at the mere thought of the fate that might befall white women and children in a "native uprising."

It was even enough to make enemies submerge their differences, at least temporarily. In 1915, when one John Chilembwe, an African convert to the Watchtower sect, led a band of fellow blacks on a vest-pocket Mau Mau rampage against the British in Nyasaland, a rumor spread that the rebellion had been instigated by the Germans. Perhaps this would have been shrewd tactics, but more like the reverse was true. At one British outpost, a Schutz-truppe officer, captured in earlier fighting, organized the defenses and actually took command of the garrison.

However, while the white man's anxiety over being driven out of Africa by hordes of murdering savages was very real, the actual danger simply did not exist, and the more rational leaders of both sides knew this quite well. The Germans, of course, had had no choice but to recruit an African army. The British had the option of changing their minds, and when they exercised it they acted wisely: if anyone could beat the enemy at his own game it was the black soldier.

As if to make up for lost time, the KAR began to expand like a balloon. In January 1917, Hoskins ordered its establishment increased from thirteen to twenty battalions—which were formed into seven regiments—giving the force a total strength of twenty-four thousand officers and men. Old hands from the veteran outfits formed cadres for the new contingents, which rapidly swelled with volunteers. Training had to be brief: rain or not, the men were needed in the lines at once if not sooner. There was barely time to give the troops the rudiments of close- and extended-order drill, to show them how to fire, strip and clean their Enfield rifles and Vickers machine guns. It was acknowledged, not without a certain anxiety, that many things usually taught in camp must be learned the hard way. Which, of course, was the only way if one survived it.

But the rookies proved willing and attentive pupils. They gave their instructors an unexpected assist by drilling for long hours on their own time. They wore the King's uniform with as much swagger as any regiment of guards, and they looked more than properly warlike in their smart khaki shorts and drill blouses, gleaming brass shoulder insignia and fire-engine-red tarbooshes. In formal parades, their esprit got an extra boost from the music of a newly formed KAR regimental band, whose ex-Lancs bandmaster composed a KAR marching song—with Swahili lyrics—to the tune of "Men of Harlech."

But most significantly, many of the new troops—perhaps the majority—were anything but green. Not atypical was the recruit who saw a company sergeant major wearing the campaign ribbon of an almost forgotten punitive expedition and demanded one for himself, claiming to have fought in the same war. This was found to be true. He had been on the other side.

White officers and NCOs also needed instruction. Most had been transferred from the Western Front and were ignorant not only of bush warfare but of local languages; crash courses in Swahili loomed large in their training. Even then, they had a tough act to follow. "The native soldier," wrote one British general, "is a very shrewd critic of those set over him. The prestige of the British officers, and . . . non-commissioned officers, who had served in the King's African Rifles up to that time was very high indeed. The askari looked up to them almost as supermen." One could not expect the fledging white leaders to meet those standards, and some—particularly shell-shock cases—fell tragically short of the mark. But on the whole they accepted their new commands with the same resolution that had helped them survive the carnage of Ypres and the Somme. They also developed a swift respect and affection for the men they led.

Much more to the point, the men developed a swift respect and affection for the new officers.

And the battalions continued to grow. Before the campaign ended, their troop strength would rise to nearly thirty-five thousand (to von Lettow's great delight). The KAR, in fact, was to become the British army in East Africa. A black man's war was in the making.

As the rains came to an end in May, Hoskins' new army prepared to bring the campaign to an end also. Never before had the British been better positioned to do so, since the Germans by now had been crowded into the southeast corner of their colony.

It was hardly a tight corner, to be sure; about the size of North Vietnam, it was also made to order for snipers, hidden gun emplacements, raids on supply convoys, ambushes of large fighting columns and, above all, the maddening dispersal into the bush which had been von Lettow's hole card for nearly three years. Yet all these assets were about to reach a point of diminishing returns. Under the relentless pressure of British armies converging from the north, west and east, the Germans would be squeezed, slowly but steadily, down to their southern border; before the year was out, they would no longer have anywhere to run. Von Lettow would be left with the choice of a last-ditch fight or surrender. Either way, it meant the end of German resistance in East Africa. The final phase of the long pursuit was at hand.

On the eve of the grand offensive, Hoskins suddenly found himself without an army to lead. Almost without notice and for no immediately discernible reason, command of the British East African Expeditionary Force had been handed over to van Deventer.

At about the same time, the lieutenant colonel commanding the Schutztruppe received a long belated promotion to major general in the German army.

18

Last Stand

WHEN SMUTS FIRST WENT OUT to East Africa, Botha had written him: "Be careful and let van Deventer always keep a captaincy with you." Van Deventer was now the sixth general to serve as British commander against von Lettow. He was also starting off with about three strikes against him.

Strike one was the widespread belief that his appointment had been political, which did not sit well with an army whose South African element had by this time shrunk to an all but negligible fraction. Hoskins, extremely well liked in the predominantly British officer corps, had been shunted off to an obscure post in Mesopotamia, and this did not ease the path for the new commander. Strike two was van Deventer's near-total lack of experience with the paperwork so dear to British staffs. He had proved himself over and over again as a fighter but until his service in East Africa he had never commanded anything larger than a regiment. The staff of his own 2nd Division was notoriously slipshod, and his personal indifference to administrative matters was regarded as slightly short of disastrous.

Strike three was the worst of all: van Deventer was a "Dutchman." Smuts had won acceptance by virtue of his genius and commanding personality, but van Deventer—especially after the departure of the popular Hoskins—could be seen at best as little more than an oafish Boer with few of the rough edges smoothed off. He not only spoke English haltingly, often relying on an interpreter, but sometimes—owing to an old bullet wound—had trouble with his own Afrikaans. He even seemed to enjoy pointing out this handicap to British officers who had fought in the Boer War, reminding them that "they" had shot him in the throat and were thus responsible for his speech defect. He always smiled when he said this, but it was hardly an auspicious way to take charge of one's former enemies.

The ice quickly melted. Suspicions of Boer prejudice were dissipated with van Deventer's immediate appointment of Sheppard—who epitomized everything British in a British general—as his chief of staff. There were approving chuckles when van Deventer heard the appeal of an Afrikaner sergeant who had been sentenced to one month's hard labor by a British court-martial for stealing some jodhpurs; the sergeant's countryman-commander made it two months. And it was presently conceded that van Deventer's weaknesses as an administrator were not really calamitous at all. Hoskins had been put in charge of the army when it cried out for reorganization; he had done his work so well that the force no longer needed a desk man but a combat man at its head. Let Sheppard do the paperwork; let van Deventer come to grips with von Lettow.

The main thrust of van Deventer's strategy, moreover, had already begun to take shape under Hoskins. A base had been established at Lindi, German East Africa's southermost port, from which a strong task force was to drive inland and place itself astride the Schutztruppe's route of withdrawal, thus accelerating the final showdown. However, since the Lindi region was ideally suited to the kind of dodging at which the Germans excelled and which could possibly be continued until the late autumn or early winter rains gave them another long reprieve, it became imperative that von Lettow be brought to book before the end of summer. This would be done not only by getting behind him and waiting for him to retreat to Lindi but also by hastening that retirement with a massive frontal assault on the main German force, which was now concentrated a few miles southwest of Kilwa. The western theatre, to be sure, had not been forgotten: Northey was still expected to round up the German columns under Wahle and Kraut. But the muscle of the offensive was to be flexed at Kilwa and Lindi.

Basically, it was to work like this: the 1st Division, now under General Hannyngton and redesignated the Kilwa Force, would roll down on the Schutztruppe Kilwa positions with flank support from the Nigerians on its right, while the Lindi columns simultaneously continued to build their strength for the vital push across the German line of retreat. By September at the latest, it was expected that the two forces would join hands and form a ring around the Germans.

While the new plan was almost identical with Smuts' abortive Rufiji encirclement—and for that matter with nearly all British strategic moves of the campaign—it benefited from one significant difference: this time, the Schutztruppe would be hemmed in on all sides. Even if the Kilwa and Lindi columns somehow failed to link up, Northey would still block off any attempted German breakout to the west, while if von Lettow continued his retreat to the south, he would march only a few miles before he had no colony left to defend. Below the German border lay Portuguese East Africa —a wilderness unknown even to the Schutztruppe. To the east was the Indian Ocean. Von Lettow's askaris could swim only so far.

The initial weeks of the British offensive were not encouraging, particularly to the troops advancing from Kilwa, who seemed unable to do much more than get lost. Colonel G. M. Orr, one of Hannyngton's column commanders, summed it up when he remarked that British knowledge of the country in 1916 had been scanty, while in 1917 it was nonexistent. The tangled land, said Orr, "gave one the feeling of working in the dark. . . . Close touch and movement by compass was usually the only safe procedure." And even compasses could be misled by maps, particularly British maps which as a rule contained either immensities of blank white space or masses of meticulously drawn misinformation. "A nice map of Switzerland with a few East African names upon it," wrote a Nigerian officer, "would have been just about as useful."

The only dependable sources of intelligence were local African tribesmen who acted as guides, but they presented a unique problem. "One of my greatest difficulties," wrote Lieutenant Christopher J. ("Buster Brown") Thornhill, an intelligence scout, "was to keep the guides when the bullets began to fly." At such times, said Thornhill, "the wretched guide would take one glance [at] the nearest bush, but the Intelligence Officer, expecting this, would hang on to the black man like grim death. . . . It was a very serious matter for all if we lost our only guide, as . . . the army could not march until a new guide was found."

In fact, recruiting local talent was seldom overly difficult. In this area, once devastated by German reprisals following the Maji-Maji uprising, Africans as a rule were glad to work for white men whom they looked on as liberators, and if they did not cooperate, the liberators simply kidnapped them. But even with local assistance, the lagging pace of the floundering advance was reduced even further by continual enemy interference. It is not extravagant to say that the southwest drive of the Kilwa Force was a skirmish that never ended. During one phase of the push British patrols were ambushed as often as two or three times a day. "I cannot think of anything quite so nerve wracking," said Thornhill, "as having to do this sort of thing for a week on end. . . . Whenever the enemy found themselves in a good position they fought desperately, and as they were able to choose their ground I think we generally suffered the most casualties."

The standard pattern of mobile defense against a bushwhacking operation was hardly designed to discourage the Germans. "One would be walking along a path," wrote Thornhill, ". . . the company doing advance-guard extended in open formation to right and left. . . . We would presently be approaching suspicious-looking country, but dare not waste time in reconnoitring; for we, the advance guard, were after all merely a buffer of the larger force and the General behind expected us to push on and take blows. Without a second's warning machine gun and rifle fire would burst out right in front of us and everyone would drop to the ground as one man, some never to rise again. . . . If the affair was to be a mere ambush by a small body of enemy sent to worry the advancing column, they would soon be driven back; but if it were to be a big affair the main body would come up and there would follow a pitched battle, perhaps lasting only a few hours, perhaps several days."

The hardest-fought of these engagements took place in mid-July, near the village of Narungombe, about forty miles southwest of Kilwa. Here, a sizable Schutztruppe detachment guarded several waterholes which the British had to capture if they were not to perish from thirst. The German force consisted of about one thousand askaris backed up by forty-eight machine guns and a pair of three-inch field pieces. Although outnumbered by two to one, their commander, Captain Eberhard von Lieberman, had deployed them on high ground behind solidly built earthworks stretching for nearly three miles across the British line of advance, and "so well camouflaged with dry grass," according to Thornhill, "as to look exactly like the surroundings." The left flank of the defenses was protected by impenetrable thorn, the right flank by a swamp, and for three hundred yards in front of the position the bush had been cleared to deny the attackers any cover.

Yet Colonel Orr, who commanded the British column, decided to crack this barrier by sending a strong force directly into the teeth of the German fire in a head-on assault. Although this seemed to guarantee that many of his men would be walking straight into the conclusion of their lives, the tactic in fact was not quite that suicidal. The attacking troops would not only have the support of simultaneous turning movements against both German flanks but would also be protected in their own advance by the deadly curtain of a Stokes mortar barrage.

These relatively new additions to the British arsenal had already proved as useful as the big field guns, especially since the Germans were without mortars themselves—and, more to the point, without any effective defenses against the weapons. Unlike conventional artillery, mortars made scarcely a sound when fired, giving no hint of their location. Their shells climbed upwards almost vertically, and the whistling of their descent could not be heard until a second or so before they burst. To all practical purposes, there was no way to take cover against these missiles that seemed to plop out of the sky like eggs laid by some invisible giant bird. The mortars, it was believed, would reduce if not entirely eliminate the German fire along the whole length of the front-line sector.

The advance began shortly after dawn. By noon, it had become a shambles. The Gold Coast Regiment, which spearheaded the attack, had been forced to dig in before being systematically ground up by the very rifle and machine gun fire that the mortars had been expected to silence. Not that the mortars were idle; it was simply that their shells kept landing far short of their target, presenting a greater threat to the Gold Coasters than the Germans. At one point, the bursts even ignited the short dry grass, forcing the Gold Coasters to expose themselves to the Schutztruppe guns once more as they leaped from their shallow rifle pits to stamp out the rapidly spreading blaze. The smoke from the fire also made the German defenses even less visible to the already rattled mortar crews, and it was not long before the Gold Coast troops were facing annihilation. With nearly all of the regiment's officers dead, African corporals and sergeants found themselves commanding platoons and companies which rapidly shrank as the German rifles and machine guns stepped up the tempo of their fire.

The enveloping colur ns were faring no better. On the British left, a newly recruited KAR battalion, in action for the first time, was almost demobilized on the spot by a German counterattack which completely ended Orr's hopes of turning that flank. The troops on the right were mired down in the swamp while being pinned down by sheets of machine gun bullets. By sunset, the attackers on all fronts had withdrawn to highly insecure lines several hundred yards to the rear. It was a staggering setback for the British, who had planned to be in possession of the waterholes before nightfall.

It was also the time to rout the British entirely, and Lieberman now ordered an all-out counterattack on Orr's right flank, held precariously by the KAR battalion which had been halted and badly bruised in the swamp that afternoon. It was a typical Schutztruppe *banzai* charge, turning the air almost solid with piercing yells, whining bullets and swishing bayonets. Even the unwounded KAR troops later found their uniforms reduced to rags. But the battalion somehow managed to dig its heels in and wait for the fury of the German onslaught to spend itself—at which point the British askaris threw Lieberman's men completely off balance in a sudden bayonet counter-counterattack. Before they could recover from their surprise, the Germans abandoned several machine guns and a large sector of their earthwork line. From this position, Orr prepared to resume the attack at sunrise.

Attack proved unnecessary. Next morning, the Germans had vanished. Although no longer able to hold the Narungombe position, Lieberman had gained his objective: to make the British pay an exorbitant price for the waterholes. And with six hundred casualties—nearly 25 percent of their force—the British had got no bargain.

Von Lettow's initial reaction to the news of the battle was one of anger. He himself was on his way to Narungombe with reinforcements when he learned that Lieberman, through no fault of his own, had been unable to obey a personal order to defend the place at any cost until the arrival of the fresh troops. Von Lettow found it infuriating to be "within reach of a most important success which was snatched from our grasp by accident"— although what was accidental about the KAR counterattack is conjectural. Presently, however, he simmered down, taking comfort in the knowledge that "in spite of his superiority the enemy had suffered a severe defeat."

That may have been putting it a bit strongly, but Orr's column had not exactly brought off a resounding triumph.

If the Germans had to fall back, slowly but visibly, before overwhelming British pressure, they continued to hold their own against nature in spite of increasingly harsh conditions. Although the troops were usually on very short commons they did not starve. Artificial drying of unripe maize had become the standard process for providing the askaris with their barely adequate cornmeal rations. Big-game hunting was risky because rifle shots could be heard at great distances, but the gamble was taken often enough to give the force at least a token protein diet from elephants, hippos and occasional antelopes. When salt ran out, the Germans emulated local tribesmen by collecting and burning plants whose ashes yielded an acceptable if less than flavorsome salt. Von Lettow personally tried his hand as a baker in experiments with wheatless bread, coming up with loaves made from millet, cassava, sweet potatoes and maize. Their taste was sometimes improved with a mixture of boiled wild rice.

By now, the officers had adjusted to their poor man's retinue of one servant and one cook apiece, and presided ingeniously over what in fact were self-contained little households that subsisted on the fruits of hunting and grubbing. The more affluent of these "families" occasionally found (or stole) poultry or a few stray goats which accompanied them on the march —although even barnyard sounds could threaten to reveal a detachment's position. Von Lettow recalled that "an order issued in one force that the crowing of cocks before 9 a.m. was forbidden brought no relief."

The medical services also managed to carry on, although standard field hospital practices were fast becoming a luxury. So hard pressed, in fact, were the force's six doctors that they recruited a seventh: an army veterinarian whose dwindling animal clientele allowed him to treat a vaulting number of human cases. Including this man, the German medical staff may have been the best in the East African theatre. It almost had to be. Medicinal stores were shrinking to dangerous lows, some stocks had given out entirely, but the shortages were overcome in countless ways. Local plants and drugs yielded up, among other things, a disinfectant, digitalis and benzine substitutes, a synthetic immersion oil and a remedy for diarrhea whose effectiveness had been demonstrated by witch doctors. Ointment bases were made from hippo and elephant fat. Particular testimony to the German doctors' skill at making do was the army's almost ridiculously low incidence of gangrene and tetanus—despite an overabundance of jagged wounds and a climate that encouraged every imaginable kind of putrefaction.

Necessity also became the mother of improvisation in the Schutztruppe's gravest medical crisis: the exhaustion of the absolutely vital quinine tablets —at a time when the whites were becoming less resistant to malaria than ever before. A quinine stopgap was devised by the senior medical officer, Staff Surgeon Moritz Taute, who had brought a quantity of Peruvian bark with him from Morogoro. When boiled, this substance produced a liquid quinine with a taste so vile as to make it all but undrinkable. Without it, every German in the force might have died of malaria. The stuff came to be known as "Lettow-Schnapps."

Even when bandages ran out, the Schutztruppe doctors came up with substitutes, resorting to African clinical practices as they learned to make dressings and compresses from beaten bark. Uniforms also augmented the bandage supply; torn up and disinfected, an officer's tunic or an askari's trousers could even be used several times over after boiling. The army began to look like a convention of hoboes but at least its wounds were covered.

And it could still march and fight.

One German column was not in retreat. While von Lettow's main force continued to withdraw slowly in the southeast, a renegade band of Schutztruppe officers and askaris was running wild in the north, cutting a swathe of pillage and terror across a huge region that had ostensibly been conquered and secured by the Allies. There had been nothing quite like it since the mugging of the Uganda Railway.

When this unexpected move began, it was almost as much an act of insubordination against von Lettow as a counteroffensive against the British. Captain Max Wintgens, who headed one of Wahle's three main columns in the west, was openly resentful of von Lettow. He believed that his own five-hundred-man detachment had been denied its fair share of new rifles from the two German blockade runners, and he blamed this on the Schutztruppe commander. Early in 1917, Wahle's detachments began edging off to the east with the objective of rejoining von Lettow at last, but Wintgens did not go along. In February, his own column was 150 miles south of Iringa. Instead of marching east, Wintgens about-faced the troops and set off in a northerly direction.

The British became confused. A rumor spread that Wintgens was heading for the Tabora district, where most of his men had been recruited, and where, it was said, he planned to disband the force. But the five hundred askaris, with their thirteen machine guns and three field pieces, did not seem ready to demobilize as they skirted the virtually unprotected borders of Northern Rhodesia, looting and laying waste the countryside on their route of march. Nor did they show any peaceable intent when they slew nineteen KAR askaris and badly cut up twenty-six others in a shootout with a British detachment that tried to block their path. A serious chase now began, with a large KAR force in full cry. If Wintgens indeed intended to cop out of the war at Tabora, he also seemed bent on giving the enemy a run for its money in the meantime.

He did that. By mid-March, although it had been kept from crossing into Northern Rhodesia, the German column remained at large, ploughing steadily northward toward Tabora through the coarse desert seaweed of the horizonless flatlands below the Central Railway. A special KAR unit was formed for the express purpose of heading Wintgens off. Perhaps suitably, this five-hundred-man posse included three hundred former Schutztruppe askaris who for one reason or another had thrown in their lot with the foe—making it necessary for their British officers to learn German words of command. Late in March, the new force set off southward from the Central line. Wintgens was now being hemmed in on his front as well as his rear. Almost casually, however, he sidestepped both pursuers and continued his swift northward advance. Even a Belgian battalion, brought in from the west, failed to slow down—much less to halt—the attacking fugitives.

Early in May, Wintgens received another honor with the formation of a miniature British army, made up of KAR, Indian and South African troops, whose only mission was to round up the renegade column. It may have been fitting that the commander of this seventeen-hundred-man force, Brigadier General W. F. S. Edwards, was a former officer of the British East Africa Police. But Edwards never got the chance to make a daring arrest. On May 21, Wintgens was knocked out of the action—not by the British but by typhus. From a litter he handed over the column to his second in command, Captain Heinrich Naumann, with orders to continue the advance while he himself remained behind to surrender.

Naumann marched off. But there was no longer any talk of disbanding at Tabora. Changing direction, Naumann struck northeast. He seemed to be making for an isolated stretch of the Central Railway, but his plans were shrouded in mystery. The war's boldest raid had begun.

By this time, a Nigerian regiment had joined the pursuit, boarding a troop train at Morogoro and clanking along westward on what was hoped would be a collision course with the German raiders. It turned out instead to be a precarious game of tag. At dawn on May 26, while the Nigerians' vintage locomotive took on fuel at a wood stack about forty miles east of Tabora, Naumann was leading advance units of his column across the tracks—or rather beneath them, through a culvert in thick bush less than two miles from the train. One of the patrols which he sent out to cover the crossing ambushed a small Nigerian party, killing two of its men and wounding five in a blast of rifle fire from a dense clump of thorn. Naumann then had the telegraph wire cut. A British repair crew came out from Tabora in a motor tractor and got into a violent skirmish with the Nigerians when each mistook the other for Naumann's band. By now, however, the Germans had left the railway far to the south; they had a commanding lead when the Nigerians finally took up the chase again.

Naumann's objective, at least for the moment, was the port of Mwanza on Lake Victoria, nearly two hundred miles north of the railway. His men would have to step off if they were to get there before being overtaken, for they were following a roundabout dog-leg route. Food was running short.

An entire day had to be wasted rustling the bony livestock of an African village. By this time the Nigerians had picked up the spoor again and were barely a day's march behind, eating up slightly less than twenty miles of thorn every twenty-four hours—although they almost lost the track several times, so heavily had it been trampled by elephant herds.

Contact was maintained, however, through the continual reports the Nigerians received of the brigands. One of these came early in June: the town of Singida had surrendered to Naumann without firing a shot, since there was not a shot to fire. Singida's two British administrative officers were treated courteously and allowed to keep their money and personal belongings—although the government safe was blown up and rifled. Shortly after this, it was learned that Naumann had reached a British-occupied German fort at Mkalama, fifty miles farther north, and had the place under siege. Reinforced by a Belgian column, the Nigerians raced to what they hoped would be not only the rescue but also the end of the Naumann nuisance.

As sieges go, this was not a long one. Under a white flag, a German officer approached the fort and demanded its surrender. The British garrison commander declined in impolite language, adding that the United States had just entered the war—possibly to give Naumann the idea that an A.E.F. infantry division was about to come charging out of the bush. Certainly the garrison could have used a helping hand. It consisted of six British officers and thirty askaris. They were outnumbered by twenty to one. Naumann hastened to exploit the odds, ordering the crews of his three one-pound guns to open fire on the fort. He had reason to expect a quick capitulation. Before the Germans abandoned the fort during van Deventer's drive from Kondoa Irangi in 1916, they had concealed dynamite charges in the walls. It was altogether likely that a shell from Naumann's pocket barrage would strike one of these spots and blow open a hole big enough to admit an army.

What Naumann did not know was that the British had discovered and removed the hidden explosives. So the one-pounders banged away to little avail; the Germans had built their forts well. But after three days, it began to look as if the British might be compelled to haul down their handkerchief-sized Union Jack: the fort's water supply was nearly exhausted, and rifle ammunition was down to seventeen rounds per man. The British askaris, moreover, had previously served in the Schutztruppe and knew that they could only expect instant hanging when Naumann entered the fort. In fact, they were preparing to desert in a body and make for the bush when advance units of the Belgian-Nigerian column were seen approaching. Thus, when the rescuers finally marched into the fort, it was Naumann's troops rather than the defenders that had taken to the scrub. A British plane tried to halt them with a rain of steel darts, but the missiles came closer to cutting up a Nigerian rifle company. One killed a cow.

At this point, Naumann decided that if he continued toward Mwanza he would be trapped. He therefore struck east, and for the next four months his dwindling force ravaged at will through the northern part of the German colony—with upwards of two thousand British, Belgian, Nigerian, Indian, South African and KAR troops in vain pursuit. For mobility, the column was split into a number of small raiding parties. They roamed the countryside like gangs of vandals, shooting up administrative posts, plundering supply depots and generally terrorizing the entire British-occupied region north of the Central Railway. At the end of August, when they reached the vicinity of the Northern line, one band carried out a bold daylight strike at the Kahe station, burning military stores, looting several stationary trains, killing a number of passengers, capturing three British officers and leaving the station building in flames. It was as if Pancho Villa had moved to Africa.

And the worst was yet to come. In September, the word went out that Naumann was preparing to cross the border into British territory. Cable and telegraph lines hummed in panic as messages flashed to van Deventer from the governor of British East Africa and other civil officials. There was even an SOS from the Colonial Secretary in London. As if van Deventer, five hundred miles to the south and with his own plate full, could have done anything to protect the colony's all but unshielded border.

Luckily the raid never came off. By the end of September, Naumann had begun to run out of steam. Most of his independent parties had finally been captured. So narrow had the gap become between his own band and the pursuing troops—nearly all of them mounted—that the German askaris did not even have time to cook meals. On September 26, the elements of the KAR, the South African Cape Corps and a South African mounted regiment (whose commander had once served in the U.S. Cavalry) managed to run their quarry into a small range of hills and surround them. A howitzer was brought up to blast Naumann from the hideout. But even then he did not quite surrender. Instead, he sent out a runner under a white flag, with a message demanding a conference. This was agreed to, and it was not until October 2 that Naumann formally capitulated, emerging from the hills with 14 German officers and NCOs, 165 askaris and 250 porters.

For some reason, von Lettow belittled Naumann's exploit. "It is to be regretted," he wrote, "that this operation, carried out with so much initiative and determination, became separated so far from the main theatre as to be of little use." The British did not agree. Naumann's little band of bushwhackers, said the official historian of the KAR, had "involved British forces in a chase exceeding 1,600 miles, created disorganization far beyond its potentialities, and diverted many units that should have been employed elsewhere."

Naumann in fact can be said to have played von Lettow's own role, writ small but far from insignificant.

More or less concurrent with the Wintgens-Naumann adventure was the gradual withdrawal of the other German forces from the western theatre. This, too, had to be a setback for the British because it was not so much a retreat as a getaway. Northey's objective had been to keep Wahle and Kraut from reaching von Lettow, but the bumpy, unshaven terrain of the southwest gave the hares an enormous edge over the hounds. Without too much difficulty, Wahle was able to sidle gradually eastwards to Mahenge, from which key position he could either link up with von Lettow's main force or move south to stiffen the German defenses outside Lindi. Kraut followed a less direct route southward. He covered his tracks well and was undoubtedly assisted by the diversion which Wintgens and Naumann had created in their sudden dash to the north.

All these divergent moves forced Northey to disperse his own troops across a five-hundred-mile front, diminishing rather than consolidating their power of pursuit. For a time, it seemed as if Northey could do little but join in football games and polo matches on mules at his headquarters south of Iringa.

And in April, Northey was almost jolted from his mule when scouts reported that Kraut had reached the Portuguese border. Here, it seemed, the German force was either raiding Portuguese frontier posts or threatening the undefended eastern border of Nyasaland. Very possibly it was both.

Now the whole western front shifted. Northey immediately moved his headquarters five hundred miles south to Zomba, one of Nyasaland's two capitals. He also ordered a massive troop transfer. A KAR battalion humped itself over the mile-high Livingstone Mountains to the north shore of Lake Nyasa, where a steamer carried the askaris to Fort Johnston, the lake's southernmost port. From this place they began marching north once more, through the shriveled, unknown wastes of Portuguese East Africa, to stave off Kraut's thrust into Nyasaland or to block off any move he might make eastward in the direction of Lindi. If they could.

Their northern drive was the usual bad dream of hunger, thirst and sickness, relieved only by occasional skirmishes with German patrols. Since Kraut's main force—nearly one thousand strong—would not be stopped unless the KAR column could overcome the near-insuperable obstacle of flushing enemy troops from the opaque vastnesses of thorn which concealed position, movement and direction, a BE2C was attached to the British force for air reconnaissance of the region. At least one long-distance flight record was broken when the plane's observer squeezed some extra petrol tins into his cockpit and managed to refuel while airborne. The craft also became the British army's first flying ambulance, carrying a badly wounded KAR officer to a base hospital in Nyasaland. What else it accomplished was conjectural. "Owing to the terribly thick nature of the country, and lack of good information and maps," wrote the KAR battalion commander, ". . . the 'Old Bee' could not help us much in reconnaissances." In due course, the KAR troops recrossed the border into German territory, but they never caught Kraut; his columns eventually joined up with other Schutztruppe forces near Lindi.

The Germans were needed there: by the summer of 1917, the Lindi region was fast taking shape as the site of the East African campaign's Armageddon.

Before its capture by the Royal Navy in the autumn of 1916, Lindi had been the chief southern port of German East Africa. It was a typical coastal city, its harbor filled with dhows, outriggers and an occasional steamer, its waterfront dominated by a huge whitewashed stone fort and a handful of two-story commercial-residential buildings with red tile or corrugated iron roofs. The rest of the town was a goat-strewn maze of mud-walled, grass-roofed African houses, partly shaded by coco palms and mangoes. A broad creek known as the Lindi river emptied into the harbor; about ten miles upstream it was fed by the much longer Lukuledi river. The Lukuledi's course ran about sixty miles north of—and parallel to—the great Rovuma river, which marked the German-Portuguese border. Between Lindi and the Rovuma stood a three-hundred-square-mile highland region called the Makonde Plateau; its slopes were thickly wooded, its crests barren. Most of the area's African population was of the Makonde tribe, well known even in 1917 for its remarkably surrealistic wood carvings.

Although Lindi and its environs were practically the only part of the German colony's southern region with any white settlement worth mentioning—a number of fairly large plantations lay a few miles outside the port—the land for the most part was unhealthy. From a military standpoint it was also, as usual, much better suited to resistance than to attack. The baobab tree was the dominant feature of the low-lying, rolling countryside. With its short, grotesquely fat trunk and multitudinous tentacle-like limbs, the baobab served well as a sniper's nest, a machine gun emplacement, an artillery observation post or concealment for scouts. In a pinch it could even furnish an emergency water supply, its trunk sometimes yielding more than two hundred gallons. In short, a useful supplement to the vast tracts of man-high thorn in which a small German force was preparing to hold off—and if possible beat back—the British drive inland from Lindi.

In October 1916, when a handful of British troops first occupied Lindi, they had barely been able to push the two defending German rifle companies more than a few miles into the scrub beyond the port. The only real armed strength in the neighborhood was a seven-thousand-man Portuguese force, whose commander, General Gil, crossed the Rovuma about this time and deployed his troops on the slopes of the Makonde Plateau. The Portuguese, however, did not seem anxious to advance much farther into German territory, having already had their fingers burned four months earlier after displaying what Meinertzhagen called the "effrontery" to declare war on Germany and announcing that they would invade German East Africa forthwith. "Let them try," Meinertzhagen had written, "and von Lettow will eat them up." They tried and von Lettow did, when a Portuguese column was dismembered on the banks of the Rovuma by the machine guns of a small Schutztruppe detachment. Said Meinertzhagen: "Those who know the Portuguese expected no more and no less." In any case, this mauling may have made 180 German riflemen look like too risky a proposition for the Portuguese army in the autumn of 1916.

But if the Portuguese were never a real cause for alarm, even a small British presence at Lindi dictated at least a token reinforcement of the German micro-army which hung on outside the town—despite the fact that in late 1916 the area had not yet become crucial to the strategy of either side. At this time, in fact, von Lettow might even have considered Lindi a sort of Siberia, for the officer whom he placed in command of the six-hundred-man Lindi relief force was an officer he may have wanted to put in exile: *Königsberg's* Captain Max Looff.

There was more to the bad feeling between von Lettow and Looff than conventional army-navy rivalry, more even than personal jealousy—although in 1916, von Lettow had not yet been promoted and Looff's elevation to a grade above his own still rankled. What really kept the mutual disharmony alive was a clash of attitudes. Looff had strong ties to Schnee, the nominal commander-in-chief; it was natural that von Lettow should hesitate to put full faith in an officer whose first loyalty did not lie with the real commander. Both men also held irreconcilable views on how the war should be waged. Von Lettow would have been content to elude the British indefinitely, without firing a shot, if this would force them to exhaust themsleves on an insignificant theatre of operations. Looff craved action and tangible victory. Perhaps Lindi was the place for him.

At any rate, when Looff set out in October on his trek from the lower Rufiji to Lindi, veteran Schutztruppe officers, behind his back, were laying odds of one hundred to one against his ever getting there. They came close to winning the bet. The march south took Looff's column through a trackless, burning morgue of tangled iron vegetation, vast stretches of which were barely known even to the Germans; the six hundred officers and askaris of the force were more like explorers than soldiers. Yet they not only reached the Lindi area intact but covered the 200 miles of their journey in three weeks. Considering that they had to drag a *Königsberg* gun all the way, it was not bad going at all.

Looff wasted no time catching his breath. So that he could devote his full attention to the British force at Lindi without Portuguese interference, he marched at once on the Makonde Plateau to dispose of Gil's seven thousand troops. He was not at all perturbed by the ten-to-one odds against him; the only people who ever seemed afraid of the Portuguese army in Africa were Portugal's allies.

The operation went off neatly. Looff himself climbed the Makonde escarpment and personally acted as observer for his *Königsberg* gun, which pumped out its shells with such accuracy that the Portuguese askaris scampered off the plateau at once and may have broken some sort of speed record as they recrossed the Rovuma. They were miles and miles inside their own territory before they stopped running. Gil took a kind of revenge by accusing the Germans of murdering prisoners and by putting a price of four thousand gold marks on Looff's head. By the time Looff learned of his outlaw status he was too preoccupied with harassing the British at Lindi to give the matter much thought.

Actually, that six-month campaign was a noisy standoff. The British, as they transformed Lindi into a major base and filled it with troops, were not quite strong enough to dislodge the Germans at once from their well-dug and well-concealed positions, while Looff, even with the *Königsberg* gun, did not quite have the muscle to paralyze the British with shellfire. But both sides never stopped trying to hurt each other. British aircraft lurched unsteadily over the German defenses nearly every day, their fifty-pound bombs transforming the bush for many miles around into a miniature moonscape of neat little craters. Although Looff's artfully camouflaged dugouts and trenches almost invariably foiled direct hits, the near-misses—which made both the earth and raw German nerve-ends jump for nearly half a year without letup—had more than just a little psychological impact.

The Germans did not give as good as they got. They gave better. If the *Königsberg* gun could not reduce Lindi to rubble, it could and did put the brakes on the British buildup there. Since Looff's ammunition was in short supply, barrages had to be confined to two or three rounds each day, but the German gunners, under the peg-legged Richard Wenig, saw to it that most shots found a target. Unlike the German positions, Lindi's harbor installations were fish in a barrel. A fair tonnage of British ammunition went sky-high while being offloaded. Two 4.1-inch shells could bracket a supply-laden dhow or a hundred-ton troop-carrying lighter, and the third could send the craft to the bottom of the harbor. Small cargo steamers or navy vessels might not be sunk, but a few days of shelling could put one out of commission for a few weeks. In the town itself, supply depots, headquarters buildings and barracks came under continual bombardment.

And there was nothing the British could do about it. Observation planes, often flying less than fifty feet above the bush, combed an inland radius of barely twenty miles in a never-ending and never-fulfilled search for the elusive gun's various hidden emplacements. Even General O'Grady, the commander of the Lindi force, became so frustrated that he sometimes went up to try his own hand at spotting. He might just as well have stayed on the ground. Without interference from a lonely relic of a ruined German cruiser's armament, Lindi's conversion into a major army base might have been completed in one month instead of five.

All this may have made Looff overconfident. In May 1917, he ordered an infantry attack on Lindi. It miscarried disastrously. The town's perimeter proved an unbreakable belt of barbed-wire entanglements, and the assaulting German askaris found themselves hung up on the wire—only to be cut down from it at once by British machine guns. Looff's losses that day were far greater than he could afford. But fresh blood was อน the way. A few days later, Wahle arrived from Mahenge with a large portion of his western army. Von Lettow had placed him in charge of the Lindi area defenses.

The change in command had nothing to do with personalities. But this time, it had become clear that the main body of the Schutztruppe must inevitably be pushed south into the Lindi region while O'Grady's force— now more than two thousand strong—drove inland to cut off any further retreat. There was no longer any doubt that the area was going to be the cockpit of the Germans' last-ditch struggle to hold the last tiny shred of their colony. It was quite natural that von Lettow would want a soldier rather than a sailor to hold the front outside Lindi until his own withdrawal brought him on the scene for the final showdown.

Wahle's arrival at Lindi ushered in what may have been the bitterest fighting of the whole campaign. Certainly it was the most sustained, raging without letup from June through November. Even in the so-called lulls between major engagements, both sides hammered each other with their big guns at distances of five miles or more, while German and British rifles and machine guns kept up an incessant dialogue at much closer ranges— whether targets were visible or not. Swahili voices sometimes had askaris firing at their own units. The sound of whispered English or German words a few yards off in the bush was enough to trigger a wild patrol skirmish that could spread into a fire fight on a mile-long front. If few of these hopelessly confused set-tos accomplished a great deal, they did underscore the new complexion of ferocity that the Lindi campaign was wearing.

The first important clash took place early in June, when O'Grady launched the long-awaited inland thrust across the German line of retreat. Like Smuts, O'Grady tended to become fidgety at his headquarters, and often alarmed his staff with inspections of the fluid front lines, where he made a habit of borrowing a rifle from an askari or sepoy for a few pot shots at the Germans. But O'Grady was more than just an Irish brawler. He also enjoyed a reputation for being as fussy as an old maid when it came to planning, and if his tactics against Wahle were simple they were no less sound. Nearly six months of steady pummeling by the *Königsberg* gun had made it clear to him that this weapon was the most intimidating barrier on the path of his advance. The gun, therefore, became the priority target in the initial step of the advance from Lindi.

At this time, British intelligence had fixed the gun's newest emplacement near the village of Mingoyo, north of the Lukuledi River and some ten miles outside Lindi. The Germans could move it farther inland quite easily, on a plantation trolley line that ran a good distance upstream, so it became imperative that O'Grady get astride that line above Mingoyo if the gun were to be captured. He therefore decided on a surprise amphibious assault, with landings carried out at night.

It was to be spearheaded by a large striking force consisting mainly of the Fusiliers and a KAR battalion; they would be towed in lighters up the Lindi River and then in the Lukuledi, to a strip of beach where they would go ashore without delay. From here, an advance through the bush would bring them to positions where they could block the German retirement down the trolley line. At the same time, another KAR battalion was to march directly overland on Mingoyo from the north, hopefully to seize the gun even before the Germans could start moving it. The total force numbered more than fifteen hundred men. Several Royal Navy warships, including two cruisers and a monitor, had also been brought down to Lindi to support the attack with their broadsides. The journey upstream was scheduled to begin at nightfall on June 9. If all went well, the *Königsberg* gun would be in British hands before the sun went down on the 10th.

The operation had the flavor of a storybook pirate raid, but its painstakingly detailed preparations took the better part of a week to complete. As pilot of the assaulting flotilla, the navy's Lieutenant Clement Charlewood had to make careful night soundings of both rivers, find locations for channel-marking lights which the Germans could not see, draw up a schedule of staggered departures from Lindi to keep the boats from colliding with each other in the dark, and outline every step of the plan to O'Grady and the naval commander, Admiral Charlton. Knowing that Wahle might expect an up-river attack, Charlewood also sought to insure the element of surprise by taking soundings, in broad daylight, near what seemed an obvious landing place. This brought his motor launch into a sleet-storm of German rifle fire, but the ruse diverted Schutztruppe concentrations from the vicinity of the real beachhead.

It also delighted O'Grady. Just before the tows departed from Lindi on June 9, he told Admiral Charlton that he would accompany Charlewood aboard the whaler *Echo,* which was acting as guide boat. "I've heard of that officer," he said. "Where he goes there's bound to be fun."

Charlewood might not have shared O'Grady's idea of fun. The creeping ten-mile voyage up the sandbank- and mangrove-clogged river saw just about everything go wrong. Almost at once, a brilliant green star rocket told the British that the Germans had discovered what was afoot; Charlewood could only hope that they had concentrated at the false landing place. The rising tide had put out one of the channel lights, causing one of the Fusiliers' boats to run aground; valuable minutes went by while the troops, taking their chances with crocodiles, jumped overboard to lighten the craft and move it into deep water. There was a bad moment when Charlewood almost missed the entrance to the Lukuledi, which he said was "like the inside of a coal mine." And just as he was breathing a sigh of relief after finally locating the landing beach, a brightly lit vessel hove in sight—violating explicit orders that all boats be blacked out. Charlewood "hailed the approaching craft in no genteel manner, only to hear the admiral's encouraging voice reply, 'Well done, *Echo*! Carry on smoking!' "

But somehow the force got ashore without serious mishap, and by sunrise on June 10 the troops were moving briskly inland through tall thorn set a-quiver by bursting shells from the big naval guns and the crunching detonation of bombs dropped by the Royal Flying Corps squadron. No real resistance was encountered until about two o'clock in the afternoon, when part of the column walked straight into an ambush that had been laid by two Schutztruppe companies under the personal command of Max Looff. "Their fire burst on us like a thunderclap," wrote Buchanan, who now found himself caught up in the longest and most violent collision of the day's operations: a seemingly interminable madman's ballet of head-down bayonet charges and countercharges, performed to a ragged orchestration of mass rifle volleys and the deafening applause of machine guns. At one point, a swarm of bees joined in the melee, almost recreating the St. Vitus' dance of Tanga for both sides. But for the moment their stings had to be ignored. "One lost all reckoning of time, all reckoning of everything," said Buchanan, "except that there was something big on that kept every energy alive and working at full speed."

It continued until sunset and it almost snapped the British spine. All that saved his own force, according to Buchanan, was the high angle of the German fire: "Had they got the correct elevation, their machine-guns alone were sufficient to deal terrible havoc along our short, hastily and half-entrenched line." In the end, the bone-weary and ludicrously outnumbered German askaris were driven back into the bush by the bayonets of the hardly less exhausted British troops. But the surprise attack had done its work. O'Grady's force was held just long enough to keep the trolley line open.

As for the northern column, it, too, was delayed—more by the matted vegetation than by German guns—and did not reach Mingoyo until June 12. When the troops finally entered the village, they saw a curious sight. Strewn everywhere were heaps of raw rubber, elephant tusks, compasses, chinaware, typewriters and even a few baby carriages. Mingoyo in peacetime had been a regional collecting point for cargoes loaded and offloaded at Lindi, and the Germans had now looted and sacked their own warehouses before evacuating the place. What they could not take with them they had simply scattered on the ground.

But the *Königsberg* gun had not been left behind; by now, it had been hauled far down the trolley line to a new position well beyond the British reach. There was nothing for O'Grady to do but order his limping columns back to Lindi to reform and try again.

The summer-long wrestling match continued as both sides built up their strength on the Lindi front. Wahle's force expanded with the arrival of several units from other parts of the theatre; Kraut's detachment was particularly welcome. Indeed, the balance in numerical strength may actually have tipped for a while in favor of the Germans. However, a continuing flow of new KAR detachments into Lindi—along with some Indian troops and a few South Africans—presently returned the overwhelming odds to O'Grady, and he exploited them with a creeping but steady advance inland.

He also had to pay for every square yard of ground he occupied. The *Königsberg* gun continued to batter his columns with effect. Vest-pocket German combat teams lashed out at supply convoys and reinforcements well behind the British lines. At a place called Tandamuti Hill, twelve miles up the Lukuledi valley, a combined KAR-Fusilier attack was halted by a solidly built thorn fence and squalls of concealed machine gun fire from a fortification near the crest. As the British troops backed off, they found that the Germans had also been busy in their rear, a company led by Kraut having scattered the KAR's long porter column with a few rifle shots and then gone on to capture a field hospital. None of the wounded patients was harmed, but Kraut's officers had made the African orderlies serve them tea—and hand over the hospital's entire quinine stock.

Toward the end of August, things almost got out of hand for the British when O'Grady tried a new ploy—or rather an old one, reverting back to a Smuts-type turning movement. About twenty miles up the Lukuledi, near the village of Narunyu, he sent a strong KAR–South African–Fusilier column on a wide sweep around the German lines to strike Wahle's force from the rear while a KAR battalion carried out a diversionary frontal attack. But as the battle progressed, the envelopers found themselves enveloped when the Germans threw out swift counter-flanking detachments which isolated and virtually surrounded the British force. The situation became so desperate for O'Grady's troops that the fighting took on a Kiplingesque flavor as Fusilier and KAR units fell back on the traditional last resort of British infantry defense, the hollow square.

That the square was not broken may have been due to the stubborn fury with which the KAR—a veteran outfit for a change—threw back an afternoonful of unusually frenzied mass bayonet assaults. Certainly the two-hundred-odd Fusiliers could never have held the position alone, and the worth of the KAR askaris seldom made itself felt with more impact. "Magnificently they fought here," wrote Buchanan, "and we, who were an Imperial unit, felt that we could not have wished for a stouter, nor a more faithful, regiment to fight alongside." Even so, it was not until long after dark that the Germans finally retired.

And the British were still far from being out of the soup. For five days, the Fusiliers and KAR hung on at Narunyu by their fingernails in perimeter camps, drenched by unseasonal rains, critically short of ammunition and food, subject to spasmodic but heavy enemy rifle, machine gun and artillery fire. So close were the Germans that in the lulls between barrages the opposing troops shouted taunts at each other, the Schutztruppe askaris reminding the KAR of Kibata, the KAR replying with ad-lib songs about how it was better to fight on the British side.

It may not have seemed better at the moment. Only the most tenuous contact could be kept with O'Grady's main force. What little food there was had to be eaten raw, as the smoke of cooking fires would have helped the German artillery spotters. When orders were finally given for a night retirement from Narunyu, many of the British porters could barely stand up under their loads, even though they had almost nothing to carry. And when the KAR and Fusiliers at last reached the safety of their own lines, the only positive result of their abortive flank attack seemed to be, as Buchanan put it, "what in the past few days we had come to dream of— tea, tea, tea."

Narunyu was the end of the line for Buchanan: "The physical exhaustion, and fever, which had gripped me for some time, began slowly to master endurance. . . . On 9th September I had not strength to walk, and later in the morning I was taken to hospital. I was beaten, hopelessly overcome, though no man likes to give in. General O'Grady came to see me when I lay on my stretcher . . . perhaps the bravest man I have fought under, and the kindest—and, in my weakness, when he had gone, I hid my face in the gloom of the low grass hut and broke down like a woman."

They could do that sort of thing in those days.

It was not all frustration for the British, who by now had begun to borrow a page from the German book with guerrilla campaigns of their own— the most successful being directed not at the Schutztruppe but at its food supplies. Extensive African maize, sweet potato and cassava acreages in the Lindi area had been taken over by the Germans and methodically organized as a catering service for their troops. Overseeing teams, composed of two or three NCOs and a handful of askaris, were posted in nearly every village of the region to see to it that a crash program of planting and harvesting was carried out—at gunpoint if necessary. But when von Lettow wrote that "the force has rarely been so well fed as in the Lindi area," he neglected to mention that the flow of food to his army was often delayed— and sometimes brought to a halt—by British sabotage. Still smarting from German reprisals following the Maji-Maji rebellion a decade earlier, the African inhabitants of the Lindi district welcomed British intelligence officers who secretly incited them to new revolts.

These were not isolated, sporadic outbursts but carefully planned conspiracies in which the British agents literally raised midget armies behind the enemy lines. "This was the best part of the whole campaign for me," wrote Wienholt, who organized and led a force of at least one hundred African irregulars. Recruited from local villages, they were formed into quasi-military units under headmen holding honorary sergeant and corporal ranks. Each man was outfitted with a pair of shorts, a shirt, a rifle and a bandolier; each quickly became expert in the use of the last two. The guerrillas knew the country even better than did von Lettow's askaris. Many had been gun bearers for white hunters before the war. All possessed an intuitive skill at bushcraft which enabled them to slip easily past German sentries in lighting raids on farm outposts, supply columns and food depots. Almost invariably, the guards were caught napping, so strong was the dose of their own medicine.

Pretorius was the arch-plotter. For nearly three months he journeyed surreptitiously through the bush beyond Lindi, meeting akidas in a large number of villages where he outlined and synchronized plans for a mass insurrection across the whole district. Maximum striking power was assured when he arranged to have two thousand rifles smuggled past German outposts and distributed among his rebels. To divert enemy attention from the arms buildup, Pretorius deliberately allowed the Germans to learn of his own presence behind their lines. Schutztruppe patrols exhausted themselves running down false leads furnished by the inventive akidas, while the gun-runners did their work undisturbed.

The second night of a new moon was the prearranged signal for the uprising to begin. Nearly every German farm outpost in the Lindi area was taken completely by surprise as fifty- and hundred-man armed flying squads stole to within a few yards of their objectives at midnight and then charged in with rifles blazing. They met practically no resistance and their prisoner haul was substantial. "It was funny," wrote Pretorius, "to see the local natives, each wearing an old sack with holes cut for his head and arms, armed with a rifle, full of martial ardor, some bringing in as many as three German Europeans, with the usual six or eight askaris." With the farms at least temporarily out of German hands, Pretorius granted his men permission to pick the fields clean of their crops, and "the whole of the district was soon as barren as a sand-dune." This may have been overstating it, but the Germans may not have thought so.

Throughout the summer of 1917, Wahle's nimble footwork against O'Grady was being duplicated farther north by von Lettow, as he carried out a stubborn and cunning retirement before the advance of the British Kilwa Force. Withdrawal was his only option. The Germans' tactical skill could delay but it could not halt; both von Lettow and Wahle were like two karate black belts trying to cope with a pair of charging rhinos. By early autumn, von Lettow's main force had been driven one hundred miles south of Kilwa and into the Lindi sector. If he and Wahle were only a few miles apart, so too were the encircling British armies that much closer to the completion of their own linkup. The Kilwa column—now called Hanforce for its commander, General Hannyngton—was forging south to join with the Lindi troops—Linforce—as they continued their stoutly resisted but visible thrust up the Lukuledi Valley. It was only a matter of a few weeks, at the very most, before the ring closed at long last around what remained of the German army.

And yet, as their situation grew increasingly hopeless, the Germans behaved more and more as if they, and not the British, were on the offensive. Schutztruppe fire discipline continually improved. After one action, wrote Cranworth, "the superior shooting of the German Askaris could be plainly discerned. . . . Our trenches were pockmarked with bullets, but from our side at 80 yards distant boughs at 8 and even 10 feet high were shot away." Nor had the Schutztruppe lost its talent for bewildering the attacking forces. Just before launching an assault on a German strongpoint, a Nigerian battalion was brought up short when the enemy bugles began sounding the regimental call of the Royal Dublin Fusiliers.

Seldom did the beleaguered German troops play the role of aggressor more convincingly than in early October, when strong elements of Hanforce drove in on Ruponda, the Schutztruppe's main supply center in the Lindi area. The three-dozen-odd defenders were outnumbered by someing like four or five dozen to one, but this did not seem to trouble them. "They knew their business," wrote Nis Kock, who had taken up a rifle himself; "they shot steadily and with judgment, and on each flank small groups were beginning to crawl out towards the enemy, carefully making use of every unevenness in the ground, and every scrap of cover. . . . In less than a minute from entering the fight they were threatening the English flanks: they acted without commands, simply on a gesture from the N.C.O. . . . and they carried out the most effective form of attack almost by instinct." Ruponda fell, of course, but as usual the British did not just walk in.

Most troublesome of all to the British was the whereabouts of the German commander: as Cranworth remarked, "General von Lettow himself commanded against Hanforce, Wahle against Linforce, but as the net constricted, the former with his picked troops seemed to be in both positions at once."

This confusion was exploited fully. "In spite of his extensive intelligence and spy systems," wrote von Lettow, "the enemy was groping in the dark. He did not know, for instance, where I was, although he seemed to place the greatest importance upon knowing. . . . It was clear to me that the enemy's obvious uncertainty about the situation would give me a great opportunity if it could be used quickly and decisively. . . . Wahle's front seemed favourable for this attempt."

"Favorable" may not have been quite the word but Wahle's front was where the two German armies finally rejoined. By mid-October, Wahle had retired fifty miles up the Lukuledi, just a mile or so from a village called Mahiwa. As von Lettow correctly guessed, the British had chosen this spot to pulverize Wahle between the battering rams of Linforce from the east and Hanforce from the north. Beves, appointed by van Deventer to take over Linforce from O'Grady, planned a direct frontal assault, with his four thousand KAR, British, Indian and South African troops, on a position held by Wahle's askaris just east of Mahiwa outside the village of Nyangao. To cut off Wahle's retreat to the west and to keep von Lettow out of the fight—he would be dealt with later—Beves ordered the Nigerian Brigade to occupy Mahiwa, which he believed to be lightly defended. The Nigerians, he said, would be "the cork in the bottle."

For some reason, Beves appeared untroubled by the fact that von Lettow had yet to be located. Nor did it seem to matter that Pretorius, now scouting for the Nigerians, had given him entirely different information about the German strength around Mahiwa. "I think we all realized," wrote a Nigerian captain on the eve of the fight, "that something big was going to take place shortly." Wisely, this officer refrained from specifying whether something big would be good or bad for his own side.

Mahiwa, the final showdown of the campaign in German East Africa, was four days of concentrated fire and brimstone. Although little more than a skirmish by Western Front standards, it was the most savagely fought battle in the history of African colonial conflict—not excluding Omdurman or any engagement of the Boer War. It was also confused beyond belief; many accounts have been written of Mahiwa, but none seems to describe the same action. Even the name is wrong: by rights it should be called the battle of Nyangao, since most of the fighting took place there and because it was at Nyangao that the issue was finally decided; for some reason, the name Mahiwa has stuck instead. Regardless of labels, however, it was the Schutztruppe's last stand in the defense of its colony.

The armies drew into position on October 15. Wahle's two thousand askaris were deployed in a rough semi-circle bulging slightly eastward from Nyangao to face a British force twice their strength. Even on the 16th, when von Lettow broke through—one might almost say he glided through—to take command, the thousand rifles of the five crack field companies he brought with him seemed inadequate reinforcement. As Beves' column rolled in on the Germans like breaking surf, von Lettow feared that his own line must soon give way.

In the past, the Schutztruppe had always dealt with this kind of superior force by the simple guerrilla expedient of filtering into the bush and living to fight another day. But now, with German East Africa all but lost, it seemed that little would be gained by running. So von Lettow sprung a surprise on Beves. Schutztruppe bugles, instead of sounding recall, began summoning all reserve companies to the center of the line. Von Lettow, at last, was making the stand-up fight which the British, for three years, had been trying to force on him.

It was an equatorial Gettysburg. "For four days," wrote von Lettow, "wave after wave of the attack broke on our front." Both sides went temporarily insane with blood lust as the fury of assault and counter-assault mounted. So closely locked were the antagonists that battery commanders often laid down their barrages with fuses set at zero. High-explosive shells tore great chunks out of battalions and regiments. Hailstorms of massed rifle and machine gun fire did not always turn back the platoons and companies that ran amok in bayonet charges; British and German trenches became ankle-deep rivers of lumpy blood from impaling and disembowling contests. Into the incessant crash of the shells and the heavy stammer of the machine guns was woven a sustained counterpoint of enraged and agonized screaming, punctuated by hoarse, high-pitched yells of command: " 'A' Company advance!" . . . *"Gefechtschiessen!"* . . . *"Tayari!"* . . . "Fix bayonets!" . . . *"Knauel!"* . . . "Charge!" . . . *"Feuer!"* . . . *"Piga!"* . . . *"Piga!"* . . . *"Piga!"*

Little of the intricate tactical ballet was evident in the battle; it was simply a toe-to-toe slugfest—a glorified riot, actually—in which acts of remarkable heroism became all but commonplace. "I take my hat off," wrote a British officer, "to one German European," who rode a horse at the head of his company in an assault "before he disappeared, never, I should think, to lead his troops on earth again, for not less than two machine guns and two score of rifles were aimed at him." A group of Nigerians in the Mahiwa sector actually halted a German attack for several crucial moments by leaping from their slit trenches and baffling the Schutztruppe askaris by going into a war dance even while bullets ripped up the thorn all around them. At Nyangao, a veteran German Sudanese sergeant put himself in the line of British fire to get a better bead on the attackers; when ordered to take cover, the old sweat refused, shouting that if the Emperor could afford to pay him faithfully for twenty years he could afford to die for the Emperor on one day.

The fighting offered little protection to generals, either. Nor did the generals seek any. Von Lettow deliberately made himself a target, wearing his full regimentals for the first and only time in the campaign. Later, he remarked laconically on the need to stay alert while drinking coffee in forward trenches, "as the enemy was keeping a fairly sharp look-out, and shot with tolerable accuracy." On the British side, O'Grady continually prowled the front-line perimeter, exhorting sepoys and askaris to "give the bastards brass, begorra!" During one determined German bayonet charge, he was seen striding atop an entrenchment in full view of the attackers, asking if anyone had seen his dog, O'Mara.

Beves did not know it, but he himself was one of the principal reasons for von Lettow's decision to hold rather than withdraw. Von Lettow had never forgotten the Kilimanjaro operations of early 1916, where Beves, at Latema-Reata, "threw his men into action regardless of loss of life and did not hesitate to try for a success . . . by repeated frontal attacks." In von

Lettow's judgment, Beves was now repeating his earlier performance, and the Schutztruppe commander had therefore decided to exploit this by making the main German line into a concrete wall against which, he felt confident, Beves would simply batter himself unconscious.

Von Lettow could afford to concentrate his force at Nyangao and not Mahiwa, for after October 16, the second day of the battle, he was no longer concerned about protecting his rear against the Nigerians. At Latema-Reata, when van Deventer's mounted troops had threatened to get behind him while he was trying to hold off Beves, he had been compelled to order a retirement. But no such threat existed now, for the Nigerians, who were supposed to be covering—or striking at—the German rear at Mahiwa, were having troubles of their own. They were preoccupied with simple survival.

On October 15, the 2nd and 4th Nigerian Regiments—half the brigade— had advanced on Mahiwa from the north, to take up the positions which would block Wahle's westward retreat from Nyangao. Hardly had they arrived, however, than they found themselves cut off from the rest of the brigade in a surprise attack from cover of high grass as a strong German detachment sent the forward Nigerian columns sprawling with rifle and machine gun fire while another force of Schutztruppe askaris scattered the Nigerian porters and got astride their supply line to the rear. The two regiments came close to being routed, and might have been, but for the spunk of several Nigerian NCOs who managed to lead tactical retirements to secure positions—sometimes in the face of four-to-one odds. So much for the light opposition which Beves had expected at Mahiwa.

Next day—the crucial 16th—the 1st Nigerian Regiment, which had been held back only three miles to the north, was ordered to the relief of the 2nd and 4th. One officer remembered the commander of the regiment's advance guard turning to a subaltern and telling him: "We've got the Boche set this time, as he's already engaged, and we shall fall on him from the rear." That remark was made only moments before the bush on all sides of the column exploded in an ambush led by von Lettow himself. If von Lettow had not then been hurrying to reinforce Wahle, his own force might easily have wiped out the 1st Nigerians to a man. As it was, the regiment's forward units barely escaped annihilation, and any immediate hope of relieving the two regiments at Mahiwa had gone down the drain.

And by now, those two regiments needed all the help they could get. Their artillery castrated by want of ammunition, they had no way of replying to a brief but pulverizing barrage by a *Königsberg* gun and a 70-mm. quick-firing piece, the latter pumping out its shells at almost point-blank range. Moreover, since their porters had bolted the day before with most of the entrenching tools, the men could barely even take cover as the shells came in like runaway steam hammers. For two days after this pasting, the baobabs and acacias around the bombarded sector dripped blood and mush from the arms, legs and torsos of officers and men who had been mashed and flattened into the branches. "The 16th October," wrote the brigade historian, "was the most disastrous day to the Nigerians since the formation of the force."

Not that the situation improved a great deal on the 17th, if one officer's diary is any indication: "We . . . find ourselves literally besieged: ammunition is very scarce, and the men have eaten their emergency ration. To add to all these troubles, the enemy have got a machine-gun and snipers posted along the water, so that our men are continuously getting hit whilst trying to obtain water. As our trenches are dug in sand, more or less out in the open, the heat in them is terrific, and the men are willing to do anything to quench their thirst . . . There is no news of any reinforcement or of a relieving column. . . . Matters are extremely critical, and if we are not relived shortly we shall meet with disaster."

Relief in fact was barely a mile away, a detachment under O'Grady having bulled and hacked through from Nyangao in the east. But O'Grady might just as well have been on the other side of Africa, so thick was the curtain of German artillery and small-arms fire that closed off the last few hundred yards of the rescuers' path. Slightly farther to the north, moreover, the 3rd Nigerian Regiment was being badly cut up by a German force while it made a desperate but futile attempt to relieve the 2nd Nigerians, who were still reeling from the body blows they had taken in von Lettow's ambush during their own effort to rescue the two regiments at Mahiwa. However, by October 18, those two beleaguered units made tenuous contact with O'Grady and finally managed to shoot and stab their way to safety through a narrow slit in the German perimeter. The remainder of the brigade also extricated itself about this time. But as a fighting force, the Nigerians had been all but emasculated.

By now, the pitched battle on the main front at Nyangao was approaching a crescendo. Although badly mauled by Beves' plunging head-on blows, the Germans continued to hold fast, mutilating the assaulting columns almost beyond recognition. Entire Indian and KAR companies had been virtually wiped out in counterattacks along the entire line. The skeleton of the Fusiliers had seen its remaining strength of 120 fever-wracked riflemen slashed down to four dozen as they covered a minor tactical withdrawal; Nyangao-Mahiwa rang down the final curtain on "the old and the bold." At least one British field piece was in German hands. Nearly half of the Linforce machine guns, alcng with their crews, had been knocked out or captured. The British were beginning to have second thoughts about how simple it would be to exterminate the Schutztruppe in a stand-up fight.

It had to stop. While there was not much left of the Germans, neither did von Lettow exaggerate when he wrote that "the enemy by the increasing fierceness of his frontal attacks was bleeding himself to death." On the evening of October 18, as if by mutual consent, the two mangled dinosaurs drew away from each other. The British hardly had the strength to gasp at their losses. Of forty-nine hundred African, Indian, British and South African troops engaged at Nyangao and Mahiwa, twenty-seven hundred had been killed or wounded, for a total casualty score of well over 50 percent. Even Tanga had not seen quite such carnage.

But von Lettow was less than correct in describing Nyangao-Mahiwa as a "splendid victory" for the Schutztruppe. With victories like that, he did not need defeats; the fighting had all but obliterated his army. Although German casualties came to only one-fifth the number sustained by the British, 519 killed, wounded, captured and missing amounted in fact to irreparable damage, since no reserves existed to fill the gaps. If Nyangao and Mahiwa had stunned the British, they would recover. But the Schutztruppe, finally, had been beaten to its knees.

Von Lettow now began a swift, forced withdrawal to the south—the only route of march left open to him as he tried to stave off the inevitable surrender. The retreat was not orderly, leaving in its wake a disarray of unburied German and African corpses, hastily abandoned field pieces, shells and other war materiel. Although the Germans, to be sure, had taken time at Mahiwa to blow up the last *Königsberg* gun—with a dynamite charge in its breech—that act itself may have been most symbolic of the Schutztruppe's impending collapse.

Indeed, it seemed very much as if desperation had finally overtaken von Lettow's army. When the pursuing British troops entered the administrative center of Chiwata, some thirty miles south of Mahiwa, they found the place aglow with Red Crosses—flying from flagstaffs and trees, painted on roofs, laid out in rock patterns on the ground—to ward off air bombardment. Even the few remaining German civilians in the town wore Red Cross armbands. A rumor spread that Surgeon-Major Taute had quarreled furiously with von Lettow over the latter's use of a hospital in Chiwata to protect his own headquarters. Reports also came in that von Lettow had been challenged not only by his senior medical officer but by growing numbers of company and detachment commanders who no longer saw any point in continuing to fight for a lost cause.

But if these acts of insubordination actually took place they were deceptive, and the British soon came to realize that von Lettow still remained capable of throwing a few hard punches before throwing in the towel. The Germans were retreating in haste, to be sure—the long-awaited linkup of the Kilwa and Lindi forces only formed a ring around thin air—but they were not bolting in headlong flight. "To the very end," wrote a Nigerian officer, "they kept their tails up, and fought a one-sided contest with indomitable courage and exemplary dash, and they never failed to leave their mark on their opponents." As always, the terrain favored the rearguard action, the ambush and the hidden machine gun that could halt a whole regiment's advance for a day or even longer. One scuffle saw half of a British mountain battery knocked out of the war by the Germans' only remaining howitzer. And, as the southward pursuit continued into November its pace began to slacken with a marked stiffening of German resistance on the bamboo-choked slopes of the Makonde Plateau. "This country . . . was far more difficult for an advancing force," said a British officer, "than anything yet experienced in German East Africa, and the fighting had now developed into regular mountain warfare." Even in its death-throes the Schutztruppe had not yet shed the sting in its tail.

In fact, it appeared for a while that von Lettow was about to order a counter-offensive, as wireless messages began pouring into van Deventer's headquarters that relief for the German army was on its way. It was coming aboard a zeppelin.

"China Show" was the German Admiralty's code name for the boldest and most quixotic operation of the East African campaign. Although the 740-foot dirigible L59 had been built in 1917 for the navy, it was decided that her first mission would serve the army: a four-thousand-mile flight from Germany to East Africa with fifty tons of arms, ammunition and stores for von Lettow's expiring force. The journey was also to be L59's last: on landing, she would be dismantled and cannibalized so that virtually every piece of her structure might serve the Schutztruppe. The balloon envelope would be converted into shelter tents, the envelope's muslin lining torn into bandages; the gas bags would become sleeping bags; small portable hutments and a wireless tower would be built from the duralumin framework. Even the catwalks had been treaded with leather for boots. The only nonessential item of cargo was a case of wine with which the dirigible's arrival would be celebrated.

In mid-November, L59's designer, Dr. Hugo Eckener, flew the airship from Friedrichshaven to Jamboli in Bulgaria, where Commander Bockholt, a regular German naval officer, took charge for the flight across the Mediterranean and two thousand miles of enemy-held Africa. The British awaited him eagerly and anxiously. "More than once," wrote Cranworth, "I was awakened during the night to decode immensely long cypher dispatches as to the necessary steps to take on [L59's] approach." Nearly every obsolescent BE2C of van Deventer's Royal Flying Corps squadron had its engines turning over continuously in anticipation of instant orders to go up and blast the lumbering German cigar out of the skies.

The skies themselves took a hand in the affair as howling Mediterranean gales forced L59 to turn back twice. On the third try, a dog-leg run over Turkey and Greece, Bockholt managed to reach North Africa and set a southward course up the Nile. Her wireless damaged by the storms, L59 was temporarily out of touch with the world. But suddenly, over Khartoum, a faint but urgent signal could be heard from Berlin. Abandon mission, said the German Admiralty; von Lettow has surrendered.

L59's volunteer crew refused to believe it. They implored Bockholt to go on, and history's first skyjacking almost took place when Bockholt ordered the airship back to Europe. Gales of even greater fury tore at the dirigible on the return flight; at one point she lost so much altitude that the lead weight of her aerial dragged on the ground, and only the jettisoning of half the cargo averted a crash. When Bockholt finally reached Jamboli, however, he had been aloft for four consecutive days and one hour, covering a total distance of 4,180 miles. Many years would pass before that record was broken.

And some time, presumably, had to elapse before Bockholt recovered from his chagrin on learning that the orders from the German Admiralty had been sent by the British. Had L59's wireless remained out of commission, a more than decent chance would have existed for Bockholt to reach his destination—with an immeasurable effect on the Schutztruppe's morale.

Still, it was highly doubtful that fifty tons of supplies would have permitted von Lettow to maintain even a precarious foothold on a few square miles of territory at the very bottom of his colony. As November drew to a close, the Schutztruppe had finally been hammered off the Makonde plateau. The force now stood with its back to the Rovuma River. There was barely enough food to keep the men going for six weeks—probably it would be even less than that, as rats had nearly emptied the grain sacks. Only a month's supply of quinine remained. The dwindling small-arms ammunition—down to twenty rounds per man—could only be used in the old Model 71 rifles, and by this time, two-thirds of the force were armed with a few modern German rifles and a large number of weapons captured from the British and Portuguese. What this meant, simply, was that the already shrunken Schutztruppe had been reduced to one-third of its effective fighting strength. Clearly, the end was at hand.

No one knew this better than von Lettow. "It would have been madness," he wrote, "to go on with this fighting, which would not bring about a favourable decision." So at long last he acknowledged his defeat.

He acknowledged it by preparing to invade Portuguese East Africa.

Arresting in its simplicity, the plan was altogether consistent with the objective which had governed von Lettow's strategy since the beginning of the war. As long as he remained in the field, however battered, his enemies must go after him. The Portuguese, incapable of defending their colony alone, would have to rely on British help, which meant a continued diversion of British resources from the Western Front. The beauty of the scheme, moreover, was that it could be carried out with greatest impact not by a large army but by a small, highly mobile striking force which would live off the land and equip itself with captured materiel. The pursuers, on the other hand, would need all the troops they could get if they were to round up von Lettow's slippery guerrilla columns, which would be roaming and raiding at will across 300,000 square miles of Portuguese territory. This in turn meant long, cumbersome British supply lines, and hence, that much more sluggish a chase—or, as von Lettow put it, "the prospect of tying down strong enemy forces and protracting the operations indefinitely."

Von Lettow did expect to augment his strength with the thousand-man detachment led by Captain Theodor Tafel, who was even then carrying out a forced withdrawal south from Mahenge following the occupation of that town by Belgian troops. Still, it was necessary to trim down the main body of the Schutztruppe if it was to be a self-contained combat team. Besides about one thousand sick and wounded men, at least one thousand more perfectly fit officers and askaris were ordered to give themselves up to the advancing British. While von Lettow was angered to observe that quite a few were openly pleased to be out of the war at last, he took a kind of perverse comfort in noting that "we had repeatedly to refuse the request of a brave Askari that he might come and fight for us." Many porters also begged to stay on, without pay or even rations. Most of the whites, too, were outspokenly reluctant to be left behind. One junior platoon commander, barely able to stand with a gaping wound in his leg, simply declared that he would disobey the surrender order. "I have seldom been so pleased," wrote von Lettow, "as at this breach of discipline."

Another who managed to stay with the force was the stump-legged Richard Wenig; von Lettow was glad to have his special skills as a gunner. Less welcome was the presence of Governor Schnee, but even von Lettow could hardly refuse the Governor if the Governor thought his duty lay with the army.

Of those who remained behind, Looff was the bitterest of all. While perhaps not overly surprised when von Lettow placed him in command of the surrendering force, he complained openly and angrily that he was being thrown to the wolves. But he had his orders and obeyed them, even keeping up the fight in his own way. When British intelligence officers asked him how many *Königsberg* guns remained with the Schutztruppe, he said he was not certain but that there were either three or four, each well stocked with ammunition. Questioned on the whereabouts of L59, he replied that not one but two dirigibles were on their way, one to bomb Tabora while the other struck at Lindi. Until that moment, he had not even known of the abortive relief flight.

Later on, Looff was able to worry the enemy a little more. Assigned to a POW camp in Suez, he and other *Königsberg* officers were put on board a British transport which sailed from East Africa with only a meager escort. For the entire voyage, Looff was carefully watched, out of fear that he and his men might somehow seize the ship and make her into another German raider. The skipper of the *Königsberg* was well known to his captors, who could hardly have forgotten the sinking of *Pegasus*. KAR askaris called Looff *"Bwana Unguja"*—Mr. Zanzibar.

One night, with British columns barely a mile away, von Lettow took his leave of the Schutztruppe expendables at a place called Nambindinga, a two days' forced march from the Rovuma. Among those who bid him *auf wiedersehn* was Nis Kock, suffering from violent attacks of malaria and the loss of an eye in the accidental explosion of a shell he had been defusing. Kock was fit enough, however, to describe the departure of the pared-down German force. "Swiftly, with hardly a sound," he wrote, "company followed company, grew out of the darkness, showed clear for an instant in the light of many fires, and were gone into the darkness again. . . . The camp-fires gleamed on fantastic shapes, black and white side by side, carrying rifles over their shoulders, butt pointing backwards. Some of the shapes were barefooted, some wore topis all askew, old felt hats, or uniform caps, and some were bareheaded. Rags of every kind of uniform sprang into sight in the firelight, and were gone into the darkness again. Camp-fire shone back from rifle barrels, or now and again from machine-guns carried by two men. More came by, and still more. . . . I could not keep count, but there cannot have been more than two thousand."

Actually, the figure was five thousand, but three thousand were porters and askaris' wives. The total fighting strength of the German army in East Africa was now three hundred white and seventeen hundred black troops. They were soon to be followed by many times that number of enemy soldiers.

Next morning, the first of the British pursuers burst into the Nambindinga camp. Kock recalled their frantic search for von Lettow. "An officer, with a dozen men at his heels . . . flourished his revolver, shouting over and over again: 'The General! Where's the General?' No one answered him, but he went on asking his question. Then one of the sick men raised his head and began to laugh: and more joined in, laughing.

" 'The General,' shouted a voice in broken English, 'the General's gone to hell!' "

Early in December, German East Africa was officially declared an Allied protectorate. The German East African Army remained in the field, a force very much in being.

PART V

THE NOMADS

19

Across the Wide Rovuma

SHORTLY AFTER SUNRISE on November 25, 1917, the askaris of von Lettow's advance column waded across the Rovuma River into Portuguese East Africa. The rains had not yet begun and in most places the river was not much more than a sluggish creek—although some of the men found deeper spots where they stopped for a swim. By noon, the main force had reached the south bank; the rear guard would follow two days later.

The Rovuma was von Lettow's Rubicon. Or, to use another parallel, von Lettow had now put himself in the position of Grant at Vicksburg, where the Union general had deliberately cut his own supply lines to get behind the Confederate stronghold on the Mississippi. Henceforth, the Schutztruppe was to be a nomadic tribe which must survive by its wits. No more reliance could be placed even on the few scattered supply dumps that had given the men a little food and ammunition during the retreat from Mahiwa. For the first time in the campaign, moreover, the army would no longer be fighting on familiar terrain. Topographically, to be sure, Portuguese East Africa was in a sense an extension of the German colony: a mad mosaic of scorched thorn and matted black rain forest, rugged mountains and aimlessly winding, crocodile-writhing rivers. The only difference was that apart from the few small columns that had previously raided some Portuguese posts in the north, the Germans knew nothing whatever of the territory which von Lettow had now chosen to invade. "Portuguese East" might just as well have been some planet yet undetected by astronomers. In its strangeness alone lay death. As the Schutztruppe entered the forbidding blank, the askaris gave von Lettow a new nickname: *"Bwana aliyefanya saanda"*—the shroud maker.

Obviously, however, the drive into Portuguese territory also brought von Lettow distinct advantages. While it was assumed—correctly—that the Portuguese army would offer little if any resistance, even the British did not expect to carry out a swift or easy pursuit. If the unknown vastness of the country was intimidating to the Schutztruppe, it must prove an almost in-superable obstacle to van Deventer's forces. They would be seeking out a small, virtually invisible column of enemy soldiers in a land nearly twice the size of Japan—a land whose only thoroughfares, apart from the treach-erous rivers and a few rough dirt roads built by the Portuguese, were game tracks. Not only must endless miles of paths be hacked out for the Carrier Corps but new supply bases must be established on the Indian Ocean and Lake Nyasa—some as far distant as one thousand miles from the army's main entrepot at Dar es Salaam. By now, most British officers were ac-knowledging freely that the nature of the country gave the Germans odds of at least three to one. The hunt for von Lettow was going to be the stalk of a wounded leopard.

Even before the sun had dried the ragged German uniforms on the south bank of the Rovuma, the men found themselves in a fight. Barely a mile away, near the village of Ngomano, was a sizable Portuguese encampment, and von Lettow, with a view to replenishing his stores, decided to attack it at once. Indeed the shooting began even while the main Schutztruppe column was still wading across the river. But it did not last long. The Por-tuguese were kept so busy ducking shell bursts as the Germans' single field piece let go on their front that they did not realize, until too late, that a large column of riflemen had worked round through the bush to strike at their undefended rear. And even when they turned to face the new attack, they could barely see the assaulting troops swarming over the barricades— so dense was the smoke from the old Model 71s. As a white flag went up, German askaris were heard to shout: *"Leo nafasi ya bunduki ya zamani!"* —today is the day of the old rifles. It must have been. Of about one thou-sand Portuguese troops at Ngomano, fewer than three hundred survived the attack.

But hardly had the Portuguese flag been struck than a new fight broke out—among the German askaris and porters—for the loot in the camp. "It was a fearful *mêlée*," von Lettow recalled. "Even the Portuguese Askari already taken prisoner, joined in the plunder of their own stores. There was no alternative but to intervene vigorously. . . . To make an example, [I] dashed at least seven times at one bearer I knew, but each time he got away and immediately joined in the looting somewhere else." The better part of the afternoon went by before order was finally restored.

Despite the riot and whatever may have been lost in the looting, however, the inventory of captured materiel at Ngomano more than compensated for the confusion and temporary collapse of discipline. The Germans now had at least five tons of supplies, enough Portuguese rifles to rearm half the force, a 40 mm. field gun, a quarter of a million rounds of ammunition, six machine guns, more than half a dozen horses, and several large loads of priceless medical stores. "With one blow," said von Lettow, "we had freed ourselves of a great part of our difficulties."

But a bad setback came on the heels of Ngomano, when von Lettow learned that he had lost Captain Tafel's thousand-man detachment which had been relied on so heavily to augment the main striking force. A few days earlier, Tafel's askaris had forded the Rovuma after marching and fighting their way across two hundred miles of barren scrub. Their food supplies were exhausted, neither crops nor game could be found, ammunition was down to barely a dozen rounds per man, and there was no sign of von Lettow. With his troops on the point of death from starvation, Tafel recrossed the Rovuma and surrendered to the pursuing 129th Baluchis.

It was unnecessary. On the south bank of the river, Tafel had been only a day's march from von Lettow. But he did not know this. Von Lettow called the surrender "a severe and unexpected blow."

There was, however, a comforting note in the news, which von Lettow received from van Deventer under a flag of truce, along with a written message urging that the remainder of the German army follow Tafel's example. Von Lettow exulted. The message, he said, "strengthened me in my belief that our escape had taken [van Deventer] by surprise. . . . Neither he nor General Smuts had ever thought of sending a summons to surrender when the situation was favourable to the English. Why should they do so in a situation like the present . . . ? Only because they were at their wit's end."

This was putting it a bit strongly, since von Lettow's crossing of the Rovuma had not been totally unexpected. In fact, as early as the autumn of 1916, after von Lettow had eluded him at Morogoro, Smuts had written to a friend that "the German commander is a tough fellow, determined . . . even to retire into the Portuguese territory rather than surrender." If von Deventer had not crossed the border before the Germans, it was at least partly because the Portuguese had declared themselves quite capable, on their own, of hurling back any hostile force at the Rovuma. It was only after the disaster at Ngomano that the Portuguese began calling for help.

Just possibly, moreover, van Deventer might have preferred to let his allies stew in their own juice. He had at last pried the Schutztruppe from its own colony, and in a sense this was all that was expected of the British. The idea that the job had been finished at last was even implied at the highest levels in England: "I heartily congratulate you and the troops under your command," King George V cabled van Deventer, "on having driven the remaining forces of the enemy out of German East Africa." But that could not be the end of it. If the Portuguese had previously discouraged a British presence in their territory, the British were now bound, by treaty and honor, to respond to the Portuguese SOS.

And yet, even those obligations might have been disregarded had not von Lettow himself remained a threat. Certainly, no Portuguese forces were going to stop the German army from slicing through their colony like a knife through soft cheese, toward border positions from which von Lettow could raid Nyasaland, Southern Rhodesia and even South Africa. In the King's cable, van Deventer and other veterans of the campaign could only have recalled Smuts' earlier pronouncement that the Germans had been crushed after the Rufiji operations at the end of 1916. "The retreat of von Lettow's force into Portuguese territory," wrote Wienholt, "was again the subject for further and very premature congratulations in high quarters, and once more the conquest of German East was hailed in the papers. The sale of the bear's skin had twice been concluded, though the animal himself, in the shape of Von Lettow and his little army of picked men, was very much alive."

Like it or not, therefore, van Deventer was obliged to keep up the chase, and his first attempt to overtake von Lettow saw the Nigerians and some Indian cavalry crossing the Rovuma in December. Actually, the chances of even finding the Schutztruppe in a southward drive were fast becoming remote, since the January rains below the Rovuma would trap the long columns of British porters in a horizonless desolation of knee-deep gumbo. The most noteworthy action of this operation was a race meeting—for a pair of silver cups—which included a mule sweepstakes. In due course the troops were pulled back, and direct pursuit gave way to a more ambitious but hopefully more feasible strategy.

Initially, van Deventer's objectives were threefold. First, he must thwart any attempt at a breakthrough back into German East Africa, and three KAR battalions were therefore deployed along the Rovuma as a sort of border patrol that could hold back the German army until reinforcements arrived. The Schutztruppe also had to be kept from wheeling west and invading Nyasaland (precautions against thrusts into Rhodesia and South Africa could come later), and to this end, an even stronger KAR force of Northey's command was held in readiness at the south end of Lake Nyasa. Presently, it would march east to apply pressure on the German right flank.

This last thrust was an arm of van Deventer's main strategy: to wear down the already weakened Germans in an unending war of attrition, striking hard blows whenever and wherever possible. These drives were to be carried out by elements of the Nyasa column and a powerful task force lunging inland from the east coast. The idea was to do more than just harry the Schutztruppe and bolt the door on areas in which the Germans might forage for food. With deft generalship and a little bit of luck, the two converging columns would either halt von Lettow's southward movement and compel another showdown fight against odds far greater than those at Mahiwa, or they would simply act as a vise and squeeze the Germans to death.

Before this could be done, however, van Deventer had to reshuffle and reorganize his entire force. With the exception of the Gold Coasters, who would remain in the theatre until July, all non–East African units were sent home early in 1918. Henceforth, to all practical purposes, the campaign was to be a contest between the Schutztruppe and the KAR. The latter body had now reached a strength of nearly thirty thousand rifles, and while not all of them were in Portuguese East Africa, those that were outnumbered the Germans by at least ten to one. And yet, in a very real sense, that numerical superiority was a handicap to the British, for it meant a proportionate inflation in the number of porters needed to serve the force. Besides, since van Deventer's plan called not for chasing the Germans but getting ahead of them and blocking their path, the army must operate along supply lines of almost unworkable length. Dar es Salaam, even Kilwa and Lindi, were of limited usefulness as bases. In December 1917, therefore, a massive troop and supply buildup was begun at Porto Amelia, nearly two hundred miles south of the Rovuma on the Portuguese East African coast.

This was not the best of places from which to launch any kind of offensive. Although situated inside a capacious natural harbor, Porto Amelia was some eight miles from the end of a "road" leading into the interior. All stores offloaded from steamers had to be transshipped across the bay in small dhows and landed on an open beach. If the wind was blowing in the wrong direction, the surf on this beach could bring the movement of supplies to a dead halt for days at a time.

Further delays at Porto Amelia were caused by minor Portuguese officials who tried to discourage recruitment of badly needed local porters because the British system of direct payment to the army's bearers had the effect of diverting hut taxes from the officials' pockets. The Portuguese did not hesitate to kidnap porters' wives, or even, in some cases, to have the porters themselves done away with, if this would keep them from their ally's employ. "It was only when we took matters into our own hands," wrote a British officer, "and showed the underlings that we intended to take very drastic steps with them, that we were able to get men." Meanwhile, supplies piled up on the beach.

All this, along with the pounding January rains, gave the Germans a head start of at least six weeks, and they made the most of it as they threaded their way southward—across sodden thorn meadows, over drenched, undulating savanna plains, through dripping rain forest dungeons, around morasses big enough to float a navy or drown an army. The nine-company force was divided into three columns, each with its own baggage train. Strung out in single file, the columns became a human earthworm twenty miles long; the forward detachment kept a full day's trek ahead of the main body, two days in front of the rear companies. A day's march usually lasted no more than six hours. In that time, ten or twelve miles could be covered. By January 1918, the troops had lanced two hundred miles into the belly of Portuguese East Africa. If they had moved in a straight line and not made several extended halts at captured posts, they would have logged upwards of three times that distance.

Little fighting took place during the early weeks of the march. Portuguese resistance was negligible. In December, three strongly fortified Portuguese outposts were captured with virtually no expenditure of ammunition. Von Lettow continually reminded his officers that speed and initiative were the keys to such attacks, that detachment leaders must strike without even waiting for orders. One company commander took this advice so literally that he and his African officer outraced their troops to storm the entrenchments of a Portuguese strongpoint by themselves. The fifty astonished askaris of the garrison surrendered to the duo without firing a shot.

The British were only slightly more troublesome. Although their patrols seemed to be everywhere, no individual intelligence unit ever numbered more than a dozen or so rifles, and could be brushed aside like a handful of stray fleas. Wienholt, whose own small party tagged at the German heels across Portuguese East Africa, spent more time in flight than in pursuit. His description of the scouting life was terse: "At 7 a.m., monarch of all one surveys in one's own little camp; at 7:15 a.m. tearing through the bush like a fugitive from justice, and wondering if one will be lucky enough to get some *ugare* (native porridge) by evening."

The main purpose of the British patrols was to keep track of the Germans' route, and while they met with only partial success here, they had more luck in a different type of effort. Von Lettow himself admitted that many of his askaris had become homesick at this time, owing to "the feeling of uncertainty as to where the campaign was going to lead them. . . . They said to themselves: 'If we go further we shall come into country we don't know. We can find our way back from where we are now, but soon we shan't be able to.' The English propaganda, by word of mouth and pamphlets, fell in many cases on fruitful ground, and . . . a number of good Askari and even older non-commissioned officers deserted."

He added, however, that "this was only a passing phase. . . . The example of the faithful Askari, who simply laughed at the mountains of gold the English promised them if they would desert, won the day."

Certainly no one could have called the Schutztruppe a beaten army. Tattered British and Portuguese uniforms and a nondescript arsenal of captured rifles and machine guns failed completely to conceal a cohesive, mobile, well-disciplined combat team of veteran professional fighting men. The companies kept good formation even in the shaggiest thorn, the tallest grass, the murkiest rain forest. No askari needed to be told to strip and oil his rifle every day, to keep his bayonet shaving-sharp at all times. More than ever, the men had to rely on the instincts that had been passed down to them through uncounted generations of bush soldiers. Patrols, points and flank guards probed beyond the columns' perimeters with the swift wariness of hunting dogs. "No movement in the bush," said von Lettow, "escaped their lynx eyes."

Behind the askari columns marched the porters. Even with their sixty-pound loads they were not much less soldierly than the riflemen; certainly they were every bit as hardened. Many walked without boots or even sandals; when a three-inch thorn pierced a carrier's bare sole or heel, he would reach down with a knife and cut the flesh away—scarcely missing a step of the brisk pace set by the askaris. At the end of a day, some porters might be too exhausted to remove their loads, and would simply sleep with the burdens as back rests. But the next morning saw them all striding off as if the trek had only begun.

A long train of African women and children also learned to keep up with the marchers. Von Lettow never wholly approved of the practice which encouraged a soldier's better half to join a campaign, noting that "it would have been better to choose an equally reliable man who was not burdened by having to drag about a wife and family." But he also bowed to the custom with good grace, perhaps knowing that half the force might have mutinied otherwise. Besides which, the bibis were anything but a decorative indulgence. Apart from fulfilling the men's biological needs, they cooked their husbands' meals and sometimes even did the work of porters. The women caused the greatest inconvenience when they became pregnant, but everyone welcomed the children born on the march; askaris occasionally went into action with babies on their backs. And the female presence also added a touch of brightness to the force, owing to the bibis' passion for gaudy colors. "After an important capture," said von Lettow, "the whole convoy . . . would look like a carnival procession."

A yeasty informality prevailed throughout the force. "Lively conversation was kept up," von Lettow recalled, "and after the plundering of an enemy camp, which often yielded rich booty, cigarette smoke rose on all sides. . . . The Askari would call out their friendly 'Jambo Bwana Obao,' or 'Jambo Bwana Generals' . . . or a little signalman would express his hope of coming some day to Uleia (Europe) and Berlin. 'Then the Kaiser will say to me, "Good day, my son," and I shall give him an exhibition of signalling. Then he will give me roast meat and present me to the Empress. The Empress will say, "Good day, my child," and will give me cakes and show me the shop-windows.' "

For the whites, a few "civilized" amenities helped take some of the edge off the strenuous life. Arriving at a bivouac at the end of a day's march, porters and "askari boys" cut branches to make frames for tents or grass-roofed huts, cooks and bibis got fires going, hunting patrols brought in game (when they could find any), women crushed corn from nearby African fields (if a region was cultivated). After eating around campfires, officers and NCOs might join in *lieder* over a few bottles of captured Portuguese brandy, or fiddle with the wireless in hopes (seldom fulfilled) of picking up a faint report from Germany. The latter offered the fun of wishful speculation on the fighting in France; von Lettow lost a bet with Staff Surgeon Taute that the German army would recapture Amiens.

Evenings also allowed the less sociable to retire to mosquito nets and read by the light of tallow dips. The whites of the Schutztruppe must have been an uncommonly eggheaded lot, at least to judge from their mobile library, which included Homer, Horace, Dante, Goethe, Schopenhauer and Schiller among other heavy going. According to Schnee, few Germans cared much for captured literature. "The English books," he sniffed, "were mostly mystery tales or other rather inferior or superficial novels. The Portuguese books gave evidence of an almost unbelievable low mentality. They were either wholly obscene . . . or cheap, emotional novels." (Schnee did make an exception of Camoens.)

Off again at dawn: "The Askari marched gaily forward," wrote von Lettow, "straight as lances, and with their guns reversed over their shoulders, as had always been the custom in the rifle regiments." The irregular pace of the columns took on a kind of rhythm with the insistent rasp of warped snare drums and the tinny dissonances of dented bugles, while a deep-throated chorus of askaris and porters gave voice to the words of the army's marching song, "Haya Safari":

> *Tunakwenda, tunashinda,*
> *Tunafuata Bwana Obersti.*
> *Askari wanaendesha,*
> *Askari wanaendesha,*
> *Tunakwenda, tunashinda . . .*

> We're on the way, we're winning,
> We're following our colonel.
> The troops are marching,
> The troops are marching.
> We're on the way, we're winning . . .

Even the officers sometimes joined in.

Not that the march was always a Boy Scout hike—especially at those times during the early weeks when the scoutmaster lost his cool. Given the pressures and responsibilities of leading the remnant of an army through a hostile terra incognita, given the uncertainty of finding food from day to day, given the vastly superior enemy forces that could pounce from bush or forest at any moment, it was hardly surprising that von Lettow should occasionally subject his officers to enraged—and usually quite unreasonable —outbursts of temper. He himself admitted that "at this time I was not always very gentle and considerate to those around me," and that "those very officers of my Staff who were working with the greatest devotion . . . and deserved the most recognition, were the objects of much unjustified reproach." He voiced gratitude to these officers "for not taking offense or allowing this to prejudice the cheerful continuation of their work."

Presumably the latter compliment did not apply to Schnee, who also felt the rough edge of von Lettow's tongue at this time and who, unlike the others, may just possibly have had it coming to him. In German East Africa, where he had been at least the nominal head of the army, Schnee had, according to von Lettow, "interpreted [his] authority in such a way as to interfere most seriously" with the conduct of the war. Von Lettow had been appalled when Schnee released detailed top-secret information on the Schutztruppe's fighting strength to German East African newspapers; at least once he had openly refused to obey a direct order from the Governor; he had even lodged a formal protest with the Kaiser over Schnee's misuse of his office. Now, Schnee was informing von Lettow that he would have him court-martialed when they returned to Germany, and Gilbertian as that threat may have seemed in an equatorial wilderness, it was more than von Lettow cared to put up with. "Now that we were outside the Protectorate," he wrote, "I attached the greatest importance to the fact that now, at any rate, I had a free hand," and he made it plain to Schnee—often quite crudely—that his presence was less useful and less welcome than that of the frailest bibi. Schnee may have regretted his decision to march with the army no matter where it took him.

Another reason for von Lettow's temporary bout of intemperate behavior was his poor health. Almost unnaturally sensitive to malaria, he endured a prolonged barrage of merciless attacks during the first few weeks in Portuguese territory. At this time also, a sand fly burrowed into one of his toes and caused an inflammation so painful that walking became all but impossible until Taute, using a local anesthetic, extracted the entire toenail. Then a blade of elephant grass pierced his right eyeball, so that for some time he could not read handwriting or even rough sketch maps. For several weeks, in fact, he was almost totally blind, since the sight of his left eye had been virtually nil ever since he had taken a head wound during the Herero campaign in South West Africa. At any rate, none of these mishaps was designed to improve anyone's equanimity.

While the health of the commander naturally had to be of crucial importance to the force, von Lettow of course was not the only member of the column to get sick. In general, the Portuguese East African campaign saw the Schutztruppe being slowly but visibly drained of the incredible physical resilience which had sustained it in the field for so long and against such crushing enemy odds. Upwards of two hundred porters had now become litter bearers. There should have been at least twice that number, but most officers and men had to stumble along and be treated in the ranks, sometimes while marching. The field hospital as such no longer existed, although the medical staff tried to work in primitive dressing stations during bivouacs—often performing operations late into the night by the flickering gleam of stable lanterns or tallow dips. As a precaution against surprise attacks, these "clinics" would be set up in the bush at a considerable distance from the main camp, with the result that patients and doctors sometimes got lost trying to find their way back to the column when it resumed the march. At least one of the dressing stations was trampled and destroyed by elephants.

In such conditions, Staff Surgeon Taute and his overworked medics and African orderlies could handle only the gravest cases. Even malaria had now come to be looked on as no worse than a bad cold, although nearly everyone was being decked by the disease. At times, malaria reduced a field company's normal complement of fifteen or twenty whites to two or three, and was even bringing down large numbers of the more resistant askaris and porters. Wounds were taking longer to heal. Superficial injuries festered swiftly; Schnee was far from being the only man in the force to march for weeks with a bloated arm in a bark bandage after getting a minor thorn scratch on his finger.

Some of the diseases seemed to run on racially segregated lines. Black-water fever was the white man's privilege, and increasing numbers of the whites exercised it freely, urinating gouts of thick black ink until they recovered or died—the latter cure taking place in at least 50 percent of the cases. The Africans had their prussic acid poisoning, caused by eating manioc which had been insufficiently cooked owing to the demand for speed on the march; as often as not, the raw manioc bellyaches proved fatal. The most integrated affliction was dysentery: a man could have a dozen or more sudden violent bowel movements in a single day—attacks of such ferocity that they left him with barely the strength to stand up after squatting. That the officers and askaris could still march, that the carriers still managed to tote their sixty-pound loads, said something about the esprit of the German force at this time.

Because the state of the troops' health depended in large measure on what—and how much—they ate, food was a never-ending source of concern. Portuguese East Africa almost invariably offered either feast or famine. Usually it was the latter—although at first, the Schutztruppe seemed to have entered a land of Goshen. When the Portuguese administrative station of Chirumba was captured, everyone gasped at the post's immense vegetable gardens and well-tailored orchards that fairly burst with mangoes and mulberries. The early route of march often crossed country abounding in game, and the men were able to barter their surplus stocks of hippo tongue and waterbuck venison for maize, fowls and eggs in large quantities. The bush itself yielded such delicacies as wild honey and a cherrylike fruit that was made into jam. Even African tobacco could be had from local tribesmen. One askari POW told a British scout that he had become tired of eating chicken. "Never have we fared so well," said a captured German officer's diary, "during the last four years."

It was not long, however, before the land began to dry up. By the end of December, the force's grain stocks were all but exhausted; more than a month would have to pass before the next harvest farther south. Once again, hippo fat—when it could be obtained—became the army's most precious staple. Sometimes the troops were reduced to raiding African villages for food—a practice they generally sought to avoid, as they relied heavily on tribal cooperation. But even these forays seldom brought in a big bag: the victims were past masters at the art of hiding produce and livestock from the Portuguese. "One after another," wrote von Lettow, "mules and horses found their way into our stew-pots."

Soon even the horsemeat ran out, and von Lettow personally helped the army stave off famine by bringing to bear his amateur's knowledge of mycology, which he had studied in Germany. He said that the baskets of mushrooms and other edible fungi which he collected were "welcome as manna to the children of Israel." But no one knew better than von Lettow that a mushroom diet was not going to keep the Schutztruppe alive indefinitely.

There was only one thing for it: the army must be split up into foraging columns. In January, Wahle broke off from the main body, leading a sizable detachment westward, while another force under Captain Franz Koehl, a resourceful Bavarian artilleryman, headed east toward the coast. (Koehl was accompanied by Schnee, no doubt to von Lettow's relief.) Von Lettow himself continued the southward thrust. He expected that at least one of the three detachments would eventually reach an area rich enough in game or cultivation to sustain the whole force.

But von Lettow had more than just logistics in mind when he trisected his army. He was certain by this time that van Deventer would deliver his heaviest blow from Porto Amelia, with a view to linking up with the force under Northey that was advancing east from Lake Nyasa. With Wahle hopefully delaying the Nyasa columns and Koehl keeping the British occupied in the east, "a situation seemed to be developing in which I could make use of my inner line to attack one part of the enemy singly. . . . This seemed to be the chance I had so long been awaiting."

In February and March, the shape of that opportunity began to materialize as the main British force at Porto Amelia gathered strength for its inland thrust. By now, the British had adopted a new and somewhat confused system of nomenclature for their various combat teams, identifying units by such abbreviations as Kartrecol, Karwunfor, Fitzcol, Shortcol, Durcol and so forth. One column at Porto Amelia, consisting of the Gold Coasters and a KAR regiment, was known as Rosecol, for the officer commanding the West African troops; another, composed of two KAR regiments, was called Kartucol. When these two contingents joined up in early April and began the drive into the interior, they became Pamforce. Altogether, Pamforce had a strength of about eight thousand rifles; this was considered more than enough to sweep aside the eight-hundred-odd Schutztruppe askaris whom Koehl had deployed astride the British route of march.

It could hardly have been otherwise, but Koehl made Pamforce work hard to dislodge him. At dawn on April 12, just outside the village of Medo, about one hundred miles from Porto Amelia, the two opposing forces collided, and the British columns almost immediately found themselves in hot water. Kartucol's advance was first slowed up by a knee-deep swamp, then stopped dead in its tracks by the fire of a dozen well-emplaced German machine guns. The KAR ammunition quickly ran short, and when orderlies were sent to the rear for more, Koehl's gunners methodically cut them down. A mine field brought the Gold Coasters of Rosecol up short; their commander, Lieutenant Colonel R. A. de B. Rose, just missed being blown apart, although he was drenched from head to foot with blood and pulp when a British artilleryman, barely three paces off, stepped on a buried 4.1-inch *Königsberg* shell.

Exploiting his initial advantage, Koehl ordered a succession of counter-attacks against the entire British line. More than once the line almost cracked. Pamforce, indeed, might have been hurled back but for the Gold Coast mortars—deadly accurate as they had not been at Narungombe—and the initiative of a few KAR African NCOs. One man, Lance Corporal Sowera, won a bar to his D.C.M. when he exposed himself to nearly all of Koehl's machine guns by climbing a tree to get an unobstructed field of fire for his own Lewis gun. As an askari handed up fresh ammunition drums, Sowera sprayed the attacking Germans without letup for more than two hours. Presently, when the NCO leading a section of recruits stopped a bullet in the head, Sowera leaped down from the tree and took over, rallying the men with a war dance which he staged while a heavy enfilading fire whined around him. Similar foolhardy acts by other black noncoms helped keep the British defenses just barely stiff enough to hold.

By late afternoon, the German counterattacks began to lose some of their sting, and when darkness fell, Koehl and his five companies had taken to the bush in full but orderly retreat southwest. The two Pamforce columns could not launch a pursuit at once. First they had to pause and regroup, bury their dead, carry more than one hundred grievously wounded officers and men to a huddle of tick-ridden grass hovels that served as a field hospital. By the time they were ready to take up the chase again, with Kartucol and Rosecol alternating in the lead, Koehl had been given a head start of more than a day. Had not von Lettow at this time been supporting one of Wahle's detachments about 140 miles to the west, Koehl might even have been able to stand his ground.

The next several weeks saw continual but inconclusive skirmishes and fire fights as the various British forces pressed in on von Lettow's columns from east and west. The objective now was to seal off the Germans from any further southward movement, and this came within an ace of happening on May 22, when Koehl made another stand at a place called Korewa. The resistance was not planned. Koehl's intention of continuing his retirement had been thwarted unexpectedly by Schnee, who for some inexplicable reason had personally moved to the head of the column and ordered a halt. Before Koehl could even adjust to this caprice, he found himself caught in a jolting crossfire spewed out by the six KAR battalions of Kartucol.

But Korewa at least proved well suited to defense, being a great jumble of steep rugged hills and colossal boulders, heavily overgrown with thorn and accessible only by direct assault through a narrow gorge which almost needed a can opener to be forced. German machine guns and snipers covered this pass so tightly as to dictate an envelopment, which meant that two KAR columns had to work some miles around Koehl's rear, while a third created a noisy frontal diversion with artillery and mortars. The fighting was hot and confused, with bullets and shell fragments setting up deafening reverberations as they caromed back and forth in the rocks of the gorge. Several times the enveloping columns seemed to have the Germans cornered, only to find that they had wriggled farther down the tunnel toward its escape hatch. But for the usual worthless maps, Kartucol in all probability would have plugged this hole and rounded up Koehl's entire force.

In fact, it was more than likely that the British could have brought the East African campaign to an end at Korewa. Von Lettow, only a few miles away with the main German body, had heard the shooting and was hastening to reinforce Koehl. If the thick country had not impeded his progress, there was every chance that he would have been drawn into the same snare in which Kartucol, only by a stroke of sheer bad luck, had failed to trap Koehl. As it was, Koehl just managed to get his companies through the door before it slammed shut. The escape cost him nearly all his supplies and ammunition, along with Schnee's personal baggage.

Schnee himself barely avoided capture, but if this disappointed von Lettow, he did not show it. "I . . . came up to help the Governor in his adversity, and honoured him with a pair of blue socks, which his wife had made me at the beginning of the war, but which unfortunately had faded."

Korewa ended the first phase of the Portuguese East African campaign: although the British armies from Porto Amelia and Lake Nyasa had joined hands, the German getaway in the Korewa gorge had made that linkup meaningless. Now began a five-week chase to the south, as von Lettow continued to forage for food, evade capture and make all the mischief he could. His primary objective remained unchanged: to keep a great deal of British soldiery tied up in a profitless pursuit. "If I only withdrew slowly enough," he calculated, "the strong enemy forces would . . . probably follow, but in view of their immense supply difficulties it would be in vain."

That was about the way it worked out. Although the Gold Coasters had gone home, dozens of large British columns—all KAR by now—remained in the field to smoke out the usually unseen German army. But, in the words of the KAR's official history, the southerly pursuit was "a monotonous series of seemingly endless marches, interspersed with minor actions against a rearguard that never stood for long. . . . Von Lettow had nothing to gain by attacking until he could obtain fresh stores of ammunition and food. . . . [The KAR] could only follow in the hope of catching him before he could capture too much." A British general put it more succinctly when he likened the chase to "feeling about for a needle in a bundle of hay. You only found it by pricking your finger, and when it dropped off your finger it was lost again."

And as if von Lettow's resourcefulness was not burden enough, the British also had to cope with their ally. They found it almost literally impossible to discern anything estimable in Portuguese strategy, tactics or general military conduct; possibly the most generous praise of the partner's role in the campaign was Cranworth's remark that "it is kinder to draw the veil." At this apparently final stage of the war, there was talk for a while of abolishing the rank of commander-in-chief, until someone remembered the clause in the Anglo-Portuguese treaty which provided that when the two nations fought side by side, the senior officer in the field must lead the combined forces. It was therefore decided that the C-in-C rank remain; the War Office might even have promoted a KAR lance corporal to field marshal before placing van Deventer under Portuguese orders.

While the Portuguese were far from being cowards, they did appear to have little stomach for the hardships and inconveniences of tropical warfare. Van Deventer's officers seldom failed to register shocked amusement at the preference of their Portuguese counterparts for being carried through the bush in hammocks rather than marching with their men. Even acts of Portuguese initiative tended to be viewed with alarm as courting blunder. A Portuguese officer once wirelessed a British field commander, requesting new instructions after reporting that his detachment had advanced ten miles and reoccupied a post from which the Germans had departed some days earlier. The orders came back instantly: remain in position and grow potatoes.

Of no less concern to the British than Portuguese military ineptitude was calculated Portuguese sadism toward the colony's Africans. At a time when forced labor and corporal punishment of "natives" were fast on the way out in Africa's white overlordships, compulsory peonage and inflicting physical pain on blacks remained firm instruments of Portuguese colonial policy. British outrage over these practices did not arise only from British notions of fair play: the system was enforced so harshly—with the bastinado, the chain gang and other coercive devices—that the result was to make a German sympathizer out of nearly every African in Portuguese territory. "The Germans," said Wienholt, "were hailed by the poor Shensis [savages] as being nothing less than heaven-sent deliverers from their cruel and cowardly oppressors"; every Portuguese post set afire by von Lettow's troops "was to the native population a little Bastille going up in flames."

Passive hostility to the Allies was bad enough, but Portugal's Africans were more than passive. In gratitude to the Germans, tribesmen across the colony, whenever possible, supplied the Schutztruppe with food, women, guides and—very often—spies against the British, who inevitably were found guilty by association. After having enlisted the aid of many black communities in German East Africa, van Deventer's command found this turning of the tables much more than a minor inconvenience.

Particularly in the matter of obtaining food, which may have inhibited the pursuit more than did von Lettow himself. Through barter or outright gifts to the Germans, African cultivators in the Portuguese colony stripped their own lands virtually bare. KAR detachments might occasionally buy a few ears of maize or a few handfuls of millet from tribal farmers, but the prices were so exorbitant that when food ran short the British askaris sometimes had to fall back on the practice of attacking and looting villages. This did not tend to increase their popularity with the local inhabitants.

To get food, however, the KAR for the most part had to depend on their ever-lengthening supply lines, which grew proportionately less reliable with every mile they extended farther south. Originally organized to resolve a grave logistics dilemma, the Carrier Corps by its very size created at least two new difficulties that were not much less critical. The porters were expected to feed the army but they also had to feed themselves. A single bearer ate the weight of his sixty-pound load in twenty days, but the trek from a supply base to the front lines and back sometimes took twenty days or more. Thus the planning of economical routes, relays, staging depots to speed the movement of supplies could become almost hopelessly intricate. It had been bad enough in the Kilwa and Lindi operations; in Portuguese East Africa, the system nearly broke down altogether.

Another problem came as an unsettling surprise. It had been assumed that the porters, like most Africans, would be less susceptible to tropical disease and hardship than whites, but in a very short time the men had started going sick in droves. The cause was not hard to find. At the end of a day's march, after plodding or wading across ten or even fifteen miles of thorn beneath a load more than a third of his own weight, a bearer was simply too exhausted to cook his ration of maize meal. Instead, he ate it half-raw—virtually guaranteeing a violent and not infrequently fatal attack of bacillary dysentery. The manpower shrinkage from dysentery among porters became particularly troublesome in Portuguese East Africa.

To combat this, the army imported a special finely-ground maize meal from South Africa, which required less cooking, and also issued meat wherever and whenever possible. These measures eased the problem but did not end it. A contingent of doctors had to be brought out from England to treat sick porters exclusively. Carrier hospitals were established at all the main supply bases and on points along the lines of communication; they had a total of fifteen thousand beds, which were almost enough. Besides the beds, twenty-six thousand graves were dug for the porters before the campaign ended.

Without the Carrier Corps, to be sure, the KAR could not have advanced a mile into Portuguese East Africa, but it could hardly be said that the

British supply machinery turned on oiled wheels. Porter convoys continually lost their way in the country's ocean of vegetation, seldom caught up with the KAR columns less than a week behind schedule, often had to eat most of the rations that were carried for the troops. KAR foraging parties, when they could find no villages to raid, were sometimes reduced to grubbing for manioc or picking berries. While no one in the British forces starved, everyone went hungry.

As for the Germans, they were enjoying a second wind. Many of the sick men had recovered, at least temporarily, and the force itself had reached a new peak of well-lubricated mobility. The rear guard commanded by Koehl was the sting in the Schutztruppe's tail—an army in microcosm, fighting an endless vest-pocket campaign on its own. The forward column of three companies doubled as a sort of dismounted cavalry, its askaris seeking out targets of opportunity several days ahead of the main body. "Portuguese bomas . . . fell before them like ninepins," wrote Wienholt, "in most cases being abandoned well before hand. . . . If not abandoned, a few shots and the Germans quickly had them."

Normally, von Lettow himself would have led the forward task force, but feeling that he was needed with the main body, he turned the command over to Captain Erich Müller, a bellicose infantryman who had been itching for a real fight after two years in a headquarters assignment. Müller was given complete freedom to act as he saw fit without ever waiting for orders; this kind of independence had its risks, but von Lettow, mindful of Müller's "very sound tactical judgment and initiative," was prepared to take the gamble. It paid off. With Müller's team as the cutting edge, the Germans knocked off Portuguese posts with almost metronome regularity while Koehl continually hurled back KAR assaults in brief but searing fire fights. "This is a funny war," remarked one of von Lettow's scouts; "we keep chasing the Portuguese and the British keep chasing us."

In the process, the Schutztruppe became what almost could have been called a caravan of swag. More than once, von Lettow had to read his officers the riot act on the rules of plunder, reminding them that all booty belonged to Germany and that whoever wished to keep a captured pocket watch, gold pencil, pearl-handled hairbrush, bone china mustache cup, silver flask or whatever was bound by law to pay for the article. The strictures were probably honored in the breach; one can even ask whether von Lettow himself enforced or heeded them.

The regulations, of course, did not apply to food, and during the march south from Korewa the land became slightly more bountiful again. Indeed, some windfalls could almost put the war into the background. After storming one large Portuguese administrative station, the Germans liberated several dozen European pigs which the garrison had been fattening up, almost as sacrificial offerings to the enemy. The approach of a KAR column received only token attention as butchers and cooks prepared a great feast of sausages, roast pork and brawn. "Our enjoyment of this unwonted luxury was so great," wrote von Lettow, "that we did not allow ourselves to be disturbed even by the shots that fell into our camp."

But if the Germans had enough to eat, they were fast running out of bullets to shoot, and by mid-June their shrinking ammunition stocks had become a matter of serious concern. Von Lettow had been told of a large ammunition depot in a large Portuguese military-administrative post in the town of Alto Moloque, which accordingly was made a priority target. Happily, no shots had to be fired in the attack on the station: Müller's detachment simply walked in and accepted the surrender of a few Portuguese officers who were drinking coffee on the veranda of a government bungalow. The rest of the German force learned of Alto Moloque's fall when Koehl picked up a Portuguese field telephone some ten miles to the rear, just as Müller, at the other end of the line, seized the instrument from a Portuguese captain and announced that he had the situation well in hand. Less pleasingly, the captured ammunition at Alto Moloque amounted to no more than a few rounds. The shortage had now become a crisis.

However, from the reports of prisoners and African spies, von Lettow was presently able to gather that a big ammunition dump might indeed be his for the taking. Although its location was uncertain, it appeared to be in a major plantation center called Namacurra, about 150 miles to the south and connected, by a 40-mile rail-river link, with the Indian Ocean seaport of Quelimane. From all indications, Namacurra was more stoutly defended than any other Portuguese strong point in the colony; von Lettow was not even certain that he could capture the place—especially since he would need at least two weeks to get there and might exhaust all his remaining ammunition against the pursuing KAR detachments in the meanwhile. But if he wanted to keep his force in the field, he had to try.

The first step of the operation was completed successfully. Toward the end of June, after a stiff forced march and some extra-slick broken-field running, the German columns were within fifteen miles of Namacurra. Seizing the position in their state of acute weakness would be another matter, but it was a task that could not wait. On July 1, Müller's three forward companies moved up in skirmish lines toward the edge of Namacurra; by the end of the afternoon they were fanning out and preparing for an attack across a sisal field.

But the Allies, for a change, were prepared to resist. Fearing a German threat to Quelimane, van Deventer had already reinforced Namacurra's 630-man Portuguese garrison with 400 askaris of the veteran 3rd KAR Regiment. Firmly dug in along a three-thousand-yard front with the KAR holding the right wing, the force was backed up by a battery of Portuguese

75-mm. field guns. Facing these defenses, Müller had barely five hundred rifles, half a dozen machine guns, no artillery and almost no ammunition. Von Lettow's main body, moreover, was at least a day's march behind.

Müller did not wait for its arrival. First he sent out patrols to cut the British-Portuguese field telephone lines. Then, as darkness fell, he ordered one of his companies to deliver a flanking blow at the Portuguese left wing, which buckled almost at once. This enabled Müller to move up another step, occupying the buildings of a sugar plantation and capturing one of the Portuguese 75-mm. guns. The piece was in bad repair and would not fire, but Müller at least held a firm position from which to throw his next punch. It did not come at once. Throughout the following day, both sides pelted each other fitfully with rifles and machine guns, accomplishing little except to reduce Müller's ammunition stocks to a fistful of rounds per askari.

That evening, however, von Lettow reached the scene. He brought with him another captured Portuguese 75, also malfunctioning. Both this gun and Müller's were quickly dismantled and their working parts reassembled into a weapon that would fire. On the following day the gun went to work, supported by the smaller 40-mm. field piece that had been captured at Ngomano seven months earlier. Both guns pumped out their few missiles with an almost desperate accuracy and soon had the Portuguese and British porters in full flight to the rear. This in turn touched off a wave of panic among the Portuguese askaris, who began throwing down their rifles and fleeing from their trenches—perfect targets for the Schutztruppe machine guns which scythed them down like weeds.

Now only the KAR on the right held fast, but their position became increasingly less tenable as the cheering German troops raced across sugar and sisal fields to fill the vacuum in the Portuguese trenches. It was not long before the British askaris found themselves all but riveted down by a cross-fire which they could not return. Their commander, Major E. A. Gore-Brown, had no choice but to order a gradual withdrawal toward a wide stream, in the hope of fording it and taking up stronger positions on the opposite bank. Suddenly, however, the usually unflappable KAR troops became infected with the Portuguese panic. Instead of retiring in order, they swarmed into the river and tried to swim across before reaching the ford. Some did get to the other side, but nearly half the force was shot dead, snapped up by crocodiles or drowned in the boiling current. Among those lost was Gore-Brown, who went under while trying to stem the rout.

Namacurra was a bonanza that surpassed all expectations. More than three hundred captured British and Portuguese rifles enabled the Germans to discard all but a handful of the old Model 71 Mausers. The ammunition shortage was relieved almost indefinitely; Imperial Navy Lieutenant Werner Besch, the quartermaster, even worried whether he had enough porters to carry it all. Namacurra's warehouses also yielded up fresh uniforms for everyone, not to mention three hundred tons of food—and far too much liquor: "With the best will in the world," said von Lettow, "it was impossible to drink it all." So, after setting aside a supply of wine for the sick and ordering several dozen immense casks emptied into the river, he then suggested that the officers and men might wish to drink up the remainder—enough to stock four or five liquor stores—on the spot. "The risk of a wholesale 'jollification' . . . was gladly taken," he wrote, "and everyone was allowed to let himself go for once, after his long abstinence."

With or without hangovers, the troops were on the march again almost at once. At this point there was nothing to stop them from occupying Quelimane or even from lunging still farther south to the Zambesi River and the soft underbelly of Southern Rhodesia. Von Lettow, however, decided against both moves, largely because he knew they were what the British anticipated. Van Deventer had now ordered all his columns to carry out forced marches on Namacurra and drive the Germans into the Indian Ocean. Correctly guessing this intention, von Lettow wheeled his troops around and headed northeast, making straight for the pursuing forces—whose commanders could hardly have expected that their prey would choose to retreat in the wrong direction.

Von Lettow was taking a huge gamble here, for if the Germans had in fact collided with the converging KAR columns, the result could only have been the Schutztruppe's sudden and violent end. But as always, the Germans had the screen of the bush working for them; at one point, von Lettow's northeast-moving troops actually passed between the two main British forces as they hurried southwest, totally unaware that their quarry was giving them the neatest slip in a campaign that fairly bubbled over with artful dodging. For two weeks, all contact with the Schutztruppe was lost.

It was not until late July that the British picked up the trail again. Von Lettow was still driving northeast, apparently making for the port of Mozambique, and two KAR battalions raced to head him off. Early in the evening of July 22, their advance units made contact with the German force near a bend in the Namirrue river. As the swiftly gathering darkness helped cover its attack, a strong KAR strike force was able to drive a Schutztruppe detachment from high ground it occupied on the river bank. Von Lettow's bold dash to the northeast had finally been checked.

For less than an hour. As it turned out, the retiring force was only Müller's forward column. Even under a full moon the ground was so confused that the British commanders had no way of knowing that von Lettow's main body was moving up rapidly to reinforce Müller. Nor did they find out until their own troops reeled under the blows of simultaneous counterattacks on their front, flanks and rear. For the first time in the campaign, the Germans were able to give the enemy a taste of his own medicine —with murderously well-directed fire from a captured mortar. The stinging crump of the shells from the unexpected barrage helped accelerate the confusion in the British lines and throw the attackers on to a wavering defensive.

Von Lettow himself almost failed to reach the scene. While groping his way through the tangled growth of the river bank in a reconnaissance along the German perimeter, he walked into a patch of the shrub known as cow-itch. So maddening was the instant rash that erupted all over his body that he barely managed to return to his command post and take charge of the counterattack. But he made his presence felt. Within two hours of the initial German assault, one of the British battalions had been all but obliterated by the mortar and its commanding officer captured while giving orders over a field telephone. Except for a single KAR company holding desperately to the spine of a hill, the rest of the British force was in full retreat. The forest being too thick to make a night pursuit feasible, von Lettow concentrated on the remaining company, mincing the hill with machine gun fire and mortar shells until a white flag went up. A German reverse had been transformed into a British rout.

The Schutztruppe was feeling its oats. In barely three weeks, von Lettow's threadbare gang of fugitives had twice turned on a heavily armed posse to beat it senseless, steal its guns and leave it lying dazed and bleeding on the ground. German esprit, which had been riding the crest of a wave since the crossing of the Rovuma, reached new peaks after the drubbings inflicted on the British at Namacurra and Namirrue. Noncombatants as well as fighting men felt the flush of victory; large numbers of porters were begging to be enrolled as askaris; von Lettow noted that even his bearded old cook, Baba, "was not disinclined to take up arms."

And the climate of buoyant camaraderie was never more conspicuous. Although the land had gone barren again and although a day's ration was usually a lump of lard or rancid hippo fat, the lunch break on the march still had the air of a company picnic. "Even the Askari and bearers, who formerly used to wait for their meal until camp was pitched," wrote von Lettow, "adopted more and more the 'desturi' (manners, customs) of the Europeans. As soon as a halt was called every black would bring out his lunch. It was very jolly when the whole force bivouacked this way in the forest, in the best of spirits."

Less enjoyable to von Lettow was his responsibility of playing nursemaid to what by now had become a small army of prisoners. Besides having to be fed—and the Germans had enough trouble feeding themselves—their mere presence inevitably reduced the pace of the march. Von Lettow found the Portuguese officers his heaviest burden: "for the most part they were infected with syphilis and were carefully avoided by the English prisoners. In addition they were not real campaigners." Dr. Ludwig Deppe of the medical staff recalled "an unforgettable incident," when a Schutztruppe corporal captured a Portuguese sergeant who was so terrified that he burst into tears, whereupon "the black caressed the white man and tried to comfort him . . . as a mother comforts her child."

Little trouble, on the other hand, came from the British prisoners, who, said von Lettow, "accepted as a matter of course the hardships of the long marches," and "bore everything with a certain humour." Some even seemed to look on their captors as the winning side in a cricket match. When Lieutenant Colonel Hugh Carey Dickinson of the 3rd KAR was captured at Namirrue, he is said to have demanded to be taken to von Lettow immediately, so that he could shake the German commander's hand.

By early August, the Schutztruppe had reached the village of Chalau, more than half the distance from Namacurra to Mozambique, and an alarmed van Deventer was regrouping his forces for another converging drive that would keep the Germans from reaching that port. Von Lettow got wind of this plan when a British officer, under a flag of truce, sought an exchange of prisoners. Something about the proposal sounded fishy, and although von Lettow was happy to unload his POW burdens, he also suspected that van Deventer "was trying to make his task easier by enticing me into a trap." Obviously, the Germans were expected in Mozambique; no less obviously they must now disappoint their hosts.

Von Lettow therefore ordered a sudden change of direction, from northeast to due west: the Schutztruppe's objective had become the eastern shore of Lake Nyasa or just possibly Nyasaland itself. Whichever it was, either target lay at the other side of Portuguese East Africa, nearly four hundred miles from Mozambique. Once again, van Deventer had to reshuffle the British columns for an entirely new operation. Von Lettow was the piper; van Deventer danced to his tune.

Now began a two-week chase across the Portuguese colony, with a strong KAR column pressing hard on von Lettow's heels, two others hurtling toward his left flank from the south and a fourth blocking what was believed would be his line of march in the west. With the British supply columns held up for days at a time, with their troops going sick in droves from eating uncooked manioc, none of the four KAR forces could quite get a bead on the Germans—although they occasionally came close enough. At least once, the askaris of KAR and Schutztruppe patrols exchanged cigarettes and small talk without either group recognizing the other's identity until long after both had gone their separate ways.

Finally, toward the end of August, a small detachment of the western column ran head-on into Müller's advance guard. The collision took place near a fortified post called Numarroe, and after Namacurra and Namirrue, euphony may have dictated that Numarroe became the third in what Wienholt called "a peculiar and unlucky similarity of names." The fight was short but decisive. Müller's riflemen and machine gunners kicked the KAR detachment back to a line of trenches that ringed the fort, and from which the British askaris were able to repel a succession of plunging bayonet charges. But the defense collapsed when von Lettow arrived with his main body, surrounded the fort and let fly with one of the captured Portuguese 75-mm. guns. When the smoke cleared, he found himself in possession of the fort, two machine guns, forty thousand rounds of ammunition, bushels of hand grenades, a badly needed stock of medical supplies, and the KAR detachment commander.

From Numarroe, an eight to ten days' march westward would bring the Schutztruppe into the heart of Nyasaland, making von Lettow the only German general of the war to occupy a British colony. Von Lettow passed up the opportunity for that distinction in favor of what he deemed a better idea: "It seemed probable that our return to German East Africa would be a complete surprise to the enemy."

It would have been no such thing: ever since the Schutztruppe's crossing of the Rovuma nine months earlier, van Deventer had been chewing his fingernails over the possibility of a breakthrough back into the German colony. But von Lettow was correct in his assumption that if he surfaced in the north again he would throw the British completely off balance. Almost certainly, they would conclude that he was making for Tabora. This meant that van Deventer would have to withdraw the bulk of his troops from the interior of Portuguese East Africa to the coast or to Lake Nyasa or both, then transport them by sea and/or lake steamer to Dar es Salaam and Kigoma for the rail journey to Tabora. By the time the whole wearying thousand-mile move was completed, von Lettow might or might not decide to make Tabora his objective. Probably not.

Meanwhile, he turned his force north.

Fighting now became more continual as the gap between British and Germans began to close. The topography, too, was getting to be more of a shambles than ever; in the mangled, chaotic intermingling of thorn and grass and forest and boulders and ravine-gashed hills, battles could be hopelessly confused, targets wrongly chosen. A Schutztruppe detachment once prepared to ambush three other German companies, the commander learning of his error at the very moment when his machine guns were being slewed into position. KAR columns sometimes opened fire on their own forward units, mistaking them for German patrols. Maps and compasses were of little use to either side; apart from their general northerly movement, both armies had virtually lost all sense of direction.

And at this stage of the campaign, the pursuers were becoming increasingly tenacious in their attacks. Most were launched by Kartucol, which had been nipping at the Germans' heels ever since the clash at Medo. Kartucol was the KAR's *corps d'élite*; its askaris by now were no less wise to the ways of guerrilla trickery than von Lettow's men, and their youthful commander, Lieutenant Colonel George Giffard, had shown himself to be one of the shrewder bush infighters of both sides. Giffard was now bringing a smart tactical innovation into play: whenever a KAR detachment made contact with a Schutztruppe column, its askaris, instead of fanning out through the bush and advancing cautiously, would attack at once, firing rapidly from the hip as they dashed straight in at the Germans. Long accustomed to the intricate and slow-moving maneuver of British assaults, von Lettow's troops were almost invariably thrown off balance by Giffard's new head-on ploy.

The British knew they had a good thing in Kartucol. "This campaign can hardly be considered either fortunate or creditable," said Wienholt, "but without Colonel Gifford [*sic*] and the K.A.R. 2nd Col. it might easily have been almost disastrous." Despite the setbacks it had sustained and the frustrations it had endured, the force's morale never flagged, and its askaris never tired—literally. In bivouac, they kept their officers awake until the small hours of every morning with *ngomas*: war dances performed to the rhythm of hands thumping on tom-toms made of empty paraffin tins. And, like their German counterparts, they had their own songs to march by— improvised and chanted in monotone across the everlasting wilderness:

> The big Bwanas
>   Stop away behind
> We others have fighting and hunger
>   What kind of business is this?
>
> The Portuguese are no good
>   When they hear a shot they run
> Nor will they stop
>   Till they reach the sea.
>
> The KAR askaris
>   Are fierce in fight
> But go carefully
>   There are lions in the bush.

By "lions" they meant Germans. KAR morale may have been soaring, but Britain's black army never short-changed its black German enemy.

On the morning of August 30, Kartucol almost took the brass ring as its columns converged on von Lettow near the village of Lioma. One detachment became caught between the German advance guard and the main body, and von Lettow immediately ordered an attack. This in itself was one of his rare mistakes: he was committing his troops to an offensive action at the very moment when enemy forces were assaulting him in strength from several directions. The error was then compounded when an inexpert guide led the main body astray and a smaller Schutztruppe column— which included most of the German sick and wounded—unknowingly marched straight into a strong attacking KAR force. By late afternoon, contact between the various German units had become hopelessly muddled and the Kartucol askaris were pressing in for the kill.

For some reason, moreover, von Lettow by now had left his own companies and joined the advance guard, which was no less inexplicably making its way along a narrow path that led up a range of steep and bulky granite hills. It was not long before this column became lost, while the echoes of rifle volleys and mortar and machine gun bursts ricocheted off the rocks and told von Lettow that Kartucol was pouring everything it had into the main German body. It was imperative that he go down and rally his own troops, but even on the footpath the descent was so precarious that he had to take off his shoes before he could find any footholds. Night had fallen when he finally reached level ground, and it was only by sheer luck that he literally stumbled into his main column.

It was also too late to do anything but take to the bush in the most orderly retreat possible under the circumstances. The Germans had been more than bruised at Lioma; but for the almost total disorder and confusion that marked the two-day action, they would have been wiped out. As it was, besides a casualty list of about one hundred officers and askaris killed, wounded, captured or missing, the Schutztruppe lost nearly fifty thousand rounds of ammunition, many loads of desperately needed medical stores, and the entire porter column of the advance detachment. Koehl's rear guard had also disappeared and did not find its way back to the force for several days. Von Lettow later said that Lioma was the German army's closest brush with annihilation.

The northward push continued through increasingly hilly and ever wilder country, von Lettow somehow managing to keep touch with his widely separated columns on a bicycle. Early in September, in the jumbled Pere hills, the force had another near thing, when it opened up with a dozen machine guns on what was mistaken for a British supply convoy. The error was not discovered until two KAR battalions, their rifles cracking like sixteen hundred bullwhips, burst from the tall grass in a counterattack. As Wienholt understated it: "Von Lettow [was] too good a soldier not to realize that he was up against rather more than he had bargained for." Indeed, he was only barely able to extricate his detachments from what could have proved at least as shattering a blow as Lioma.

In any case, the casualties in that action were far greater than the Germans could afford. The two-thousand-man combat team which had invaded Portuguese East Africa in the autumn of 1917 had now been whittled down to fewer than two hundred Germans and barely fourteen hundred askaris. This was the equivalent of no more than a pair of KAR battalions, and it was shrinking steadily. As usual, battlefield wounds were less serious than sickness—and sickness almost got out of hand in the summer of 1918, as the Schutztruppe was smitten by three consecutive epidemics.

They were minor visitations, to be sure, but they contributed competently to the further enfeeblement of an already infirm army. Despite the vaccination of all troops and the most careful hygienic precautions possible, smallpox had broken out in the columns; in some companies 20 percent of the askaris were aflame with suppurating rashes. Facilities for proper isolation did not exist, and it was only by the weirdest of miracles that none of the Europeans became infected. Shortly after Numarroe several men were seized by the fevers and convulsions of cerebro-spinal meningitis; soon the medical staff diagnosed seventeen cases. Once again sheer good fortune kept the affliction from running amok. Certainly the doctors could have done little to halt it. Their hands were full enough with an outbreak of croupous pneumonia which slew at least two dozen of the 250 infected officers and askaris before running its course.

Even among those untouched by the epidemics, few in the Schutztruppe at this time could have passed the physical examination of an under-quota draft board. With the officers of one column laid low by fever and wounds, the only European fit to command was *Königsberg's* one-legged Richard Wenig. Another officer was leading his troops on a stretcher; in action, he could fire his rifle only from the prone position. But he was far from the only member of the force who had to be carried. The German army's most conspicuous feature by now had become its long, ragged millipede of litter-bearers and their gasping, vomiting, defecating, raving human burdens.

The even longer file of walking wounded and sick may have been kept on their feet by their own delirium. "With some," wrote Dr. Deppe, "this psychotic state had less than unpleasant symptoms. . . . The eternal marching, often for hours in the tall grass, which struck boots and leggings as waves strike the hull of a ship, could make one so drowsy that dreamlike visions of the homeland fluttered about us and we believed ourselves to be there. Thus, this curious form of homesickness usually had a liberating effect."

Which was just as well. "We could not afford many halts," said von Lettow.

On September 28, 1918—nine months, three days and fifteen hundred miles after crossing the Rovuma into Portuguese territory—von Lettow led his scrofulous band of marauders across the river again to re-enter German East Africa. *"Bwana Obersti anarudi!"* shouted the exultant askaris as they re-formed on the northern bank—the Colonel's back.

On its own soil once again, the force took a new lease on life. In the high country of the Songea region, the bracing air hastened the recovery of the last pneumonia cases. The steeply rolling, fertile hills yielded up an abundance of maize, wheat and fresh fruit. Game proliferated. A less heartening development was the desertion of some of the porters. They were members of the Angoni tribe, who made their homes in this part of the colony—for which reason the defections did not surprise von Lettow: "It would after all have been asking too much of human nature to expect that these men, who had not seen their people for years, should now march straight through their native district." Von Lettow also took comfort in the knowledge that the shrinkage in his bearer ranks was canceled out by the bulk acquisition of local African livestock: the herds simply became a mobile larder that did not have to be carried.

Meanwhile, the British had gone into a perfect panic. As the Schutztruppe continued to advance northward along the eastern shore of Lake Nyasa, von Lettow's earlier prediction of van Deventer's strategy on the Germans' return to their colony proved even more accurate than he had expected. Not only were KAR columns rushed to Tabora but other detachments made forced marches to stiffen the defenses of Iringa and Mahenge, should the German commander decide to invest those places. Even the Belgians received an SOS.

The Allied moves were also a waste of effort. By mid-October, von Lettow had reached the northern end of the lake—which was probably as far north as he had ever intended to go. Certainly the recapture of Tabora appealed to him, but he also knew that the chances of bringing this off, in the face of almost immeasurable odds, were remote. On the other hand, he would be confronted by little more than token opposition if he turned west—to invade British territory for the second time in the campaign with a drive into Northern Rhodesia.

Before striking off on the new route, he pared down the force again, leaving all sick and wounded in charge of Wahle, himself too ill to continue the march. Also at this time, captured British newspapers gave the Germans their first tidings of the European conflict in many weeks. The news was not good: Bulgaria had been knocked out of the war; on the Western Front, Cambrai, St. Quentin and Armentières had fallen to the Allies. A little wishful thinking might not have been out of order: "Positions could be given up for so many reasons," said von Lettow, "that I did not attribute any decisive importance to this news."

As October drew to a close, the German columns were fast approaching the Northern Rhodesia border post of Fife, where a large British supply depot was believed to be located. Although Kartucol by now had been disbanded, van Deventer had already ordered two other KAR detachments to take its place and check the German advance. One unit was marching south from Tabora, the other sailing northward aboard three troop transports to the upper end of Lake Nyasa, while two companies of Northern Rhodesia Police were digging in at Fife itself. As things turned out, von Lettow bypassed Fife; after making a tentative pass at the town, he concluded that a direct assault might cost him too many casualties. (He nearly became one himself; for half an hour he had to lie prone in the grass as British machine gun bullets almost literally parted his close-cropped hair.) But his advance was halted only momentarily: early in November, with its four hundred head of cattle raising enough dust for an army corps and a KAR column hot on its heels, the Schutztruppe began the invasion of Northern Rhodesia.

The new and unfamiliar terrain, sodden with swamps, interlaced with a cobwebbing of small rivers, did not lend itself to a rapid march—especially since the livestock tended to act as a brake. It was von Lettow's good fortune that his pursuers found the going just as stiff, if not more so, since they were being misled by their maps—or rather by their lack of them. Owing to some wondrous malfunction in van Deventer's administrative machine, the only guide available to the commander of the KAR column was a schoolroom atlas of the world with a scale of two hundred miles to the inch, reducing the whole region of the chase to an area slightly larger than a man's heel print. Partly as a result of this, von Lettow was gradually able to put a little distance between himself and the KAR, even picking up some speed in the process as his detachments changed course from west to southwest.

By November 12, in fact, the Schutztruppe had advanced 150 miles (or three quarters of an inch by the atlas) inside the border, and the chances of being overtaken in force had become remote.

The time had also come for von Lettow to plan the next phase of his campaign. He must now decide whether to continue the march south toward the Congo-Zambesi watershed, where he could dynamite Belgian copper mines in Katanga, or to thrust westward into the Congo—and thence, perhaps, to the Portuguese West African colony of Angola. The latter route made it possible that the Germans might even reach the Atlantic coast, thirteen hundred miles away. Following either path, however, the force now had enough arms and supplies to go on raiding, looting and fighting for at least another year.

At any rate, those were the prospects as von Lettow saw them on November 12. The Schutztruppe had now occupied the town of Kasama, a key post on an important British supply route, and was ready to move out at once. Although the KAR force was closing the distance again, its forward elements at that moment were being slowed down by the rifle fire of several German companies on a river bank a few miles to the north. Neither von Lettow nor his pursuers realized then that this skirmish was the last battle of the First World War.

Or that it was being fought a day after the war had ended.

20

Strange Surrender

IT WAS ENTIRELY in keeping with the aggressiveness of von Lettow's army that it should have learned of its own defeat by capturing the news.

On November 13, a British motorcyclist was intercepted near Kasama by an askari patrol of Koehl's rear guard. The rider was carrying urgent dispatches from van Deventer to the commander of the KAR battalion which had been trying to overtake the Schutztruppe. Riffling through the papers, Koehl found an announcement of the Armistice and the draft of a message to von Lettow, calling on him to order a cease-fire among his troops, as van Deventer had already done with his own army. "Our feelings were mixed," wrote von Lettow.

They surely must have been. After nearly a year of being all but hermetically sealed off from developments in Europe, von Lettow and his officers had no way of knowing that the armies of the Fatherland had finally been brought to their knees on the Western and Eastern fronts. Von Lettow, therefore, could only remain "convinced that the conclusion of hostilities must have been favourable, or at least not unfavourable to Germany."

But his eyes were opened almost at once with the receipt of a telegram— forwarded under a flag of truce—from van Deventer, stating that Germany had agreed to the unconditional surrender of the Schutztruppe and its arms. Von Lettow might have taken some pride in learning that a special clause had been written into the Armistice permitting this surrender to take place within a month after November 11. He might also have felt consolation in van Deventer's personal gesture which allowed the Schutztruppe officers to keep their weapons "in consideration of the gallant fight you have made." But it was cold comfort. The otherwise harsh demands "showed the desperate situation of the Fatherland. Nothing else could account for the surrender of a force still maintaining itself proudly and victoriously in the field."

The extent of his country's collapse was brought home further the next

Majestät Berlin
General Deventer teilt offiziell mit, daß
nach den von Deutschland unterzeichne-
ten Waffenstillstandsbedingungen bedin-
gungslose Übergabe der Schutztruppe zu
erfolgen hat Ich werde entsprechend
verfahren
                    Lettow
        14. 11. 18

written in my presence, on the bank of the
Chambeze river Northern Rhodesia, on the
morning of the 14th day of November 1918

            H. Croad.
            Provincial Commissioner
            retired.

Von Lettow's message to the Kaiser acknowledging the Armistice

day, when von Lettow met with a retired British provincial commissioner
to discuss arrangements for the cease-fire; this man told him of the revolution in Germany, the mutiny in the Imperial fleet and the as yet unconfirmed report of the Kaiser's abdication. The news was still not altogether
credible. At this time, von Lettow may have been in something like a state
of shock. It was as if he had spent the previous four years leading an army
of astronauts in a war for possession of some distant planet, only to discover that Earth had been attacked and conquered in the meanwhile. "All
our troops, native as well as Europeans," he wrote, "had always held the
conviction that Germany could not be beaten in this war. . . . The strategic
situation at the moment was more favourable than it had been for a long

time. The Askari, it is true, saw that our numbers were dwindling . . . but whenever I discussed this topic with one of my orderlies he always assured me: 'I will always stick by you and fight on till I fall.' Many others spoke to the same effect, and I am convinced that it was not merely a case of empty words."

Still, there was no longer any doubt that the war had ended, and von Lettow could only hand the British official a telegram for the Kaiser, "in which I reported what had happened and . . . that I would act accordingly." This simply meant compliance with van Deventer's terms.

Not that every condition was accepted supinely. As further details of the Armistice reached him, von Lettow learned that "unconditional surrender" also meant "unconditional evacuation"—in effect, the handing over of German East Africa. Several official protests brought no results—not even an acknowledgment—and von Lettow eventually had to tell himself that the matter "seemed a small point." Which was quite true, in the sense that he was powerless to do anything about it.

Another point on which von Lettow took a strong stand was not mentioned in the surrender terms, although he considered it at least as important. This was the question of the back pay owed to his askaris and porters, and which he felt had become a British responsibility. For several years, the bankrupt German colonial government had been unable to pay its African forces, "yet it was a matter of honour for us to see that these people, who had fought and worked for us with such devotion, should receive their rights." The arrears came to about 1.5 million rupees—barely $500,000, or considerably less than $200 per man—and at the first opportunity, von Lettow made a formal request to the British for this "relatively small" sum. He ran into a stone wall. "We were told at different times and places that the matter was 'under consideration' by the War Office, and there it remained." The best von Lettow could do was see to it that each askari and carrier was given an IOU.

The most urgent of van Deventer's demands was that the Schutztruppe march without delay to the Northern Rhodesian town of Abercorn, about one hundred miles north of Kasama, and there lay down its arms. En route, the Germans met the KAR battalion that had been chasing them southwest from Fife. The British askaris had been jubilant since learning of the Armistice—when they had formed a circle around their equally exultant officers and gone into a wild victory dance—but there was no crowing as the former enemy approached. Lieutenant Colonel E. B. B. Hawkins, the battalion's thirty-year-old commander, invited von Lettow and his staff to lunch, and although von Lettow felt obliged to decline, he said he was gratified by "such an expression of chivalry."

One reason for not accepting the invitation may have been the British force's bare larder. When Hawkins told von Lettow that his battalion's food supplies had been exhausted for nearly a week, the German commander came to the rescue, cutting out a large portion of the Schutztruppe's cattle herd and turning it over to the famished KAR askaris.

Von Lettow made the rest of the journey to Abercorn in a British staff car. It had been sent down for him by Brigadier General Edwards, the one-time British East Africa policeman who had failed to apprehend Wintgens and Naumann in 1917 and who was now in charge of the final surrender negotiations. If von Lettow found this ironic he did not say so, although he mentioned his appreciation of Edwards' kindness to him and his staff. The discussions went off smoothly enough, von Lettow only registering protest that the Schutztruppe rank and file must hand over their weapons. His demurrer, however, was no more than a formality; he knew quite well that he had no real say in the matter.

When the German askaris arrived in Abercorn, however, it looked for a while as if they might have a great deal to say. They told von Lettow—and anyone else who cared to listen—that they had no intention whatever of giving their rifles or their bayonets or their machine guns to an enemy who had never beaten them. Edwards and his staff began to fear that the surrender formalities might degenerate into a pitched battle, which could very well have taken place had not von Lettow intervened personally. "Without the exercise of his influence," wrote a British officer, "there might have been grave difficulties, for we had not sufficient men on the spot to enforce surrender of arms by the askaris, had they declined to deliver them up." And as it was, the German Africans obeyed their commander only with the greatest reluctance.

But obey they did. One man stepped from formation to speak for the whole army. With him was his bibi, and his infant son was perched on his shoulder. "I have been asked to say this to you, Bwana Obersti. Where you go, we will go with you. And if the time is not now, then wait until this *mtoto* of mine grows up to be an askari, and he will take my place and go with you."

On Sunday, November 25, 1918, as a Union Jack drooped from an improvised flagstaff in a pelting rain, Hawkins' KAR battalion and a detachment of Northern Rhodesia Police drew up on a patch of open ground in Abercorn to form a guard of honor for a slightly ludicrous ceremony: the capitulation of an army that had not lost to an army that had not won. Photographers cursed the weather, but the correspondent of the Bulawayo *Chronicle* was able to record the event in detail:

Von Lettow, whose striking presence is a good index of what must be a wonderful personality, came in at the head of his first detachment. . . . After these troops had been quickly formed into three lines in close formation, von Lettow advanced a few paces, saluted the flag, then, taking out a pocket-book, read therefrom his formal statement of surrender in German. He repeated it in English, whereupon General Edwards replied, accepting his surrender on behalf of his Majesty King George V. Von Lettow was then presented to the officers present, and in turn introduced his own officers. . . .

Then followed the most dramatic moment of the proceedings, when von Lettow called upon his troops to lay down their arms, the Europeans alone being allowed to retain theirs in recognition of the splendid fight they had put up. The Askari laid down their rifles, took off and deposited their equipment, and were then marched off by companies. . . . The above ceremony was repeated twice, and by 4 P.M. the last German Askari had laid down his arms. . . . It was a most impressive spectacle. The long motley column, Europeans and Askari, all veterans of a hundred fights, the latter clothed with every kind of headgear, women who had stuck to their husbands through all of these years of hardships, carrying huge loads, some with children born during the campaign, carriers coming in singing in undisguised joy at the thought that their labours were ended at last. All combined to make a sight that was unique.

Altogether, the shabby cavalcade numbered about four and a half thousand, but with porters, women and children deducted, the total fighting strength came to 155 Germans and 1,156 askaris: 1,311 soldiers remaining of a force that had once been ten times that size—a force which, for four years, had stood up to the best that a quarter of a million enemy troops could throw at it. A partial idea of that accomplishment was had when the Schutztruppe askaris handed over their arms and the weapons were stacked. Apart from seven German machine guns and a handful of the old Model 71s, the rest of the arsenal had been captured; among other items it included 208,000 rounds of small-arms ammunition, 40 artillery shells, a Portuguese field piece, 30 British machine guns and 1,071 British, Belgian and Portuguese rifles. It was less a surrender of arms than a return of borrowed articles.

With the ritual of submission completed, the German askaris were packed into a small enclosure surrounded by a tall thorn boma and heavily guarded by British African troops. Resentment flared almost at once. Hardly had the last man been herded into the compound than a Schutztruppe *effendi* started to walk out. When halted by a KAR sentry with fixed bayonet, the African officer glared haughtily at the askari and told him that no *shenzi* (savage) was going to stand in his way, whereupon the askari brought his rifle to present arms and the *effendi* stalked off. Other German troops had less luck trying to break out, but they refused to accept their enforced status as captives. Trouble began to brew. Several mass riots were only narrowly averted.

Von Lettow, whose good grace in the surrender formalities had been remarked on by the British, now became less sporting. He backed up his men with an angry telegram of protest to van Deventer, noting later that "we were not ordinary prisoners of war, whose escape he had to fear, but had given ourselves into his hands voluntarily." Van Deventer could only reply, in a apologetic tone, that "I have no choice but to act in accordance with the orders of the War Office, and treat your force as prisoners of war."

This only made matters worse; as the askaris continued to simmer over what struck them as a humiliating injustice, their disaffection spread to the Germans. Many of von Lettow's officers approached him with a plan to storm the British camp, recapture the surrendered weapons and resume the campaign. The scheme was far from being harebrained: the relatively weak detachment then guarding the Schutztruppe would have been hard put to stave off a surprise attack, even by unarmed askaris and officers carrying only pistols. It took all of von Lettow's persuasive powers to convince the plotters that the thing could not work over the long pull. Besides which, he reminded them, they had given their word as German officers that they would no longer fight.

Not that he was in any way displeased by the conspiracy: "I could only feel glad and proud of such a revelation of true soldierly spirit."

Inactivity as much as indignation may have accounted for the army's unrest at this time. (Only von Lettow's adjutant, Captain Walter von Ruck- teschell, seems to have exploited the enforced idleness constructively, sketching countless portraits of African tribesmen; a number of the draw- ings later illustrated von Lettow's book about the campaign.) But the seeds of revolt quickly withered in early December, after the troops had been marched from Abercorn to the port of Bismarckburg on Lake Tanganyika. The British had now decided that the German askaris would be interned for the briefest possible time at Tabora, while the Europeans would be taken to Dar es Salaam and sent back to Germany at once. The knowledge that they were going home at last removed any lingering incentives among the men to continue fighting.

The first leg of the journey, by steamer from Bismarckburg to Kigoma, witnessed a renewal of good feelings between the Germans and their cap- tors. When one of the famous Lake Tanganyika "typhoons" struck the four-ship convoy, Royal Navy bluejackets were quick to come up with blankets and dry clothes for the drenched prisoners on deck. On arrival at Kigoma, still under Belgian administration, von Lettow was agreeably surprised to be greeted by the victims of the 1914 atrocities "with a hos- pitality which could not have been anticipated." Wine was served to the officers, and the tables laid out for them even had tablecloths—"a sight we had not seen for years." After boarding the train for Dar es Salaam, "it was like peace time to get a good night's rest by letting down the bunks and using a leather pillow."

As the train rolled eastward, so too did the red carpet. The prisoners' journey to Dar es Salaam, in fact, was more like the triumphant return of a conquering army. German civilians turned out in large numbers at nearly every station; some wanted to complain to von Lettow of looting by Belgian and British troops, but most had come simply to cheer their soldiers until their throats went hoarse. On reaching Morogoro, the officers found that the German women of the town had already laid out tables, with fresh rolls, cakes and fruit, on the station platform. And the former enemy continued to shower its charges with goodwill—of various sorts. Von Lettow particularly recalled being cornered at Morogoro by a "tall, lanky corporal who had apparently drunk a whole series of glasses to our health before the train arrived. I managed to slip away from him at last."

At Dar es Salaam, comfortable tents awaited the Germans in a prison camp which also offered a private mess and all the food they could eat. Clothes, shaving kits and other luxuries were available to the prisoners at low prices in the British army canteen. The compound itself was only a token jail, since the inmates were free to come and go as they pleased, taking sightseeing strolls through their former capital in the company of a British escort officer. The latter, more a bodyguard than a watchdog, was not really needed: wherever they went, the Germans were no longer Huns but honored guests. Only one untoward incident took place, when a KAR company marched past Richard Wenig, its askaris singing "a shameless satirical song" about the Kaiser. But Wenig's anger quickly abated: he had just come across the cracked barrel of the *Königsberg* gun which he had blown up on the last day of the battle of Mahiwa. It was decorating a lawn. Wenig stroked it fondly.

Von Lettow got the full hero treatment. Van Deventer's chief of staff, General Sheppard, personally conducted the Schutztruppe commander to the handsome white house that had been set aside for him and a few members of his staff. When they arrived, they found that a luncheon had been arranged for them by van Deventer himself. A car and a driver were placed at von Lettow's disposal. If King George's coach of state had been in Dar es Salaam it could not have attracted more attention, for von Lettow was fast becoming an object of something just short of adulation among his captors, having gained "more esteem and affection," as one British officer put it, "than our own leaders." "Everyone was anxious to see the man who had shown himself to be such a wonderfully able commander," wrote Brigadier General C. P. Fendall of van Deventer's staff. "He had the bearing of a Prussian guardsman, but none of the bluster and swagger usually attributed to such. His manner was just what it should have been, courteous and polite. He talked extremely good English." (Which was more than could be said for Fendall.)

By comparison, Schnee could only suffer. He struck Fendall as "a man of the less presentable lawyer class, full of cunning, by no means a fool, but not a gentleman." Poor old Schnee.

If von Lettow enjoyed occupying the limelight he was also anxious to escape it. He could not have felt comfortable at the sight of Dar es Salaam, once the sapphire in the diadem of the German colonial empire, now under foreign occupation. (By way of twisting the knife unwittingly, the British army made its administrative headquarters in the spacious house where he had lived before the war.) Perhaps he took some hope for the future in conversations with certain "intelligent Englishmen," among whom he "found the view prevailing that Germany must have colonies on economic grounds, as well as on account of her over-populousness." But perhaps he did not delude himself. Despite the courtesy and warmth with which he and his men were treated, all could only feel like strangers in the city that was no longer theirs.

But their hosts would not let them go. Although the British had moved the Germans swiftly and efficiently from Bismarckburg to Dar, with a view to putting them aboard a Europe-bound steamer by mid-December at the very latest, the last leg of the journey home became mired down in red tape. Christmas and New Year's Day came and went. Troop transports came and went. The Germans stagnated. Their homesickness was compounded by a more tangible malady when the worldwide Spanish flu epidemic swept into East Africa and cut down 10 percent of the Schutztruppe's remaining Europeans. (In Tabora, large numbers of interned German askaris also succumbed.) It was not until January 17, 1919, that 114 German officers and NCOs, along with 107 German women and children, finally boarded ship for the Fatherland. More than two months had gone by since their scheduled embarkation date.

And it was exactly five years to the day since von Lettow had first stepped ashore at Dar es Salaam.

Early in March, the last surviving remnant of the Schutztruppe's Germans came home. Led by von Lettow on a black charger, the men were wildly acclaimed by solid masses of cheering, hat-waving Berliners as they marched through the streets of the capital to the Brandenburg Gate. Their formation was as ragged as that of any patrol in the East African bush. Even in the mild pre-spring weather, their battered sun helmets and frayed tropical uniforms looked almost clownishly alien. It did not matter. No one needed immaculate, goose-stepping gray ranks to be reminded that Germany's only undefeated army was giving the beaten nation its only victory parade. The mayor of Berlin was waiting to honor von Lettow and his men at a formal banquet.

Then he cancelled it, fearing that the celebration might be interrupted violently by mobs of German revolutionaries. It would have been a bright red feather in their cap to humiliate the Junker general and his imperialist bandits.

Epilogue

Haya Safari

On a sparkling blue-gold-green tropical morning in 1953, the Union Castle liner *Rhodesia Castle* steamed into the harbor of Dar es Salaam on her regular run between Europe and Capetown. Among the passengers on the upper deck was von Lettow. He was paying his first visit to the old battleground in nearly four decades, and he saw at once that the torpidly busy East African seaport had undergone little outward change in his long absence. Apart from a few new steamer berths and commercial buildings—and, of course, the Union Jacks which flew from rooftops in the capital of the British territory of Tanganyika—the place looked much the same. The coco palms and casuarinas on the shorefront seemed never to have stopped their contented sighing in the Indian Ocean breezes. The tiny, lateen-rigged coastal dhows called *jahazis,* with their ancient cargoes of mangrove poles and simsim, came and went as they always had, lurching with awkward grace over the harbor's short chop. One of the first things that caught von Lettow's eye was the spire of the Lutheran church that his countrymen had built when the colony was still theirs. And he probably smiled to himself when *Rhodesia Castle* changed course in the channel to avoid the wreckage of a sunken floating dock; a German naval officer under his command had scuttled that dock to discourage Admiral King-Hall's cruisers at the start of the East African campaign. It was almost as if a time machine had carried von Lettow back to 1914.

But he was not likely to be deluded by surface appearances. Once a German and now a British colonial capital, Dar es Salaam would soon be neither. The Second World War had left in its wake a ferment of nationalism that bubbled with angry vigor in all the hot countries of the world that were still ruled by white men from harsher climates. Britain had already handed over India. The Dutch had been ousted unceremoniously from their Indonesian islands. France was about to get the same treatment in Laos, Cambodia and Vietnam. And Africa had to be next. Harold Macmillan had not yet coined the expression "the wind of change," but the wind was blowing. Like any thinking man of the 1950s, von Lettow could hardly have failed to feel it.

Certainly his own life had witnessed more than its share of changes since his triumphal return to Germany thirty-four years earlier. Almost inevitably, that life had been an anticlimax, although not without its moments. For a brief time he had commanded a Reichswehr division—appropriately named for him—and helped suppress a Communist uprising in Hamburg, but this was the last military action of his career. In 1920 he resigned from the army and entered politics, serving for ten years as a deputy in the Reichstag. He also wrote several books, and his personal memoirs of the East African campaign may have found as many readers in England as in Germany. For von Lettow was anything but forgotten by his onetime foes. In London in 1929, he was the guest of honor, seated next to Smuts, at an anniversary dinner of the British East African Expeditionary Force.

In 1930, as Nazis began emerging from the woodwork, a disillusioned von Lettow resigned his Reichstag seat. Five years later, he was given the opportunity to re-enter public life when Hitler offered to make him ambassador to England. The suggestion, interestingly, had come from von Lettow's friend, retired Colonel Richard Meinertzhagen, during a visit to Berlin to meet with Hitler on behalf of German Jews. Meinertzhagen reported that Hitler enthusiastically endorsed the first idea and went into a volcanic tantrum over the second. Von Lettow was no less affronted by Hitler's overture, and declined with frigid hauteur.*

After that (possibly even before that) he was on the Nazi blacklist, and although Hitler was not quite up to doing away with the one man who had consistently humiliated Germany's enemies in the First World War, he could see to it that von Lettow was subjected to every possible indignity short of a concentration camp. He was kept under continual surveillance. SA troops sacked his office. No opportunity was lost to slander him. It did not matter that both of his sons were killed in action with the German army in the Second World War.

When peace came, the seventy-five-year-old general was destitute, subsisting for a time on the food parcels sent to him by Meinertzhagen and Smuts. With Germany's postwar recovery, however, he presently came to enjoy comfortable circumstances again. And even in his ostensibly declining years, his mind remained as alert as it had been on the day when he ordered the 13th Field Company to counterattack at Tanga.

---

* During a conversation not long ago with the grand-nephew of a German marine who had fought in the East African campaign, the author brought up the subject of the spurned ambassadorship, remarking: "I understand that von Lettow told Hitler to go fuck himself." "That's right," was the reply, "except that I don't think he put it that politely."

If anything, those mental facilities had become even more acute when, at the age of eighty-three, von Lettow stepped nimbly down *Rhodesia Castle's* gangway to board the lighter that would bring him ashore at Dar es Salaam. Noting a sizable crowd of Africans on the dock—many as old as he, some older—he asked one man whether any of them might have served with the Schutztruppe. Broad grins broke out at once, and the names of long-forgotten field companies and obscure battles were croaked back and forth among the venerable blacks. But why did this old *Mzungu* want to know? One great-grandfather, stooping but dignified in his nightshirt-like *kanzu,* turned to von Lettow and asked: *"Na wewe, Bwana? Ni jina lako?"* —and who might you be, sir? *"Pumbavu!"* roared von Lettow. Idiot! Don't you recognize your old colonel? Whereupon the graybeard fell to his knees and clasped von Lettow around the legs. Tanganyika's deputy governor had just arrived at the dock to escort von Lettow to a reception at Government House, but no one paid any attention to the white official as the swarm of doddering ex-askaris hoisted their commander to their bony shoulders and carried him off.

In due course he kept his appointment at Government House, whose stately Arab style archways seemed no less graceful to him than they had when the place was called the Governor's Palace and was occupied by Schnee. Another kind of memory returned shortly afterwards when he stood in the reviewing stand at Colito Barracks and took the salute of the 6th KAR Regiment. As the askari companies passed by in stiff, well-tailored khaki ranks, the band struck up the regimental march. Von Lettow recognized the music at once. He should have. The lyrics, of course, had been changed, but there was no mistaking the jaunty upbeat lilt of *"Haya Safari."*

The last decade of von Lettow's life witnessed few if any signs of senility. Visitors to his home in Hamburg-Altona inevitably remarked on the general's bright eye, his steel-trap mind, his crystal-clear recollection of the old campaigns and all their details. He even enjoyed a half-joking flirtation by mail with an elderly Danish baroness whom he had met in 1913 when both were passengers on the same ship for Africa—he bound for the German colony, she for the British. Von Lettow had given the young woman an autographed picture of himself. When the war broke out and she took four ox-wagons to the border with supplies and ammunition for the East Africa Mounted Rifles (no white men were available for the mission), she also carried the photograph as insurance—should she be captured by a Schutztruppe patrol. In 1958, the author Isak Dinesen visited von Lettow and told him of the trek she had made to the border. She also said that she regretted not having kissed him when she left the ship at Mombasa, and that, with his wife's permission, she would do so now. Two years later, on von Lettow's 90th birthday, she sent him flowers and wrote that another kiss was enclosed. Von Lettow replied that she would have to deliver the next one personally.

He faded away in 1964. Anyone fancying symbolism can read something into that year. It was not only half a century since von Lettow had arrived in Dar es Salaam to take command of the Schutztruppe; 1964 was also the year in which his askaris finally got their back pay. The funds had been voted by the Bundestag in Bonn, but payment was made, fittingly, through the African government of Tanzania. By no means all of the claimants were still alive, but at least three hundred old men gathered at the Lake Victoria port of Mwanza, where a temporary cashier's office had been opened in a commercial building.

Then a problem of identification arose. Some of the men wore tattered scraps of Schutztruppe tunics, torn uniform trousers or frayed kepis. Several showed what they said were battle scars; one man lowered his shorts to reveal a long-healed wound on his left buttock. But only a small handful could produce the faded certificates that von Lettow had given them in 1918. Might not the others be masquerading as veterans?

The German banker who had brought the money came up with an idea. As each claimant stepped forward, he was handed a broom and ordered in German to perform the manual of arms. Other German commands were barked out: Attention . . . About turn . . . March . . . Present arms . . . Halt . . . Slope arms . . . Not one man failed the test.

The few who are left today have probably forgotten those alien words. But it has not yet become entirely beyond the realm of possibility for a visitor to Tanzania, should he happen to ask some village elder about himself, to hear the reply: "*Mimi ni askari Mdaichi.*" I am a German soldier.

Bibliography

Admiralty; Geographical Section of the Naval Intelligence Division, Naval
   Staff: *A Handbook of German East Africa;* London: H.M.S.O., 1921.
Armstrong, H. C.: *Grey Steel;* London: Arthur Barker, 1937.
Arning, Wilhelm: *Vier Jahre Weltkrieg in Deutsch-Ostafrika;* Hanover: Verlag
   von Gebrüder Jänecke, 1919.
Bee, David: *Curse of Magira* (fiction); New York: Harper & Row, 1964.
Bell, R. M.: *The Maji-Maji Rebellion in the Liwale District;* "Tanganyika Notes
   and Records" No. 28, January 1950.
Boell, Ludwig: *Die Operationen in Ostafrika;* Hamburg: Walter Dachert, 1951
   (privately printed).
Bruce, J. M.: *British Aeroplanes, 1914–1918;* New York: Funk & Wagnalls,
   1957.
Buchanan, Capt. Angus: *Three Years of War in East Africa;* London: John
   Murray, 1919; reprinted 1969 by Negro Universities Press, New York.
Calvert, Albert F.: *German East Africa;* London: T. Werner Laurie, 1917; re-
   printed 1970 by Negro Universities Press, New York.
Cane, Col. L. B.: *S.S. "Liemba";* "Tanganyika Notes and Records," No. 23,
   June 1947.
Charlewood, Comdr. C. J.: *Naval Actions on the Tanganyika Coast, 1914–
   1917;* "Tanganyika Notes and Records;" No. 54, March 1960; No. 55,
   Sept. 1960 (reprinted from Comdr. Charlewood's book, *Channels,
   Cloves and Coconuts;* North Devon: The Western Press, n.d.).
Chatterton, E. Keble: *The "Königsberg" Adventure;* London: Hurst & Blackett,
   1932.
Churchill, Winston S.: *The World Crisis,* Vol. I; New York: Scribner, 1923.
Clifford, Sir Hugh.: *The Gold Coast Regiment in the East African Campaign;*
   London: John Murray, 1920.
Collyer, J.: *The South Africans with General Smuts in German East Africa,
   1916;* Pretoria: Government Printer, 1939.
Corbett, Sir J. S., and Newbolt, B.: *Official History of the Great War—Naval
   Operations,* Vols I, II, III, IV; London: Longmans, 1920–31.
Cranworth, Lord: *Kenya Chronicles;* London: Macmillan, 1939.

Crowe, Brig. Gen. J. H. V.: *General Smuts' Campaign in East Africa;* London: John Murray, 1918.

Davies, W. J. K.: *Light Railways of the First World War;* Newton Abbot: David & Charles, 1967.

Deppe, Dr. Ludwig: *Mit Lettow-Vorbeck durch Afrika;* Berlin: Verlag August Scherl, 1919.

Dolbey, Capt. R. V.: *Sketches of the East Africa Campaign;* London: John Murray, 1918.

Downes, Capt. W. D.: *With the Nigerians in German East Africa;* London: Methuen, 1919.

Eberlie, R. F.: *The German Achievement in East Africa;* "Tanganyika Notes and Records" No. 55, Sept. 1960.

Ellis, Chris: *Military Transport of World War 1;* New York: Macmillan, 1970.

Falls, Cyril: *The Great War;* New York: Capricorn Books, 1961.

Fendall, Brig. Gen. C. P.: *The East African Force, 1915–1919;* London: Witherby, 1921.

Foran, W. Robert: *The Kenya Police, 1887–1960;* London: Robert Hale, 1962.

Fosbrooke, H. A.: *Arusha Boma;* "Tanganyika Notes and Records;" No. 38, March 1955.

————*Kondoa Boma;* "Tanganyika Notes and Records;" No. 32, January 1952.

Freeman-Grenville, G. S. P.: *In Search of the History of the "Tabora Sovereign;"* "Tanganyika Notes and Records;" No. 13, June 1942.

Gardner, Brian: *On to Kilimanjaro;* New York: Macfadden Books, 1964; published in England as *German East;* London: Macrae Smith, 1963.

Gillman, C.: *A Short History of the Tanganyika Railways;* "Tanganyika Notes and Records;" No. 13, June 1942.

Goldsmith, F. H.: *John Ainsworth, Pioneer Kenya Administrator;* London: Macmillan, 1955.

Gregory, J. R.: *Under the Sun;* Nairobi: The English Press, n.d.

Hancock, W. K., and van der Poel, Jean: *Selections from the Smuts Papers;* Vol. III, June 1910–November 1918; Cambridge: The University Press, 1966.

————*Smuts: The Sanguine Years, 1870–1919;* Cambridge: The University Press, 1962.

Hatch, John: *Tanzania, A Profile;* New York: Praeger, 1972.

Hatchell, G. W.: *The British Occupation of the South-Western Area of Tanganyika Territory, 1914–1918;* "Tanganyika Notes and Records;" No. 51, December 1958.

————*The East African Campaign–1914 to 1919;* "Tanganyika Notes and Records;" No. 21, June 1946.

————*Maritime Relics of the 1914–18 War;* "Tanganyika Notes and Records;" No. 32, January 1954.

Henderson, W. O.: *Studies in German Colonial History;* London: Frank Cass, 1962.

Hill, M. F.: *Permanent Way;* Nairobi: East African Railways and Harbours, 1949.

Holtom, E. C.: *Two Years' Captivity in German East Africa;* London: Hutchinson, 1919.

Hordern, Lt. Col. Charles: *History of the Great War: Military Operations, East*

Africa; Vol. I, August 1914–September 1916; London: H.M.S.O., 1941.

Howes, Wing Comdr. A. M. D.: *Some Details of the First Twenty-Five Years of Flying in Tanganyika, 1914–1939;* "Tanganyika Notes and Records;" No. 50, June 1958.

Hoyt, Edwin P., Jr.: *The Germans Who Never Lost;* New York: Funk & Wagnalls, 1968.

Huxley, Elspeth: *Red Strangers* (fiction); London: Chatto & Windus, 1939.

———*White Man's Country;* Vol. II; London: Chatto & Windus, 1935; reprinted 1968 by Praeger, New York.

Inhülsen, Otto: *Wir ritten für Deutsch-Ostafrika* (first printing entitled *Abenteuer am Kilimanjaro*); Leipzig: Koehler & Amelang, 1926.

King-Hall, Admiral Sir Herbert: *Naval Memories and Traditions;* London: Hutchinson, 1926.

Kock, Nis: *Blockade and Jungle;* London: Robert Hale, 1941.

Lane, L. P.: *Naval Visit, Dar es Salaam—November 1914;* "Tanganyika Notes and Records;" No 16, December 1943.

———*The T.R.S. "Mwanza;"* "Tanganyika Notes and Records;" No. 6, December 1938.

———*To Utete by Ship;* "Tanganyika Notes and Records;" No. 20, December 1945.

Lettow-Vorbeck, Gen. Paul von: *Mein Leben;* Biberach an der Riss: Koehlers, 1957.

———*My Reminiscences of East Africa;* London: Hurst & Blackett, 1920; published in Germany as *Meine Erinnerungen aus Ostafrika;* Leipzig, 1920; U.S. edition entitled *East African Campaigns* with introduction by John Gunther; New York: Robert Speller & Sons, 1957.

Lewin, Evans: *The Germans and Africa;* London: Cassell, 1915.

Looff, Vizeadmiral a.D., Max: *Kreuzerfahrt and Buschkampf;* Berlin: Neudeutsche Verlags-und Treuhand-G.m.b.H., 1927.

Lord, John: *Duty, Honor, Empire; The Life and Times of Colonel Richard Meinertzhagen;* New York: Random House, 1970.

Lucas, Sir Charles (ed.): *The Empire at War;* Vol. IV; London: Oxford University Press, 1924.

Macdonald, Alexander: *Tanzania: Young Nation in a Hurry;* New York: Hawthorn Books, 1966.

Macpherson, Maj. Gen. Sir W. G. (ed.): *History of the Great War: Medical Services. Diseases of the War;* London: H.M.S.O., n.d.

Meinertzhagen, Col. R.: *Army Diary, 1899–1926;* Edinburgh: Oliver & Boyd, 1960.

———*Kenya Diary, 1902–1906;* Edinburgh: Oliver & Boyd, 1957.

Migel, Parmenia: *Titania; The Biography of Isak Dinesen;* New York: Random House, 1967.

Millais, J. G.: *Life of Frederick Courtenay Selous, D.S.O.;* London: Longmans, Green, 1919.

Mosley, Leonard: *Duel for Kilimanjaro;* London: Weidenfeld & Nilcolson, 1963; New York: Ballantine Books, 1964.

Moyse-Bartlett, Lt. Col. H.: *The King's African Rifles;* Aldershot: Gale & Polden, 1956.

Nielsen, Thor: *The Zeppelin Story;* London: Allan Wingate, 1955.

O'Neill, H. C.: *The Royal Fusiliers in the Great War;* London: Heinemann, 1922.

Orr, Col. G. M.: *Random Recollections of East Africa, 1914–1918;* London: "The Army Quarterly;" Vol. XI, October 1925—January 1926.

————*Smuts v. Lettow: A Critical Phase in East Africa; August to September, 1916;* London: "The Army Quarterly;" January 1925.

Pretorius, Maj. P. J.: *Jungle Man;* New York: Dutton, 1948.

Reitz, Deneys: *Trekking On;* London: Faber & Faber, 1933.

Rodwell, Edward: *With a Light Touch;* Nairobi: "Spear," publication of East African Railways Corporation; Vol. III, No. 10.

Schmiedel, Dr. Hans: *Bwana Sakkarani: Captain Tom von Prince and His Times;* "Tanganyika Notes and Records;" No. 52, March 1959.

Schnee, Dr. Heinrich: *Deutsch-Ostafrika im Weltkriege;* Leipzig: Verlag Quelle et Meyer, 1919.

Schoen, Walter von: *Auf Vorposten für Deutschland;* Berlin: Deutscher Verlag, 1935.

Seaton, Henry: *Lion in the Morning;* London: John Murray, 1963.

Shankland, Peter: *The Phantom Flotilla;* London: Collins, 1968.

Shann, G. N.: *Tanganyika Place Names of European Origin;* "Tanganyika Notes and Records;" No. 54, March 1960.

Shorthose, Capt. W. T.: *Sport and Adventure in Africa;* London: Seeley Service, 1923.

Sibley, Maj. J. R.: *Tanganyikan Guerrilla: East African Campaign, 1914–18;* New York: Ballantine Books, 1971.

Stierling, Dr.: *The Hehe Royal Graves;* "Tanganyika Notes and Records;" No. 46, January 1957.

Taute, Dr. M.: *A German Account of the Medical Side of the War in East Africa, 1914–1918;* "Tanganyika Notes and Records;" No. 8, December 1939.

Taylor, A. J. P.: *A History of the First World War;* New York: Berkley Medallion Books, 1966.

Thatcher, W. S.: *The Fourth Battalion, Duke of Connaught's Own, Tenth Baluch Regiment in the Great War, 129th D.C.O. Baluchis;* Cambridge: The University Press, 1932.

Thornhill, Christopher, J.: *Taking Tanganyika;* London: Stanley Paul, 1937.

du Toit, P. J.: *Notes on the Coinage of German East Africa;* "Tanganyika Notes and Records;" No. 31, July 1951.

Walmsley, Leo: *So Many Loves;* London: Collins, 1944.

Weidmann, W.: *A Short History of the Klub Dar-es-Salâm;* "Tanganyika Notes and Records;" No. 41, December 1955.

Wenig, Richard: *In Monsun und Pori;* Berlin: Safari-Verlag, 1922.

Wienholt, Arnold: *The Story of a Lion Hunt;* London: Melrose, 1922.

Wylly, H. C.: *The Loyal North Lancashire Regiment;* London: Royal United Service Institution, 1933.

Young, Francis Brett: *Jim Redlake* (fiction); London: Heinemann, 1930.

————*Marching on Tanga;* London: Collins, 1917.

Index